Validity Evaluation in Language Assessment

D1809968

Language Testing and Evaluation

Series editors: Rüdiger Grotjahn
and Günther Sigott

Volume 11

PETER LANG

Frankfurt am Main · Berlin · Bern · Bruxelles · New York · Oxford · Wien

John M. Norris

Validity Evaluation
in Language Assessment

PETER LANG
Internationaler Verlag der Wissenschaften

Bibliographic Information published by the Deutsche Nationalbibliothek
The Deutsche Nationalbibliothek lists this publication in the Deutsche Nationalbibliografie; detailed bibliographic data is available in the internet at <http://www.d-nb.de>.

ISSN 1612-815X
ISBN 978-3-631-54946-9

© Peter Lang GmbH
Internationaler Verlag der Wissenschaften
Frankfurt am Main 2008
All rights reserved.

Printed in Germany 1 2 3 4 5   7

www.peterlang.de

This book is dedicated to Lourdes Ortega,

in gratitude for her support and encouragement.

Contents

Acknowledgements

The work reported in this book would not have been possible without the interest, participation, support, and encouragement of numerous individuals as well as several institutions. Above all, I am very much indebted to the faculty, staff, graduate teaching assistants, and students of the Georgetown University German Department for their patience and critical participation over several years of intensive work. I am profoundly grateful to Heidi Byrnes and Peter Pfeiffer for countless hours of intellectual exchange and pragmatic effort, and, most importantly, for their educational vision and a commitment to engaging in worthwhile assessment practices. In addition, Cori Crane, Susanne Kord, and Hiram Maxim contributed substantial time and energy at various points throughout this work. I would like to thank Rüdiger Grotjahn, both for making available extensive resources on C-test research and development, and for his interest in my work. I also value the support and critical commentary offered by my colleagues at the University of Hawai'i: J. D. Brown, Paul Chandler, Craig Chaudron, Thom Hudson, Gabrielle Kasper, and Richard Schmidt. I would like to acknowledge the very generous financial support of portions of this project through a Mellon Foundation doctoral research fellowship at the National Foreign Language Center (Johns Hopkins University), a U.S. Department of Education Language Resource Centers Program grant (University of Hawai'i), and direct funding from the Georgetown University German Department. Finally, once again, I am indebted to Lourdes Ortega for her unflagging encouragement, commentary, and feedback during all phases of research and writing.

Chapter 1
Evaluating Educational Assessment

1.1 Introduction: Ubiquitous assessment

Assessment plays an integral role in contemporary educational practice, and its use is ubiquitous across all formal education contexts. Teachers and students devote a large proportion of their class time to assessment activities (Stiggins & Conklin, 1992), and most of what researchers, parents, and policy makers know about what students are learning comes from the use of assessments (Brookhart, 2003; Light, 2001; National Research Council, 2001). Increasingly, practitioners in primary and secondary education, including teachers as well as administrators, are expected to understand the principles of assessment (and be certified in them via assessment) and to engage in sound assessment practices within and beyond the classroom (e.g., Elliot, 2003; NCATE, 2002; Schafer & Lissitz, 1987; Stiggins, 1999; Wise, 1993). Curriculum and instruction are also more apt to be integrally linked with, or even driven by, assessment practices and the forms that they take (e.g., Angelo & Cross, 1993; Huba & Freed, 2000; Wiggins & McTighe, 1998). Furthermore, current educational policy at all levels has been gripped by a veritable frenzy to hold teachers, programs, schools, and institutions accountable to the public through assessments (Shavelson & Huang, 2003). In response, testing professionals have devoted extensive energies to the development of assessments based on organizational, state, and national standards of student learning across a variety of content areas and disciplines (Cizek, 2001, 2003; Phelps, 1998; Popham, 1999). Along similar lines, assessment figures prominently in national education policies (e.g., No Child Left Behind, 2001) and the federal funding (or non-funding) of educational research (e.g., Education Sciences Reform, 2002). Even in the once 'off-limits' arena of higher education (including graduate education, see Haworth, 1996; Maki & Borkowski, 2006), faculty are being asked to engage in the structured and well-informed assessment of student learning, not only for the purposes of degree-program and institutional accreditation (e.g., Chun, 2002; Hernon & Dugan, 2006; Maki, 2002; Peterson & Einarson, 2001), but also as a means for understanding and improving student learning, and for revising curriculum and instruction (e.g., Bryan & Clegg, 2006; Cross, 1999; Lopez, 1998; Suskie, 2000).

Despite this ubiquity, or perhaps because of it, what constitutes a 'good' or 'appropriate' assessment in education has proven to be a highly contentious question, the answers to which range considerably depending on the purposes, uses, users, and contexts for assessment. Indeed, even arriving at a definition of the term *assessment* invites disagreement, with some arguing sharp technical distinctions among terms like assessment, measurement, and testing (e.g., Embretson & Hershberger, 1999). By contrast, others, like Popham (2000), contend that each of these terms can be defined identically, at least within education, as "A process by which educators use students' responses to specially created or naturally occurring stimuli in order to make inferences about students' knowledge, skills, or affective status" (p. 3).

As definitions have differed, so too have prioritized qualities of educational assessments. For example, some have argued that large-scale, norm-referenced testing of students based on national or state standards of achievement will ensure the accountability of teachers and schools, resulting in positive consequences for student learning outcomes (e.g., Cizek, 2001, 2003; Mehrens, 1998). Others have countered that this focus on accountability, and the concomitant demand for highly discriminating instruments based on traditional testing formats, is inappropriate for evaluating the quality of schools and teachers, and that it causes a reductionist approach to curriculum and the denigration of instruction and learning (e.g., Bryk, 1998; Popham, 1999, 2003b). In a similar vein, so-called 'alternative' assessments, including in particular performance and portfolio assessment, have been advocated for use in meeting both classroom- and curriculum-based purposes as well as for high-stakes achievement testing (e.g., Aschbacker, 1991; Wiggins, 1989, 1993b; Wolf, Bixby, Glenn, & Gardner, 1991). By assessing authentic, complex performances and samples of student work, it has been argued, teachers and students will focus on valued learning outcomes as opposed to figuring out how to score well on test items that have little to do with such outcomes. In response, others have emphasized perceived problems with reliability, domain sampling, population biases, and related concerns in suggesting that such 'alternative' assessments may not provide the most appropriate alternatives (Cizek, 1991; Eisner, 1999; Haertel, 1999; Mehrens, 1992). Still others have promoted distinct qualities for educational assessments, including, for example, a focus on the feedback potential of classroom-based assessments (e.g., Angelo & Cross, 1993), a prioritization of educative over auditing properties of assessments (e.g., Wiggins, 1998), and the clarity of objectives and relevance for instructional decision making of criterion-referenced and curriculum-based assessments (e.g., Glaser, 1994; Nitko, 1995, 2001; Popham, 1994).

While the nature of 'appropriate' or 'good' assessment continues to be debated, it is clear that assessment exerts an undeniable influence on educational practice and participants in the 21st century. The consequences of assessment use, and the qualities of assessments that are used, will in all probability persist in shaping how education proceeds and how education is experienced for some time to come. On the basis of assessments, students will be accepted, placed, promoted, informed, instructed, motivated, and rewarded, or they will be denied access, retained, misplaced, misled, discouraged, and embittered. Teachers will be hired, promoted, supported, encouraged, and developed, or their contracts may not be renewed. The public, and educational policy makers, will be thoroughly informed or they will be willfully (and often willingly) deceived. Likewise, on the basis of assessments, educational institutions, schools, and programs will be accredited and funded, or not. Standards and curriculum will be challenged, evaluated, endorsed, revised, or dismantled. Instruction will be supported, developed, and improved, or it will be degraded, undermined, and ignored. Even assessment itself will be judged, revised, and improved—or alternatives will be adopted—on the basis of its quality and the consequences that it engenders.

1.2 The challenge of educational assessment

Because its use is integral to educational practice as we know it, because it has the potential to do considerable harm or good, and because it may take a wide variety of (not necessarily agreed upon) forms in attempting to meet a variety of purposes, assessment presents contemporary educators with a major and complex challenge: to *ensure* that appropriate and high-quality assessment practices are being designed, developed, and employed in order to meet specific purposes and bring about positive consequences within the educational contexts for which their use is intended. It is clear that professional educators—teachers, administrators, researchers, academics— will be held ultimately responsible for what happens in the name of, through, and as a result of assessment as it is implemented in classrooms, schools, universities, and wherever structured educational efforts occur. No one else besides the professional educator is in a better position to be blamed or praised for assessment, or, more importantly, to do something about how assessment is perpetuated (or perpetrated). Therefore, whether for externally mandated assessments or with their own internally developed practices, it is up to educators to respond to this challenge by: (a) questioning whether assessment in general, as well as each specific instance of assessment, is functioning as intended within education; (b) seeking thorough and well-informed answers to these questions; and (c) doing something about it; in other words, making decisions and taking actions on the basis of the information entailed in those answers.

However, in order for this process of questioning, investigating, and acting on educational assessments—this process of *evaluating* assessments—to result in an improved understanding of, and lead to improvements in, assessments, the process itself begs careful design and implementation that is mindful of a variety of issues. When should assessments be investigated (e.g., during development, after adoption and use)? What features of an assessment demand attention (e.g., items, scores, score interpretations, associated decisions, consequences for students)? What kinds of questions should be asked about which features or qualities of assessments? Which questions should be prioritized for investigation, or do all possible questions need to be addressed? How much information is required to answer each question in an adequate way? When does the questioning stop, or does it? How should information from these investigations be put to use and by whom? Who should make these determinations? In short, what is required in order for educators to meet this challenge, to answer these questions, is a conceptual approach and a practical (i.e., practicable) method for evaluating educational assessments.

To some extent, of course, educators have responded to this challenge, through the development of a professional and academic discipline of educational measurement, with its standards of practice, theories and debates, and research, development, and dissemination activities. Over the past century, educational measurement has prioritized a finite, well-rationalized set of questions about assessment quality, focusing on the extent to which an assessment is measuring what it was intended to measure, as well as the extent to which interpretive and action inferences that are based on the measure are warranted (Messick, 1989). In practice, this means that questions are posed about the relationship between assessment designs, the items and tasks that examinees respond to and perform, the resulting scores and how they are determined, and the kinds of claims that are made about examinees' abilities or knowledge on the basis of those scores. In addition, these assessment *validity* questions are accompanied by a standard set of scientific techniques, which have been developed over the years into a comprehensive methodology for investigating the measurement qualities of assessments (AERA, APA, NCME, 1999). Clearly, the current practice of assessment *validation* presents educators with one professionally endorsed and highly refined approach to ensuring the quality of assessments as measurement instruments, and it is typically undertaken by measurement experts with the know-how to do so.

However, as thoughtful contemporary educators have developed particular assessment practices in response to the specific demands of their educational contexts, questions have begun to emerge regarding the feasibility, utility, and meaningfulness of conventional assessment validation processes stemming from this measurement tradition. To what extent, they ask, are prescribed validity questions and methods adequate to the challenge of evaluating and ensuring assessment quality, especially when that evaluation entails an expectation that resulting information will be used for improving assessment practice *in situ*. For example, where performance assessments have been developed in order to emphasize the real-world value of instructional outcomes, many have questioned the prioritization of validity concerns with measurement qualities over other important qualities like the impact of assessment on teaching and learning, the feedback potential of complex performances, the perception of assessment authenticity by the public, and the student motivational outcomes of targeting real-world tasks (e.g., Eisner, 1999; Linn, Baker, & Dunbar, 1991; Miller & Legg, 1993; Moss, 1992; Quellmalz, 1991; Wiggins, 1989, 1993b, 1998; Wolf, Bixby, Glenn, & Gardner, 1991).

Along similar lines, it has been argued that educational measurement has become so "hyperspecialized" (Popham, 2003a), so focused on a truncated set of assessment types used for meeting only a finite range of purposes, that the profession has lost sight of the extent of the challenges presented by assessments as they are actually developed and used throughout all corners of education today. For example, until very recently (e.g., Brookhart, 2003; McMillan, 2003; Moss, 2003), the discipline had specifically abdicated any responsibility for evaluating and ensuring the quality of classroom-based assessments (persistent attention from concerned measurement practitioners notwithstanding; e.g., Stiggins, 1988, 2001; Stiggins & Bridgeford, 1985; Stiggins & Conklin, 1992), to the point that the most recent standards for professional practice (AERA, APA, NCME, 1999) clearly stated this dissociation.

Despite such concerns, it would be foolish for educators to argue that a conventional educational measurement approach to assessment validation has nothing to offer in response to the challenge of evaluating and ensuring assessment quality. However, it does seem necessary to examine the extent to which the current conceptual approach and practical methods for validation can provide an adequate and applicable framework for raising relevant questions, investigating meaningful answers in feasible ways, and utilizing findings for understanding and improving assessments within the full range of educational contexts for their use. Will conventional validity practice enable the individuals responsible for evaluating assessments to do so for the particular assessment types that are being used for meeting specific purposes within specific settings?

A fitting response to the assessment challenge will depend equally, in turn, on the characteristics of assessment within each particular educational context. Different domains of education may differ considerably in terms of the demands and impetuses for assessment, the traditions of assessment, the extent to which a given discipline has accepted responsibility for assessment, and the associated treatment of assessment through research, development, and practice. For example, in some contexts, assessment may be perceived only as an external accountability demand (e.g., accreditation in higher education), while assessment in other contexts may be required as a fundamental component of daily educational practice (e.g., to meet feedback purposes in learner-centered, electronically-mediated instruction; see Bitter & Pierson, 2002; Frederick, 2002; Muirhead, 2002). Assessment may have enjoyed lengthy institutionalized traditions in certain contexts (e.g., standardized achievement testing in secondary education), or it may be a very new and evolving process (e.g., awarding college credit through the assessment of adult experiential learning outside of the classroom; see Keeton, 1999). Certainly, unique educational domains will have very distinct perceptions regarding assessment as a core professional responsibility, and the development of and standards for educational practitioners will vary accordingly. For example, primary and secondary school teachers and administrators will have been exposed to at least some course-work in principles and practices of educational assessment via their certification requirements, while it is unlikely that the majority of college faculty members in the non-education disciplines would have received any formal training in assessment, or in education for that matter.

Finally, the nature and treatment of assessment within a given context will also depend on the extent to which that locus for assessment has served as a subject of research, development, and practice, either from within or beyond the professional discipline. The educational measurement profession has clearly focused much greater efforts on certain purposes and contexts for assessment (e.g., university entrance testing, large-scale state and national achievement testing in public education, aptitude testing in the military) than others (e.g., classroom assessment, student learning outcomes assessment in higher education). Likewise, assessment may or may not provide a valued professional focus within unique contexts of education, as revealed by the existence or absence within a given discipline of journals which publish articles on assessment, professional organizations which address assessment standards, conferences at which assessment forms a major theme, and/or expectations for academics to engage in assessment as a part of their professional responsibilities.

1.3 Responding to the challenge: The current work

Given the unique characteristics which define assessment within each educational context, and given the potential incongruity of conventional validation practices sanctioned by the educational measurement profession, how, then, are educators to respond to the challenge of evaluating and ensuring the quality of assessments? On what basis might a conceptual approach and practical methods for meeting this challenge be identified? This precise problem served as the point of departure for the current work, which explored the notion of *validity evaluation* as a means for reconciling assessment validity concerns with the contextual realities of assessments in use and the particular needs of educators in evaluating them.

My purpose in this work was twofold. First, I sought to understand and address the exact nature of the challenge to evaluate and ensure the quality of educational assessments by: (a) scrutinizing the characteristics of assessment within a representative educational domain (U.S. college foreign language education); (b) unpacking and illuminating the relevant recommendations and shortcomings of conventional validity theory and practice in educational measurement; and (c) reconceptualizing assessment validation in order to provide a workable solution for evaluating assessments within specific educational settings. Thus, in the current work I did not simply design yet another validation study for a given educational assessment following conventional questions and methods. Rather, I sought first to found an approach to designing evaluations of assessments that would enable the actual, responsible educators to prioritize and investigate important qualities of assessments (including conventional validity qualities, where relevant) as they are actually used to meet specific purposes within a particular educational context. In addition, rather than simply gathering prescribed validity information, I sought to incorporate into evaluation design the intended uses of such information within the corresponding educational domain, thereby tailoring methodology to the overriding purpose of ensuring assessment quality (i.e., doing something about it, rather than just doing it).

Second, I then examined how the resulting *validity evaluation* methodology could be applied in designing and implementing the needed evaluation of assessment practices within a specific, innovative German language program at a U.S. university. In a three-year case study, I engaged the responsible local educators in the evaluation of assessment practice, thereby enabling a thorough exploration of the kinds of questions that were actually asked and prioritized about assessment, the methods that made sense in responding to these questions, and, most importantly, the ways and extent to which validity evaluation processes and findings were actually used to ensure assessment quality. The details of this particular evaluation were, of necessity, locally contextualized to the specific assessment uses and the educational program and domain. Naturally, the assessments in question focused on aspects of German language knowledge and ability. However, outcomes of this in-depth investigation offer key insights into how the validity evaluation approach proceeded and how it motivated changes in assessments and in a 'culture of assessment' within the program. These insights may help elucidate the assessment challenges experienced in diverse educational contexts, foreign language and others alike. Moreover, the processes and outcomes of the current work illustrate one mechanism for fundamentally reconceptualizing validity and the ways in which educational assessments are currently evaluated.

The foundation, structure, and findings of this work are presented as follows. Chapter 2 characterizes assessment in U.S. college foreign language education, from the perspective of its traditions, impetuses, professional responsibilities, and research and development activities, in order to contextualize the challenge of evaluating and ensuring assessment quality within this domain. Chapter 3 traces the origins of recent notions of measurement validity and reflects on their relevance for evaluating educational assessments. Chapter 4 explores the reconceptualization of validation in educational assessment from the perspective of program evaluation theory and practice. Chapter 5 introduces the validity evaluation model and methods proposed for meeting assessment evaluation needs in college foreign language education, and it outlines the major characteristics of the specific foreign language program within which it was applied. Chapter 6 then details the questions, methods, findings, and uses from each of a series of evaluation studies conducted over three years of assessment development and practice within this program, with particular focus on a single assessment used for placing students into the German undergraduate curriculum. Finally, Chapter 7 discusses the local and broader implications and limitations of the validity evaluation approach, and concludes with recommendations for additional work that is needed in order to meet the serious and complex challenges of educational assessment, paying particular attention to the U.S. college foreign language education context.

Chapter 2
The challenge of assessment in
U.S. college foreign language education

College foreign language (FL) education in the U.S. constitutes a unique educational context, with its own subject areas and curricular objectives, its instructional theories and practices, and its proprietary organizations and intellectual forums. From within this milieu, unique traditions of assessment have emerged as well. In order to come to grips with the specific nature of the assessment challenge—that is, how college FL educators might best go about ensuring the quality of their assessment practices—a characterization of assessment within college FL education will provide the background necessary for identifying key concerns and for situating evaluation needs, constraints, and possibilities. The three sections of this chapter review U.S. college FL assessment from the perspective of its distinct traditions and impetuses, its priority within the professional concerns of FL educators, and the amount and focus of assessment research and development efforts in this context.

2.1 Traditions of assessment in U.S. college foreign language education

Much of why and how assessment occurs within contemporary U.S. college FL education is related both to a substantial history of FL assessment, which developed hand-in-hand with FL teaching methodologies, and to a range of distinct purposes to be fulfilled by assessment. Of course, the origins of testing, measurement, and assessment can be critiqued from a variety of sociological and historical perspectives (e.g., Foucault, 1979; Madaus, 1990; Toulmin, 1990), and there is little doubt that early efforts to measure mental abilities (e.g., Thorndike, 1904) have influenced deeply the nature of all educational assessment as we know it in the U.S. today (Gould, 1981), including language testing (Spolsky, 1995). Nevertheless, the specific practices of assessment in college FL education have been most immediately determined, on the one hand, by widely promulgated views regarding how foreign language knowledge/ability can best be measured, and on the other, by the exigencies of decision making, accountability, and 'good practice' in institutionalized higher education.

2.1.1 How to assess?

Although language testing in general has a complex and lengthy history (see reviews in Barnwell, 1996; Spolsky, 1995), current trends in college FL assessment practice derive from a handful of 20th century traditions that forcefully argued *how* language should be measured and provided FL educators with instruments for doing so. Principal influences were: (a) an early focus on standardization and objectivity, especially in receptive tests; (b) structuralist demands (in the 1950s and 1960s) for testing discrete components of language knowledge; (c) an emphasis on testing communicative ability (in the 1970s and 1980s); and, most prominently, (d) the proficiency movement's particular take on communicative competence—in the form of proficiency guidelines, scales, and tests.

During the first half of the 20th century, much attention was paid in the U.S. (e.g., Coleman, 1929; Henmon, 1929, 1934; Lundeberg, 1929) to the development and dissemination of standardized testing procedures for use in determining progress and achievement in college FL learning. For example, in conjunction with the *Modern Foreign Language Study* (Henmon, 1929), tests were developed to focus on the following language skill areas: (a) reading comprehension, (b) vocabulary recognition and production, (c) knowledge of grammatical rules, (d) aural comprehension, and (e) written composition. The intent of these 'new-type' tests was to enable interpretations about what students were actually learning in language classrooms and programs of study. Given the subjective nature of grading practices ('old-type' tests, often based on translation exercises), educators sought to standardize the measurement of language ability through the introduction of more objective methods. Thus, tests featured new item formats which could be scored with consistency (e.g., multiple-choice and true-false), much larger numbers of items to increase reliability, and the use of rating protocols and descriptive scales in written constructed-response tests (e.g., compositions). Likewise, the content of tests was based objectively on the minimal expectations associated with college FL curriculum and instruction of the time (hence a heavy focus on receptive skills and grammatical knowledge).

Common to these early FL tests, then, was an overarching emphasis on the careful measurement of language knowledge and/or ability, and tests were to be applied and interpreted in equivalent ways across the variety of college contexts in which language skills were being taught (Henmon, 1934). However, beyond very generic allusions to progress or achievement purposes, no particular attention was paid to the variety of possible educational functions to which tests might be put—good assessment was equated with standardized, objective, and accurate measurement (as observed by Spolsky, 1995), but not necessarily with meeting particular educational needs. This emphasis on measuring language with the 'new-type' tests quickly took hold, and the content, format, and structure of these early college FL assessment practices—especially a focus on testing receptive skills and grammatical knowledge—has been sustained over most of the 20th century, including the ongoing practice of large-scale FL assessment in U.S. colleges and universities (e.g., the *Advanced Placement* foreign language exams, the *SAT II* language subject exams, and commercial assessments like the *Foreign Language Achievement Tests* from Brigham Young University). What is more, the emphasis on standardization, objectivity, and accurate measurement came to mark most subsequent language tests (Spolsky, 1995).

Discrete-point testing. The tradition of "discrete-point" testing (a term coined by Carroll, 1961) emerged from these early years as perhaps the major influence on how assessment was done. It sought to measure accurately finite bits of a learner's knowledge about specific components of the target language (phonological segments, grammar rules, vocabulary meanings, etc.), typically in the form of selected-response (e.g., multiple choice) or very limited constructed-response (e.g., word completion) items. A range of such items, for example, based on contrastive distinctions between the target and first languages of a learner, could be compiled into a test instrument and scored objectively as correct or incorrect, and the sum of these item scores was presumed to provide a trustworthy indication of the learner's mastery of a given component of the target language. Perhaps best represented in the work of Lado (1961), discrete-point testing of this sort was clearly linked with structuralist linguistics and behaviorist models of learning and teaching (especially audiolingualism, e.g., Fries, 1945). As such, it was considered to provide a much more trustworthy measure of language knowledge than did so-called "integrative tests" (Carroll, 1961), in which a focus on contextualized communication interfered with a direct interpretation about learner mastery of the structural building blocks of the target language. Despite theoretical and practical arguments against the measurement of language in this manner (Brière, 1971; Spolsky, 1973), and early alternative models from the English-language testing industry (e.g., Oller, 1971), there is little doubt that discrete-point assessment continues to be practiced throughout college FL education (Barnwell, 1996), particularly in the form of teacher-developed tests. For example, in a collection on the training of FL graduate students, Mason (2000) recommended the inclusion of Lado's (1961) discrete-point treatise as a "standard language testing manual" (p. 121) for meeting FL teachers' needs.

Communicative testing. Largely in response, a subsequent tradition, which sought to provide a more direct means for measuring a learner's ability to communicate, emerged during the 1970s and 1980s with developments in communicative language teaching (e.g., Canale & Swain, 1980) and evolving notions of linguistic competence and performance (e.g., Hymes, 1967). From this perspective, given the shifting focus in language teaching away from the structural pattern drills of audiolingualism and towards the development of learners' creative abilities to use the language (e.g., Savignon & Berns, 1984), assessments also needed to emphasize contextualized communicative performance rather than decontextualized display of knowledge. Appropriate measures of communicative competence were to be based on simulated language use situations in which the learner received and produced (typically aural/oral) real-world messages, and measures were to be scored according to a criterion of communicative success rather than linguistic accuracy (e.g., Canale, 1984; Swain, 1984). As with communicative language teaching, so too were extensive efforts made to describe how best to test 'communicatively' (e.g., Canale, 1984; Henning, 1990; Magnan, 1991). However, as was the case in discrete-point testing, the focus of assessment continued to be how best to measure accurately the language knowledge or ability construct of interest, in this case communicative competence. Little attention was paid, in these prescriptions for how to test communicatively, to the educational uses to which tests might be put or how test qualities might need to vary accordingly.

Proficiency testing. While the communicative language teaching and testing groundswell spawned a new wave of language education practices around the world (e.g., Munby, 1978; van Ek, 1976), in U.S. foreign language education it was quickly incorporated into the hugely influential proficiency movement, beginning in the early 1980s. This 'movement', which came in response to several national surveys and reports on the crisis of FL teaching and learning in the U.S. ("Report", 1978; "Report", 1980), was driven by the American Council on the Teaching of Foreign Languages (ACTFL) and its search for universally agreed upon standards of FL learning. According to Higgs (1984b):

> We have called proficiency 'the organizing principle' because literally every-thing that students, teachers, and teacher trainers know and understand about active, spontaneous *use* of language and productive cultural interaction can be subsumed under the proficiency movement's watchwords of *function*, *content*, and *accuracy*. (p. v, emphasis in original)

Ability to use language, rather than passive knowledge about language, was the order of the day from a proficiency perspective. The key to this organizing principle was a set of scales developed by ACTFL (1982, 1986), and ostensibly generic to all foreign languages, that described the constellation of communicative functions, content, and accuracy at each of a series of proficiency levels, from novice to superior, germane to the perceived learning needs and limitations of U.S. FL students. These "proficiency guidelines" were ostensibly based on descriptions and experiences of learners using the language, rather than prescriptions or theories about language competence, and as such they could be trusted to provide a 'common yardstick' against which to measure learners' actual, real-world abilities (Liskin-Gasparro, 1984a, 1984b). Although distinct scales were developed by ACTFL for each of the four skills, the proficiency descriptions were originally based on a similar scale from the Foreign Service Institute's Oral Interview procedure, which was used to assess the preparation of U.S. diplomats and other government employees for dealing with the speaking demands of overseas assignments (Lowe, 1988).

Along with these proficiency guidelines, assessments were also needed that would provide an accurate indication of where, within the novice to superior scale, a learner's global language proficiency was located. Of primary importance were assessments of speaking proficiency, which provided the most direct and comprehensive reflection of this new approach to communicative competence (Byrnes & Canale, 1986; Liskin-Gasparro, 1984b). However, given the complex descriptions of proficiency at each scale level, test scores could not be based on mere communicative success, although that certainly played a role, but they also had to account for the extent to which an examinee met each of the minimal characteristics which described a given level, including features such as fluency, grammatical accuracy, appropriate vocabulary, and pragmatic sensitivity, in addition to the ability to handle a range of distinct tasks, communicative situations, and topics. In order to operationalize the complex proficiency guidelines via assessment, then, ACTFL also appropriated the format of the FSI Oral Interview as its primary approach to measuring proficiency. In the ACTFL Oral Proficiency Interview (OPI), an examinee interacted with an interlocutor who was trained both to elicit language performance relevant to the various scale level descriptions and to rate the qualities of this performance according to the same (Buck, Byrnes, & Thompson, 1989; Clark & Clifford, 1988).

This approach to speaking assessment promised a comprehensive measurement of language based on a set of proficiency scales endorsed by the U.S. FL community, yet independent of any particular teaching method or curriculum. OPI ratings were championed as unadulterated, direct, and objective indications of a learner's language proficiency (e.g., Liskin-Gasparro, 1984a, 1984b; Omaggio, 1986). However, in order for such measurement to actually occur objectively and to produce accurate and trustworthy scores, it became clear that FL educators would need to be provided with considerable assistance in the administration of OPIs and the rating of examinee performances. ACTFL thus initiated an extensive (not to mention expensive) rater training program, whereby FL educators could be certified as OPI raters, in order to standardize proficiency assessment practices across FL education settings (Barnwell, 1996). In addition, to extend the benefits of an accurate proficiency measure to the less commonly taught languages, in which trained raters were only rarely available, ACTFL also sponsored the initial creation of Simulated Oral Proficiency Interviews (SOPIs), which were tape-based and self-administered, but which could be submitted for official ratings according to the ACTFL Guidelines in much the same manner as OPIs (e.g., Clark, 1988; Stansfield, 1996; Stansfield et al., 1990; Stansfield & Kenyon, 1992).

As the appeal of these standardized proficiency measures spread, and was promoted by ACTFL, additional efforts were pursued in order to: (a) tailor proficiency scales in each of the four skills to distinct expectations across different FLs (e.g., ACTFL, 1987a, 1987b, 1988, 1989); (b) revise the original ACTFL proficiency guidelines in response to perceived weaknesses (e.g., ACTFL, 1999); (c) develop more specific guidelines, as well as instruments and procedures for measuring proficiency in listening, reading, and writing (e.g., Breiner-Sanders, Swender, & Terry, 2002; CARLA Assessment Team, 1998a, 2000a, 2000b); and (d) explore new methods for accurately and efficiently measuring speaking proficiency (e.g., computerization, see Kenyon & Malabonga, 2001).

The influence and import, perceived as well as real, of the proficiency movement and associated assessments have indelibly marked U.S. college FL assessment as it occurs today (Barnwell, 1996). In descriptions of the proficiency movement's role in FL education, terms like "Holy Grail" (Higgs, 1984a) and "revolution" ("The quiet revolution", 2002) have been used not infrequently, and assessment practices based on the ACTFL proficiency guidelines figure prominently in FL teacher development as well as in the college FL assessment research literature (see below). In practice, proficiency assessment has been advocated for and applied to a variety of purposes in college settings, from the operationalization of a foreign language learning requirement to classroom assessment to just about every other use, including:

13

"academic placement, student assessment, program evaluation, professional certification, hiring, and promotional qualification" ("The quiet revolution", 2002, p. 593).

The assessment traditions outlined above—from early notions of standardized objective measurement to discrete-point, communicative, and proficiency testing—have called for and resulted in obviously divergent practices for the assessment of language knowledge and/or ability in college FL education. However, underlying apparent differences in the forms of assessment, these distinct approaches have all subscribed to a single tradition that perpetuated a 'how-to' mentality. In Lado's (1961) words, "Since the student has to learn language, it is language that we must test" (p. 20). While their accounts for what constitutes 'language' have differed substantially, in association with developments in language pedagogy, their approaches to assessment have all sought to operationalize language knowledge, ability, competence, proficiency, etc., in the form of standardized measurement instruments and procedures. These measures were to be applied with utmost consistency across all contexts of use, with the goal of providing a maximally accurate interpretation of the language knowledge and/or abilities of students. Likewise, the primary qualities of a good assessment had to do with the fidelity of this interpretation; in the words of the College Entrance Examination Board (1937), in discussing FL exams, "The index of genuine significance is that of validity, or the extent to which an examination actually measures what it purports to measure" (p. 31).

Thus, despite claims by proponents that the ACTFL OPI "stood language assessment on its head" ("The quiet revolution", 2002, p. 589), the proficiency movement simply offered one more argument for *how* language should be measured. What none of these traditions pursued, however, was the relationship between their well-advocated measures and the various roles that assessment was actually being asked to play within college FL education contexts. Nor did they offer any evaluative evidence for why their particular measures provided the most fitting means of informing the specific uses of assessment by FL educators. Instead, they instructed FL educators that standardized, objective measures of language were the appropriate focus in developing and evaluating college FL educational assessments. This decontextualized measurement emphasis on 'how to assess', then, reflects the primary legacy that these traditions have passed along to contemporary college FL assessment practice. This tradition has led most FL educators to engage in assessments of the sorts described above (often in the form of ready-made commercial solutions) because of the perception that good measurement is all that is needed for good educational assessment.

2.1.2 Why assess?

While considerable attention has been paid over the years to how language should be measured, there has been, until very recently, much less discussion regarding why the assessment of students actually needs to occur within the particular context of U.S. college FL education. Even historical reviews of FL assessment (e.g.,

14

Barnwell, 1996; Spolsky, 1995, 2000) have made almost no mention of the specific impetuses for engaging in language assessment or its educational roles, in college FL settings or elsewhere. At the same time, some language testers have argued that the most important consideration in developing, adopting, or adapting educational tests is the use or uses to which test-based information will be put (e.g., Bachman, 1990; Bachman & Palmer, 1996; Brown, 1996; Norris, 2000), and it is becoming increasingly apparent that there are many possible uses (indeed, many required uses) for assessments in contemporary college FL settings, as in all of education.

Of course, various sources on college FL educational assessment, and particularly textbooks on FL assessment or teaching, have paid perfunctory homage to the notion that assessments might need to meet distinct purposes. For example, Lado (1961) cited achievement, diagnostic, and aptitude uses for language tests, while Larson and Jones (1984) distinguished between proficiency and achievement tests, and Valette (1992) described the three main assessment roles in college FL education as placement, achievement, and proficiency testing. Many FL educators have drawn a basic distinction between formative and summative assessments (e.g., Omaggio, 1986; Swain, 1984), although for some this is simply a temporal distinction (during instruction versus at the end) rather the identification of different ways of *using* assessment information (e.g., ACTFL, 2002). Other educators have focused on 'types' of assessment. For example, The College Board (1996) identified the four most important types of assessment in FL education to be achievement, prochievement, proficiency, and performance-based. Still others have discussed a much wider variety of uses for assessment, as did Finocchiaro and Sako (1983), who provided over fifteen distinct answers to the question "why do we test" and then categorized these according to three overarching uses: (a) student measurement; (b) instructional evaluation; and (c) curriculum evaluation.

Each of these examples, and others like them within FL education, has indicated the potential diversity in applications for FL assessment, ranging from very generic distinctions between types of tests to much more particular delineations of their specific intended uses. However, as these sources have each gone on to describe the characteristics that constitute good assessment practice, they have generally failed to consider that this diversity in intended uses for assessment might call for a parallel diversity in the form of distinct designs that emphasize unique qualities of assessment most appropriate and effective for meeting these different purposes. Instead, they have emphasized the need for assessments to be designed according to traditional principles of good measurement—objectivity, reliability, fairness, etc.; in short, the validity characteristics that make a test (any test) a good measure of what it was intended to measure.

There is an apparent gap, then, between prescribed notions of good measurement in FL education and the ways in which these good measures might or might not be applied in resolving the actual challenges of unique assessment uses, users, purposes, and intended consequences in FL settings. This gap between the 'how' and the 'why' of assessment is further exacerbated by opaque proclamations from authoritative sources, for example, in The College Board's (1996) recommendation that "[t]he use

15

of alternative assessment practices can help teachers to meld curriculum, instruction, and student evaluation into a coherent whole" (p. 31)—what exactly assessment is intended to do remains undefined in their treatment, but the message makes clear that teachers should be practicing assessment and that it should be of the 'alternative' variety.

Meanwhile, whether or not the characteristics and qualities of language measures are aligned with their purposes and uses, assessments are regularly applied within college FL settings (a) for making real decisions about students, (b) for informing instruction and learning, and (c) for meeting increasing demands for accountability and program improvement from within and beyond institutional walls. These three educational perspectives account for most of the impetuses to assess within U.S. college FL education today. Recently, individuals have begun to recognize the gap between these assessment impetuses and the information and processes that they require, on the one hand, and the qualities that are emphasized within an array of available language measurement practices, on the other. Following in particular the first wave of the proficiency movement and its promulgation of one-size-fits-all-purposes assessment, some FL educators have sought to raise the awareness of others regarding the need to design and evaluate college FL assessments with their distinct purposes in mind. In an early example, Shohamy (1992) discussed the ways in which language assessments can be designed and used in responding to the critical feedback needs of both students and teachers within classrooms, as well as how such assessment information might be extended to provide feedback at the FL program and curriculum level. In a similar vein, Delett, Barnhardt, and Kevorkian (2001) devoted several years to the development of a framework for using portfolio assessments in FL education. Key to their recommendations was initial identification of the ways in which the portfolio was intended to be used, including classroom-internal as well as program-level uses, the careful design of the portfolio to meet those particular uses, and the evaluation of the portfolio assessment according to those uses. More recently, Phillips (2003) highlighted increasing external demands on college FL departments to meet accountability expectations in the form of both institutional and professional accreditation, and she called for the careful development of performance assessments that would provide evidence for the range of student learning outcomes valued by FL programs.

These examples suggest that FL educators are beginning to realize the need to align assessment qualities with the uses to which they will actually be put. What is more, these educators have taken a critical step beyond the mere advocacy of 'how' to assess and towards the explicit linkage of particular ways of doing assessment with particular reasons for doing so. By way of summary, then, one might ask what basic intended uses for assessment have been identified within contemporary college FL education. The following list, which expands on and details assessment from the three educational perspectives above, compiles a range of such uses raised within various corners of the college FL literature over the past decade. Assessment is used in U.S. college FL education for:

1. Making decisions about students, including: admissions, placement, awarding of college FL credit, determining fulfillment of exit requirements, grading, advancement or retention, awarding scholarships/grants, and certification of language abilities.
2. Informing instruction and learning within the classroom, including: the provision of feedback to teachers (for diagnosing needs of individual learners, for understanding student learning outcomes, for revising instruction, etc.); the provision of feedback to learners (for describing the extent to which they are meeting expectations, for identifying what to emphasize in studying, etc.); and focusing, sustaining, and improving the motivation of students.
3. Meeting programmatic and institutional purposes, including: the provision of feedback on the effectiveness and appropriateness of curricular expectations and instructional methods (e.g., for program-internal decision making); the demonstration of student learning outcomes vis-à-vis expectations (e.g., for program review and accreditation); the demonstration of the *use* of assessment for program and instructional improvement (e.g., for contemporary approaches to institutional accreditation); and the communication of program worth to students, teachers, the institution, and the public.

This list provides an initial idea of the generic range of demands that college FL educators typically must respond to via their assessments. However, in order to meet such demands through local practice, individual college FL educators and programs will have to respond to their own unique set of impetuses to assess, in conjunction with the particular students, teachers, curriculum and instruction, and institutional requirements that characterize a specific educational context.

2.2 Assessment responsibility and professional development

Faced with the very real, increasing, and increasingly divergent demands for educational assessment, as well as a variety of received traditions, to what extent and how has the U.S. college FL profession responded? What is the status of assessment within the ranks of college FL faculty and practitioners, and at what level of sophistication are they prepared to act on the challenge to ensure the qualities of assessments within FL education? While language testers and other educational measurement specialists may or may not apply their expertise to college FL assessment issues (see section 2.3), it is clear that FL department administrators, faculty, instructors, and teaching assistants will engage most directly in the use of assessments for meeting demands of the sorts listed above. Therefore, the qualities of assessment that are valued, how it is practiced, and the ways in which it might best be evaluated will depend in large part on: (a) how assessment has come to be perceived and addressed as a professional responsibility within college FL departments and the FL discipline in general, and (b) the extent and nature of FL educators' professional development in assessment-related knowledge and skills.

2.2.1 A professional responsibility to assess

Turning to current configurations of FL departments, of major concern is the "deskilling of professional teachers" (Crookes, 1997, p. 68) and a generally denigrated status of educational topics, including assessment, among FL professionals. It has been observed that FL teaching in the U.S. is typically not treated as a profession, with its own knowledge base, standards, and areas of research expertise (e.g., Bernhardt & Hammadou, 1987; Hammadou, 1993; Schrier, 1993). In addition, the "anti-intellectual" perception of FL education has reinforced the notion of language teaching as a craft to be passed across generations rather than an area for serious professional development and inquiry (Jarvis & Taylor, 1990), and the marginalized status of education topics and specialists within FL departments is well-attested. For example, in characterizing FL departments of the early 1980s, DiPietro, Lantolf, and Labarca (1983) found that only 3% of courses in U.S. FL graduate programs dealt with language pedagogy (never mind assessment), while 73% addressed literature and criticism, and the remainder focused on linguistics. Furthermore, in a survey of 154 language program directors in the U.S., Teschner (1987) found that only 13% had completed dissertations in what he termed 'educational linguistics', while 19% had focused on theoretical linguistics and 59% on literature.

It has also been observed more recently (e.g., Byrnes, 2001; Byrnes & Kord, 2001; Ortega, 1999) that the predominant structure of FL departments features a bifurcation of 'language teachers' and 'content teachers'. This divide has been linked, in turn, to antipathy on the part of the content-teaching majority for the importance of *language* education issues, to the lack of articulation within FL undergraduate curricula and courses, and to a failure in the preparation of FL graduate students to face the educational realities of future professional demands (e.g., Byrnes, 2001; Graman, 1988; Pfeiffer, 2002; Shanahan, 1997; Tedick & Walker, 1994, 1995). Indeed, a dismal picture of FL professionalism vis-à-vis educational concerns emerged during the 1990s, reflecting an emphasis in language teaching practice on the implementation of prescribed 'methods' over well-considered and researched pedagogy (Azevedo, 1990; Tedick & Walker, 1994). Consequently, Crookes (1997) observed that, "At a technical level, teachers are not given the tools to do the job even when the job of S/FL teaching is depicted at a level of nonprovocative liberal discourse: to educate children and adults in second and foreign languages" (p. 75).

At the same time, and in part as a result of these awareness-raising discussions, the FL education community has devoted some attention to the unavoidable educational responsibilities that face college FL programs. As they have defined the scope and focus of these responsibilities, assessment has been included, albeit most often as a minor concern. Thus, while Spolsky (2000) observed that, historically, FL educators have downplayed the importance of assessment in language teaching, assessment demands have triggered its inclusion within recent recommendations for the basic professional needs of FL departments (e.g., Bernhardt, 2002; Byrnes, 2001; Phillips, 2003; Schulz, 2002). For example, Lariviere (2002) argued that, in order to foster effective language instruction, FL departments must be staffed to cover a "complex of professional concerns ranging from basic pedagogical techniques to innovative assessment of student learning" (p. 245).

Unfortunately, that these observations are continually repeated within professional discourse is probably indicative of the minimal ways in which assessment expertise has been incorporated into expectations for language teachers and language program administrators. On the one hand, some educators expressed an early awareness of the lack of assessment expertise within college FL programs, as did Valette (1992), who pointed out that "[m]ost college language departments do not have a testing specialist on their faculty" (p. 199). On the other hand, assessment was also treated within these observations as a narrow technical skill and therefore beyond the scope of most FL educators. Again, Valette (1992) noted, "In fact, the great majority of foreign-language professors are unfamiliar with psychometrics and uncomfortable with statistics" (p. 199). That educational assessment within language programs might entail something more and different than just psychometrics and statistics has typically not been acknowledged.

Where assessment has been addressed as a responsibility of FL educators, it has come in the form of a watered-down set of expectations, or it has been relegated to the 'language' specialists within FL departments. For example, Rivers (1992a) observed that FL teachers, regardless of their disciplinary affiliations (e.g., literature, linguistics), expend a great deal of their professional time in developing and delivering language courses; as such, she sought to outline the areas of knowledge that all members of the FL professoriate should command. Regarding assessment, she advised that all FL educators "should understand principles of assessment and evaluation of learning and be able to apply these in quizzes and examinations at all levels" (p. 298). However, she made no mention of the capacities or knowledge which might underlie these principles and applications, of the assessment demands that might or might not be fulfilled by "quizzes and examinations", or of the need for educators to evaluate and ensure the qualities of their assessments. In addition, for "language teaching and culture specialists" she recommended some competency in "psychometrics", and she suggested that their research and publications might include "problems of language learning in formal settings, including testing" (p. 300). However, for "language program directors and coordinators" she did not include assessment as an area of concern.

In general, then, although assessment has been identified as an area in need of attention within FL departments, it has not been afforded a very central status among the responsibilities of most FL educators. Moreover, the role to be played by educational capabilities has remained ambiguous within FL departments, despite increasingly apparent needs for a distinct FL educational knowledge base, including language assessment. As discussed in the following section, this ambiguity is further reflected in the discipline's treatment of just how best to develop emerging FL professionals.

19

2.2.2 Professional development in assessment

Perhaps most revealing of the status of assessment within the FL milieu is its role in professional preparation. Of interest in related discussions is the amount and type of attention that has been paid to assessment, and specifically the development of teachers' abilities to understand its various uses, to design and engage in relevant practices, and to evaluate its processes and outcomes. While the professional development experiences of individual educators will clearly differ across graduate degree programs, faculty mentors, and other circumstances, the following review of associated topics that have emerged within the FL education literature provides basic insights into the likely status quo of assessment within professional development experiences.

Foreign language educator development has been addressed since the early days of the proficiency movement, when it became clear that the FL profession was going to be held responsible for the language learning outcomes of U.S. college students (e.g., "Report", 1980). This realization, in conjunction with the dramatic shift in language teaching practices towards more communicative techniques, spurred several educators to express concern with the lack of training among most FL practitioners for engaging in assessment practices that were relevant to the new ways of teaching. For example, Canale (1984) worried that "teacher training in this complex and crucial component of any curriculum has been minimal" (p. 79), and consequently that "[r]eliance on existing tests and assessment techniques as a means of compensating for the relative lack of teacher training in this area raises concerns about the suitability of a given test" (p. 79). As such, he argued that teachers needed to be trained in methods for measuring "core aspects of communication" (p. 87). Others echoed the primary concern that FL educators were practicing discrete-point testing while they were learning to teach in communicative ways, and they emphasized the need to train teachers in the application of tests that supported and 'washed back' positively on communication-oriented curriculum and instruction (e.g., Byrnes & Canale, 1986; Higgs, 1981; James, 1984; Morrow, 1984; Omaggio, 1986; Swain, 1984).

Along these lines, proponents of the proficiency movement argued that FL educators obviously needed to be trained in proficiency-based assessment procedures, and particularly the OPI, given the goal of the movement to "interpret every aspect of a program—materials and activities, student and teacher behaviors—into a larger conceptual framework" (Muyskens, 1984, p. 197). As the organizing principle of the ACTFL proficiency guidelines was being disseminated and used to transform teaching (Higgs, 1984b), so too were principles of proficiency assessment advocated for teacher development and incorporated into its practice (e.g., Omaggio, 1986). For example, as a foreign language oral proficiency requirement based on the ACTFL guidelines was introduced into undergraduate education at the University of Pennsylvania (Freed, 1984), it became clear that FL faculty and teaching assistants would have to understand the ACTFL guidelines and be able to use the OPI, in order to "provide for and maintain an intimate connection between training, teaching, and testing" (p. 225). Similarly, Muyskens (1984) advocated a proficiency-oriented approach to all of FL teacher preparation, including training in the OPI and other means of directly measuring proficiency, with the clear intent of altering teacher behaviors: "Once prospective teachers are aware of the proficiency goals, they will no longer want to give only traditional discrete-item achievement tests" (p. 194).

Recommendations along these lines, emphasizing the positive effects on teacher behavior of training in proficiency assessment practices, have continued to surface over the intervening years (e.g., Kenyon & Tschirner, 2000; Larson & Jones, 1984; Nuessel, 1991; Omaggio-Hadley, 2001). Indeed, on the 20th anniversary of the introduction of the OPI, ACTFL's director of testing and research, Elvira Swender ("The quiet revolution", 2002), advocated that all FL teachers receive thorough training in the ACTFL guidelines and proficiency testing techniques, in particular via OPI tester training workshops, with the justification that "[a]fter all, if teachers do not know how to *measure* what students can do with language, how will they be able to determine whether their students are *measuring* up to the expectations of the 21st century?" (p. 591, my emphasis). Common to these recommendations from proficiency movement advocates, then, was that FL educators be trained (and encouraged) to objectively administer, score, and interpret measures based on the ACTFL proficiency guidelines. However, virtually no mention was made of developing teachers' abilities to judge the extent to which proficiency testing might or might not meet the various assessment demands within their classrooms and programs, nor, for that matter, how FL educators might best evaluate its use.

Beyond predictable recommendations from the proficiency movement, the newfound interest in FL teacher development also spawned a number of individual articles and edited collections that sought to outline the main areas of competence in which FL educators should be prepared. However, while proficiency proponents were at least consistent in acknowledging the importance of teacher development in proficiency assessment, from other perspectives, the inclusion of assessment as a component of teacher development was much more variable.

Several overview articles during the 1990s addressed needed reforms in the professional preparation of FL educators, but they did not include assessment capabilities among key teacher competencies. For example, Jarvis and Taylor (1990) made the critical point that "[t]he future of foreign and second language teacher education is increasingly dependent on our connection with inquiry being done outside our field and on our ability to use that knowledge to conduct our own inquiry" (p. 160). However, they made no mention of assessment as a serious focus of FL teacher inquiry, although they did include pedagogy, curriculum, and instruction as important teacher-education knowledge bases in need of development. In a similar overview for the *ADFL Bulletin*, Roche (1996) called for thorough education of language teachers in the following six subject areas in order to encourage professionalization of the discipline: (a) culture and xenology, (b) psycholinguistics, (c) acquisitional linguistics and intercultural communication, (d) descriptive linguistics and pragmatics, (e) sociolinguistics, and (f) didactics and methodology. No mention was made of assessment within this otherwise very broad list. Finally, in discussing the range of professional development needs for FL graduate teaching assistants, Fox (2000) ignored assessment, despite very detailed attention to other areas of knowledge, including "contrastive analysis, error analysis, the acquisition/learning distinction, cognitive style, discourse analysis, and the relationships among theories of linguistic analysis, the psychology of learning, and teaching methodologies" (p. 200).

Similar indifference to assessment also surfaced in edited collections on the priorities of contemporary FL education in the U.S. (e.g., Birckbichler, 1990), including those specifically compiled as resources for defining the scope and focus of FL teacher development. For example, Guntermann (1993) assembled eight chapters that reviewed the major implications of the FL reform movement during the 1980s on teacher professional preparation. No chapter among these eight explicitly addressed assessment competencies expected of teachers, but individual chapters did address the importance of developing teachers' research abilities (Hammadou, 1993) and their expertise in curricular design and implementation (Schrier, 1993), among other areas.

At the same time, others did recognize the need for some degree of teacher preparation in basic assessment competencies beyond the use of proficiency measures. For example, in an edited book (Bardovi-Harlig & Hartford, 1997) covering the basic components of language teacher education, Gradman and Reed (1997) offered a chapter on language testing and argued that "an understanding of and practice in language testing is a crucial component of second language teacher education" (p. 198). However, while their coverage of assessment briefly addressed several approaches to measuring language skills, it made no effort to consider the various uses for tests within language programs or how particular test types might best meet particular uses. Likewise, while the chapter intimated the importance of validity and consequences in language testing, it made no recommendations regarding who might be responsible (teachers, administrators, 'experts'?) for evaluating the qualities and outcomes of test use or how such an evaluation might proceed.

Assessment was also addressed in discussions regarding the course work via which FL graduate students should be formally introduced to the various valued aspects of educational practice. Infrequently, recommendations were made for the inclusion of an entire course on assessment in FL graduate degree programs (e.g., Omaggio, 1986; Omaggio-Hadley, 2001), and some even proposed advanced graduate courses to prepare students for the assessment demands associated with specific professional roles in FL education. Thus, Mason (2000) included extensive coverage of assessment skills and knowledge within a proposed seminar for future language program directors, because "language testing may not get attention in the first-level methods course due to time limitations" (p. 119). However, others who advocated for multiple teacher development courses (e.g., Lalande, 1991) did not perceive assessment as important enough to warrant its own course. For example, Murphy (1991) did not mention assessment in recommending at least three courses for developing FL graduate students' capacities to respond to the educational demands of FL programs, including: (a) language acquisition theory, (b) applied linguistics, and (c) a "linguistically oriented methods course" (p. 137).

Much more common than these multiple course models of graduate student development has been the assumption of a single methods course. Frequently referred to as language teaching methods courses, or simply 'the methods course', these nearly ubiquitous components of FL graduate degree programs have come to occupy a central role in most college FL departments as the principal locus for disseminating disciplinary knowledge about the educational side of the FL profession. While assessment skills have been included within recommendations for the methods course, they clearly compete with many other potential professional development needs. In a survey of the content covered by methods courses in 157 U.S. FL programs, Grosse (1993) found that testing skills of some sort were addressed in 78% of the courses, but she also found that participants devoted on average only two to three class meetings to the topic. Little wonder, then, that recommendations about the range of assessment knowledge and skills to be addressed within the methods course have been quite limited. For example, VanValkenburg and Arnett (2000) mentioned in passing that FL teachers should learn "how to evaluate students" (p. 3) and to engage in "test preparation" (p. 4), but they did not expand on the implications of these skills. Similarly, in their advocacy for a revised professional development course, Barnett and Cook (2000) included simply "how to write and grade tests" in the "practical aspects" (p. 92) of the course.

To summarize, despite some attention over the past several decades to assessment competencies within FL professional development concerns, it is questionable to what extent college FL educators have been sufficiently prepared via associated courses, training, and other experiences to ensure the quality of assessments as they need to be used for meeting the various purposes that exist within college FL programs.

2.3 Research and development in U.S. college foreign language assessment

A professional responsibility for engaging in assessment might best be characterized as incipient, and professional development as largely lacking, within U.S. college FL education. However, individual FL educators as well as language testing specialists have, at times, undertaken to develop and research particular assessment practices within this context. A brief review of the frequency and focus of this work provides further insights into the extent to which U.S. college FL education has been deemed a valued arena for assessment research, and it helps to clarify the nature of existing patterns in the evaluation of FL assessments.

2.3.1 College FL assessment articles in representative publications

There are many possible venues for publishing research and development activities related to language assessment, including the foreign language education and applied linguistics journals, as well as related books and edited collections, and potentially the extensive educational measurement literature. However, by reviewing a few selected journals here—the most likely venues for publication of work focused specifically on the college FL assessment context—an initial indication of the status quo is provided. The selected journals offer these relevant perspectives: (a) the *ADFL Bulletin* reflects the interests and concerns of U.S. college FL department chairs; (b) *Foreign Language Annals* is the official research and practice publication of the American Council on the Teaching of Foreign Languages; (c) the *Modern Language Journal* is the leading refereed publication for research on FL instruction; (d) *Language Testing* has been the primary source for articles on the theory and practice of assessment in language education since its inception in 1984; and (e) *Die Unterrichtspraxis* is typical of the journals associated with the teaching of specific foreign languages in the U.S. (in this case, German, which is particularly relevant for the current work).

In order to estimate the focus and amount of recent work published on FL assessment, all of the full-length research and/or practice articles (excluding short reports, letters, book reviews, and similar non-article-length entries) that appeared in each issue of these five journals between 1984 and 2002 were reviewed and categorized according to the focus and context of the article. The starting point of 1984 was selected as a watershed point in the potential publication of FL assessment articles, given the appearance that year of the first issue of *Language Testing*. First, the number of articles published in each journal issue and for each year was tallied and summed. Second, each article was then categorized as "assessment-focused" or not, based on whether or not it directly addressed the theory, research, or practice of assessment; categorized as 'not' were articles which had nothing to do with assessment as well as articles in which language assessments or measures were employed (e.g., for research purposes) but did not themselves constitute the focus of the article's content. Third, each of the "assessment-focused" articles was further attributed to one of the following contextual categories: (a) English-language assessment (including foreign and second language assessments); (b) U.S. college FL assessment (including an additional sub-categorization for assessments related to the ACTFL proficiency guidelines); (c) other FL assessment (including primary and secondary school FL assessment in the U.S., FL assessment other than English outside of the U.S., and the assessment of professionals or of teacher practice in FL education); (d) other assessment (including de-contextualized assessment theory and issues, and non-language topics, such as the assessment of learning disabilities or affective variables); or (e) mixed assessment (articles which addressed two or more of the other categories).

While articles in any of these categories might entail implications for the practice of language assessment in U.S. college FL education, the purpose of this review was to identify those articles which did, in fact, specifically relate research and development work to that particular context and its concerns. Clearly, of primary interest for the current study were articles which reported on *student* assessment within this context; hence, teacher and professional assessments were treated separately under the 'other FL' category. In addition, it should be noted that English-language assessment articles were addressed independently for two reasons: (a) because they are not directly related to the primary concerns of U.S. college FL education; and (b) because of the enormous industry and energy surrounding the testing of English as a second or foreign language, and the associated potential for over-generalization of assumptions to all of language assessment based only on research into English-language assessment. In other words, the assessment of English language ability, whether foreign or second in nature, has developed into its own unique research and development domain, quite distinct in scope, history, economy, and other features from all other language assessment practice in all other contexts worldwide (Barnwell, 1996; Spolsky, 1995). Accordingly, it was treated as its own separate category in the current review.

Figure 1 summarizes only the FL-relevant findings from the review in terms of the overall percentage and type of assessment articles published in each journal between 1984 and 2002 (with each column from left to right representing a sub-set of the previous column). Note that very few articles were identified within the 'mixed' category (effectively 0% for each journal) and are not included here. Looking first at the overall amount of assessment publication activity, it is apparent that, with the exception of *Language Testing* (where, obviously, 100% of the articles treated assessment), assessment-focused articles constituted only a meager percentage of the work published during the period under review, totaling between 5% and 10% for each of the other four journals. Nevertheless, non-English FL assessment of some kind (indicated by the second column of diagonal striped bars in Figure 1) did constitute the majority of the assessment-focused work addressed in each of these four journals (and all of the assessment articles in the *ADFL Bulletin* and *Die Unterrichtspraxis*). In *Language Testing*, by contrast, non-English FL articles accounted for only around 15% of the total. Thus, since the inception of this principal forum for discussing the theory and practice of language assessment, 57% of the *Language Testing* articles have focused on English language assessment, with the majority covering topics related to large-scale English-language testing, while another 28% have concerned other (non-FL) assessment topics.

Turning to the specific case of assessment in U.S. college FL education contexts (indicated by the third column of solid white bars in Figure 1), the findings indicate even weaker overall interest. In each of the five representative journals, articles focused on this context constituted between 4% and 8% of the total work published during the 19-year period. Furthermore, it was found that, in each of the five journals, the majority (between 3% and 5% of the total) of these context-relevant articles addressed the single topic of assessment based on the ACTFL proficiency guidelines (indicated by the final column of light grey bars in Figure 1). Therefore, between the years of 1984 and 2002, only approximately 1% to 3% of the total research and practice articles that appeared in five representative journals addressed any of the considerable number of other assessment concerns or impetuses associated with U.S. college FL assessment.

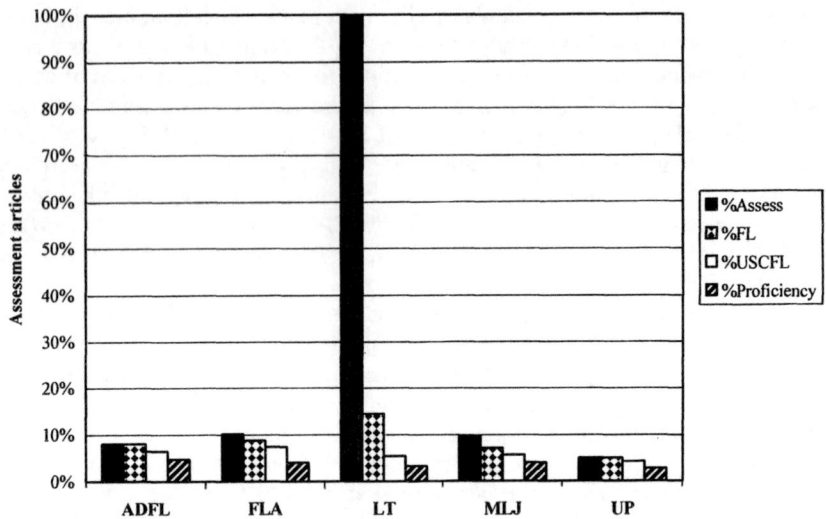

Figure 1. Percentage and type of FL assessment articles in five journals, 1984-2002

Note: Abbreviations are as follows: ADFL = *ADFL Bulletin*; FLA = *Foreign Language Annals*; LT = *Language Testing*; MLJ = *Modern Language Journal*; UP = *Die Unterrichtspraxis*; %Assess = percentage of assessment-focused articles; %FL = percentage of total non-English FL assessment articles; %USCFL = percentage of assessment articles related to the U.S. college foreign language context; %Proficiency = percentage of articles related to assessment based on the ACTFL Proficiency Guidelines.

Figure 2 sheds additional light on these findings and the characteristics of assessment work with direct relevance to U.S. college FL education. Each bar in Figure 2 displays the highest yearly percentage (top of the bar) and the average yearly percentage (either a + or – sign) of articles on U.S. college FL assessment published in each journal during the first (1984-1993) or the second (1994-2002) half of the period surveyed. In other words, the first column indicates that, between 1984 and 1993, U.S. college FL assessment articles in the *ADFL Bulletin* comprised as much as 29% of the articles one year, and an average of 10% over the ten year period. The minus sign in the second column indicates that the average for the *ADFL Bulletin* dropped to a mere 2% of yearly articles on U.S. college FL assessment for the following period of 1994-2002. While this drop was most precipitous for the *ADFL Bulletin*, it is obvious for each of the other four journals that a similar decrease occurred in the yearly percentage of articles published on U.S. college FL assessment from one period to the next. Thus, interest in, or at least publications about, research and development of assessment in the U.S. college FL context seems to have declined considerably over the most recent period. Note also that the highest yearly percentages of relevant articles, which occurred during the 1984-1993 period for each of the five journals, were all associated with either special issues of the journals devoted to proficiency testing based on the ACTFL guidelines or with a rash of articles researching, promoting, critiquing, or simply commenting on the same.

It is apparent that work on the research and development of assessment in U.S. college FL education has been published only sporadically, and decreasingly so, over the past several decades in the journals reviewed. Furthermore, this low degree of interest has been equally evident across a variety of publication types, from the more practice-oriented association-sponsored journals, to FL education research journals, to the primary journal for language testing theory and research. However, although infrequent, when FL educators and language testers have attended to and published on U.S. college FL assessment (in these forums and others), it is worth inquiring into the nature of their research and development interest, and the extent to which this work has contributed to a potential foundation for ensuring the quality of FL assessment practice. The following two sections characterize the nature of this work, first from the 'insider' view of U.S. college FL educators, and then from the 'outsider' view of language testers. While the distinction is somewhat artificial, with particular individuals working occasionally from both perspectives, it serves to highlight the different aspects of assessment that have (or have not) been emphasized from unique points of view on the U.S. college FL assessment context.

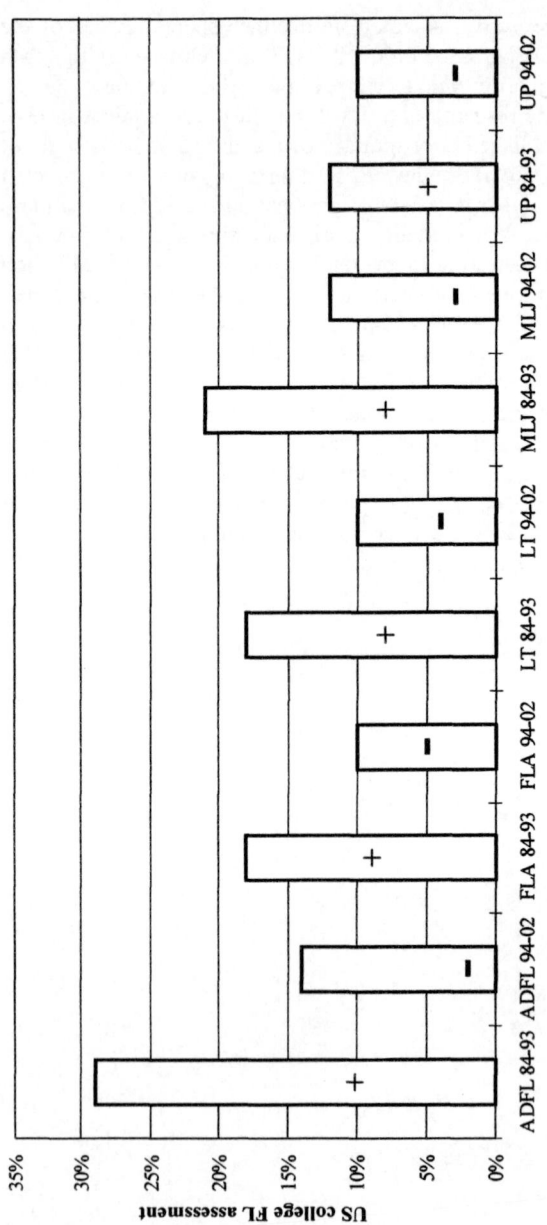

Figure 2. High, low, and average yearly percentage of articles on U.S. college FL assessment, 1984-1993 and 1994-2002

Note: Abbreviations are as follows. ADFL = *ADFL Bulletin*; FLA = *Foreign Language Annals*; LT = *Language Testing*; MLJ = *Modern Language Journal*; UP = *Die Unterrichtspraxis*.

2.3.2 FL assessment research and development from the inside

From the internal perspective of U.S. college FL educators addressing their own assessment concerns, research and development work has taken several forms. Perhaps most common are articles which argue for, and detail the format and implementation of, instruments and procedures that respond to particular perceived assessment needs. For example, Carduner (2002) advocated the introduction of classroom assessment techniques (cf. Angelo & Cross, 1993) into FL composition instruction in order to meet formative and feedback needs of teachers and students. Similarly, Egbert and Maxim (1998) recommended the integration of critical thinking and problem-solving skills into the construction of large-scale business German exams, with the purpose of improving curriculum and instruction within this domain as a result of such changes. Liskin-Gasparro (1995) also suggested the use of a range of different assessment procedures in undergraduate college FL programs, including standardized exams, oral proficiency assessments, portfolios, interviews, and surveys, for meeting both program-external accountability demands for evidence of student learning outcomes, as well as program-internal uses such as the improvement of FL curriculum and instruction. Finally, a number of others have advocated intensively the use of assessments based on the ACTFL proficiency guidelines as a means for operationalizing a proficiency-based language requirement in undergraduate education (e.g., Barnes, Klee, & Wakefield, 1990; Bernhardt, 2002; Freed, 1984, 1987, 1992; Schulz, 1988) as well as for meeting a variety of other purposes (e.g., Larson & Jones, 1984).

These examples, and other articles of this type, have performed a critical service in identifying a variety of actual and distinct needs for assessment development and use specific to the college FL education context. However, generally missing from their proposals is systematic attention to (a) why the assessments that they advocate are most appropriate for meeting these specific needs, or (b) on what basis these assessments might best be evaluated or investigated (or any recommendations that they should be). Thus, while their discussions of instrumentation and implementation provide potentially useful recommendations for responding to clearly identified needs for assessment, what is missing is a rationale for how the particular qualities of these recommended practices will provide assessment users with information that can most appropriately meet such needs (not to mention what these users would actually do with the information). Likewise, without this rationale, it remains unclear how the qualities of these assessments should be evaluated and ensured vis-à-vis their intended uses.

In addition to individual articles, several books and edited collections have highlighted certain roles for assessment in the specific context of U.S. college FL education, generally advocating particular types of assessment. For example, Finocchiaro and Sako (1983) reviewed assessment uses, such as student placement, feedback on teaching, profiling language acquisition, and researching instructional outcomes, and they presented concrete recommendations for the development of language assessments by teachers for meeting such purposes. However, in their discussion of the qualities of effective FL assessments, they drew no connections between how assessments should be evaluated and the particular contextualized uses to which they are applied. In a similar vein, the chapters in Teschner's (1991) edited collection on assessing college undergraduates highlighted a variety of student assessment needs, and, for the most part (cf. Hammerly, 1991, for an opposing viewpoint), they took issue with a perceived lack of alignment between contemporary testing practices and communicative language teaching. Accordingly, they recommended the development of assessments based on principles of communicative language testing (e.g., Canale, 1984; Henning, 1990) in order to support changing emphases in curriculum and instruction. However, when the contributors addressed the evaluation of such tests, they focused on questions about measurement qualities such as "what do the tests actually measure" and "are the tests accurate measures" (Bernhardt & Deville, 1991, p. 47), without attending to issues of how the tests were put to use. One exception is Heilenman (1991), who echoed Shohamy (1990) in suggesting that qualities like utility, feasibility, and fairness should be investigated in addition to measurement accuracy, although she provided no systematic approach for doing so. In a more recent example, the College Board (1996) advocated the use of authentic, performance-based, portfolio, and alternative assessments in conjunction with the release of the *Standards for foreign language learning* (1996), but they made no suggestions regarding what qualities of these kinds of language assessment should be evaluated. Thus, while these books have presented arguments for particular types of college FL assessments in response to a range of purposes, they have done little in the way of linking the qualities of such assessments or the uses to which they are put to their evaluation; instead, they have prescribed how to align closely language assessment formats with evolving notions of effective language teaching.

Obviously, when they do address assessment, college FL educators focus on recommending and developing practices for meeting various purposes, but researching the use of assessments for meeting such purposes has received less attention from within the discipline. Very occasionally, efforts have been made to research specific prioritized concerns with the use of assessments within U.S. college FL settings. For example, Kondo-Brown (2002) applied item response theory techniques to explore the nature of rater agreement and biases in the assessment of students' FL Japanese writing on a university placement exam, with the intent of improving the consistency of norm-referenced decisions based on constructed-response performances. In another example, several researchers have investigated the relationship between years and/or type of college FL instruction and the development of varying levels of proficiency, in order to provide an evidentiary basis in setting assessment standards for undergraduate language requirements (e.g., Thompson, 1996; Tschirner & Heilenman, 1998) or for assessing language learning outcomes associated with various types of FL study (Milleret, Stansfield, & Kenyon, 1991; Norris & Pfeiffer, 2003).

While these examples highlight research that has addressed a few priority issues in the contextualized use of assessments for meeting particular needs, research has focused much more frequently on de-contextualized validation studies of U.S. college FL assessments. Thus, for example, a rich opus of work has investigated the measurement qualities of several assessments based on the ACTFL proficiency guidelines, including research on inter-rater reliability, score comparability among test types, the nature of examinee performances, and the inter-relationship between the proficiency scale construct, examinee performances, and rating processes (e.g., Clark, 1988; Clark & Clifford, 1988; Halleck, 1995; Henning, 1992; Johnson, 2001; Kenyon, 1997; Kenyon, Malabonga, & Carpenter, 2001; Kenyon & Tschirner, 2000; Kuo & Jiang, 1997; Magnan, 1987; Norris, 1996, 1997a, 1997b, 2001b; Sasaki, 1996; Shohamy, 1994; Stansfield & Kenyon, 1992; Stansfield et al, 1990; Thompson, 1996; Young, 1995; Young & He, 1998). Although this type of research has done much to help the discipline interpret the measurement construct (or to dispute it) underlying the ACTFL proficiency guidelines, and to establish the accuracy and trustworthiness of associated test instruments and procedures, it has done very little to advance our understanding of how such assessments might best be used (or not) for meeting actual purposes within U.S. college FL education. Indeed, in response to recommendations for such situated, evaluative work that attends to the specific uses for proficiency assessment (e.g., Norris, 2001a; Salaberry, 2000), test developers have countered that "[t]he validation of the way in which users use assessment results based on the ACTFL scale will be a mammoth and lengthy undertaking" (Kenyon, Malabonga, & Carpenter, 2001, p. 107), and they have pushed ahead, instead, with the further creation and dissemination of proficiency measures (e.g., "100 days—100 languages", 2003; Kenyon & Malabonga, 2001).

Research efforts from within U.S. college FL education, then, have generally focused on a few selected, among many possible, concerns with contextualized assessment use, or they have ignored assessment use and concentrated instead on investigating a range of measurement qualities. In addition, FL educators have clearly paid greater attention to developing and disseminating assessments than they have to studying the qualities of assessments in use (see similar findings in Spolsky, 2000). Thus, while FL educators have identified a range of assessment targets within the U.S. college context, and provided extensive recommendations for measuring them, what has been lacking—in response to the challenge of evaluating and ensuring the quality of FL educational assessments—is a means for identifying the qualities of assessment instruments and procedures that are relevant to meeting particular intended uses, on the one hand, and for prioritizing and investigating the relationship between these qualities and the actual uses of assessments, on the other.

2.3.3 FL assessment research and development from the outside

Given these gaps in the assessment research and development literature from within U.S. college FL education, one might hope that language testing experts would have taken a serious look at the range of contextualized uses identified by college FL educators, and that they would have responded with the development of relevant instruments and procedures and, in particular, with guidance on researching the qualities of FL assessments as they are put to use. Unfortunately, when language testers have infrequently paid attention to U.S. college FL assessment, they have generally done so from a perspective that is by and large unaware of (or uninterested in) the range of actual purposes for and constraints on assessments. Instead, they have typically opted to criticize the psychometric qualities of FL assessments, from the point of view of measurement theory, or to generalize about 'good' practice in researching and developing FL measures based on their experiences in other language testing domains.

One laudable, if circumscribed, area of exception has emerged over the past ten years through collaborations between language testers and FL educators that have been sponsored by National Foreign Language Resource Centers at several institutions across the U.S.. For example, at the University of Minnesota's center, several long-term projects have sought to provide college FL educators with instruments and procedures relevant to proficiency-oriented instruction. One such project developed an extensive array of proficiency assessments for classroom and curriculum purposes in conjunction with statewide FL teaching articulation efforts (McCarthy, Scott, Shiba, & Thornton, 1998; Posse, Shifman, & Sweet, 1999; Tedick, 1997, 2002). A second project reviewed the uses for existing FL entrance and graduation tests at the University of Minnesota (e.g., Chalhoub-Deville, Sweet, Schmidt, & McCollum Lozier, 1996), and then proceeded to develop and disseminate 'contextualized' proficiency assessments directed at meeting these needs in each of the four modalities (e.g., CARLA Assessment Team, 1998a, 1998b, 2000a, 2000b). Similarly, collaborative projects at the University of Hawaii have resulted in the development of models for college FL assessment practice, as well as a variety of instruments, in response to a range of perceived needs, including performance and task-based achievement testing (Brown, Hudson, & Kim, 2001; Long et al, 2003), computer-based assessment in the less commonly taught languages (Hudson, 2000), placement testing (Kondo-Brown & Brown, 2000), and other areas (e.g., Hudson, Detmer, & Brown, 1995; Yao & Ning, 1998). In a third example, researchers at the National Capital Language Resource Center interacted with FL educators across the U.S. in developing a framework for implementing portfolio assessments within FL classrooms (Barnhardt, Kevorkian, & Delett, 1998; Delett, Barnhardt, & Kevorkian, 2001).

Clearly, these recent collaborative efforts have introduced a considerable degree of language testing expertise into the development of assessments for fulfilling certain purposes specific to U.S. college FL education contexts. However, while occasional research has been conducted on these assessments, it has generally taken the form of isolated investigations of measurement qualities of the instruments and procedures as they are being developed and pilot-tested (e.g., McCollum Lozier & Chalhoub-Deville, 1997). Only rarely have the projects incorporated recommendations for evaluating the actual uses of assessments for meeting specific purposes in practice (e.g., Barnhardt, Kevorkian, & Delett, 1998), and reports of such evaluations have not been forthcoming.

While language testers in the projects listed above have taken a serious look at the actual assessment uses, needs, and constraints of college FL educators in the U.S., attention from language testing experts has come more commonly in the form of criticism directed at the measurement qualities of assessments developed within FL education, regardless of their intended uses. By far the most frequent target in this context has been the ACTFL proficiency guidelines and associated assessments, the qualities of which have been widely analyzed and discussed from the point of view of construct validity concerns (e.g., Bachman, 1988; Bachman & Savignon, 1986; Lantolf & Frawley, 1985; Spolsky, 1985; Stevenson, 1985), as well as occasionally investigated in order to challenge or defend validity claims (e.g., Dandonoli & Henning, 1990; Fulcher, 1996; Halleck, 1995; Henning, 1992; Lazaraton, 1992; Norris, 1996; 2001b; Young, 1995). Although this attention has highlighted clear weaknesses in the measurement qualities of tests based on the ACTFL proficiency guidelines, and has highlighted directions for improvement, it has failed to address the relationship between proficiency assessment and the purposes it may or may not fulfill in college FL education. Indeed, these critiques and research into the validity of the ACTFL proficiency construct and associated interpretations have underscored a rather singular emphasis among language testers as they consider the qualities of FL assessments—that is, a priority focus on the meaning of test scores as measures of language ability constructs, independent of the uses to which they may be put, and at the exclusion of other possible concerns with assessment use in actual FL education contexts. Similarly, the minimal collection of studies in which language testers have researched other U.S. college FL assessments has taken this decontextualized measurement tack as well (e.g., Chalhoub-Deville, 1996; Ginther & Stevens, 1998).

Sadly, on other, rare occasions when language testers have attempted to contextualize assessment research, development, and evaluation practices for the specific U.S. college FL context, their efforts have frequently gone awry. For example, one contribution on assessment was recently solicited for inclusion in a volume published by the Modern Language Association for the general audience of college FL department faculty members. This volume was intended, according to the editor (Byrnes, 1998b), to "address the issues and dilemmas that foreign language departments face" (p. 4) and to "make clear that the research reported does not exist in isolation but, instead, speaks to the problems of foreign language education in the United States that urgently need to be resolved" (p. 13). Along these lines, Shohamy's (1998) contribution from the language testing expert's perspective began laudably by arguing that "[a]ssessment is shaped by its specific context, its purpose, the type of knowledge it addresses, the procedures it selects, by the different criteria for determining success, by different interpretations and different ways of reporting results" (p. 258). However, in stark contrast to this argument, no mention was made within the chapter of the U.S. college FL education context (to which the work was supposed to be directed), nor was there any attempt to isolate and respond to the particular assessment "issues and dilemmas" faced by college FL educators. What is more, as an extended example of the contextualized assessment development, use, and validation process, a description was provided of assessments used for determining the *second* language Hebrew proficiencies of *child immigrant* learners in Israeli public schools; arguably, a more unrelated context could not have been selected for exemplifying assessment problems in need of response within U.S. college FL education.

In general, then, language testers have adopted a critical, but not necessarily contextual, view of assessment within U.S. college FL education, and they have offered little in the way of guidance directed specifically at FL educators seeking to evaluate and ensure the qualities of their assessments as they are actually used. Moreover, language testing experts do not seem particularly interested in taking seriously the details of this context for assessment, choosing instead to focus on theoretical, generalizable issues in the measurement of language ability rather than practical, local concerns with the uses for assessments in foreign language education. This perspective was forcefully demonstrated in Spolsky's (2000) review of articles on language assessment published over the course of the 20th century in the *Modern Language Journal*. Spolsky's primary question of this body of work was whether any of the articles constituted "serious contributions to the field of language testing" (p. 536), and he found, not surprisingly from this point of departure (i.e., the 'expert' external perspective), that they mostly had not. Accordingly, he recommended that the *Modern Language Journal* should concentrate its assessment reporting efforts on disseminating developments from the field of language testing to the foreign language teacher audience. Not asked by Spolsky was whether the field of language testing has made any serious contributions to research and development on college FL assessment, nor whether it has provided adequate guidance in responding to the challenge of evaluating and ensuring the quality of assessments as they are actually used for meeting the specific demands of college foreign language education.

2.4 Summary of the contextual challenge

To summarize the preceding sections, several threads may be brought together to characterize contemporary assessment perceptions and practices in U.S. college FL education. First, assessment is generally portrayed within FL education to be the development and use of instruments and procedures for measuring language knowledge or ability. Thus, historical traditions as well as trends in contemporary assessment practice have revealed an overarching focus on how best to measure language, although language has been defined in unique ways over the years, resulting in several distinct forms of assessment that characterize most of what occurs in its name within college FL education today. Without a doubt, assessments that reference the ACTFL Proficiency Guidelines represent the single most dominant of these approaches to measuring language within the college context. Second, it is apparent that a variety of different purposes and uses for assessment has emerged recently within U.S. college FL education, in the form of distinct impetuses from various quarters, including student decision-making, instructional feedback, and program accountability demands. However, efforts in FL assessment development, research, and practice have by and large ignored the potential differences among such uses for assessment, choosing instead to advocate for and attend to idealized measurement qualities rather than other qualities of assessments as they are actually used for meeting various educational purposes. Therefore, little attention has been paid to the link between intended uses for FL assessments and the ways in which they might best be developed and, consequently, how they might best be evaluated. Third, while assessment has been treated peripherally within the professional responsibilities and development of college FL educators, this treatment has emphasized assessment as a technocratic skill in measurement rather than a fundamental, valued professional competency. Some college FL educators may be prepared to administer and score language tests, and to recognize the types of language measures that have been promoted by professional organizations; however, they are generally not prepared to: (a) identify and understand the intended uses for assessment in response to specific impetuses and demands particular to this context; (b) design or select assessment instruments and procedures as appropriate to each of these uses; or (c) evaluate and ensure the qualities of each assessment in a manner that systematically and comprehensively examines the relationship between intended uses, designs, and outcomes for the educational context.

Unfortunately, it also seems apparent that the proximate discipline of language testing has offered input and guidance of a very limited nature. When they have, rarely, attended to problems in U.S. college FL assessment, language testers have focused on generalizable concerns with whether FL tests can be trusted to measure what they are intended to measure (i.e., measurement validity), thereby reinforcing the perception within the FL community that good measurement practice is all that is needed for good educational assessment. Furthermore, although some recent efforts have been made to develop assessments in response to the particular demands of college FL education contexts, almost no direction has been provided in researching the relationship between the *uses* of these assessments and the measurement (or other) qualities that are being stressed in developing them.

More broadly, while language testers have proposed extended, if generic, frameworks for the evaluation of language assessments and their use, even couching the qualities of tests in terms of their "usefulness" as did Bachman and Palmer (1996), these frameworks have clearly prioritized the evaluation of "essential measurement qualities"—that is, reliability and validity—"because these are the qualities that provide the major justification for using test scores—numbers—as a basis for making inferences or decisions" (p. 19). Thus, even though Bachman and Palmer (1996) in this example, and many other language testers in other validity discussions and related work (e.g., Alderson, Clapham, & Wall, 1995; Bachman, 1990; Brown, 1996; Brown & Hudson, 2002; Chapelle & Douglas, 1993; Chapelle, 1999; Cumming & Berwick, 1995; Davies, 1990; Genesee & Upshur, 1996; Henning, 1987; Hughes, 1989; Kunnan, 1998, 2000; McNamara, 2000; Weir, 1990), have acknowledged the potential need for investigating other qualities of language assessments as they are used (albeit not in the particular context of U.S. college FL education), they have, virtually without exception, subjugated such concerns to the primacy of measurement validity investigations, in conjunction with their perception of the primary function of language tests to be the measurement of language knowledge or ability constructs.

As will be seen in the following chapter, language testers have simply followed suit from traditions within the broader educational measurement discipline in emphasizing a truncated set of measurement qualities as the primary concerns for the validation of educational tests. However, it will also be seen that this long-standing primacy of test validity concerns has led some educational assessment practitioners to question the extent to which contemporary notions of validity are appropriate for framing the needed evaluation of assessments as they are applied in educational settings. Likewise, for foreign language educators, it remains to be seen how best to evaluate the quality of assessments as they are actually applied in meeting the demands of college FL education contexts—that is, which qualities should be investigated for which assessments used in what ways? Furthermore, perhaps the most important problem to be resolved is how evaluations themselves can be developed and implemented such that FL educators can actually do something with evaluative information and via evaluative processes that will fulfill the primary goal of ensuring (i.e., informing, improving, changing) the quality of their assessment practices in support of their educational efforts.

Chapter 3
From test validation to validity evaluation
in educational assessment

The issues raised in Chapter 2 characterize the unique nature of college foreign language assessment as it is practiced in the U.S., and the details of this educational context will play an important role in determining why and how assessments will need to be evaluated. However, the underlying emphasis on the development and validation of 'good measures' has not been unique to FL assessment or even to the broader field of language testing. Indeed, over the second half of the 20th century, language testers adopted very much the same prioritization of measurement development concerns, the same themes in debating validity theory, and the same methods in practicing test validation, as did the educational measurement mainstream (see overview in Chapelle, 1999).

Within educational measurement, the evolution of validity theory and practice during this 50-year span was marked by several key iterations, to which contemporary notions about test validity may be attributed and within which the origins of current challenges—and possible solutions—for the validation of educational assessments, including language assessments, may be found (for historical overviews see Anastasi, 1986; Bachman, 1990; Cronbach, 1971; 1989; Kane, 2001, 2006; Messick, 1989; Moss, 1992; Shepard, 1993). In this chapter I survey the evolution of validity theory and practice, and I highlight critical gaps that must be addressed if validity is to achieve educational relevance.

3.1 Validity 'types' and early validation practice in educational measurement

From the 1950s through the 1970s, validation practices in educational measurement generally focused on 'types' of validity that were associated with a few specific tests. During this pragmatic and empirical phase (Angoff, 1988), certain kinds of discrete evidence were sought to demonstrate that a test was measuring what it was purported to measure (Guilford, 1946; Gullickson, 1950). Thus, the earliest codified test validity standards (APA, 1954) presented four different types of validity for four distinct testing purposes: (a) *content* validity for achievement tests; (b) *predictive* validity for placement and selection tests; (c) *concurrent* validity for short-cut approximations or replacements of existing tests; and (d) *construct* validity for tests of theory-based psychological traits and states. This approach to defining different validity types for different tests was perpetuated through the 1970s (APA, AERA, & NCME, 1966; 1974; see also Popham, 1981), although the 1974 standards referred in passing to the logical "interrelatedness" of the different types (p. 26). The only major development during this period featured the reduction of predictive and concurrent validity into the single "criterion-related" type in the 1966 standards.

In practice, validation of a test proceeded as the selection of one or another recommended validity type and the subsequent collection of (typically minimal amounts of) evidence directly bearing on only that type. Kane (2001) observed that during this period, "the practice developed of using the different models as a sort of toolkit, with each model to be employed as needed in the validation of educational and psychological tests" (p. 323). Validation studies often resulted in the production of a single criterion-predictor correlation (the so-called 'validity coefficient'), or a single set of expert judgments about content coverage and relevance, as the sole and sufficient body of evidence in support of a given test (Cronbach, 1971; Guion, 1980; Hambleton, 1984; Landy, 1986; Tenopyr, 1977). For educational tests in particular, validation studies tended to emphasize either content or criterion-related types (Angoff, 1988; Jonson & Plake, 1998; Shepard, 1993).

Setting the stage for years of practice to come, several influential concepts and methodologies emerged from this 'types' approach, which Guion (1980) labeled the "trinitarian doctrine" of content, criterion-related, and construct validities. First, validity was characterized as a quality of test instruments rather than the interpretations based on test scores and the uses to which they were put. In other words, it was presumed that the validity of a test could be demonstrated through a validation study, and once established, validity inhered within the test regardless of how or with whom or why it was used. This widespread interpretation of validity as a demonstrable quality of tests—rather than test *uses*—persists today, despite years of effort to counter the fundamental misconception (e.g., Cronbach, 1969, 1971).

Second, from this early perspective on validity, the principal purpose of educational tests was to provide accurate measurements of variables for a few discrete decision types. This portrayal of tests as measures may have been due in large part to the origins of testing standards within the American Psychological Association and that organization's overriding interest in the measurement of psychological variables. Indeed, the original testing standards were developed exclusively by the APA (1954); the APA served as lead author on the next two revised standards documents (APA, AERA, & NCME, 1966; 1974); and it was not until the 1985 edition that the order of authors for the testing standards became alphabetical (AERA, APA, & NCME, 1985). Whatever its origins, this conceptualization of the principal role of tests as accurate *measurement* devices reinforced narrow notions of validation. All that validity required was a demonstration of the extent to which a test is measuring what it was intended to measure, a prevailing assumption which persists in educational 'measurement' today (see, e.g., the thermometer metaphor for educational testing employed by Mehrens, 1997). Within this tradition, little or no attention was paid—at least in association with the concept of validity—to the wide variety of actual uses and users for tests within applied educational settings, where measures of psychological variables may or may not play a useful assessment role.

Third, the test validation process became a relatively mechanical and limited endeavor which fell under the purview of test developers, whose responsibility it was (because it was mandated in the standards) to demonstrate the validity of their tests as measures of what they were intended to measure. Validation of this sort was restricted to two principal sources/methods for gathering evidence: either correlations with criterion measures or expert judgments of test-content representativeness and coverage. The practice of validation proceeded in this narrow vein despite criticisms that criterion-related techniques relied on circular reasoning and "blind empiricism" (Anastasi, 1986; Guion, 1974) and that content validity judgments nearly always suffered from confirmatory bias because the content judges were virtually always the test developers themselves (e.g., Guion, 1977).

Finally, within the 'types' of validity tradition, little attention was paid to the reasons and intended uses motivating the validation process itself, beyond appeals to a general responsibility for maintaining scientific rigor and the need to publish some type of validity evidence in test manuals. As such, virtually no consideration was given to concerns such as: (a) how much evidence was needed? (b) which among the many available methods of inquiry might be pursued? (c) how should validity studies be organized and by whom? (d) how should a validity judgment be reached? (e) to whom should validity findings be communicated? and (f) what should be done with the findings of a validity study? These and related questions remained largely unaddressed in educational assessment practice, and only recently have they become a focal issue in related discussions (see below).

Despite the problematic notions which emerged in conjunction with the 'types' approach to validation, this early pragmatic-empirical phase did offer straightforward methodological options, and in this sense validation remained a viable (if impoverished) endeavor which could be pursued for any test. For example, Kane (2001) has pointed out that the criterion-related validity model provides a simple, practicable strategy:

> The scores from less direct measures can then be used to estimate or predict these direct measures and can be validated through the criterion model, with the direct measure serving as the criterion. This is a limited but reasonable methodology, and the basic model is still appropriate in many contexts (e.g., in selection and placement testing). (p. 321)

In addition, although based on a narrow understanding of test use, early treatments of validity also provided a key piece of logical guidance for test developers, by recommending that distinct validation strategies be tailored to distinct test types. Unfortunately, the implications for validation practice were not linked to broader conceptions of the actual uses for educational assessments, despite sage and early counter-proposals such as Cureton's (1951) thoughtful definition of validity as "how well a test does the job it was employed to do" (p. 621). Instead, the prevalent reductionist view of tests as *measures* would lead further developments in validity theory and practice in a very different direction.

3.2 Prioritizing construct validity in test validation

While, in *practice*, the validation of educational tests remained largely within the 'types' of validity tradition, validity *theory* between the 1950s and 1980s was marked by considerable development. In particular, a focus on construct validity and associated methodologies came to define the domain, despite unassuming beginnings. Construct validity was first introduced with the 1954 testing standards in response to the desire of the APA testing committee to include methods for validating clinical assessments linked to psychological theories (Cronbach, 1989; Kane, 2001). Thus, the original standards (APA, 1954) advised that construct validity be investigated for those tests where theoretical interpretations were at stake and where no acceptable criterion measures existed. As such, construct validity was portrayed as an *additional* type to be applied in validating theory-based psychological tests, but not necessarily as an appropriate way of validating educational or other tests.

In their widely influential follow-up to the first standards document, Cronbach and Meehl (1955) defined construct validation as the empirical testing of theoretically posited relationships between test constructs and observable behaviors. They explicitly reserved this type of validation for those tests which invoked explanatory theory as the basis for interpretations. In its original form, then, as developed by the APA (1954) and Cronbach and Meehl (1955), construct validity was not intended as an organizational framework for all of validity theory (Kane, 2001). Indeed, this distinction between construct and other types of validity was maintained within the standards (APA, AERA, & NCME, 1966; 1974) and by its creators (e.g., Cronbach, 1971) until the 1970s.

Despite such careful articulation, the appeal of scientific methodology and rigor within Cronbach and Meehl's (1955) proposal quickly led measurement theoreticians to adopt construct validity as the whole of test validity (e.g., Loevinger, 1957). By employing "scientific theory testing to confirm (or disconfirm) the interpretation of test scores" (Shepard, 1993, p. 416), construct validity dovetailed with realist philosophies of science (e.g., Popper, 1962) and positivist social science epistemologies (e.g., Campbell, 1957) that predominated at the time (Moss, 1992). From this psychometric perspective, the 'job' of a test was to provide an accurate measure of variables which were perceived to have definite and discernable values within examinees. These variables corresponded to constructs (which defined the unobservable mental traits or states behind behaviors), and the relationships among constructs were clearly laid out in explanatory theories. Accordingly, construct validation of tests was to proceed as scientific hypothesis testing—pure and simple—based on the explicit statement of proposed relationships between test scores and other variables, and attempts to falsify these hypothesized relationships (e.g., Campbell, 1960). This approach to validation took hold within educational and, especially, psychological measurement discussions to the extent that, by 1975, Messick advocated "all measurement should be construct referenced" (p. 957) and, in 1980, that "...construct validity is indeed the unifying concept of validity that integrates criterion and content considerations into a common framework for testing rational hypotheses about theoretically relevant relationships" (p. 1015).

Although validation practice for most educational assessments did not (could not?) involve elaborate construct validity investigations, sophisticated research methodologies were nevertheless called for in order to better examine the psychological constructs that all tests were (suddenly) presumed to measure (Angoff, 1988). The key for an adequate validation study was to employ scientific hypothesis testing as a means for structuring the investigation (Landy, 1986). Thus, construct validation required initial detailed explication of a theory and the role of the construct within it, the proposed interpretations about the construct to be based on test scores, and the hypothesized relationships between test scores and other variables (Kane, 2001; Moss, 1992). Once clearly defined, the proposed test construct could be investigated both internally (item-level analyses) and externally (criterion-related analyses), using correlational as well as experimental techniques, and pursuing evidence not only for convergent validity (i.e., the test is measuring the construct) but also for discriminant validity (i.e., the test is not measuring something other than the construct) (Shepard, 1993). In particular, challenges to proposed construct interpretations came to be valued in the form of investigating 'plausible rival hypotheses' (Campbell, 1957) which might explain test behaviors equally well or better than the intended construct. The multitrait-multimethod matrix (Campbell & Fiske, 1959) enjoyed widespread appeal in this regard (even "reification" according to Shepard, 1993), due to its operationalization of both convergent (criterion-related support) and discriminant (plausible rival hypotheses) sources of evidence within a single validity framework.

The commitment of educational and psychological measurement communities to a "strong program" (Cronbach, 1988) of construct validation via scientific hypothesis testing further shaped trends in the practice of validating educational assessments. First, by focusing on theoretical constructs, the primacy of *psycho*metric views of tests was reinforced, and other aspects of tests and test use were presumed of secondary importance for validation, a perspective which has enjoyed sustained support (e.g., Mehrens, 1997; Popham, 1997; Wiley, 1991). The purpose of validation, then, became primarily explanatory, in seeking to confirm/deny that a test measures the intended construct, at the expense of other potential roles for validation (e.g., functional, operational, political, economic; see Cronbach, 1988).

Second, while the strong program of construct validation provided a sophisticated and rigorous scientific methodology for validating tests that were based on well-formulated constructs, such explanatory theories and tests designed according to them exist only rarely in applied (especially educational) assessment settings, as Cronbach (1971, 1988, 1989) himself pointed out repeatedly. Thus, in the absence of a formalized theory to be tested, construct validation became diluted to the search for *any* available validity evidence which might support a given interpretation of test scores (Kane, 2001). This "weak program" (Cronbach, 1988) of construct validation provided no guidance regarding how much and which types of evidence are relevant and necessary to support the validity of a test score interpretation. As such, it inevitably reinforced the collection of evidence biased in support of the test (Cronbach, 1989; Kane, 2001).

Third, the commitment to construct validation resulted in the prioritization of particular research methodologies and sources of acceptable validity evidence, but these methods and sources did not provide educational assessment practitioners with criteria or guidelines for validating most educational assessments in terms of non-theoretical questions about test interpretation and use—that is, whether the test is doing its job (Moss, 1992; Shepard, 1993). Furthermore, a strong program of construct validation demanded such technical levels of expertise (see, e.g., the multitrait-multimethod matrix in Campbell & Fiske, 1959) that only highly trained researchers would be able to carry out appropriate studies, and interpret and evaluate the results.

On the positive side, the emphasis on construct validity did lead to several clear improvements over the 'types' approach to validation. Test developers were called upon to state exactly what interpretations about examinees were going to be made on the basis of test scores, and the focus of validation (at least in theory) shifted away from test instruments per se and towards these interpretations (Cronbach, 1969, 1971). In addition, the requirements of an adequate construct validity study introduced rigor into the validation process, by calling for a clear understanding of test score interpretations and the theories upon which they were based, careful planning of the study, the incorporation of multiple lines of evidence, and the need to consider challenges to score interpretations (Kane, 2001). Finally, for the particular use of test scores as measures of well-defined theoretical constructs (e.g., within research settings), a useful validation methodology was created and elaborated, and this methodology remains applicable in such contexts today (Chapelle, 1998; Norris & Ortega, 2003; Norris, Ortega, & Mislevy, 2003).

3.3 Incorporating test use and consequences into validation

By the 1980s, several lines of thought within educational measurement crystallized into a much more comprehensive notion of validity and the methodologies of validation practice. First, consensus emerged, and was codified in the testing standards (AERA, APA, & NCME, 1985), that validity should be treated as a unitary concept, that validity was "the most important consideration in test evaluation" (p. 9), and that validation involved collecting a variety of interrelated *evidentiary* types bearing on test score inferences. Investigations of distinct validity 'types' associated with different tests were no longer adequate, although the presentation of the trinitarian framework persisted in many measurement textbooks (e.g., Cronbach, 1990; Gronlund & Linn, 1990; Popham, 1981, 1990). Second, as the centrality of construct validity within this unitary view came to be generally accepted (Moss, 1992; Shepard, 1993), exclusively psychometric notions of what was meant by construct validity were also challenged. Building especially from Cronbach's (1969, 1971) arguments that validation should focus on the interpretations occurring in conjunction with specific applications for tests, the consensus on construct validity expanded to incorporate not only the theoretical meanings attributed to test scores but also the meanings implied by the ways in which these scores were used for applied purposes (e.g., educational decision making). In practice, this expansion of construct validity meaning implied that, on its own, theory-based hypothesis testing of measurement constructs would prove insufficient in judging the comprehensive construct validity of most tests, because test score meanings could not be separated from the uses to which they were put. Finally, by expanding construct validity to include the uses to which tests are put, consideration of the consequences of test use also emerged as a critical function of validation. Thus, both Cronbach, (1980) and Messick (1975, 1980, 1981), echoing others, recommended that validation pay particular attention to the social and ethical dimensions of test-based interpretations and how those interpretations are used in practice.

This emerging consensus on validity was formalized in Messick's (1989) hugely influential (and huge) chapter on validity in the third edition of *Educational Measurement* (Linn, 1989). In just over 100 pages, Messick laid out his conceptualization of a unified and comprehensive approach to validity, including both philosophical underpinnings and methodological implications for how validation practice should proceed. The first sentence of his treatise (by now a ubiquitous quote included in every major treatment of test validity written since) summarized the watershed changes that had taken place:

> Validity is an integrated evaluative judgment of the degree to which empirical evidence and theoretical rationales support the *adequacy* and *appropriateness* of *inferences* and *actions* based on test scores or other modes of assessment. (p. 13, emphasis in original)

Messick portrayed validity first as a purposeful judgment, thereby immediately distancing it from previous depictions of validity as a quality or characteristic of tests themselves. The validation process, then, was at once a theory- and an evidence-driven evaluative endeavor, incorporating the construct validity requirement of a clear theoretical basis for the test and empirical evidence to support the theory. However, Messick pushed much further. A comprehensive approach to validation also had to attend to evidence and consequences about intended *uses* for tests (which he termed "action inferences") as well as the proposed test score *meanings* (which he termed "interpretive inferences") that inform those uses. Validity included much more than an appraisal of the extent to which a test was 'measuring what it was intended to measure', since tests themselves were intended to do much more than simply provide accurate measures of constructs. Indeed, Messick argued, the very act of interpreting test scores in meaningful ways was itself grounded in societal values, and these values were linked to the decisions and other actions for which tests had been designed in the first place. The test construct was no longer merely a theoretical argument; rather, it emerged from the values-laden inferences (both interpretive and action inferences) that were based on social uses for tests. Messick summarized these arguments in the form of a four-celled matrix which presented the requisite facets of a comprehensive approach to validity, including: (a) construct validity (theoretical rationale and evidence supporting the meaning of intended test score interpretations); (b) relevance and utility (evidence supporting the usefulness of test score interpretations for the actual applied uses to which they are put in real-world settings); (c) value implications (the social and ethical consequences of adopting a particular test and construct theory); and (d) social consequences (support for the actual outcomes for individuals, and society in general, of an intended use for a test).

According to Messick (1989), "[t]he function of test validation is to marshal evidence and arguments in support of, or counter to, proposed interpretations and uses of test scores" (p. 32). In practice, validation required working progressively through the facets of the validity matrix (a-d above), pursuing systematic investigations of each component. Primary concern was afforded construct validity, which Messick cast as a necessary but not sufficient condition for comprehensive validation: "The meaning of the measure, and hence its construct validity, must always be pursued— not only to support test interpretation but also to justify test use" (p. 17). Given evidence in support of score meaning from a construct point of view, subsequent investigations pursued lines of evidence for the remaining components, calling upon a range of epistemologies appropriate to each type of inquiry. Messick argued that a comprehensive approach to validation was consonant with, indeed required, epistemological flexibility in that "philosophical foundations of validity and validation combine elements not only from multiple philosophical but also from multiple methodological perspectives" (p. 30). However, methodological opportunism and confirmatory bias were to be countered by deriving lines of validity inquiry "mainly from the construct theories themselves and the theoretical expectations about data patterns therefrom, which provide a rational basis for linking the specific inferences to be made to the forms of evidence needed to support them" (pp. 33-34). Thus, Messick did not advocate that all possible social consequences of test use be investigated; rather, only those consequences derived directly from intended score interpretations and test uses had bearing on a validity judgment. For example, where performance assessments were to be implemented for effecting change in educational systems, these systematic concerns had little to do with the meaning of scores inferred from the given assessment instrument, and their investigation was not directly implied within the validation framework (Messick, 1994, 1995).

While Messick (1989) formalized the full range of considerations implied by the new consensus on validity, he offered scant additional instruction on organizing and implementing practical validity investigations. His advice was basic: (a) construct validity was the primary consideration, and construct theory should motivate all validation efforts; (b) construct underrepresentation and construct irrelevant variance were the primary threats to validity and should receive closest scrutiny; (c) all components of the comprehensive validity framework required investigation, including intended and unintended consequences of intended test use; (d) validation was an ongoing process, punctuated by judgments about adequacy and appropriateness of test use in light of what was known; and (e) adequate validation efforts lay well beyond the scope of individual practitioners. In addition, Messick acknowledged that "[d]ifferent kinds of inferences from test scores may require a different balancing of evidence, that is, different relative emphases in the range of evidence presented" (p. 15), and he summarized the possible types of validity evidence according to six concise categories: (1) analysis of content in relation to the content of the domain of reference; (2) analysis of the ways in which individuals respond to test tasks; (3) analysis of the internal structure of test responses; (4) analysis of the relationship of test scores with other measures and background variables (external structure); (5) investigation of differences in test processes and structures over time, across groups, and in response to experimental interventions; and (6) consideration of the intended and unintended social consequences of using test scores in particular ways.

Messick's presentation of a unified theory of validity, which incorporated test use and consequences alongside test score meaning, broadened considerably the domain of validity inquiry, and in doing so it addressed many of the theoretical concerns with previous approaches to validation. However, with this increased scope and the requirements imposed by his comprehensive validation framework, numerous questions were also raised regarding practical implementation. In particular, Messick's (1989) chapter sparked debate throughout the 1990s in two areas of specific interest to educational assessment: (a) validating performance, classroom, and so-called 'alternative' assessments; and (b) addressing the consequential aspects of validity.

3.3.1 Validating performance, classroom, and 'alternative' assessments

Of particular concern to those working within educational settings were the implications of Messick's approach for the validation of emerging assessment instruments and uses, which bore little resemblance to the selected-response, standardized tests of traditional focus for validity investigations. Performance assessments, which employed publicly valued, authentic, and complex performance tasks for educational assessment at a variety of levels, but especially for high-stakes accountability and certification purposes presented several problems (see Delandshere & Petrosky, 1998; Eisner, 1999; Haertel, 1999; Khattri, Reeve, & Kane, 1998; Madaus & O'Dwyer, 1999; Moss & Schutz, 1999; Stiggins). On the one hand, societal and educational values from some quarters demanded the replacement of traditional standardized multiple-choice testing with extended, authentic performance assessments. Fundamentally, this movement sought to improve learning by improving instruction which inevitably 'taught to the test'. At the same time, the use of these new assessments for high-stakes decisions raised serious concerns about consistency in administration, reliability in scoring, and generalizability/comparability of scores across tasks and testing contexts. Caught in a conflict between consequential and construct validity, practitioners posed legitimate challenges for validation, including: (a) what criteria should be applied in evaluating these high-stakes uses for performance assessments? (b) how should particular criteria be weighted differentially in making validity judgments? (c) how should the apparent conflict between desired consequences and measurement score accuracy be resolved? and (d) what guidelines were available for ensuring an appropriate and adequate validation process?

Answers from the educational measurement community varied (and continue to vary) considerably. Messick (1994) advocated a comprehensive approach which investigated *all* aspects of validity, including intended consequences of performance assessment (in the form of washback on instruction and learning) and unintended consequences (in the form of bias/fairness concerns for examinee populations). However, he also emphasized that both performance assessment and its validation should remain construct-driven, with priority given to investigations of construct underrepresentation and construct irrelevant variance (see examples in Bond, 1995; Brennan & Johnson, 1995; Green, 1995; Jaeger, 1995; Messick, 1995). In contrast, Linn, Baker, and Dunbar (1991) argued that "the criteria for judging the assessment must correspond to the purpose" (p. 20), and they proposed eight criteria specific to the validation of performance assessments, based on their perceived educational purposes: (a) educational consequences, (b) transferability of performances, (c) fairness of performance tasks and scoring, (d) actual versus intended cognitive complexity of performance tasks, (e) meaningfulness of assessments to teachers and students, (f) content quality and coverage, and (g) cost of assessment. From a third perspective, more recently, Kane, Crooks, and Cohen (1999) proposed that validation of performance assessments be tailored to the specific inferential argument implied by the assessment, with a focus in particular on the weakest parts of that argument. For performance assessments, they prioritized three inferential problem areas: (a) scoring complex performances; (b) generalizing from performances to a target domain of tasks or performances; and (c) extrapolating beyond the performance and the domain to a universe of performance abilities. Given the distinct criteria and guidelines offered from these three perspectives, it is clear that high-stakes performance assessment remains an elusive target for current validation practice.

In a similar vein, increasing attention to classroom assessment and other forms of so-called 'alternative' assessment led practitioners to question the applicability of comprehensive, construct-driven approaches to validation. Stiggins and Bridgeford (1985) foreshadowed these concerns in observing that:

> [M]easurement research...concentrates on assessment methods that have the least utility for teachers' decision making. As researchers, our focus must be redirected to include assessment methods and quality control issues in the classroom environment that affect student learning and instruction. (p. 283)

From the point of view of assessment as an integral component in the classroom instruction and learning process (Shepard, 2000), prioritized purposes and qualities of assessments did not necessarily match those in other test use contexts. Within the classroom, where assessment serves as an "educational medium" as opposed to an accountability tool for "temperature taking" (Eisner, 1999), it was argued that assessment is intended for a variety of purposes, including among others: (a) modeling valued performances, behaviors, and criteria; (b) providing rich feedback to learners and teachers; (c) enabling instructional and learning adaptations; (d) demonstrating the value of knowledge and skills learned; (e) enabling contextualized and individualized judgments by teachers; (f) fostering curricular improvements; and (g) enabling self-assessment and self-determination by students (Miller & Legg, 1993; Shepard, 2000; Stiggins, 1988, 2001; Stiggins & Conklin, 1992; Wolf, 1993; Wolf, Bixby, Glenn, & Gardner, 1991). In order to validate assessments designed to meet such localized purposes, Glaser and Silver (1994) argued, "Evidence must be produced to demonstrate that changes in assessment result in classroom activities that are conducive to improved student learning" (p. 413). Similarly, Wiggins (1989; 1993a, 1993b; 1998) emphasized that, unlike large-scale standardized assessments used for auditing purposes (which prioritize qualities such as efficiency in administration and scoring, reliability, and generalizability), assessments intended to function "educatively" at the classroom and curricular level depend upon other qualities and processes, such as: (a) authenticity to learners, curricular objectives, and the public; (b) provision of timely, ongoing, rich, and useful feedback to students and teachers, as well as other assessment constituents; and (c) clear improvements in teaching and learning as a result of assessment. Finally, Moss (1994, 1996) suggested that standard approaches to validation, which prioritized reliable and accurate interpretations of test constructs, could constrain educational assessment practices and in turn hinder teaching and learning. She proposed that validation strategies borrowed from interpretive research traditions (e.g., Lincoln, 2001; Mishler, 1990) would prove more appropriate under conditions where assessment prioritizes the value of teachers' contextualized judgments and seeks to support students' own purposes and processes in learning (e.g., portfolio assessment; see Moss et al, 1992). While issues surrounding the validation of classroom and 'alternative' assessments have spurred considerable discussion and even acrimonious debate (e.g., Cizek, 1991), guidelines and criteria for implementing validation strategies appropriate to these purposes continue to defy consensus (Stiggins, 2001).

3.3.2 Investigating consequences in test validation

Messick's (1989) inclusion of *consequential* aspects of test interpretation and use within a unified theory of validity also triggered substantial debate, and it led practitioners to raise critical methodological questions. Within educational measurement, many disagreed with the incorporation of consequences into definitions of validity and practices of validation. Prominent voices (e.g., Mehrens, 1997; Popham, 1997, 2000; Reckase, 1998; Wiley, 1991; Yalow & Popham, 1983) argued that validity should be restricted to an appraisal of the accuracy of test score interpretations as indicators of constructs. They asserted that the inclusion of decisions, actions, and other consequences ensuing from various possible uses for score-based measurements only serves to confound the *quality* of the measure with the efficacy or appropriateness of using it in particular ways. Clearly, this position presumed that tests are used psychometrically, that is, as instruments for estimating theory-based constructs. The persistent appeal to psychometric validity arguments made by psychologists is telling in this regard (e.g., Boorsboom, Mellenbergh, and van Heerden, 2004; Tenopyr, 1996).

Other prominent voices (e.g., Linn, 1997; Shepard, 1997) countered that the uses for tests, and therefore the consequences for individuals and society, should be a core consideration for validation, and that if consequences of test use are not included in the notion of validity, they will be ignored in practice. In addition, they contended that test score meaning itself is determined in most cases by the uses to which tests are put (i.e., because tests are generally designed to inform particular uses), and that separating test scores from test use and consequences only serves to dilute the actual meaning of the interpretation. Validation, then, must include evaluation of the meaningfulness, appropriateness, usefulness, and outcomes of interpreting and using test scores.

Despite contention regarding the role of consequences in a unified theory of validity, general consensus emerged that the consequences of test use require investigation (AERA, APA, & NCME, 1999), and even those voices opposed to including consequences within definitions of validity agreed that the consequences of test use must be evaluated (e.g., Popham, 2000). However, methodological questions also emerged, as in Linn's (1997) observation: "This, of course, does not mean all conceivable consequences of all possible uses. As in any good evaluation, priorities need to be established in the investigation of possible consequences" (p. 14). Thus, moving beyond the methodologically useless truism that positive consequences of testing should outweigh negative consequences, practitioners from several perspectives (e.g., Green, 1998; Lane, Parke, & Stone, 1998; Linn, 1998; Moss, 1998; Shepard, 1997; Taleporos, 1998) raised much more complex concerns, including: (a) who is responsible for investigating consequences (test developers, test publishers, test users, policy makers, the educational measurement profession, all stakeholders, etc.)? (b) which consequences should be investigated (putative benefits, unintended negative side effects, social impact of adopting particular construct theories and test methods, effects of the test development process per se, washback on teaching and learning, etc.)? (c) when and for how long should consequences be investigated (immediate versus long-term outcomes for examinees and society, during test development, after test publication and deployment, etc.)? (d) what types of evidence will provide useful insights into consequences (surveys of constituents, observations of test use, documentation of effects on individuals and educational systems, experimental studies, in-depth case studies, educational program values and mission statements, etc.)? and (e) for what purposes should the findings from consequential investigations be used (judging and communicating about test worth, continuing or abandoning testing practice, revising test interpretation and use, generalizing to other related contexts, litigating against testing practices, etc.)? In terms of validation practice, then, methodologies for investigating test uses and consequences remained the focus of speculation and discussion, while frameworks lacked for guiding practice *in situ*.

3.4 Prioritizing validation practices for educational assessments

Messick's (1989) unified theory of validity, and its codification in the latest *Standards for educational and psychological testing* (AERA, APA, & NCME, 1999), synthesized over four decades of thought, discussion, and experience from the educational and psychological measurement professions into a framework which organized, located, and drew logical relationships among principal concerns for tests and the uses to which they are typically put. However, substantial challenges remain for the practice of validating assessments and the myriad ways in which they are applied in specific educational settings. Indeed, in this respect, it has been argued that Messick's framework and the current standards have detracted from efforts to help educators engage in useful validation work. According to Brennan (2001), instead of "demystify[ing] validation so that practitioners find it to be an approachable goal" (p. 13), the scope and complexity of a unifying framework for validity has led to the unordered accumulation of vaguely focused studies in the name of validation. Brennan also argued that, instead of all-encompassing theories, "those who are actually responsible for validation almost always require detailed and concrete guidance for conducting validation activities, and the 'unitary' notion is simply not helpful for them" (Brennan, 1998, p. 7). More specifically, several key deficiencies in the practice of validating educational assessments have been identified in contemporary approaches to validity.

3.4.1 Deficiencies in validation practice

Most prominently, the unified notion of construct validity has been criticized for being overwhelming in its scope and therefore largely unfeasible for most practitioners responsible for validating actual educational assessments (Kane, 2001). Shepard (1993) observed that "the complexity of Messick's analysis does not help to identify which validity questions are essential to support a test use" (p. 427). Validation is typically perceived to require some investigation of *all* of the facets of the comprehensive validity framework. In this regard, the current testing standards (AERA, APA, & NCME, 1999) are unambiguous: "The present *Standards* continues the tradition of expecting test developers and users to consider all standards before operational use" (p. 2). Over 200 individual standards comprise the most recent recommendations. Little wonder that the depiction of validation as an 'ongoing' process is often interpreted as a *never-ending* process that is beyond the capabilities of most educational assessment practitioners (Shepard, 1993).

Second, considerable attention has been paid to the lack of contextualization, and therefore the lack of accessibility, utility, and meaningfulness, in contemporary approaches to validation. It is clear from the depiction of educational assessment in a variety of texts (e.g., Angelo & Cross, 1993; Nitko, 1996; Popham, 2000; Wiggins, 1998) that assessment enjoys a wide variety of uses by a range of users for a number of distinct purposes, and that it impacts unique groups of stakeholders in both intended and unintended ways. Likewise, the ways in which assessment instruments and procedures are designed, implemented, and utilized vary considerably from one educational setting to the next. However, despite the highly contextualized nature of educational systems and the roles of assessments within them, little attention has been paid to the corresponding demands on validation, in the form of distinct: (a) audiences and stakeholders for the validation process; (b) individuals or groups responsible for validation; (c) reasons for engaging in validation; (d) questions for validity inquiry; (e) appropriate methods for investigating these questions; (f) useful sources of evidence; or (g) means for summarizing, synthesizing, and using validation results to meet immediate local needs.

Here again, the standards and contemporary approaches to validation prove particularly inadequate and even contradictory. On the one hand, the most recent standards (AERA, APA, & NCME, 1999) seek to direct and model validation and the evaluation of testing in general: "The purpose of publishing the *Standards* is to provide criteria for the evaluation of tests, testing practices, and the effects of test use" (p. 2). However, in the chapter on educational testing and assessment, the authors are quick to qualify that, in fact, the standards are only intended for large-scale testing, testing for selection in higher education, and individualized/special needs testing (e.g., for learning disabilities). Moreover, the standards are explicitly "not intended for tests used by teachers for their own classroom purposes" (p. 137). Apparently, then, the standards are only intended to inform validation practice for a handful of the actual assessment uses within education, not including what is arguably the most common application for tests (within the classroom; see Stiggins, 2001). Such standardized validation practice reserved for only 'standard' types of assessment undermines any utility for resolving the actual, contextualized validation demands of most educational assessments.

Further, the standards repeatedly appeal to the authority of measurement professionals in dealing with the difficulties presented by validation. For example, while they acknowledge that "[e]valuating the acceptability of a test or test application does not rest on the literal satisfaction of every standard in this document, and acceptability cannot be determined by using a checklist" (p. 4), they suggest that "professional judgment" should prevail in determining the specific balance of evidence needed. Furthermore, while ostensibly "[v]alidation is the joint responsibility of the test developer and the test user" (p. 11), it turns out that the primary responsibility of test users is:

> documenting that their test uses and score interpretations are supported by *measurement authorities* for the given purpose, that the inferences drawn from their instruments are validated for use with a given population, and that the results are being used in conjunction with other information, not in isolation. (p. 112, my emphasis)

The higher authority of measurement professionals' validation purposes clearly prevails over the meaningfulness or utility of such standardized validation practice for the actual contexts within which educational assessments occur. Validation should occur, from this perspective, principally because it is a mandated professional responsibility, not because it is a useful process which may provide information to a variety of constituents for understanding, improving, or otherwise evaluating test use *in situ*. The priority 'context' of validation, from the *Standards* point of view, seems to be the measurement profession, rather than the stakeholders, audiences, and purposes for assessments as they are used for making decisions and taking actions within educational systems (Frederiksen & Collins, 1989).

Along similar lines, Kane (2001) has observed that, by portraying all validity as construct validity, the unified approach has led test users and measurement professionals alike to assume that all test-based inferences must be validated in the same way (i.e., starting with the construct theory). He has argued that this uniform approach is unwieldy in educational assessment, and in many cases not possible, due to the fact that theory-based construct definitions and associated measures have little to do "with the work of teachers, policy makers, and others making day-to-day decisions based on test scores" (p. 325). For example, in the case of performance assessment, Kane points out that test users are often interested in qualities of "observable attributes" per se (e.g., how well an examinee can perform on specific, educationally valued tasks) rather than theoretical constructs posited to underlie these performance qualities. Insisting on the primacy of construct validation (e.g., Bachman, 2002) ignores the fact that specific uses for tests in applied settings may call upon very different inferential processes than do measures of theoretical or research constructs, and thus, that different assessment uses cannot be validated equivalently according to the same kinds of prescribed methods and evidence (Shepard, 1993). Therefore, following Kane (2001), "Unless we are willing to assume that all validations are to follow the same pattern of inference and evidence, we need some criteria for what to include in each validation" (p. 331). Similarly, Moss (1992) has echoed others (Anastasi, 1990; Cronbach, 1971, 1988) in calling for the contextualization of validation practice according to the inferential boundaries of tests and their uses; in other words, validation should only seek to investigate generalizations and extrapolations about construct meanings in test scores insofar as tests themselves are used to do so in practice.

A third deficiency in contemporary approaches to validation, related to the first two, issues from the lack of clear guidelines for focusing and organizing actual practices and procedures in validating educational assessments. Moss (1992) summarized that "[t]he problem for validity researchers is finding the appropriate set of criteria and standards to simultaneously support the validity of an assessment-based interpretation and the validity of its impact on the educational system" (p. 230). Beyond appealing to professional judgments, the only organizational advice offered by the current standards (AERA, APA, & NCME, 1999) is that a sound validity argument should integrate all of the sources of evidence into a coherent account. Such minimal advice reflects Shepard's (1993) indictment that:

Validity standards are not organized in a coherent conceptual framework. Therefore, they do not help answer the question "How much evidence is enough?" nor do they clarify that the stringency of evidential demands should vary as a function of potential consequences. (p. 429)

Likewise, Kane (2001) has questioned "If an essentially infinite number of studies are relevant, where should one start, and how much is enough?" (p. 327). Unfortunately, the most recent authors of the standards did not follow Shepard's (1993) recommendation to "find a simpler model for prioritizing validity questions, one that clarifies which validity questions must be answered to defend a test use and which are academic refinements that go beyond the immediate, urgent questions" (p. 407).

In this regard, educational measurement textbooks also lack solutions to the problems of organizing and implementing useful validation practices. For example, Popham (2000) recommends the following five categories for evaluating educational assessments:

1. Instructional contribution
2. Validity (content, criterion-related, and construct)
3. Reliability
4. Absence of bias
5. Comparative data

However, while he discusses ways of evaluating each in useful detail, he does not provide guidance for ordering, weighing, comparing, communicating, making a decision upon, or otherwise *using* the constellation of evidentiary types issuing from these categories to actually accomplish concrete evaluative objectives. Instead, he simply states:

Based on the five evaluative factors described in the next five chapters, an educational leader could come up with a readily usable five-factor framework for evaluating educational tests. Certain of the factors always apply. Certain of the factors apply only in certain situations. (p. 63)

Structured recommendations regarding which of the factors to investigate when, or in what order, or to what depth of detail, or with what concrete objectives, are not offered.

In sum, some educational assessment practitioners have argued forcefully that Messick's unified approach to test validity, and its standardization/promulgation by professional organizations, fares poorly when its own comprehensive criteria are focused inwards on the resulting validation practice. How relevant/useful are current notions of validity for illuminating the effectiveness or appropriateness of particular assessment practices? What are the values implications of adopting a unified and comprehensive approach to validation (i.e., whose values are represented and whose are ignored)? What might be the consequences, for various groups of stakeholders (besides educational measurement professionals), of insisting on the application of the standards for all assessments? From the point of view of those who seek to understand educational assessment practice within actual applied settings, and to utilize that information to ensure its quality, contemporary notions of validity continue to be found lacking.

3.4.2 Proposals for improving validation practice

In response to these deficiencies, initial solutions have been proposed for organizing, focusing, and prioritizing procedures and evidentiary sources for the validation of educational assessments. Underlying these proposals is the common argument that, rather than a scientific theory-testing framework, or sets of exhaustive standards based on a unified theory of validity, a more effective and practicable approach to validation may be provided by adopting a program evaluation model. Cronbach (1988) summarized, "Validation of a test or test use *is* evaluation (Guion, 1980; Messick, 1980), so I propose here to extend to all testing the lessons from program evaluation" (p. 4, emphasis in original). Messick (1988) also considered the potential of such an approach:

> Moreover, the practical use of measurements for decision making and action is or ought to be *applied* science, recognizing that applied science always occurs in a political context. Indeed, social and political forces are sometimes so salient that we may need a new discipline to deal explicitly with the politics of applied science, which is what the field of program evaluation shows signs of becoming. (p. 43, emphasis in original)

Cronbach (1989) later spelled out more explicitly how "test evaluators" would go about their work. Following Cronbach (1982), he suggested that the focus of test evaluation should be derived from an initial identification of the most relevant questions and the subsequent prioritization of these questions based on considerations of uncertainty, information yield, cost, leverage with stakeholders, etc.:

> After weighing these criteria, the evaluator will probably choose a few questions for intensive research, with other questions covered incidentally by inexpensive side-studies, or not at all. This prioritizing steers the evaluator away from *Dragnet* empiricism. (Cronbach, 1989, p. 165)

More recently, these initial ideas have been explored in some detail by assessment professionals seeking to resolve practical validation dilemmas via an evaluative approach (Kane, 1992, 2001; Moss, 1992, 1998; Shepard, 1993, 1997). While their recommendations for "validity evaluation" (Shepard, 1993) vary in the specifics, they share the following overarching features.

In order to contextualize and frame the validation process such that it provides useful information, Shepard (1993) recommended that "[a]ny validity evaluation must start by identifying not only the test but its intended use" (p. 432). Likewise, Kane (2001) suggested that "[i]n order to evaluate a proposed interpretation of test scores, it is necessary to have a clear and fairly complete statement of the claims in-cluded in the interpretation and the goals of any proposed test uses" (p. 329). Thus, in order to prioritize questions, methods, and sources for validity evaluation of edu-cational assessments which are designed to do anything beyond simply measuring constructs, the evaluation stage must first be set with a clear understanding of in-tended test use, including not only the interpretations that are to be based on the test but also the decisions and actions that will derive from the test. Building from this clarification of what (among many possible educational roles) an assessment is claimed to do or accomplish, the possible scope of evaluative activities can be con-strained to focus on the specific inferential arguments (both interpretive and action inferences) that are relevant to test uses and users within the educational setting (see also Cronbach, 1988, 1989; Cureton, 1951; Glaser & Silver, 1994; Kane, 1992; Moss, 1992).

Given a clear understanding of intended test use, a finite set of particular validity questions to be addressed can be identified according to the associated inferences; in turn, the particular constellation of evidentiary requirements will depend on these questions. Kane (1992) observed that "[t]he amount of evidence and the types of evidence needed in a particular case depend on the inferences and assumptions in the interpretive argument" (p. 534), and he later added that "...a unified argument-based approach to validation suggests the need for different kinds of validity arguments to support different kinds of interpretive arguments, involving different patterns of in-ference" (Kane, 2001, p. 332). Procedurally, Kane's argument-based approach involves the following steps: (a) decide on statements and decisions based on test scores; (b) specify the inferences and assumptions from test scores to these interpre-tations; (c) identify competing interpretations; and (d) seek evidence supporting proposed interpretations and refuting others. Shepard (1993) has also advocated this approach to tailoring validity evaluations, and both Kane (2001) and Shepard (1993) have recommended that evaluation questions be prioritized by focusing on what are likely to be the weakest parts of the interpretive argument.

The types of inferences to be evaluated may include not only test-score interpre-tations, but also the decision and action inferences that inhere in test uses. For Kane (2001), the interpretive argument extends from test development, through admini-stration, scoring, score interpretation, and score reporting, to decision making and associated consequences. Inferences within each of these stages may be prioritized for validity evaluation, with each calling for unique types of evidence, such as: (a) elicitation and observation (procedural evidence); (b) generalization (evidence for scoring reliability, sources of error); (c) extrapolation of scores to non-test behav-iors/abilities (content and criterion-related evidence); (d) theory-based explanation (construct rationales, hypothesis testing evidence); (e) decisions (evidence for out-comes and consequences); and (f) technical uses and specifications (evidence for test form equating, item fit, norming, etc.). While any of these aspects may be prioritized, it is clear that applied educational assessments will always call for evidence bearing on the impact of test use on the individuals with a stake in that process (Moss, 1992; Shepard, 1993). Kane (2001) observed that consequences determine the bottom line for any applied testing procedure, and thus "[t]he validation of decision procedures has always depended on the evaluation of the consequences of the decisions" (p. 339).

Because educational assessments are used by specific individuals for making interpretations and decisions which result in positive and negative consequences for other individuals, it has also been recommended that validity evaluation be framed at least in part according to the interests of stakeholders in the assessment process (Shepard, 1993). Cronbach (1989) in particular advocated the inclusion of stakeholders, both assessment advocates and critics, in order to frame and prioritize validity questions and as critical sources of evidence about assessment use (see also Moss, et al, 1992; Moss, 1998). Stakeholders, and especially test users, are often the most direct sources for determining which portions of the assessment argument are most in need of investigation, due to their proximity to assessment applications. In addition, the responsibility for validation of testing in practice frequently falls to the test user (Angoff, 1988).

In order to carry out investigations appropriate to a variety of test uses, the specific inferences associated with them, the range of questions that may be asked by stakeholders, and the evidence required to answer such questions, validity evaluation obviously demands epistemological flexibility (Moss, 1992). Evaluative methods and sources of evidence may vary considerably, depending on the specific purposes for validation within the given educational assessment setting—scientific hypothesis-testing using experimental methods (e.g., Campbell, 1957, 1969) will not answer all questions that may be prioritized about test interpretation and use. Thus, for example, an investigation of the consequences of score-reporting formats from high-stakes assessments may necessitate interviews, case-study methods, and otherwise "highly contextualized, sustained interpretive work" (Moss, 1998, p. 11). On the other hand, the evaluation of an employment-related performance assessment might initially call for a focus on task, rater, and rating consistency in the form of a generalizability study (Kane, 2001).

Finally, validity evaluation may be pursued from a variety of perspectives for a variety of evaluative purposes, not simply in response to mandates from professional standards or for the sake of scientific rigor. Clearly, a major purpose for validity evaluation is to provide formative information for improvements, especially during test development and initial stages of implementation (Cronbach, 1988). For such formative evaluation purposes, Kane's (2001) argument-based approach may prove particularly appropriate for ferreting out information that is directly tied to specific, questionable, or "weak" inferential components of an assessment. In addition, according to Cronbach (1988), validity evaluation may be called upon to provide evidence from functional, economic, operationist, political, or explanatory perspectives, depending on who is mandating or requesting the evaluation. Thus, the reasons for engaging in validity evaluation, and consequently the questions asked and the evidence gathered, will depend as much (if not more) on the ways in which validity information itself is intended to be used as it will on the intended uses for educational assessments per se.

3.5 Committing to validity evaluation in educational assessment

Notions of test validity and methods for validation practice have evolved considerably since the 1950s, progressing from the "trinitarian" approaches to content, construct, and criterion-related validity types, through psychometric emphases on score meaning in the form of theory-based construct validity, and culminating in Messick's (1989) theory of validity which unified test score meaning with the uses and consequences of tests. Along the way, educational and psychological measurement experts have recommended a variety of methodologies and evidentiary sources for the investigation of validity, and these have been summarized and disseminated periodically in the form of professional testing standards (most recently in AERA, APA, & NCME, 1999). While the scope of recommended validation practices has expanded, the continued primacy afforded construct validity has prioritized a few scientific models of inquiry and the accumulation of evidence bearing primarily on test score meaning. However, educational assessment practitioners have raised concerns about the feasibility, meaningfulness, and utility of current unified approaches to validation. These concerns have illuminated the lack of coherent and practicable guidelines and criteria for engaging in the validation of actual tests as they are used for a variety of actual decision-making and other purposes within specific educational contexts. In response, recent proposals have begun to approach validation from the perspective of program evaluation, thereby enabling the prioritization of particular validity questions relevant to specific interpretations and uses for tests. Based on these meaningful questions, evaluative methods and evidentiary sources can be articulated. To be clear, these proposals have not suggested that construct theory or validation be done away with. Rather, they have sought to provide frameworks for focusing the questions, methods, and uses of validation, such that its processes may lead to educationally relevant and usable outcomes, whether the focus is on theoretical constructs or other features of assessment.

Although the proposed shift to "validity evaluation" has the potential to structure an accessible validation methodology resulting in useful information about educational assessments, the full implications of a commitment to program evaluation have yet to be explored. Missing from the proposals thus far are practical answers to several questions, including:

1. Who is responsible for initiating and implementing the validity evaluation and, more importantly, for making methodological decisions along the way? Cronbach (1989), Kane (2001), and Shepard (1993) all attribute control over the evaluation process to an external test evaluator expert. However, depending on the context and purpose for the validity evaluation, responsibility and decision making may more appropriately involve program-internal individuals, groups of constituents, or a mix of internal and external participants. A praticable validity evaluation model will need to address issues of ownership, responsibility, and decision making among potential participants.

2. How should the purposes for validity evaluation be determined, and what is the value of engaging in the process? Program evaluation may occur for a variety of reasons, from formative improvement-oriented purposes to summative judgments regarding the perpetuation or termination of practices. Likewise, there may be numerous purposes for evaluating educational assessments and their uses, including those proposed by Cronbach (1989) as well as others. An argument-based approach (Kane, 1992, 2001; Shepard, 1993) assumes that validation occurs in order to evaluate the inferences occurring within a given test use; however, it does not address what gets done with the findings, to whom they are communicated, of what value they may be to the educational system and its constituents, or what decisions or actions are intended on the basis of the evaluation. Therefore, an adequate validity evaluation model will need to provide a mechanism for clarifying the purposes of the evaluation itself.

3. How should potential questions be prioritized and types of evidence weighted in validity evaluation? Depending on the reasons behind a given evaluation effort, decisions will also be made about the questions to be asked and the types of evidence required in answering them. It may not be the case that all available evidence bearing on test interpretations and uses will prove relevant or necessary for the intended evaluation purposes. Furthermore, it may be the case that particular sources of evidence far outweigh others or that particular questions are dramatically more important than others for the constituents in the particular educational context. A validity evaluation model will require a straightforward means for prioritizing among and balancing potential questions and sources of evidence.

4. How is validity evaluation best translated into practice? Adequate evaluation projects may involve a number of phases, including stage-setting and fact-finding, stakeholder identification, negotiation of evaluation purposes/goals/objectives, development of research questions and methods, data collection and analysis, interpretation and judgment, reporting and dissemination, etc. Depending on the purposes for evaluation, these phases may occur over a short or long span of time, may involve cycles of investigation-reporting-reassessment-investigation, may be renegotiated and shift focus, and may require the commitment of considerable time, money, and effort. In order to make validity evaluation happen, various implementation phases will need to be planned and structured according to models of effective evaluation practice.

The idea of recasting test validation as validity evaluation has opened the door for validity to be reconceived as an educationally relevant concept rather than a preoccupation of psychometricians. However, a commitment to validity evaluation will require that educational assessment practitioners take a serious look at the purposes, models, and methods of program evaluation, as well as lessons learned from their implementation, in order to achieve such relevance.

Chapter 4
Learning from program evaluation in validating educational assessments

An evaluative approach to validating educational assessments may provide the missing framework for organizing meaningful and useful validation efforts, for prioritizing and focusing validity questions, evidence, and criteria, and for communicating and explicating the value of validation to assessment stakeholders. The theory and practice of program evaluation provide methodologies and guidance for: (a) clarifying the context and stakeholders for programs and their evaluation; (b) determining the intended uses and audiences for evaluation; (c) identifying priority evaluative questions or problems, and appropriate types and amounts of evidence for addressing them; (d) designing and implementing feasible and accurate evaluation studies; (e) establishing, weighing, and balancing the social and political values inherent in programs as well as evaluative judgments about them; and (f) ensuring the utility and use of evaluation processes and findings (Joint Committee on Standards for Educational Evaluation, 1994). Where assessment is implemented as a component of an educational program, or, indeed, as an educational program unto itself (i.e., with its own goals, objectives, practices, outcomes, and consequences), these program evaluation processes may provide the means for dealing with the concerns raised in chapter 3. However, program evaluation models abound, with each model emphasizing unique techniques in response to the perceived purposes and contexts for evaluation (Stufflebeam, 2001). In addition, the program evaluation profession itself has engaged in extensive debate regarding exactly what these purposes for evaluation should be (e.g., Campbell, 1969; Fetterman, 1988, 2001; Guba & Lincoln, 1989; Scriven, 1997; Stake, 1997; Weiss, 1980), resulting in considerable discord among some of the existing methodological and procedural recommendations.

In this chapter, I review recent debate (and current consensus) regarding the purposes and uses for program evaluation, and I briefly survey associated evaluation models and methods. I then argue that a commitment to *validity evaluation* in educational assessment will call for a reconceptualization of conventional assessment validation practices. Finally, I outline the fundamental tenets of an evaluative approach to validating educational assessments.

4.1 Purposes and practices of program evaluation

Like educational measurement, program evaluation has emerged as a professional and academic discipline over the past century in response to intellectual and societal demands for certain kinds of applied research activities (see historical overviews in Cook, 1997; Cronbach & Associates, 1980; Fetterman, 1988; Guba & Lincoln, 1989; Rossi, Freeman, & Lipsey, 1999). In the first half of the twentieth century, social scientists sought to systematize judgments about the effectiveness and value of social programs by applying scientific methods in researching large-scale public health, education, criminal justice, and employment initiatives (Freeman, 1977). These early evaluation practices focused nearly exclusively on measuring the outcomes or 'products' of social programs in order to justify decisions about their perpetuation or termination (Guba & Lincoln, 1989; Scriven, 1991; Weiss, 1998b). However, the last three decades of the 20th century witnessed considerable diversification in the focus and applications of evaluation. On the one hand, an expanding array of programs, projects, and policies, the values of a range of evaluation sponsors, stakeholders, and audiences, and a variety of program components (e.g., inputs, participants, processes, products) fell under the program evaluation lens (Mohan, Bernstein, & Whitsett, 2002; Rog & Fournier, 1997; Rossi, Freeman, & Lipsey, 1999). At the same time, evaluation techniques came to be applied for new and varied reasons. Thus, within the space of a few critical developmental years, Cronbach (1963) and Stufflebeam (1966) recommended a shift in the purpose of evaluation towards program improvement, Stake (1967) advocated the description of program rationales and processes in addition to outcomes, and Scriven (1967) formalized the distinction between formative and summative perspectives on the evaluation of educational curricula. In short order, the potential roles for evaluation increased considerably beyond the measurement of program outcomes, to accommodate purposes such as program description, learning, improvement, justification, accountability, and public relations, among others (Rossi, Freeman, & Lipsey, 1999; Weiss, 1998a).

Currently, there is a very general level of consensus within the discipline (with some notable exceptions, e.g., Scriven, 1997), that evaluation seeks to illuminate and enable understanding of both program processes and program outcomes via applied research activities. In addition, according to the *Program Evaluation Standards*, programs are evaluated "in order to determine their quality and gain direction for improving them" (Joint Committee on Standards for Educational Evaluation, 1994, p. 1). Therefore, Rossi, Freeman, and Lipsey (1999) present as a fundamentally accepted premise that program evaluation involves the use of a variety of research procedures "to systematically investigate the effectiveness of social intervention programs" and "to inform social action in ways that improve social conditions" (p. 20). It is in this sense that program evaluation is most readily distinguished from other forms of research, by committing *a priori* to at least some degree of intended use of evaluation processes and findings in the service of understanding, judging, and improving programs. According to Weiss (1998a), "Even when use is less direct and immediate, utility of some kind provides the rationale for evaluation" (p. 15).

However, beneath this apparent consensus about what program evaluation generally seeks to do, there has been extensive debate within the domain regarding why and how evaluation should be done and specifically what should be accomplished via evaluation practice. As a result, the methods that have been promoted for evaluation studies have varied considerably, with different purposes dictating differences in who conducts evaluations, when, how quickly, based on what evidence, with whose participation, and for what audiences. Given the specific demands to be met through validity evaluation of educational assessments (raised in chapters 1-3), a careful articulation of practices fitting to these purposes will be required, and review of recent purpose-to-practice arguments within the evaluation discipline will provide a fitting foundation.

Beginning in the 1960s, several prominent positions on the social roles for evaluation were argued from philosophical, and especially epistemological, perspectives, often reflecting unique settings for the application of evaluation. Accordingly, evaluators introduced increasingly disparate models of practice. While methodological details of these models overlapped in some cases, and similar purposes were met with radically different methods in others, each approach represented a distinct and comprehensive advocacy regarding the responsibilities of evaluation and the associated methods to be employed (Stake, 1991). In the following sections, I summarize three major emphases that have characterized recent program evaluation practice.

4.1.1 Knowledge generation evaluation

An early and persistent rationale argued that the purpose of evaluation was the generation of new and trustworthy knowledge about programs and policies, although this rationale has been associated with often dramatically different perspectives on what counts as 'trustworthy' or 'knowledge'. The prominence of this conceptualization of evaluation is clear from its representation in recent categorizations of evaluation purposes, including Shaw's (1999) "academic-driven evaluation", Weiss's (1998a) "enlightenment evaluation", and "knowledge generation evaluation" in the writing of both Rossi, Freeman, and Lipsey (1999) and Chelimsky (1997).

From this perspective, evaluation might take the form of in-depth, cumulative inquiry in order to illuminate and explain program effectiveness or deficiency (Chelimsky, 1997), or it might seek to test causal relationships underlying explicit program theories (Rogers, Hacsi, Petrosino, & Huebner, 2000). At the same time, evaluation might focus on the generation of understandings from alternative points of view. For example, it might challenge the hegemonic portrayal of program worth by engaging in the hermeneutic interpretation of multiple realities associated with a program (Schwandt, 1997), or by continuously deconstructing proposed truths about programs (Mabry, 1997; Stronach & MacLure, 1997). More broadly, knowledge generation evaluation may be pursued as a means for highlighting program history, goals, and objectives, ensuring accountability to the public, understanding social interventions, and contributing to theory building (Weiss, 1998a).

Common to the dramatically varying models within this tradition is an overriding commitment to a particular paradigm for evaluation research, and a specific epistemic stance within that paradigm. The practice of evaluation is therefore driven, first and foremost, by rigorous adherence to associated methodologies, regardless of the intended uses for evaluation information or the particulars of program and stakeholder contexts and needs. Evaluation achieves its purpose not by enabling immediate change or improvement in programs and policies, but rather by shedding new, more accurate light on what is known about programs through the application of 'good science'—whatever that might mean within the evaluator's chosen paradigm.

Evaluation for the purpose of generating trustworthy knowledge was perhaps best characterized by Campbell's (1969, 1991) notion of the 'experimenting society', in which the principal goal was to render truthful judgments about causal relationships between social and educational reform programs and their outcomes for society. Working from the perspective of philosophical realism and rationalism (Popper, 1962), Campbell championed the use of experimental and quasi-experimental research designs for providing credible evidence about program effects. His model of evaluation prioritized rigorous standards for applying experimental scientific methods (e.g., Campbell & Stanley, 1966; Cook & Campbell, 1979), in particular the reduction of threats to internal validity of the inferences being made between causal and outcomes variables. Through experimental hypothesis testing, true and comprehensive findings about program outcomes and relationships could be produced, and once disseminated, it was assumed, these findings would be channeled into thoughtful decision-making about program theory, structure, implementation, and perpetuation.

In a similar vein, Scriven (1997) argued that evaluation should seek "to get things right, to uncover and report the truth, the effort that is an ideal of every scientist" (p. 491). The fundamental purpose for evaluation was to render a truthful judgment regarding the merit or worth of a program, most often for informing summative comparisons of outcomes among an array of possible program alternatives. Accordingly, evaluators were to maintain maximal distance from the program context and stakeholders in order to achieve objectivity, accuracy, and public credibility (Scriven, 1972). In Scriven's "goal-free evaluation" model, any attempt by evaluators to work from within program settings, understand program processes and constraints, interact with participants, suggest improvements, or advocate for programs and policies interfered with the truth and trustworthiness of evaluative claims about program effectiveness.

Ultimately, both Campbell and Scriven argued that the only socially responsible role for evaluation was to inform policy makers and the public by contributing clear-cut findings about program effectiveness—uses of evaluation for purposes other than discerning the truth were distracting, if not deleterious, to this end. Although they generalized their advocacies to all of evaluation practice, Campbell (e.g., 1969) and Scriven (e.g., 1969) were primarily interested in large-scale (often federally funded) social, and especially educational, programs and reforms, and they sought to inject rigorous experimental research processes into what they perceived to be scientifically uninformed debates and policies surrounding these program settings.

Both Campbell's and Scriven's work had tremendous impact on the theory and practice of program evaluation, and throughout the 1960s and 1970s experimentation assumed *de facto* predominance as the most telling test of program effectiveness, and therefore the ultimate goal of evaluation research (Shaw, 1999). Their focus on the generation of trustworthy knowledge, and a commitment to experimental science for doing so, continues to exert an enormous influence today, for example, in the U.S.

government's definition of 'scientifically based research standards' in education (e.g., Education Sciences Reform, 2002; Eisenhart & Towne, 2003; No Child Left Behind, 2001).

It was in large part because of the sweeping impact of this approach to evaluation that critical challenges were quickly mounted, eventually sparking what came to be known as the 'paradigm wars' in program evaluation (Cook, 1997). Throughout the 1970s and 1980s, evaluators took issue with both the philosophical foundations and the methodological restrictions of quantitative experimentation (often incorrectly interpreted as 'scientific positivism'; see discussion in Campbell, 1996; House & Howe, 1999; Shaw, 1999), and they proposed a range of alternatives, primarily under the rubric of 'qualitative evaluation' (e.g., Fetterman, 1988). Absolute distinctions were drawn between the two sides of this 'war', and debate raged to acrimonious degrees (e.g., Guba & Lincoln, 1988, 1989). However, despite clear ontological distinctions, the overriding purpose of evaluation from these alternative perspectives remained the generation of trustworthy understanding and knowledge.

Most representative and vociferously argued of the alternative paradigms was the radical constructivist evaluation model promoted by Guba and Lincoln (1989) under the title of "Fourth Generation Evaluation". Rather than seeking to discover the objective truth about a program's effectiveness or worth (as had previous 'generations'), constructivist evaluation rejected the possibility of truth and objectivity, adopting instead a relativist ontology and interpretive epistemology (e.g., Geertz, 1973; Reason, 1988). Fundamental were the assumptions that reality was radically undecidable and knowledge was inevitably socially constructed. The purpose of evaluation, according to Guba and Lincoln (1989), was to facilitate the "evolution of consensual constructions about the evaluand" (p. 252) via "a process that creates reality" (p. 255) rather than discerns it. This process followed a hermeneutic tradition in identifying the full array of program stakeholders, eliciting "as many constructions ... as possible" (p. 73) about the program and associated concerns, engaging in dialectical reasoning to interpret shared versus contentious constructions, and negotiating a consensual joint construction of knowledge about a program (which might or might not include agreement on needed changes). Methods for controlling variables, testing outcomes, and interpreting causal relationships (derived from the 'positivist' paradigm) were strictly rejected in lieu of prescribed interpretive qualitative research practices (e.g., Denzin, 1978; Lincoln & Guba, 1985). Similarly, specific goals for evaluation studies and the targeted uses of findings could never be determined in advance, given the constructivist ascription of equal value to all possible perspectives on a program and the likelihood that individuals would disagree on goals, uses, and the like.

Thus, despite the radical distinctions in how, methodologically, evaluation should take place, constructivist evaluators argued (as did experimentalists from their own epistemological perspective), that the disciplined interpretive construction of knowledge would prove "catalytic in producing action" (p. 259). Of particular interest were local contexts and circumscribed program issues, although there was little detail as to how the use of evaluation findings might be facilitated or evolve in practice. In the end, then, proponents from both sides of the paradigm wars reflected very similar commitments to the promotion of their specific methodologies for engaging in evaluative work. For both, the generation of knowledge about programs was presumed much more important than any actual or immediate uses for such knowledge.

4.1.2 Pragmatic evaluation

While knowledge generation models and associated paradigm-inspired debates dominated much of the disciplinary rhetoric in program evaluation into the early 1990s, practicing evaluators argued increasingly that the overriding focus on epistemic distinctions, and the ensuing methodological inflexibility, only served to undermine the utility of evaluation for fostering actual improvements in programs and society. For one, it was quickly observed that paradigmatic distinctions tended to be overdrawn and artificial, based on false dichotomizations of available epistemologies and scientific methods (e.g., 'qualitative' versus 'quantitative' ways of knowing), and marked by straw-man argumentation (Patton, 1988; Reichardt & Cook, 1979; Reid, 1994). From this perspective, there was no reason why so-called 'quantitative' and 'qualitative' methods and data could not both be used as needed within a single evaluation study. Furthermore, drawing heavily on the thinking of 20th century U.S. pragmatic philosophers (e.g., Dewey, 1938; Rorty, 1979, 1982), many evaluators began to advocate for a focus on the practical ends of evaluation studies (i.e., in the form of questions to be answered, problems to be solved, decisions to be made) as a basis for selectinng the appropriate methods and tools of inquiry, rather than vice-versa (e.g., Brisolara, 1998; Cook, 1985; Patton, 1988; Reid, 1994; Reid & Hanrahan, 1982). Finally, it became increasingly clear that the knowledge being generated by paradigmatic approaches to evaluation, and particularly Campbell's experimenting society (Caracelli, 2000), was simply not being put to use for understanding and improving programs (Cronbach & Associates, 1980; Davis & Salasin, 1975; Leviton & Hughes, 1981; Patton, 1978).

In contrast with knowledge generation models, evaluations within the pragmatic tradition sought to provide information that was maximally and immediately useful for decision-makers and simultaneously tailored to the needs of clearly identifiable program stakeholders (Cronbach & Associates, 1980). Alternately categorized as "practice-driven" (Shaw, 1999), "improvement" (Rossi, Freeman, & Lipsey, 1999), "developmental" (Chelimsky, 1997), or "instrumental" (Weiss, 1998a), pragmatic evaluation approaches shared an overriding emphasis on the utilization of evaluation findings, as well as processes (Patton, 1998), for enabling program understanding, decisions, and improvements. More specifically, evaluation might focus on eliciting, prioritizing, and responding to stakeholder needs through a variety of participatory processes (e.g., Cousins & Whitmore, 1998; Greene, 1988; Huberman & Cox, 1990; Stake, 1980; Torres & Preskill, 1999), or it might be driven by a commitment to practical issues such as mid-course adjustments, program design improvements, the development and testing of new program components, the monitoring of program implementation, the identification and measurement of outcomes indicators for program feedback, or decisions about perpetuation and funding (Chelimsky, 1997; Weiss, 1998a).

An early proponent of pragmatic, use-driven applications for evaluation was none other than Lee Cronbach, whose work in educational and psychological measurement had proved fundamental to the development of notions of test construct validity (as described in chapter 3). Cronbach (1982, 1986) and colleagues (Cronbach & Associates, 1980) drew a sharp distinction between scientific validity and research standards, on the one hand, and situated or practical validity and evaluation practice on the other. From their perspective, Campbell's (1969) insistence on internal validity standards via controlled experimentation proved trivial compared with the exigencies of actual program contexts and stakeholders' needs for meaningful and timely information (Cronbach, 1982). The purpose of evaluation was to understand and explain the mechanisms of programs as they functioned within real contexts (versus randomized experimental conditions) in order to facilitate the work of individuals who needed to make inferences about the specific participants, settings, and interventions that characterized social programs. According to Cronbach and Associates (1980):

> An evaluation pays off to the extent that it offers ideas pertinent to pending actions and people think more clearly as a result. To enlighten, it must do more than amass good data. (pp. 65-66)

Programs and participants were not entities to be controlled—they could not be expected to "play statue" while evaluators did their work (Cronbach & Associates, 1980, p. 56). Rather, programs were to be thoroughly understood and formatively critiqued *in situ*, such that improvements could be immediately recommended and generalizations to other programs enabled through the adequate characterization of how programs actually functioned. To achieve these pragmatic ends, Cronbach advocated a flexible methodological approach to evaluation studies, with a particular emphasis on the use of case studies. Further, as Shadish, Cook, and Leviton (1991) have pointed out, he did not want "a particular conception of scientific methods to trivialize the process of asking important questions" (p. 349). Key to enabling the use of evaluation studies was the frequent reporting of features of the evaluation to program stakeholders, including not only study findings, but also questions and methods. Cronbach (1982) assumed that a pluralistic state of affairs determined actual program decision making and policy development, and he therefore reasoned that political interaction would have to be included from the outset in evaluation planning and implementation. The role of the evaluator, then, was to contribute scholarly advice on the range of methodological possibilities and to ensure evaluation use among key program constituents via the balanced mediation of their views throughout the evaluation process.

Many others have argued the case for pragmatic approaches to evaluation, and a variety of specific models have been formulated and promoted during the intervening years. Most prominent among these are approaches which seek to ensure evaluation use through varying degrees and types of participation by program stakeholders (e.g., Brisolara, 1998; Patton, 1978, 1986; Preskill & Torres, 2000; Torres & Preskill, 1999; Whitmore, 1998). Within "practical participatory" evaluation models, according to Cousins and Whitmore (1998), "professional evaluators collaborate in some way with individuals, groups, or communities who have a decided stake in the program" (p. 5), in order to enhance relevance, ownership, and use of the process and outcomes. Through the careful maintenance of sustained interactivity between the evaluator and practitioners, rigorous evidentiary sources can be tailored to specific needs or priority problems within programs (Huberman & Cox, 1990), and there is mounting evidence for increased action, change, decision making, and program improvement as a result (e.g., Cousins, 1996; Greene, 1988).

In the most practice-oriented of these participatory approaches "evaluators tend to work in partnership with potential users who have the clout to do something with the evaluation findings or emergent recommendations" (Cousins & Whitmore, 1998, p. 11). Patton (1978, 1986, 1997) has provided a detailed evaluation rationale and methodology based on the incorporation of "primary intended users" into the evaluation process from the very beginning of problem identification through to the reporting and, of course, use of findings. His *utilization-focused* evaluation model seeks to bring appropriate and useable data to bear on priority program issues, and the nature of both the issues and the data are to be determined through interaction between an expert evaluator and the primary intended users. While the evaluator helps maintain methodological rigor and a "commitment to empirical evaluation" (Patton, 1988, p. 128), participation by the intended users ensures relevance and use of the process and outcomes (Patton, 1998). Clearly, a very wide array of research methods must be available to the evaluator in order to advise and respond appropriately to the actual prioritized needs of the primary intended users. As Stufflebeam (2001) has pointed out, utilization-focused evaluation has worked best when applied to discrete programs with well-defined parameters or to interventions with clear targets, and he has rated Patton's model as one of the "strongest and most promising for continued use and development beyond 2000" (p. 80).

Other evaluation professionals have similarly advocated and explored a focus on utilization as the primary heuristic for informing evaluation practice (e.g., Alkin, 1990; Christie & Alkin, 1999; Johnson, 1998; Leviton & Hughes, 1981; Shulha & Cousins, 1997), emphasizing a fundamental pragmatic commitment to providing specific decision makers and other constituents with the information they need for understanding and improving their programs.

4.1.3 Social agenda evaluation

Working from an initial pragmatic commitment to stakeholder participation, some evaluators recently have reconceptualized evaluation purposes and practices to address explicitly their undeniably political and power-laden nature. From this perspective, frequently referred to as "social agenda/advocacy" (Stufflebeam, 2001) or "transformative" (Cousins & Whitmore, 1998) evaluation, it has been observed that models which emphasize practical utility may unintentionally serve to support the status quo, by prioritizing the views of existing empowered decision-makers. As a result, evaluation may ignore the needs of under- or non-represented minority stakeholders (e.g., House, 1995; House & Howe, 1999). While pragmatism focuses evaluation on the achievement of concrete, real-world ends, social agenda evaluators argue that the nature of those ends should be grounded in philosophies of social and political justice (e.g., Freire, 1970; Kymlicka, 1991; Rawls, 1971) rather than utility. More important than providing information that is useful for decision-makers is the responsibility of evaluation to transform programs, and decisions about them, such that equity and fairness are promoted for all stakeholders (Cousins & Whitmore, 1998; Fetterman, 2001; House & Howe, 1999; Torres & Preskill, 1999).

Thus, rather than informing immediate program practice (or pursuing scientific knowledge, for that matter), evaluation can best help people and communities by incorporating processes which, in their application, serve to advocate for the rights of all individuals impacted by programs and/or to democratize social and program change. Such evaluations might seek to engage with representatives of all stakeholder groups in order to clearly establish their concerns and recommend responses (Greene & Abma, 2001), or they might promote processes of information dissemination, learning, and critical reflection to ensure equal control over the production of knowledge among the entire range of constituencies within a given organization (Cousins & Earl, 1995; Preskill & Torres, 2000). Other social agenda evaluators work for the empowerment of marginalized or disenfranchised communities by providing individuals with the tools, resources, and encouragement to create their own local knowledge and solutions in lieu of externally imposed policies (Vanderplaat, 1995, 1997).

Common to social agenda models is an overriding commitment to 'process uses' for evaluation, in which the effects of implementing evaluations take precedence over the use of findings (i.e., the process of thinking and acting evaluatively is the objective, rather than the specific findings of evaluation studies). Thus, evaluation designs are characterized by methods that ensure full stakeholder participation or representation; individual reflection and learning; inter-individual dialogue, critique, and deliberation; and improvement in the social conditions of individuals and communities. Priority is given to the collection, analysis, and use of data which contribute most effectively to the improved understanding of relationships between programs and stakeholders, and especially to the portrayal of stakeholders' unique perspectives.

One of the most well-articulated and widely applied models within the social agenda tradition is *empowerment evaluation* (Fetterman, 1994a, 2001; Fetterman, Kaftarian, & Wandersman, 1996), which was "designed to help people help themselves and improve their programs using a form of self-evaluation and reflection" (Fetterman, 2001, p. 3). Drawing extensively on community empowerment theory (e.g., Zimmerman & Rappaport, 1988) and action research methods (e.g., Stenhouse, 1993), Fetterman based this approach on processes for legitimizing the values, knowledge, and experiences of individuals within disenfranchised communities, such that they might achieve power and self-determination over policies and programs which directly affected their lives. A clear commitment to process use and advocacy is reflected in the key methodological elements of empowerment evaluation, including: (a) identification and participation of those stakeholders most affected by programs; (b) use of self-reflection, critique, and individual-group interaction to elicit priority issues and set agendas; (c) tailoring of data for understanding and use within (rather than beyond) the community; and (d) decision-making as a public interactive and collaborative process. These characteristics of empowerment evaluation reflect its principal application in well-defined and small-scale settings where communities are able to come to agreement on priority local issues that impact the rights and welfare of individuals, where relevant data may be efficiently collected and disseminated, and where solutions may be effectively debated and chosen through participatory democratic processes (e.g., Fetterman, 1994b, 2001).

Democratic participation also drive's evaluation processes within "deliberative democratic evaluation" (House & Howe, 1999; Ryan & DeStefano, 2000). However, while disenfranchised individuals and communities are carefully included, the ultimate goal of evaluation from this perspective is to seek a reasoned collective consensus on the worth of social programs and policies through explicitly democratic processes. Deliberative democratic evaluation does not seek primarily to empower communities; rather, it pursues principles of democracy in order to best achieve objective knowledge and conclusions about programs. Underlying this goal, though, is a detailed rationale for what constitutes 'objectivity' (House & Howe, 1999), which is clearly not to be understood as a value-neutral seeking of facts and the truth (cf. Campbell, 1969). Instead, because facts are assumed to be value-laden representations of social belief systems, objectivity can only be sought through the unbiased inclusion in an evaluation of the perspectives of all parties with an interest in the evaluand. Therefore, it is the responsibility of the evaluator to advocate for democratic processes which promote such unbiased inclusion (Ryan & Johnson, 2000) and to facilitate their implementation, specifically in three methodological phases. First, all relevant program interests must be identified and included, and their balanced representation during evaluation must be ensured. Second, all parties engage in extended dialogue in order to expose their "real interests" (House & Howe, 1999, p. 100) in a program or policy; such dialogue may take a variety of forms, such as the presentation of data summaries or the use of metaphors for explaining each group's position to the others. Third, all parties deliberate over the exposed viewpoints—in face-to-face meetings, discussions, and conflict-resolution sessions—collectively weighing what is now known about the program, in order to achieve a consensus regarding its worth. It is through this process of democratic social determination that evaluation fulfills its role in society, which House and Howe (1999) portray as a means for keeping powerful *non*-democratic social institutions, such as advertising and the mass media, in check. While they acknowledge that the ideal of deliberative democracy may not "be achieved once and for all in any one study" (p. 103), they argue that it provides a guide for good practice and a means for encouraging evaluators to take seriously their responsibility to redress the imbalances of power that inhere within social programs and policies.

4.1.4 Resolution in contemporary practice

The models reviewed above represent some of the principal roles advocated for program evaluation in recent years, and they highlight the wide range of methods that have been recommended for practice. Clearly, arguments for the purposes and practices of evaluation have originated in conjunction with varying settings, constituencies, and audiences for evaluation, but they have also been determined by competing philosophical notions regarding the nature of rigorous, effective, or socially responsible research and work. There are, of course, many other specific program evaluation models, just as there are other ways of categorizing the purposes for evaluation. For example, in Stufflebeam's (2001) review of 22 well-articulated evaluation models, he identified four overarching categories: (a) pseudo-evaluations (focus on public relations); (b) quasi-evaluations (focus on *a priori* methodologies); (c) improvement/accountability evaluations (focus on merit judgments); and (d) social agenda/advocacy evaluations (focus on social justice). Nevertheless, despite different categorizations, a common set of intellectual tensions underlies Stufflebeam's distinctions and those drawn above as well as elsewhere (e.g., Chelimsky, 1997; Rossi, Freeman, & Lipsey, 1999; Shaw, 1999; Weiss, 1998a):

- Should evaluation pursue systematic inquiry via rigorous methodologies in order to provide ever more trustworthy knowledge, or should it respond to the practical imperatives of organizations, programs, and people?
- Should evaluation judge program merits based on outcomes, or should it seek to understand the dynamics of program implementation?
- Should evaluators mandate the nature of questions, data, and uses to ensure objectivity, or should stakeholders participate directly in all phases of evaluation practice to ensure relevance?

These and related questions continue to determine why and how evaluations are conducted; likewise, critiques continue to be mounted on the basis of underlying tensions. For example, Henry (2000) has argued from a social advocacy perspective that intended uses for evaluation should not dictate methods, reasoning that "In their efforts to provide information that will get used, evaluators can lose sight of what information is needed to inform the discourse leading to social betterment" (p. 87). Similarly, House and Howe (1999) have contended that the hyper-egalitarianism of social constructivist evaluations belies any possibility of achieving consensus solutions to program concerns because there will always be individuals whose disagreement with proposed actions must be accepted. On the other hand, Stake (2000) has taken issue with a prioritization of democratic processes, arguing that "The purpose of program evaluation is to acknowledge merit and shortcoming, not to promote democracy" (p. 97) and that "a vigorous political advocacy by the community of professional evaluators would stand a good chance of violating public expectation and confidence" (p. 98).

Nevertheless, despite the apparent contentiousness of these ongoing debates, contemporary evaluation practice has entered into a 'post-paradigm-war' period of détente (Cook, 1997). Rather than continuing to advocate monolithic positions on evaluation purpose and practice, according to Weiss (1998), some time in the 1990s evaluators "concluded that evaluation was a house of many mansions and had room for a variety of approaches" (p. 14). In fact, evaluation as a discipline has adopted a broadly *anti*-monolithic approach to its current research work and the portrayal of its role in society. For example, in a letter from the American Evaluation Association to the U.S. Department of Education, evaluators argued that the federal government's notion of 'scientifically based research' was inaccurate and reductionist in prioritizing only causal inference (and experimentation) as the priority of educational evaluation. They pointed out that "constraints in the proposed priority would deny use of other needed, proven, and scientifically credible evaluation methods, resulting in fruitless expenditures on some large contracts while leaving other public programs unevaluated entirely" (Richard Krueger, President, American Evaluation Association, December 01, 2003).

Currently, then, evaluators agree that no single model or approach can resolve all of the questions and problems posed to the evaluation field (Chelimsky, 1997) and furthermore, that it is high time to move beyond the "belief that a single type of question should be dominant in evaluation" (Cook, 1997, p. 35). They also accept that a variety of social science research methods are needed in order to accommodate the actual range of purposes for evaluation (e.g., Fetterman, 2001; Patton, 1997; Reid, 1994; Rossi, Freeman, & Lipsey, 1999). Of much greater interest to contemporary evaluators, in lieu of continuing the exhaustive epistemological debates of previous decades, is the detailed exploration of: (a) what evaluation purposes and questions make the most sense in what social, political, organizational, and program settings; and (b) what evaluation practices best enable these purposeful ends to be met. Therefore, according to Chelimsky (1997), because "the purpose of an evaluation conditions the use that can be expected of it" (p. 18), "the place to start is with the evaluation purpose and the question that has been asked" (p. 23), and to proceed by allowing "purpose and question [to] dictate method, and not vice versa" (p. 25). While the intellectual tensions raised above continue to frame much evaluation work, they are no longer resolved by evaluators taking sides. Rather, they are incorporated into practice as heuristics for the careful contextualization of evaluation purposes to program settings and the careful articulation of evaluation methods to prioritized purposes.

4.2 An evaluative approach to validating educational assessments

The feasibility, meaningfulness, and utility of conventional test validation practices have been challenged recently, in particular from an educational assessment perspective. It has been proposed that adopting an evaluative approach may answer such challenges and transform validation into an educationally relevant process (see chapter 3). However, given the range of program evaluation approaches outlined above and the tensions that distinguish among them, it is unclear exactly what shape the validity evaluation of educational assessments might take. In fact, it is very likely that a serious commitment to validity evaluation (i.e., a serious commitment to the educational relevance of validation processes) will require a fundamental reconceptualization of assessment validation in order to bring its practices in line with contemporary notions of evaluation—that is, as a purposeful, contextualized endeavor which may meet a variety of ends through a variety of means, including conventional construct validation methods on occasions where those are required. However, simply ascribing validation to the realm of evaluation, or simply adopting one of the available models reviewed above, without attending to the actual purposes and practices which have evolved through years of disciplinary deliberation, would ignore critical implications of the transformation that is being advocated. More specifically, in order to take advantage of the benefits that program evaluation has to offer, a legitimate effort at validity evaluation will require: (a) the treatment of educational assessments as complex programs rather than mere tools; (b) acceptance of multiple legitimate purposes for assessment validity evaluation; (c) clear specification and contextualization of the purposes for each validity evaluation of a given assessment program; and (d) close articulation of the appropriate, among many possible, evaluation methods for meeting these specified purposes.

Conventional approaches to assessment validation (AERA, APA, & NCME, 1999; Messick, 1989) fall short of these desiderata for program evaluations. To recap briefly, the singular focus of current validation practice, as repeatedly emphasized in virtually every textbook definition for validity within language testing and educational measurement, is the extent to which an assessment is measuring what it was intended to measure. From this perspective, assessments or tests are simply measurement tools used to inform trustworthy interpretations about theoretical constructs. The sole (monolithic) purpose for validation, then, is to marshal rigorous scientific evidence regarding the extent to which an assessment is measuring what it was intended to measure; the sole use of that information is for judging whether or not construct interpretations, in the form of test-based inferences and actions, are warranted. As Messick's (1989) treatise on the unified notion of validity made clear, construct validity is the whole of assessment validation. Validation processes seek to answer only a prescribed and circumscribed set of questions about the relationship between test scores and construct interpretations. Thus, despite the incorporation of methodologies for investigating test uses, values, and consequences, the only reason for doing so is to provide a more comprehensive evidentiary basis for understanding the construct interpretations that are actually being made, or are implied, throughout the assessment process—all resulting evidence is folded into a judgment about the meaning of scores generated in assessment use.

In practice, conventional validation is contextualized only to the extent that each use of an assessment should be investigated for introducing potential variability into score meaning, through differences in assessment conditions, test-takers, etc. However, the validation process, per se, is generic from one assessment setting to the next. Once the (unspecified amount of) evidence has been gathered and a judgment rendered, there is no special concern or planning for how this information might then be used, by whom, for what specific ends (e.g., assessment improvement, learning, accountability, advocacy). Consequently, validation information is not tailored to the needs of specific intended users for meeting specific intended uses which might be prioritized within a particular assessment program context. Stakeholders, such as test users, play no active role in the determination of validation purposes, methods, or uses; rather, they are responsible for receiving the validation wisdom of the measurement profession and seeing to it that their uses of assessments fall within those warranted by measurement professionals. Thus, validation is portrayed in current standards as a professional responsibility of measurement experts, who exclusively own its highly technical and prescribed methodologies. The commitment to assessment validation is a core professional ethic, a commitment to rigorous science and the production of trustworthy knowledge about the meaning and accuracy of measures. Clearly, conventional measurement validation most closely approximates the knowledge-generation approaches to evaluation outlined above. The methods of validation, then, are explicitly articulated to only this purpose, and the range of methodological possibilities are essentially the same for all assessments.

It is apparent that current approaches to assessment validation resonate little with contemporary consensus on program evaluation, this despite persistent (if not necessarily consistent) recourse within educational measurement rhetoric to the idea of evaluation as fundamental to the nature of validation and what it seeks to achieve (e.g., Cronbach, 1988, 1989; Kane, 1992, 2001; Messick, 1980, 1988; Shepard, 1993). Of course, the program evaluation discipline has only recently come to consensus regarding the status of evaluation as a multi-purpose, multi-method, contextualized undertaking, rather than a monolithic approach to judging program worth. In terms of validating educational assessments, then, the critical question is whether a shift to this contemporary program evaluation framework can resolve the challenges that conventional validation presents to educators who seek guidelines for understanding, improving, or adjudicating their assessments (or those that impact on their educational efforts). Validation endures as the principal mandated, and perceived, requirement for the implementation and perpetuation of assessments within education; however, it is precisely *within* educational settings that the value of validation, the functional scope of its ends, and the suitability of its means, remain indeterminate. A critical first step towards addressing these challenges has been taken by assessment experts in alluding to the potential use of evaluative processes as a guide for validation studies. In addition, I argue that the following steps are now required in order for the validation of educational assessments to proceed as, and have the potential to garner the benefits of, truly evaluative endeavors.

First, the treatment of assessments as tools for providing accurate information about constructs will need to be revised to incorporate additionally the full purpose and scope of assessment practice. Educational assessments do not occur in a purposeless vacuum, and it is fruitless to evaluate them as if they did. Unlike tools designed only to meet instrumental functions (e.g., knives, thermometers, paint-brushes), and despite a penchant in the educational measurement community to invoke instrumental qualities when describing assessments (e.g., the 'temperature-taking' metaphor so frequently used in conjunction with the *National Assessments of Educational Progress*), educational assessments are complex, context-dependent processes involving the use of a wide array of instruments and procedures in inten-tional ways. Educational assessments cannot be adequately defined without addressing: (a) who uses them, (b) what kinds of information they provide about whom or what, (c) why and how that information is sought, (d) what decisions and actions are taken on their basis, and (e) what consequences are intended (and not in-tended) to occur as a result—in short, elements which define social programs (i.e., inputs, processes, outputs, outcomes; cf. Rossi, Freeman, & Lipsey, 1999). Clearly, the potential answers to these questions are many, in conjunction with the variety of actual roles for assessments within education (e.g., locating learners within ability-appropriate instruction; providing feedback to teachers and students about student learning; understanding and revising curricular expectations; holding educators and institutions accountable for learning outcomes; effecting change on the values of educational systems). By understanding educational assessments as coherent pro-grams designed to accomplish these and other purposes in particular settings, an evaluative approach to validation is both enabled and required. On the one hand, the specification of answers to questions (a) through (e) outline important variables of the program context within which evaluation will occur, setting parameters on what is and is not expected of an assessment program, identifying the key stakeholders, and limiting the range of questions that might be posed to those features which de-fine the program. At the same time, it is clear that a comprehensive evaluation design will be required in order to adequately address the complexities of educational as-sessments in use. A validation approach which does not treat the full program context of an assessment risks both inaccuracy (by not attending to the entire range of factors which determine how the assessment program functions) and irrelevance (by not responding to the actual exigencies of assessment programs and stakeholders *in situ*).

Second, given the considerable variety of assessment programs in education, each proceeding according to its own purposes and within its own context, it makes sense that there will be a number of distinct reasons for wanting to engage in validity evaluation. Accountability, knowledge generation, development, improvement, learning, advocacy, and other rationales each may be posited as the primary driving force behind a validity evaluation. For example, in conjunction with a small-scale assessment being developed to inform discrete decisions within a single curriculum, evaluation might be employed to provide local assessment developers and users with formative information tailored to their needs in understanding and improving the ef-fectiveness and efficiency of the assessment program. For a large-scale national assessment used in holding schools accountable for educational outcomes, evaluation might be required to provide trustworthy information regarding the accuracy and equivalence of test scores across schools with distinct student demographics. From another perspective, for the same assessment, an evaluation might seek to promote the inclusion of educational researchers, teachers, and students, in addition to government policy-makers, in the process of adjudicating the continued use of the assessment program. In another setting, where an alternative assessment program is introduced into classrooms in order to wash back on how students learn and teachers teach, evaluation might focus primarily on identifying the range of intended and unintended consequences in terms of student and teacher behaviors and perceptions.

Each of these examples, and many potential others, constitute legitimate purposes which might be prioritized for the validity evaluation of assessment programs in education. While conventional approaches to assessment validation mandate an exclusive focus on the generation of specific types of scientific knowledge about the accuracy of construct interpretations, without any particular intention for how validity information will be used, it should be apparent that a variety of questions may be raised about assessment programs by distinct stakeholders and audiences. Likewise, the intended uses for evaluation processes and findings will vary considerably across different assessment programs, as well as within a given assessment program over time. Thus, in addition to the generation of trustworthy knowledge about assessments and their constructs, validity evaluations will sometimes be required to meet more immediate pragmatic purposes, or to promote social and educational agendas, or to accomplish numerous other specific ends within educational settings. By accepting that a variety of legitimate purposes may need to be addressed through validity evaluation, evaluators will be better prepared to respond with practices that support, rather than dismiss, the various actual ends that are sought.

Third, in order for validity evaluation to proceed as a meaningful endeavor, the exact purpose of the evaluation will need to be prioritized and contextualized according to the nature of the assessment program. In other words, rather than a 'one-size fits all' approach or a willful selection of evaluation purposes and questions by an expert evaluator, the particular features of a given assessment context will interact to determine what purposes for evaluation make the most sense. Educational assessment programs function in a wide variety of settings and with considerable differences in scope, from within the classroom, to across the curriculum, to the institutional, district, state, and national levels. Likewise, the audiences for validity evaluations will differ in type and size between these various assessment program settings, and distinct individuals and groups will have a stake in the evaluation, depending on their level of investment in the particular program. For example, teachers and students may constitute the primary audiences and stakeholders for validity evaluations of classroom-based assessments, while the evaluation of institutionally required assessments of student learning outcomes will primarily interest administrators and accrediting agencies, and they will have consequences for entire programs as well as individual teachers and students. In addition, a range of interested parties may mandate or request a validity evaluation at different points over the timeline of an assessment program—from the identification of a need for new assessments, to the development of assessment instruments and procedures, to their pilot-testing and revision, to on-going program implementation—with concomitant differences in the intent of the evaluation.

Clearly, each educational assessment program will be tied to a unique constellation of potential audience and stakeholder communities, as well as mandates and timelines for validity evaluation. Therefore, before designing and implementing an evaluation, the specific purpose to be pursued—why it is taking place and what it seeks to accomplish—will need to be thoroughly rationalized, based on the ways in which the prioritized purpose responds to a given mandate, how it provides information and services required by particular targeted audiences, and what kinds of consequences it seeks to engender for relevant program stakeholders. By detailing the relationship between program context and purpose for validity evaluation, the focus of resulting evaluation practices will be sharpened, and their use defended.

Finally, given a reasoned purpose for the validity evaluation of an assessment program, fitting methods will need to be identified and put into practice. Clearly, a wide range of scientific methods may be called upon for gathering, analyzing, and interpreting data in response to specific validity questions, including various 'quantitative' and 'qualitative' techniques. These will include methods both precedented within construct validation traditions and heretofore untapped in the evaluation of educational assessments. However, beyond research practices, additional methods may be required for: (a) identifying and ensuring the participation of important stakeholders; (b) eliciting, negotiating, and prioritizing validity questions; (c) identifying appropriate types of evidence that will be relevant for use by specific audiences; (d) interpreting and judging evaluation outcomes; (e) reporting and otherwise disseminating findings; and (f) ensuring the use of evaluation findings and processes in intended ways. Key to the accomplishment of evaluation intentions will be an informed yet flexible approach, which seeks to balance the information and procedural needs of the evaluation purpose and context with rigorous and defensible practices; evaluation expertise may play a critical role in this respect. By articulating methods to the actual prioritized purposes for validity evaluation within a given assessment program context, rather than insisting on only those methods that have been sanctioned by the professional measurement community, validity evaluation will stand a much better chance of providing workable guidelines, criteria, and procedures for framing educationally relevant practices in the name of validation.

In order to achieve alignment with fundamental tenets of contemporary program evaluation practice, a reconceptualization of the validation of educational assessments will be required along the lines of the four steps described above. However, this proposed shift in the way validation is understood and practiced is not intended to rule out any of the various possible purposes for assessment validation that may exist. Indeed, the intent of conventional approaches to validation fits very closely within the rubric of knowledge generation evaluation, by seeking to provide ever more trustworthy iterations in our understanding of how assessments function to inform construct interpretations. Rather than dismissing this viable end (which may be of particular interest, for example, to communities of researchers), a validity evaluation approach requires that the purpose be rationalized and justified, rather than mandated on the basis of professional standards of good science. That is, the shift to validity evaluation seeks to transform validation into a worthwhile and relevant endeavor by making its purposes explicit and by contextualizing its use within a specific community with clearly defined interests in a particular assessment program. As a result, validity evaluation should be able to meet the full range of actual purposes for validating assessment programs by tailoring its methods to specific and well-defined intended uses within particular education contexts. Given the reconceptualization of validity evaluation along these lines, each of the program evaluation models reviewed above (and others) may prove useful for framing the specific practices which will best inform distinct purposes within particular assessment program contexts. For the validity evaluation of educational assessments in collegiate foreign language contexts, it may well be that one particular model will provide an adequate means for meeting the range of current purposes, and I turn to the exploration and application of this model in the following chapter.

Chapter 5
Articulating assessment context and validity evaluation method

Clearly, in advocating a move away from prescribed validity questions and techniques, and toward a purposeful and contextualized undertaking with the ultimate goal of educational relevance, critical demands are made on the emergent practice of validity evaluation, and it remains to be seen what its outcomes will be. On the one hand, the weaknesses raised in chapter 3 with conventional validation practices will have to be addressed, such that the process is transformed into a meaningful, feasible, and useful endeavor for interested parties, and especially for local users of specific educational assessments. If a program evaluation approach is to inform this transformation, basic questions will have to be answered, including: (a) how can educational assessments be conceived as full-blown programs rather than mere tools? (b) how can purposes and uses for validity evaluation of assessments be identified and prioritized within specific assessment contexts? (c) how can evaluative methods be articulated with these purposes, such that they result in useful information for specific audiences? and (d) how can educators be encouraged to act on validity evaluation findings, in order to ensure the qualities of their assessment programs?

At the same time, in order to pursue validity evaluation within college foreign language education (like any other education setting), the very real constraints of that particular context will have to be taken seriously, and it is likely that the nature of assessment uses and impetuses in FL education will indicate the need for specific evaluation models and methods. In other words, it is probably not the case that all program evaluation models will meet the particular requirements of assessment validity evaluation in college FL education. Given traditional perceptions of FL assessment as simply the measurement of language, a general lack of professional development in basic assessment concepts and capabilities, and, especially, inattention to the relationship between assessment practices and the impetuses and uses they are intended to meet (as reviewed in chapter 2), it is uncertain how validity evaluation can be translated into workable guidelines for practice in this particular context. In addition, it remains to be seen what the outcomes of the process will be—what will, and what will not, happen in the name of validity evaluation—and whether it will actually help college FL educators meet the challenge of evaluating and ensuring the quality of their assessments. A key factor in this regard will be the extent to which a guiding evaluation framework can be identified for responding adequately to these particular issues.

In the remainder of this work, rather than simply describing how assessment validation occurred and what was found about the 'validity' of measures of language ability or knowledge—the standard approach in reporting language assessment validation studies—I subscribe to current program evaluation practice by providing a rationale for (as well as a detailed account of) how assessment validity evaluation occurred and what was found, based on why it was pursued and for what ends it was intended. In the current chapter, I argue that, from among the many current approaches to program evaluation (as reviewed in chapter 4), *utilization-focused* evaluation provides one comprehensive framework that is particularly well-suited to meeting the specific validity evaluation demands within the college FL education context.

5.1 Utilization-focused evaluation

As the name implies, utilization-focused evaluation seeks to enable and promote the *use* of evaluation processes and findings by specific intended users for addressing priority questions about social programs and their effectiveness. Developed principally through the work of Michael Quinn Patton (1978, 1986, 1997), this approach is driven by a fundamental commitment to the utility, feasibility, and propriety of program evaluations in helping "real people in the real world" (Patton, 1997, p. 20) actually do something on the basis of evaluation processes and findings. In this sense, program evaluation is distinguished from scientific research, as observed by Patton (1997): "Research aims to produce knowledge and truth. Useful evaluation supports action." (p. 24). To be sure, scientific research methods play an important role, but particular methodologies are not slavishly adhered to in the search for 'truth' or knowledge. An explicit appeal to pragmatism leads utilization-focused evaluators to eschew ontological/epistemological paradigms, as well as prescriptive (and exclusionary) scientific standards, in favor of a methodologically flexible, but nevertheless rigorous, approach for responding to those questions and concerns that are actually posed by the intended users of evaluations. Rather than dictating *a priori* how the merit, worth, or value of a program should be determined, then, evaluation starts by clarifying exactly why a program is being judged and what will be done on the basis of these judgments—the determination of program evaluation uses, according to Patton, is too important to be left to evaluators to decide or prescribe. Instead, utilization-focused evaluation directly incorporates primary intended users of a program evaluation—typically local program constituents—into all aspects of its design, implementation, and, most critically, its use for making decisions, improving programs, or whatever other ends might be prioritized. It is the responsibility of the evaluator to ensure this participation, to elicit the priority concerns and needs of program stakeholders, and to offer technical advice and support in seeing to it that these concerns are addressed and needs are met through directly relevant *and* empirical, evidence-based procedures.

Of course, utilization-focused evaluation has not been without its critics (as summarized in Fetterman, 1988; Patton, 1997; and Stufflebeam, 2001). From a social-advocacy perspective, concerns have been expressed with the potential for bias among primary intended users and a lack of representation of other stakeholders' interests and values. Alternately, from a knowledge-generation point of view, it has been argued that, because program stakeholders are explicitly involved in determining the questions and methods of utilization-focused evaluation, the rigor of evaluative methods is unavoidably denigrated. At the same time, these criticisms have issued from specific *a priori* assumptions regarding the purposes for evaluation, something that a utilization-focused approach explicitly avoids. According to Patton (1997), "The fundamental value-premise of utilization-focused evaluation is that intended users are in the best position to decide for themselves what questions and inquiries are important" (p. 367). In committing to "intended uses by intended users" as the principal heuristic for motivating evaluation ends and means, then, it is certainly possible that the advocacy or truth-seeking goals above might emerge as priorities of the intended users, and in such cases, careful stakeholder representation and/or rigorous evidentiary procedures for inferring causality or the 'truth' about programs can be pursued through evaluation. However, what is certain, and certainly distinct from other approaches, is that an explicit rationale for the evaluation of a program will be required before any methods are selected or judgments rendered, and this rationale will inform exactly what gets done in the name of evaluation and not vice-versa.

In this sense, then, a utilization-focused approach to evaluation addresses one of the most fundamental concerns with conventional practices of assessment validation, by incorporating procedures for determining exactly what is to be accomplished by whom through validation inquiry, and what methods best meet these purposes. Rather than motivating assessment validation according to a fixed set of research questions and scientific methods, utilization-focused evaluation offers a framework for rationalizing particular questions and methods that best meet the priority information needs of actual decision makers. To be clear, investigations of theoretical construct hypotheses, social consequences and values judgments, and formative questions alike are all potentially viable concerns for assessment validity evaluation from this perspective. What utilization-focused evaluation provides (and requires) is a mechanism for figuring out which of these, or other, types of inquiry will be pursued to meet what actual ends within particular program contexts with clearly specified stakeholders and audiences for evaluation outcomes. Unlike knowledge-generation or social advocacy (or other) approaches to program evaluation, then, utilization-focused evaluation is not based on the presumption of a monolithic purpose or set of purposes. Instead, it grounds each evaluation activity in an initial clarification and commitment to the particular targeted purposes that will help specific and well-defined communities act on well-justified priorities in understanding and improving programs.

While there are no pre-set circumstances for its application, a utilization-focused approach may be particularly well-suited to contexts wherein program purposes and boundaries can be clearly defined, stakeholders can be readily identified and fairly represented, decisions can be made feasibly and efficiently by key program constituents, and the use of evaluation processes and findings is valued as a legitimate and necessary action. Therefore, as Stufflebeam (2001) pointed out, this approach offers distinct advantages in small-scale contexts where information for program improvement and decision-making is sought by local program constituents. In educational assessment terms, then, it may be that certain assessment programs are more appropriately evaluated via a utilization-focused approach to validity evaluation than are others. For example, large-scale or research-program assessments that are used across multiple teaching and learning contexts might prove particularly challenging for a utilization-focused approach, due to the range of stakeholders, the scope of assessment use, the difficulty of prioritizing evaluation questions or negotiating consensus on implications of findings for assessment change, etc. However, for assessments that are developed and used within college FL education settings, where evaluation audiences and program decision-makers are clearly identifiable, assessment uses are constrained to specific purposes and stakeholders, and there is a priority on directly useful information about assessment quality, a utilization-focused approach may provide a particularly appropriate framework for initiating much-needed validity evaluation processes.

5.1.1 Steps in utilization-focused evaluation

In concrete terms, utilization-focused evaluation proceeds according to several principled steps which seek to ensure, on the one hand, the justification of intended uses for evaluation by intended users, and, on the other hand, the application of relevant and trustworthy empirical methods for informing these uses. Initially, stakeholders for the program of interest (and its evaluation) are identified—that is, people who are responsible for and impacted by the program—and, among these, the primary intended users of an evaluation are established, thereby narrowing the range of direct participants to those who are most likely to actually employ the evaluation for achieving some program-relevant purpose. According to Patton (1997) primary intended users consist of "strategically located people who are enthusiastic, committed, competent, interested, and assertive" (p. 52), and they should be incorporated into evaluation design and implementation from the outset.

Next, a range of possible uses for evaluation are elicited from these primary intended users, in the form of questions, concerns, issues, or problems that they pose about the program of interest. Uses may vary considerably, including the use of findings about program outcomes for making judgments about its worth or perpetuation, about program strengths and weaknesses for facilitating improvements, or about program theory and practice for generating and disseminating basic knowledge about programs to other parties. Furthermore, an evaluation's processes, rather than merely its findings, may be used explicitly for enhancing shared understandings among program constituents, for driving and supporting program development per se, or for increasing stakeholders' engagement with program practices. Any or all of these potential uses may be identified in primary intended users' initial questions and concerns, but they are subsequently narrowed to a set of the most meaningful and feasible target uses, through negotiation and prioritization procedures. These procedures require primary intended users to consider the stage of a program (e.g., nonexistent, under development, early implementation, established practice), the interests and needs of stakeholder groups, the potential for particular questions to produce useable findings, and the actual constraints on time, resources, expertise, etc. As a result, the most essential and relevant uses are clearly focused and specified before further efforts are undertaken. Patton (1997) summarized the importance of this step as follows:

> Because of limited time and limited resources, it is never possible to look at everything in great depth. Decisions have to be made about what's worth looking at. Choosing to look at one area in depth is also a decision not to look at something else in depth. Utilization-focused evaluation suggests that the criterion for making those choices of focus be the likely utility of the resulting information. Findings that would be of greatest use for program improvement and decision making focus the evaluation. (p. 190)

Following these critical stage-setting steps, appropriate designs and methods are determined. Clearly, a variety of methods may be called upon in light of the wide range of potential concerns of primary intended users. Key to the selection of methods is both their relevance in responding to particular intended uses and their rigor/appropriateness for providing actual users with information that is both credible and useful—methods are not selected simply because they have been endorsed by scientific or professional communities (who may or may not have any understanding of or concern for the particular program context). Thus, depending on the program stage and intended uses, evaluative methods may include, among others: (a) identification and specification of program goals and objectives; (b) development of program intervention techniques, guidelines, and processes; (c) observation and documentation of program implementation; (d) investigation of program outcomes; (e) analysis of program effectiveness in terms of its goals and objectives; and (f) interpretation of program impact and consequences. The specific techniques employed and the data gathered are determined according to the clearly identified needs of the primary intended users, and the proof of their selection lies in the extent to which they are understood and used in intended ways.

Here again, just as no evaluation questions are ruled out *a priori*, the point in selecting methods is not to rule out any scientific techniques (including those advocated in relevant standards, such as those for educational assessments). Instead, utilization-focused evaluation poses the additional requirement that methods of inquiry be selected according to a criterion of relevance. Beyond basic concerns with rigor or an appeal to the endorsement of professional communities, evaluations must include a justification of how particular methods respond to prioritized questions and intended uses by specific users. Without this justification, evaluations risk considerable (or even total) irrelevance, despite the scientific rigor that may inhere within their methods.

Finally, the observations, findings, or other outcomes of evaluation are analyzed, interpreted, and reported, and decisions and actions are taken on their basis. Key to the use of data for actually doing something is their presentation to intended users and other audiences (i.e., those who may not directly participate in evaluation but will have an interest in the outcomes) in a format that can be understood and directly linked to original questions or concerns. At the same time, the meanings that may, and may not, be attributed to data must be carefully outlined, such that claims to be made about programs are warranted on the basis of what was actually done methodologically; 'anything goes', absolute relativist, and willful interpretations are clearly ruled out in this regard. Assuming a balanced and warranted understanding of data, deliberation among intended users is then called upon to enable judgments regarding the implications of these data for understanding or determining the worth of programs, for making summative or formative decisions, or for grounding recommendations of further program and/or evaluative actions to be taken. Thus, the local expertise of primary intended users is again required in this step, such that evaluation outcomes can be used in program-meaningful ways. However, procedures may be incorporated for requiring primary intended users to consider the impact of decisions and actions from the perspective of various program stakeholders, and consensus may be sought from stakeholder groups on any recommendations that are made. In addition, the empirical limits of evaluative methods and their resulting data serve as a frame of reference within which particular uses—decisions, actions, and recommendations—may or may not be sufficiently warranted.

In order for the preceding steps of utilization-focused evaluation to take place, and to result in useful, fair, empirically warranted, and trustworthy outcomes, it is obvious that considerable organization, facilitation, interaction, negotiation, implementation, communication, and even educational efforts will be required. Within Patton's (1997) framework, a program evaluator is called upon explicitly to advance these various efforts in a systematic way, and in particular to provide the expertise necessary for responding with appropriate methodological recommendations to the intended uses for evaluation. Thus, at each of the steps in the evaluation process, the evaluator plays an advisory/consultant/facilitator role in recommending specific actions that will make evaluation happen, and happen with consistency. The evaluator oversees the identification and involvement of primary intended users; elicits their priority questions, concerns, and uses; proposes methods for meeting these needs; assists in gathering, analyzing, and reporting empirical data; advises on program claims that may and may not be warranted on the basis of these data; and facilitates the negotiation of decisions and actions to be taken. Throughout these processes, then, the evaluator is responsible for *procedural* considerations, with the ultimate goal of informing intended uses by intended users via the provision of relevant and trustworthy methods. However, while the evaluator may suggest areas of potential concern, the evaluator does not determine *substantive* considerations regarding why programs should be evaluated; rather, the evaluator facilitates the generation of contextually fitting substantive decisions by primary intended users. Patton (1997) summarizes the role of the evaluator as "active-reactive-adaptive" in seeking to understand the program context, respond to the needs of its stakeholders, provide situationally meaningful advice, and maintain an empirical focus throughout the evaluation endeavor.

To summarize, utilization-focused evaluation provides a unique framework for wedding external evaluation expertise with local program-based expertise, in order to meet the dual requirements of *rigor* and *relevance*. By incorporating into evaluation planning and implementation those key stakeholders who will act on findings and other outcomes of the process, questions and methods with direct relevance to the specific program are prioritized. At the same time, accusations that utilization-focused evaluation is subject to total relativism—that is, any questions or methods or uses may be prioritized by users, regardless of whether they are appropriate to the program or to standards of evaluation practice, or whether they will produce rigorous scientific knowledge—are countered in several ways. First, the direct involvement of an evaluator with fitting expertise maximizes the probability that rigorous methods will be employed, interpretations of findings will be warranted, and claims about programs will be justified (and often limited) in terms of their evidentiary bases. Intended users of evaluation do not simply gather 'sloppy' data and interpret them at will; rather, the evaluator assists them in ensuring that scientific methods most appropriate to their questions are carefully selected and implemented, and interpretation of findings occurs in a structured and empirical way. Second, key questions about programs are prioritized through careful deliberation by primary intended users and the evaluator; within these deliberations, the needs/interests of program stakeholders are explicitly considered. Furthermore, resulting uses for evaluation must be justified in light of the need for and contribution of particular questions and investigations, and findings and related actions must be reported to program-wide constituencies. These mechanisms provide an important 'check' on the possibility that idiosyncratic, willful, or biased uses for evaluation will ensue. In the end, then, utilization-focused evaluation asks for and enables not only scientifically *rigorous* and defensible methods, but it also demands their explicit justification in terms of *relevance* for specific, program-based uses.

5.1.2 Responding to validity evaluation demands in college FL assessment

It should be apparent that a utilization-focused approach offers considerable potential for responding to the major challenges in validity evaluation of educational assessments, and in particular to the challenges of college FL assessment. First of all, it provides a directly applicable framework for clarifying who is responsible for validity evaluation, how its purposes should be determined, which immediate or most urgent questions are prioritized, how much evidence of what kinds is called for, and what specifically gets done (i.e., the decisions and actions that should be taken) as a result of validity evaluation. Instead of simply adhering to conventional prescribed questions and methods which address only certain measurement qualities of educational assessments (and which are not rationalized in terms of specific, actual uses), a utilization-focused approach clearly enables the kinds of contextualization for local educators—in terms of both priority questions and methodological flexibility—and the meaningfulness, feasibility, and utility that have been called for in criticisms of contemporary assessment validation practice (see chapter 3). Nothing is prescribed or ruled out from the outset of evaluation (including theoretical construct investigations), but the questions and methods that are pursued must be rationalized according to their intended uses by particular audiences, especially audiences of local educators, where they are the stakeholders most likely to be held responsible for assessment practices and consequences (and this is exactly where conventional validation practice has been found most wanting).

Second, utilization-focused evaluation informs the systematic treatment of desiderata for an explicitly *evaluative* approach to the validation of educational assessments (see chapter 4). Following a utilization-focused approach, assessment validity evaluation would be undertaken as a purposeful endeavor, contextualized with respect to a particular assessment program, its stakeholders and audiences, its goals and objectives, its processes, and its outcomes and consequences. The reasons for evaluating a given assessment program, among multiple possibilities, would be specified and justified from the outset by individuals in a position to represent assessment stakeholders and to act on evaluation outcomes, and the methods for doing so would be articulated with their intended uses. At the same time, the clearly advantageous relevance provided by these local processes would be balanced through an empirical scientific focus contributed by the external evaluator. Finally, the results of the evaluation process would be used by educators for judging, sustaining, revising, improving, disseminating, and otherwise *doing something about* their assessment practices, rather than merely producing more or less applicable findings about the validity of assessments (without any intended use of such findings).

In addition, a utilization-focused approach should prove particularly appropriate to the validity evaluation of assessment practices within college FL education contexts. Specifically, the small-scale local practices of assessment (e.g., placement, classroom-based assessment, student learning outcomes assessment), the likelihood of clearly identifiable primary intended users for evaluation (e.g., departmental administrators and faculty), and the present need for considerable attention to development, improvement, and decision-making vis-à-vis assessments, make the college FL context an ideal setting for this kind of evaluation approach. Its systematic sensitivity to the needs, and especially the constraints, of program contexts and intended users should provide for evaluation methods that both elicit and respond to the immediate questions and concerns of FL educators. Furthermore, by treating assessments as programs, it will call for an initial specification of the goals and objectives of assessment practices, thereby requiring resolution of the gap between the 'how' and the 'why' of distinct assessment uses in college FL education. In this respect, utilization-focused evaluation will not simply demand such a resolution, but will also offer the means for accomplishing it. It provides an immediately applicable framework for integrating critical local expertise about assessment uses and needs with the critical scientific methodological expertise for making assessment programs and their evaluation happen (i.e., exactly the kind of serious treatment of the 'how' and 'why' of assessment that seems to be missing from college FL professional development and responsibilities; see chapter 2). By explicitly incorporating the facilitative participation of an evaluator, an immediate, if short-term, answer may be provided to the lack of assessment capabilities in college FL departments, at least on a case by case basis. In addition, beyond short-term advice on and organization of evaluation activities at all stages of assessment program development, implementation, and sustained practice, it may be that utilization-focused evaluation processes will enable the long-term development of local capacities to understand and act on contextually meaningful aspects of assessment in empirically sound ways.

5.2 Exploring validity evaluation in a college FL assessment context

While there are good reasons for believing that program evaluation practices in general, and a utilization-focused approach in particular, can respond in directly applicable ways to many of the apparent weaknesses that have been identified within conventional practices of educational assessment validation, it is certainly an empirical question whether and to what extent such weaknesses will be resolved and undesired side-effects will be avoided. Accordingly, in order to begin to provide evidence in response to these uncertainties, the current work was designed as an in-depth and long-term case study for investigating *what would happen if* a utilization-focused approach were applied to the validity evaluation of assessments within one college FL education context.

More specifically, the current study set out to explore *what would happen if*: (a) the demands and constraints of the local education context were taken seriously as the starting point for assessment validity evaluation; (b) validity evaluation were designed and implemented with respect to the intentional roles for assessment programs as they actually occurred within that context; (c) the primary intended users for evaluation of a given assessment were identified; (d) their (carefully justified) priorities for evaluating specific assessments were adopted; (e) empirically fitting and purposefully articulated evaluative methods were implemented; and (f) findings were reported, interpreted, and used for informing various local decisions and actions that needed to be taken. Thus, the current study did not seek to prove or disprove the value of a validity evaluation approach; nor did it seek to 'demonstrate the validity' of a given assessment. Rather, it sought to provide initial evidence regarding the potential for understanding and improving college FL assessment practices if assessment validation were treated as an evaluative undertaking.

Within this study, then, a utilization-focused approach was implemented for validity evaluation within a single college FL educational assessment context, with the intent of providing initial evidence about what happened, including what kinds of questions were posed, methods employed, and findings used for evaluating assessments. In this section, I first describe key characteristics of the college FL setting within which the exploration of validity evaluation took place, including its students and departmental constituents, the specific educational program of interest, and the nature of assessment within it. Subsequently, I outline the basic procedural components of the validity evaluation approach, in order to complete the overarching framework for the current study.

5.2.1 Characterizing the FL educational assessment context

The Georgetown University German Department (GUGD) constituted the educational context in which the use of validity evaluation was explored. As a long-standing FL department in a large and well-regarded private institution, the GUGD presented many characteristics common to other college FL programs around the U.S., including a range of impetuses for and constraints on assessment. At the same time, several features unique to this context, and in particular a department-wide commitment to the improvement of educational practices, enabled the pursuit of an innovative response to the challenge to evaluate and ensure assessment quality.

Like many other U.S. college FL departments, the GUGD administers both undergraduate and graduate degree programs in German, including emphases in literary/cultural studies as well as applied linguistics. However, the major instructional focus (in terms of number of courses taught and students served) is comprised by a comprehensive undergraduate German-language studies program, with enrollments ranging from 200 to 250 students per semester. This student population includes primarily language majors and minors, individuals fulfilling two-year foreign language learning requirements in other degree programs, and students from the Georgetown School of Foreign Service seeking to meet a language proficiency requirement. Common characteristics of most students within this target learner population include a background of considerable academic success, high levels of motivation toward specific academic and professional goals, some degree of language learning experience (in German and/or other FLs), and the general expectation of acquiring FL knowledge and abilities directly relevant to their needs. Responsibilities for addressing students' academic needs, via the implementation of the GUGD's educational programs, fall to several key departmental constituencies, including a department chair, a curriculum developer, an undergraduate curriculum coordinator, the faculty (approximately 10), graduate teaching assistants (8 to 10 each semester), and administrative staff.

Beginning in the spring of 1997, the GUGD initiated major renewal efforts within its undergraduate German-language program in response to emerging perceptions among department faculty of a number of fundamental challenges, including: (a) a lack of articulation between the program's instructional focus and students' language-learning, intellectual, and professional needs and goals; (b) a mismatch between theoretical tenets and empirical research findings in instructed second language acquisition and the program's pedagogic approaches, materials, and activities; (c) the realization that students' and employers' advanced-level language acquisition expectations could not be achieved within the typical two-year college foreign language requirement; (d) an over-emphasis in program courses and related materials (i.e., commercial textbooks) on the development of decontextualized language knowledge at the expense of intellectual content and the ability to communicate about it in valued ways; and (e) the perceived 'demise' of foreign language education in the United States, in the form of disappointing learner outcomes accompanied by decreasing enrollments, as well as a sense of 'disintegration' into service department status within the institution. In order to address these challenges, a multi-year program development project was undertaken, in the form of innovative restructuring and development of all aspects of curriculum and instruction (see Byrnes 1998a, 2001; Byrnes & Kord, 2001; Eigler, 2001; Pfeiffer, 2002). Primary intellectual influences throughout the curriculum and instruction innovation included notions of focus on form in instructed second language acquisition (e.g., Doughty & Williams, 1998), systemic functional linguistics and associated pedagogies (e.g., Christie, 1999; The New London Group, 1996), and task-based language teaching (e.g., Long, 1985; Long & Norris, 2000; Skehan, 1998).

From the outset, departmental constituents agreed that the fundamental goal of the undergraduate German-language program would be to foster learners' abilities to communicate in sophisticated ways about topics of intellectual interest to them and their professional or academic domains. Thus was born within the GUGD the notion of 'developing multiple literacies', wherein various kinds of literate communication constituted the priority program outcomes. At stake, then, was adult language use for more than conversational purposes, and in particular the ability to produce and comprehend German-language texts across a variety of targeted genres and for a variety of communicative purposes. Ensuing efforts sought to provide an instructional sequence that was appropriate and interesting to students (and teachers), and in which the acquisition of literate language abilities could be fostered in conjunction with the development of students' capacities to deal with worthwhile intellectual content and, what is more, such that one supported the other. This program development effort was entitled *Developing Multiple Literacies* (*Multiple Literacies*, for short), and it instigated a host of curricular, instructional, and administrative changes within the GUGD over the ensuing years (for a thorough historical and conceptual overview, see *Developing Multiple Literacies*, 2003).

Program innovation in pursuit of the *Multiple Literacies* goal was realized through several principal developments. First, a dual, integrated focus on content and language instruction was introduced into all undergraduate German courses. This content-plus-language approach sought to enable students to become competent and culturally literate second language users by linking German language acquisition with learning about the German-speaking world. Critically, this explicit attention to content-embedded language acquisition was to inform the structure of all courses within the *Multiple Literacies* curriculum, from the very beginning (first year, first semester) through to the end (fourth and fifth years) of the undergraduate sequence. Unlike most college German programs in the U.S. (e.g., Barnes, Klee, and Wakefield, 1990), the new curriculum did not distinguish between 'lower-division' (typically, the first two years of *language* instruction) and 'upper-division' (typically, *literary/cultural content* instruction) courses, or between 'language program instructors' and other faculty. *All courses* throughout all years were planned and sequenced according to this content/language focus, and all faculty (and graduate teaching assistants) were intended to teach regularly at all curricular levels.

Second, all aspects of instruction, including materials as well as pedagogic activities, were revised in order to engage students in literate, adult communication from the start, and to embed this literacy focus within structured attention to students' development of the German language. In principle, revisions were intended to integrate meaning-oriented communicative activities with focus-on-form instructional techniques and a concomitant sensitivity to German interlanguage development. The resulting pedagogy stressed: (a) the use of German for content-relevant communication purposes; (b) the linking of meaningful L2 use with the learning of corresponding L2 forms; and (c) a balanced and cyclical emphasis on developing accuracy, complexity, and fluency in L2 use. In concrete terms, this pedagogic overhaul featured the replacement or supplementation of commercial German language textbooks with in-house activities and materials (produced jointly by graduate students and faculty) across all curricular levels.

Third, these revised learning goals and instructional methods were arranged into a carefully planned, multi-year curricular sequence that encompassed the entire undergraduate program. Within this sequence, each semester and year targeted particular content emphases, associated textual genres, and expected student performance outcomes, particularly in terms of abilities to accomplish specific communication tasks. As students progressed through the curriculum, expectations increased in terms of both accuracy/complexity/fluency of language use, as well as abilities to process and produce an expanding array of texts (oral and written) for a variety of communicative purposes. These expectations were formalized as learner profiles for each curricular level, and they served as the basis for syllabus construction in all individual courses taught within the undergraduate program.

Table 1 outlines the five sequential levels of the *Multiple Literacies* curriculum that emerged from this multi-year development effort. The first column identifies the curricular level according to its content-related title; the second shows the available courses at each level; the third indicates the number of hours of instruction for each course; and the fourth provides a curricular-level/semester abbreviation used throughout the current study. Each of the first three curricular levels is comprised of a total of six hours of instruction per level, which may be completed either in two, non-intensive 16-week semesters (3 contact hours per week), or in one intensive semester (6 contact hours per week). Note that expected student learning outcomes for one intensive semester are identical to those for two non-intensive semesters within a given level. Following the first 18 credit hours of instruction (Levels I-III), the sequence culminates in the required "Text in Context" course, for students who wish to proceed with level IV and V classes. This course (4 hours per week) requires one semester to complete, and it synthesizes and expands considerably upon the L2 and textual processing abilities introduced during the first three curricular levels. After completing "Text in Context", students may, depending on their individual goals, enroll in a variety of additional level IV and V courses, each of which fosters continued L2 acquisition in the context of literary, cultural, and other content areas.

Unlike the intensive efforts that had been expended since 1997 in renewing curriculum and instruction in order to meet student needs, at the time of my initial contact with the GUGD (early 1999), assessment had received little attention in conjunction with other program development efforts. While there were various impetuses and demands for assessment of students' learning, knowledge, and abilities—from within the classroom, to across the program, to the institutional level and beyond—minimal explicit attention had been paid to exactly what educational purposes assessment was intended to accomplish or to the alignment of particular assessment instruments and procedures with these specific purposes. Existing assessments, by and large, had simply been carried over in much the same manner as they had occurred prior to program development efforts; for example, a placement exam developed some two decades prior was still in use for locating students within the newly restructured curriculum.

Table 1. Sequence of instructional levels in the *Multiple Literacies* curriculum

Level	Courses	Credit hours	Abbreviation
	Introductory German 1	3	1.1
I. Experiencing the German-speaking world	Introductory German 2	3	1.2
	Intensive Basic German	6	1.Int
	Intermediate German 1	3	2.1
II. Contemporary Germany	Intermediate German 2	3	2.2
	Intensive Intermediate German	6	2.Int
	Advanced German 1	3	3.1
III. Stories and Histories	Advanced German 2	3	3.2
	Intensive Advanced German	6	3.Int
	Text in Context	4	4
IV. Text in Context	(other subsequent courses)	(3 each)	--
V.	(post-sequenced courses)	(3 each)	--

In this respect, the GUGD shared considerable similarity with most other college FL programs in the U.S. As described in chapter 2, assessment was not a particular focus of faculty expertise within the GUGD, and graduate teaching assistants, not to mention other teachers, did not receive much in the way of professional development in educational assessment capabilities. Although one faculty member had participated extensively in assessment-related activities within the FL community, these had all focused on 'how to measure' language, in conjunction with the proficiency movement (and it is to that individual's credit that those previous assessment experiences were acknowledged to be only peripherally relevant to their current needs). Needless to say, there had been no attempts to evaluate the qualities of existing assessment practices, in order to ensure their appropriateness, effectiveness, or positive consequences for the language education context, or for the GUGD students in particular. Nor, for that matter, had attention been paid to the need to translate the implications of the new curriculum into new assessment practices.

However, one additional unique characteristic of this context was the willingness of departmental constituents to seek input and expertise regarding all features of the undergraduate German-language program, in order to maximize its chances of resolving the problems that had inspired innovation in the first place. After the initial two years of program development work, they agreed that the educational functions of assessment had to be addressed explicitly along with other aspects of the *Multiple Literacies* curriculum. In addition, they agreed that external expertise would be required in order to attend to assessment needs in an educationally responsible manner.

5.2.2 Applying a utilization-focused approach to validity evaluation

Beginning in January, 1999, the GUGD initiated wholesale revision of its assessment practices in order to bring them in alignment with the educational premises of the *Multiple Literacies* curriculum. From the outset, departmental administrators and faculty had decided that a visiting researcher/consultant should be invited to oversee this process, and to provide expertise in all aspects of language assessment development, use, and validation. In the official capacity of visiting researcher, I assumed an advisory role on assessment-related concerns within the GUGD, and, from 1999 through 2002, intensive attention was devoted from both my external and their local perspectives to planning and implementing a curriculum-based, use-driven assessment framework. In brief, the activities that took place during this period included the critique of existing assessment practices, the specification of intended uses for all assessments, the development of assessment instruments and procedures to meet these intended uses, the on-going implementation of assessments for various targeted purposes, and the validity evaluation of assessment practices in order to understand, improve, and ensure their quality in meeting intended uses. In addition, these activities took place at multiple levels of assessment use, responding to classroom-based, cross-curricular, and program-external impetuses for assessment. Over the three-year revision period, I advised on and participated in all of these activities at all of the program levels. Outcomes of this working relationship took the form of extensive departmental assessment policies, guidelines, and specifications; a wide variety of new and revised assessment instruments and procedures; washback on and considerable refinement of curriculum and instruction; enhancement of the assessment capabilities of educators within the FL context; and a number of specific research projects, findings, and dissemination efforts.

Validity evaluation efforts proceeded from the very beginning of these assessment revision processes. Thus, one of the primary contributions that I sought to provide (as well as explore empirically) was a systematic means for helping the local

FL educators evaluate and ensure the quality of their assessment practices. In order to do so, the basic notions and procedures of utilization-focused evaluation were integrated into all assessment-related activities. In other words, validity evaluation was not treated as a post-hoc concern, to be dealt with only once assessments were in use; rather, evaluation informed every stage of the programs that evolved in response to the educational assessment needs of the GUGD. The following procedural components framed the validity evaluation of assessments throughout the current study (as well as for those assessments not reported in detail here). Note that this description is only intended to frame the basic steps in the validity evaluation process pursued in the current study; detailed description of participants, methods, findings, etc., is provided in chapter 6.

First, throughout the three years of intensive assessment revision efforts, I provided direction to all validity evaluation endeavors, in the form of procedural and methodological recommendations, and I organized and facilitated related activities. As described above, recommendations took an active-reactive-adaptive form, in which I proposed a variety of procedures that would help GUGD educators advance their efforts towards the resolution of particular assessment needs. Specifically, I sought to respond to the GUGD context by initiating a framework that would help local educators first clarify and understand the educational roles of assessment within the *Multiple Literacies* curriculum, then develop and engage in assessment practices that would fulfill these roles, and finally judge and improve the qualities of resulting assessment programs.

Second, in light of the complex assessment needs of the GUGD, discrete validity evaluation activities were designed (by me and the local educators) and pursued in accord with unique demands at each of a series of assessment program stages. Thus, it was clear from the outset that much of the existing assessment practice would have to be replaced entirely in order to bring it in alignment with the revised *Multiple Literacies* curriculum. Validity evaluation procedures were applied, then, in order to provide an empirical basis for distinct assessment-related decisions and actions that needed to occur at each of the following program stages: (a) specification of intended uses for assessments; (b) development of assessment instruments and procedures; (c) implementation and revision of assessment programs; and (d) sustained assessment program practice. At each of these distinct stages in the emergence of each individual assessment program (e.g., placement testing, student learning outcomes assessment), utilization-focused procedures were employed in order to figure out what needed to happen in the first place and then to actually make it happen in situationally relevant ways—that is, in ways that GUGD educators would understand and be able to use in advancing their assessment practices. Once again, it should be stressed that validity evaluation was not simply focused on the outcomes of operational uses for assessment, but it also was used to elucidate the purposes for assessment programs in the first place, as well as their corresponding development.

Third, through negotiation with the local educators, I identified primary intended users of validity evaluation from among the range of assessment stakeholders who were in a position to make decisions and take actions on the basis of evaluation. In general, throughout all stages, I interacted with a core group of primary intended users, including the GUGD department chair, the curriculum developer, and the curriculum coordinator, in negotiating the basic procedural steps to be followed. In addition, then, at each program stage, additional users for evaluation were identified, such that empirical questions, methods, and findings could be tailored to their interests, needs, and potential constraints to the extent possible.

Fourth, at each program stage, I elicited priority intended uses for validity evaluation from the primary intended users. This elicitation occurred in distinct ways at each stage, and included the investigation of questions, concerns, and problems with existing assessment practices, surveys of teacher and student stakeholders regarding the functions of assessment within the GUGD, full-department meetings in which key assessment issues were debated, and small-group meetings, conversations, and e-mail discussions in which the specific questions and concerns of primary intended users were voiced. Here again, while I organized and facilitated these elicitation occasions, the primary intended users and other GUGD constituents provided the substance of the intended uses for validity evaluation. In addition, validity evaluation efforts at all program stages, with the obvious exception of the initial specification of intended assessment use, were informed by the findings from previous program stages. Thus, once the intended uses for a given assessment program had been specified, validity evaluation questions and methods were directed explicitly at key concerns with the particular assessment program, and these concerns varied from one assessment to the next according to the distinct features of each.

Fifth, based on these prioritized intended uses for validity evaluation, I formalized a set of assessment questions to be addressed via validity evaluation. These focal points provided direction for the subsequent recommendation of methods and data that would enable an empirical basis for targeted decisions and actions about assessment programs. The primary intended users and I then debated the relative merits of methodological possibilities, and they offered key insights into the contextual constraints on specific research proposals. In response to each intended use and associated questions, we jointly determined a final set of evaluation methods, and I undertook the corresponding research activities in conjunction with other implicated individuals and groups within the GUGD.

Finally, at each program stage, I reported evaluation findings to primary intended users, and to broader audiences of GUGD constituents. Reporting consistently took the form of written documents that were disseminated to stakeholder audiences and tailored to their information needs. In addition, targeted decisions and actions were taken in the context of: (a) large-scale meetings of departmental constituents wherein major assessment program efforts and/or changes were negotiated; and, more frequently, (b) small-scale discussions in which the primary intended users considered the implications of findings and made specific decisions, took actions to improve assessment practices, or offered recommendations for assessment program features in need of further attention.

In sum, these principal utilization-focused components framed the practice of validity evaluation throughout the GUGD assessment revision project:

1. Active-reactive-adaptive direction and facilitation of all evaluation processes by an external evaluator.
2. Treatment of assessment programs according to stage of development and implementation, with unique evaluation questions and methods articulated with the program stage.
3. Identification of primary intended users of validity evaluation at each assessment program stage.
4. Elicitation of priority intended uses by intended users at each assessment program stage.
5. Implementation of evaluation methods tailored to primary intended user audiences and their priority intended uses.
6. Reporting and use of findings for intended decisions and other actions.
7. Cyclical attention to steps 3-6 for subsequent assessment program stages and/or new validity evaluation priorities.

Of course, as each assessment program stage unfolded in response to each impetus for assessment use within the GUGD, validity evaluation efforts took a unique shape in addressing the particular prioritized concerns and questions of primary intended users, the methods that would provide fitting evidence in answer to these concerns, and the ways in which evaluation processes and findings were used by primary intended users. Indeed, the outcomes of validity evaluation—in terms of what actually happened, and what didn't happen—offer valuable insights into the extent to which this approach may help transform validation into a practicable and educationally relevant undertaking, as well as the extent to which scientific rigor can be maintained throughout the process. Therefore, in chapter 6, these outcomes, and the validity evaluation processes that led to them, are described and displayed in detail for three distinct stages of one assessment program that received immediate attention as a major priority for improving educational assessment practice in the GUGD.

5.3 Record-keeping and reporting of validity evaluation activities

The following chapter takes the form of a program evaluation report, in which I summarize in detail the validity evaluation processes and outcomes associated with a single assessment program that emerged in response to a priority need (placement testing) within the GUGD. Each of the three sections in chapter 6 reports on the validity evaluation efforts carried out during three distinct stages in the assessment program. Within each of these stages, evaluative questions were raised by educators, methods designed and implemented to address these questions, evidence gathered and interpreted, and findings used for specified purposes. Thus, at one level, chapter 6 adopts a familiar research report format in detailing: (a) research questions, (b) research methods, (c) results/findings, and (d) discussion.

However, unique to the current work—and a result of the application of utilization-focused methods as described above—is the addition of a situated rationale for each of these investigations, that is, how and by whom the research questions were generated, why particular methods were pursued, and what kinds of findings led to what kinds of decisions and other actions within the assessment program. Therefore, in addition to the conventional research report categories above, each of the three main sections in chapter 6 also includes an initial discussion of: (a) the characteristics of the assessment program stage (timing, purpose, constraints, etc.); (b) the specific primary intended users for evaluation and their roles in the assessment program; (c) techniques employed for eliciting and prioritizing areas of concern with the assessment program from these intended users; and (d) the basic intended uses for validity evaluation at each program stage. To be clear, the following chapter does not simply report the research questions, methods, and results of validity investigations (i.e., the standard reporting format for conventional validation studies). Rather, each section in the chapter first provides a contextualization of and rationalization for the particular questions and methods pursued, based on the intended uses for evaluation findings at the given assessment program stage, and each concludes by providing a summary of exactly *what happened* as these findings were reported and put to use by specific actors.

The detailed summaries in chapter 6 are intended to offer a foundation for understanding exactly what happened (and what did not happen) as a result of the implementation of validity evaluation from a utilization-focused approach. The description of evaluation processes—including in particular the generation of priority assessment concerns from the point of view of local educators—and the nature of methodological and practical decisions should enable considerable insights into why and how particular validity investigations were pursued and what was done on the basis of their findings. In turn, these insights will inform further considerations about the educational value of the validity evaluation approach pursued here (and I return to this basic issue in chapter 7). It bears emphasis here that chapter 6 takes the form of a *summary report* of multiple years of multiple evaluation activities, and it is intended to reflect most closely the reporting format of other program evaluations. While a number of features in the report, including in particular the descriptions of local educators and their participation in various aspects of validity evaluation procedures, may resemble aspects of interpretive ethnographic and other qualitative research traditions, this report by no means approximates the epistemological and methodological requirements of such research—nor was it intended to do so! However, the report does offer a comprehensive and detailed summary of exactly what happened as validity evaluation efforts unfolded within the GUGD for one priority assessment program.

To provide an evidentiary foundation for the following report, I maintained a variety of records over the three years of intensive validity evaluation efforts covered in the current study, including:

- all documents that were created in relation to the focal assessment program during the stages under consideration here;

- all electronic communications about the validity evaluation process and the assessment program;
- researcher notes on key decision-making junctures during assessment program development, implementation, and evaluation;
- all artifacts of assessment program development and use; and
- all data and analyses from each validity evaluation activity.

The collection of these evidentiary sources enabled not only the reporting of conventional research categories (questions, methods, findings), but also informed the additional treatment of how and why particular research activities were carried out and what happened as a result. However, the raw data from these sources amounted to much more than can be reported feasibly here (indeed, they constituted numerous boxes of paper documents and audio tape cassettes, very large computer files, etc.). Accordingly, in chapter 6, I condense these diverse and extensive sources of data into a coherent summary of the primary features of validity evaluation processes that unfolded during the study. Where especially informative, I include key evidentiary sources in the text of chapter 6.

Chapter 6
Validity evaluation of a college foreign language assessment program

Over three years, from 1999 to 2002, a utilization-focused approach to validity evaluation framed the emergence and development of a variety of distinct assessment programs in response to distinct assessment needs in the GUGD. These programs included classroom-based as well as cross-curricular assessments, and their uses ranged from motivating students to providing instructional feedback to improving the scope and sequence of the new curriculum. However, common to all assessments was their transformation into purposeful and contextually relevant practices, the qualities of which were determined and ensured by local educators. Of interest for the current study was how this transformation took place, as utilization-focused procedures were deployed, and what specific concerns with assessment came to shape the questions, methods, findings, and uses of validity evaluation.

This chapter details the processes and outcomes of validity evaluation as it was applied to one priority assessment program within the GUGD, and three distinct program stages are considered. In section 6.1, I first examine how intended uses were specified for *all* assessment practices within the GUGD, and I highlight the process whereby *one* major cross-curricular assessment program—the placement exam—was prioritized for immediate attention. I then summarize the development of placement assessment instruments and procedures in response to this priority. In section 6.2, I report on the evaluation of key validity concerns that arose during the initial two years of placement program implementation, illuminating in particular the decision-making and program-improvement orientation of validity evaluation efforts. Finally, in section 6.3, I report on the shifting nature of validity evaluation concerns as the placement exam entered into a phase of sustained program practice.

The summary evaluation report for each of these program stages is structured as follows. First, as an introduction to each program stage, I outline the general context and purpose, I identify the individuals who acted in the role of primary intended users at that stage, and I introduce the principal means and ends of validity evaluation efforts pursued. These introductions serve to contextualize what happened in the name of validity evaluation at the particular point in the emergence of the focal assessment program. Next, I present the rationale for specific evaluative *questions* that were posed by primary intended users at each stage, and I list the final negotiated set of priority questions that informed investigations. I then outline the particular *methods* used for gathering appropriate evidence in response to these questions, and I detail the *findings* that resulted from their implementation. Finally, and most critically, I discuss and summarize the ways in which evaluation findings were actually put to *use* by primary intended users.

Note that throughout these summaries, I employ the passive voice to indicate decisions and actions that were undertaken *jointly* on the basis of negotiated consensus among the primary intended users. The majority of interpretations, decisions, and actions were of this sort. Where specific individuals, including myself in the role of consultant evaluator, or groups undertook unique actions during validity evaluation processes, I describe their roles explicitly. It is well beyond the scope of this work to detail individual contributions (never mind the sources of recorded evidence from which they were gleaned) for each and every decision or other evaluative activity that occurred. Therefore, throughout, readers should bear in mind that: (a) all summaries of validity evaluation procedures and their outcomes are based on the sources of evidence listed in 5.3 above (i.e., passive constructions do not indicate 'arbitrary' interpretations by me in reporting); and (b) where assessment-related actions are reported in the form of passive constructions, they indicate precisely that consensus among the listed primary intended users (or other individuals as explicitly indicated) was the basis for the given action.

6.1 Specifying and developing an assessment program

Validity evaluation efforts in the GUGD began in January, 1999, with initial interactions between myself and departmental stakeholders (i.e., faculty, staff, graduate teaching assistants and researchers, and administrators of the department). Primary concerns at this stage centered on (a) staking out the territory for assessment, in terms of its specific roles within the department and especially the *Multiple Literacies* curriculum, and (b) engaging in development activities that would bring assessment in line with the new curriculum. Thus, both departmental stakeholders and I began assessment program revisions, and associated validity evaluation efforts, by seeking to illuminate the 'why' and to articulate the 'how' of assessment as a foundation to further practice.

Prior to formalized validity evaluation efforts, I initiated a variety of informal stage-setting activities in order to better understand the nature of the GUGD educational context, the specific actors within it, and especially the general functions of existing assessments. In addition, these activities provided an opportunity for the local stakeholders, in particular the teachers and administrators who owned the GUGD educational programs, to get to know me in the role of visiting researcher and to establish with me the kinds of validity evaluation endeavors that would, and would not, be feasible and situationally relevant. The following stage-setting efforts summarize this initial three-month period:

- Invited presentations on assessment by the visiting researcher
- Interviews with GUGD teachers and administrators
- Observations of classroom instruction and assessment
- Collection and review of curriculum and assessment documents
- Discussion of assessment practices within curricular-level meetings
- Initial program-wide surveys of teachers and students on assessment practices, purposes, and values

On the basis of these activities, it became clear to both me and departmental stakeholders that gaps between their understandings of 'why' to assess and the 'how' of existing assessment practices were substantial; indeed for many assessments, teachers and administrators were not immediately able to articulate exactly what they were supposed to be accomplishing. However, they did identify specific and basic needs for assessment in the form of guidelines for practice, criteria for performance expectations on distinct instruments, methods for ensuring consistency in administration/scoring/decisions/feedback/etc., the alignment of test types with curricular emphases, and a system for encouraging cooperation among teachers in engaging in classroom and curricular-level assessments.

These initial outcomes helped to indicate the concrete directions that validity evaluation efforts would have to take in the immediate future, and they also underscored the key quality that was valued for all assessments within this context: the extent to which their use contributed as intended to the educational success of GUGD students. Another important outcome of this stage-setting phase was the identification of a core group of *primary intended users* (PIUs) for validity evaluation. Thus, while most departmental stakeholders participated in one form or another in some aspect of ensuing evaluation activities, I sought a handful of "strategically located people who are enthusiastic, committed, competent, interested, and assertive" (Patton, 1997, p. 52) to serve as a sounding board and advisory panel on all assessment-related decisions and actions that needed to occur. Individuals who fit the bill in all of the ways defined by Patton were easily identified in the form of the GUGD *department chair* and the *curriculum developer*, both senior faculty members in the department (and with later participation by a newly hired *curriculum coordinator*, as described below). Departmental stakeholders agreed in initial meetings that these individuals would collaborate directly with me in determining the nature of all assessment efforts.

6.1.1 Specifying intended uses for assessment

By the middle of the Spring 1999 semester, it became apparent (to me and the PIUs) that, in order for awareness-raising efforts to bear fruit, it would be necessary to formalize concrete policies and recommended practices of assessment that could be translated consistently into operational instruments and procedures, and that would serve as the basis for evaluating assessments in use. Therefore, as the first formal step in validity evaluation, departmental stakeholders were asked to specify the intended uses for all assessment practices in the GUGD. Similar to the clarification of goals and objectives as a foundation for any educational or social program, the purpose of this step was to elicit from those who knew best—the teachers and administrators of the educational context—exactly why assessment was, or should be, occurring, and exactly how it was, or should be, contributing to the overall educational ends of curriculum and instruction. Furthermore, via this elicitation process, educators were required to commit to a rationale for and direction in assessment (and its evaluation), by making the valued qualities of their assessments explicit.

99

In order to do so, and to encourage a programmatic, rather than technocratic, perception of assessment, I developed a series of specification activities (Norris, 2000) which would result in concrete answers to the following basic questions, asked for each and every instance of assessment use within the GUGD:

(a) Who uses the assessment for making what kinds of interpretations?
(b) What information is needed to inform the targeted interpretations of assessment users (i.e., what do assessment users want to know on the basis of assessment)?
(c) How is that information used for making decisions and/or taking actions; what is the purpose of assessment?
(d) Who or what is impacted by the consequences of this use for assessment, and in what ways?

In addition, in order to further flesh out the various roles played by assessment and to seek consensus on initial steps in developing assessment programs, questions were asked about the general practices of assessment within the GUGD:

(e) What are the intended uses for assessment within each curricular level as well as across all curricular levels?
(f) What are the priority needs for assessment development?
(g) What are the principal constraints on assessment practice?

Answers to these specification questions were sought in order to provide a clear mandate for each use of assessment in the GUGD, to build a consensus on the valued practices and qualities of all assessments, and to negotiate the priorities for further needed work. At this stage, in addition to the main PIUs, other intended users included all departmental teaching stakeholders (faculty, administrators, graduate teaching assistants), as well as me in the role of consultant evaluator.

Methods. During April and May of 1999, a series of meetings, workshops, and development activities took place with the goal of formalizing the intended uses for assessment as it was implemented at all levels of the GUGD, from within the classroom to across the multiple curricular levels. While I facilitated the steps of identifying, negotiating, and coming to agreement on the intended uses for assessment, I did not participate in proposing, debating, or otherwise influencing the nature of these specifications. I had stressed from the outset, and all stakeholders had (eventually) agreed, that the uses for assessment had to be defined and owned by those responsible for assessment and its outcomes, in this case, the teachers and administrators within the GUGD language education context. Clearly, they would have to accept the results of this specification process, incorporate assessment changes into their practices, use the information for making decisions and taking other actions, and live with the consequences, as would their primary constituents—the students in the GUGD.

The specification process proceeded through several discrete steps, each with its own objectives, and it culminated in the production of a range of documents that spelled out the uses for all assessments. Participation was sought and encouraged from all departmental faculty and teachers (including graduate teaching assistants and graduate students who would teach in the near future), labeled here as the departmental stakeholders. Wide-spread participation was considered essential, such that the diverse perspectives of actual test users could be incorporated into the process, and in order to ensure that the results were endorsed by the full range of stakeholders. Efforts were made at each step to promote the views of individuals as well as the development of group consensus. Thus, a process of transactional negotiation informed the activities that were undertaken, by building into each step both an individual reflection phase, to prompt all participants to formalize their own ideas, and a dialogic presentation/reaction phase, wherein these ideas were shared, discussed, and further developed. In addition, those who facilitated the various meetings (GUGD faculty members) were instructed to ensure the balanced presentation and discussion of viewpoints from all individual participants, especially in the development of consensus on final notions of assessment use. Finally, during all steps in the specification process, participants were requested to complete each activity by producing a clear outcome in the form of a written statement about intended assessment use. While these statements were not expected to provide polished documents for public consumption, they did establish a clear target for each activity, and they helped to push participants towards concretization of their ideas rather than mere discussion and debate (a pattern that had been noted in previous meetings).

Formalized efforts at specifying intended uses for assessment were initiated with a meeting of the departmental stakeholders in April 1999. The meeting began with a review of key observations about assessment practices in the GUGD. While a number of positive features of assessment had been found, it was clear to most stakeholders that assessment as practiced in the GUGD at that time suffered from several weaknesses, which they themselves had raised on previous occasions, including: (a) lack of coordination; (b) lack of guidelines and criteria; (c) no teacher training; (d) no attention to consistency in administering, scoring, and using; and in particular (e) no alignment between most assessments and the instructional emphases of the new curriculum. I summarized these observations by proposing that the key missing component within the GUGD context was a clear understanding of the purposeful nature of assessment, in the form of a specification of intended uses for all assessment activities.

The meeting then proceeded with a general discussion of how a specification of intended uses for assessment would enable the GUGD to establish a foundation for developing, implementing, and evaluating assessments. In order to resolve the challenges above, I argued that departmental constituents should first provide answers to the basic questions in Figure 3 for each and every assessment activity that needed to take place.

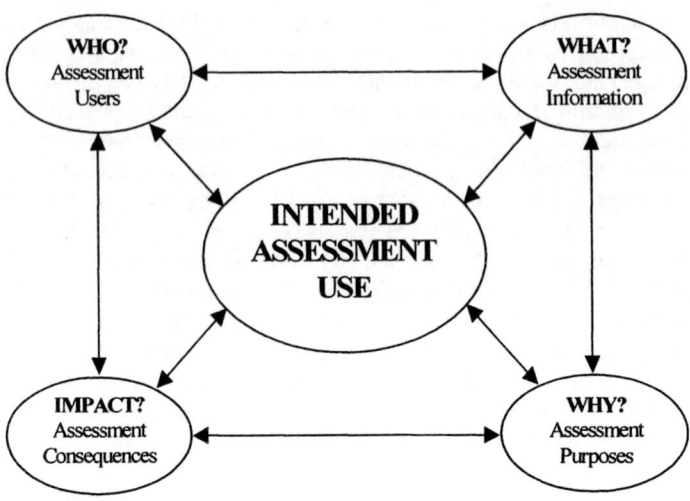

Figure 3. Specification of intended assessment use (from Norris, 2000)

Where these questions could not be answered about an assessment practice, serious thought needed to be given to whether or not that assessment was particularly necessary, at least in its current form. Furthermore, I pointed out that without a clear specification of intended uses for assessment along these lines, there was little basis for motivating any evaluation of whether an assessment was accomplishing what it was intended to accomplish.

Following this discussion, a proposal was put to the participants that all assessment activities within the GUGD, extant or to be developed, should be reviewed and their intended uses specified along these lines. Debate ensued among the participants, primarily over whether a general set of specifications could be drawn up in the form of policies for all departmental assessment practice, or whether each and every assessment use required specification, with administrators arguing the former and teachers arguing the latter. This debate was resolved with a general agreement among participants that both overarching policies and specifications for each assessment practice were needed.

Based on this agreement, the remainder of the meeting was devoted to setting out exactly how assessment uses should be specified. First, committees were formed to tackle the specification process at each of the curricular levels, and an additional committee was charged with creating general policies for assessment and identifying any cross-curricular assessment uses. Second, I provided guidelines for informing the process of individual-group transactional negotiation, and materials were distributed that covered the basic components required of an intended use specification. Third, objectives and a timeline were set, and it was agreed by participants that draft specifications would be due from each committee by the semester-final meeting in May. Fourth, sources of information for the specification process were discussed, and I emphasized that the perspectives of all assessment users, including students, should be considered, and that potential consequences for all stakeholders, including particularly students, should also be considered.

Over the four weeks following this initial meeting, committees at each curricular level (I-IV) were charged with completing an initial specification of intended assessment use. Within each committee, a level coordinator organized the specification activities and sought to ensure input from all participants as well as achieve consensus on final documents. Participation was requested of all faculty teaching at the given curricular level, as well as any graduate teaching assistants or other graduate students with particular interests in that level. In general, committees pursued the following recommended course of action. First, they met as a group to review the current assessment practices that occurred within the given curricular level and to establish a time-line for further specification activities. Second, each group member individually reflected on these extant assessment practices, and drafted notes on an initial specification of intended uses for assessment at the given level, based on personal impressions of what was happening, what should not be happening, and what needed to happen in the name of assessment. Third, each committee met again, and all members shared their perspectives on intended uses for assessment at the given level. Committees were to finalize a working document for presentation at a follow-up workshop meeting in mid-May, 1999.

Simultaneous with this committee work at each curricular level, another committee pursued very similar procedures in formulating a specification of intended assessment use for curriculum-wide assessment practices and policies. This committee consisted of the PIUs, and it sought input from the assessment coordinators of each of the curricular level committees. The initial charge of this committee was to draft a general statement regarding assessment practices within the GUGD, covering broad goals, objectives, and principles that ostensibly applied to all assessments within the *Multiple Literacies* curriculum. In addition, and following the procedures described above, the committee identified any assessments that were to be applied across the entire undergraduate curriculum and drafted corresponding specifications of intended use for these assessments. Finally, they tentatively prioritized immediate needs in terms of the development of key assessment programs, instruments, and procedures.

In May, 1999, following this one-month period of committee-based work on specifying intended uses for assessment, another formal meeting and workshop was held with the full group of departmental teaching stakeholders. The aims of this half-day event were to (a) produce final working specifications of intended use covering all assessment practices in the GUGD, (b) finalize general assessment policies, and (c) identify and prioritize needed assessment development work for the immediate future. The meeting proceeded as follows, with an initial outcomes presentation phase, a subsequent workshop phase, and a final prioritization phase. First, as a means of further highlighting strengths and weaknesses in existing GUGD assessment practice, I presented general findings on student and teacher perceptions from a recently completed survey. The presentations then shifted to potential changes in assessment practices, as each curricular level committee presented the main points from their draft intended use specifications, followed by a brief question/comment period. A final presentation was then made by the curriculum-wide assessment committee on general policies and practices, again followed by a question/comment period. Throughout these presentations, participants were encouraged to note any issues or concerns, and to raise questions that they deemed particularly relevant to the finalization of their intended use specifications.

The second phase of the meeting involved a series of workshop activities designed to provoke further thought, provide feedback, and generally inform the revision and finalization of working specification documents. First, cross-curricular discussion groups were composed based on representation by individuals from each of the curricular-level committees, and these groups addressed any questions or concerns with the curriculum-wide assessment policies and practices document. Discussion ended with each group presenting their recommendations for improvement to this document. Next, in order to provide feedback to each curricular-level group, the level coordinator from each group led a discussion about the corresponding intended use specifications with the members of another level group, who offered their suggestions for improvement. Thus, the level I coordinator discussed that level's specifications with the level II group, and vice versa, while the level III and IV coordinators also discussed their specifications with each others' groups.

The final hour of the workshop was then devoted to identifying and prioritizing needed work on assessment development activities. Each curricular-level group first spent a few minutes discussing their primary needs, establishing a timeline for development, and distributing future responsibilities within the group. Subsequently, a full-group discussion sought to identify immediate needs in terms of developing cross-curricular assessment practices, based on those intended uses that had been specified by the cross-curricular committee. This discussion resulted in a clear consensus among those departmental stakeholders present, in the form of a list of priorities for developing particular assessment programs within the GUGD.

Findings. Given the multiple steps completed during this stage, numerous findings emerged in conjunction with each methodological iteration, as individuals and committees drafted, discussed, revised, presented, and re-drafted their specifications for the intended uses of assessment in the GUGD. Beyond this multitude of intermediate findings, three outcomes that had been targeted by PIUs emerged from the process: (a) specifications of intended uses for assessments at each curricular level, (b) general policy statements for all assessment practices in the GUGD, and (c) prioritized needs for assessment development.

Findings from the *curricular-level specifications* of intended assessment use produced an interesting overview of similarities and differences in assessment practices across the four targeted curricular levels (specifications are available on the curriculum web-site, *Developing Multiple Literacies*, 2003). Common to all levels was the

104

use of: (a) daily, weekly, or unit-end quizzes for providing focused feedback to teachers and learners on language and content learning targets; (b) assessment of class participation and homework as a means for motivating students to engage with instruction; (c) periodic formalized writing performances for checking and providing focused feedback on development of language/content knowledge and abilities as appropriate to valued genres; and (d) oral presentations, interviews, and other speaking tasks for checking and providing feedback on development of planned and extemporaneous speaking ability. Each of these assessment uses also provided a basis for the calculation of semester-final course grades, although their relative weighting varied from level to level.

Key differences in intended uses for assessment were found in several respects across the levels. First, greater importance was placed at the lower levels on the assessment of discrete knowledge about language elements, such as vocabulary and grammar rules, and the use of more traditional assessment formats for doing so, such as quizzes and final exams. Second, as curricular level increased, so did the role played by performance assessments in speaking and, in particular, in writing, and there was an increased emphasis on assessment being used to support instruction, especially through feedback to learners and to teachers about student development. Third, clear content distinctions at different curricular levels resulted in the incorporation of specific bodies of knowledge into assessment practices (e.g., the coverage of contemporary historical events in essay writing). Fourth, as curricular level increased, and especially at level IV and beyond, assessments adopted an explicitly individualized approach, in recognition of the distinct language use needs and academic/intellectual developmental trajectories of these very advanced students.

Finally, perhaps the most interesting and useful findings from these curricular-level specifications came in the form of questions and uncertainties about assessment. For one, considerable consternation was engendered at all levels due to the existence of assessment practices that could not be easily explained in terms of purposes, including, for example, daily quizzes and final exams. Associated discussions led to important awareness-raising outcomes among teachers, as well as to the revision of such practices. Furthermore, it was also pointed out repeatedly that existing formats for assessment did not match well the goals and objectives of the *Multiple Literacies* curriculum, specifically in terms of opportunities for assessing and providing explicit feedback on students' developing abilities to communicate about intellectual content for authentic (i.e., needs- and curriculum-based) purposes. Two other major concerns were (a) the lack of consistency and guidelines/criteria for scoring assessments and providing feedback to students, and (b) the lack of communication to both students and teachers regarding the specific intended uses for assessments.

Findings from the *general policy statements* on assessment (see Appendix A), which were drafted by the cross-curricular assessment committee and then revised and approved during the final specification workshop, revealed the basic values and uses for assessment within the GUGD, and they reflected many of the themes that had been raised by curricular-level committees. These policies outlined the principles upon which assessments at all levels, including classroom as well as cross-curricular assessments, were to be developed, implemented, and evaluated, and they were explicitly intended to communicate to teachers, students, and external parties that the GUGD attended to assessment in conjunction with other aspects of its educational efforts. The following points summarize in brief the initial assessment policies that were endorsed by the GUGD departmental stakeholders in May, 1999:

- All assessment focuses on students' abilities to use the language for communication.
- Students should have ample opportunity to develop and demonstrate the content, linguistic knowledge, and performance abilities reflected in classroom and cross-curricular assessments.
- Assessment tasks are gauged at the particular level of instruction (as determined by the curriculum) and reflect suitable expectations in terms of L2 acquisition.
- Assessments require clear scoring criteria that are communicated to and agreed upon by students and teachers.
- Assessments provide a clear rationale for the weighting of content and language performance elements in scoring, grading, and feedback.
- Students are made aware of the specific uses for assessment outcomes.
- The overall balanced development of accuracy, complexity, and fluency of L2 performance is emphasized within classroom assessment.
- Multiple assessment formats are required for addressing holistic as well as specific aspects of student learning.
- Assessment outcomes are conveyed to students and other score users in the form of rich and interpretable feedback in addition to simple grades or scores.
- Feedback and scores enable both criterion-referenced interpretations, in terms of instructional expectations, and individual-referenced interpretations, in terms of individual student needs and progress.
- Assessment and pedagogy emphasize the curriculum in similar ways, and one supports the other.
- Assessment reflects a balanced emphasis on communication modes (listening, speaking, reading, writing), as appropriate to a given course at a given curricular level.
- Target performance tasks serve as an organizing principle for both assessment and pedagogy.
- Teachers require training in the use and interpretation of assessment practices appropriate to curriculum and instruction.
- Teachers and administrators cooperate in developing, using, and revising assessments, and coordination of assessment is designated to particular individuals at each level of use (classroom, curricular-level, and cross-curricular).

These general assessment policy statements provided a potent and, critically, a consensus-driven basis for assessment practice in the GUGD, and they were to play a central role in subsequent development and evaluation activities.

Findings from *prioritization sessions* at the final specification meeting indicated key areas in need of immediate work, both within curricular levels and in terms of cross-curricular assessment practices. First, it was clear that, overall, considerable efforts were needed in order to bring all assessment practices in alignment with the content and task orientation of the new curriculum, and with the specific performance expectations for student learning outcomes that characterized each level. Second, at all levels, considerable concern was expressed regarding the consistency of grading and feedback practices from one classroom to the next, in particular with written and spoken performance assessments, and within-level guidelines and criteria to be followed by all teachers were targeted for immediate development. Third, much more explicit treatment and communication of the purposes, practices, and criteria were called for at all levels for four specific assessment types: (a) daily/weekly quizzes; (b) class participation; (c) oral assessments; and (d) final exams. Finally, generally improved communication with students about assessment was prioritized at all levels, and it was targeted to include general descriptions of assessment purposes and practices in the course syllabus, in-class discussions about various assessments and their uses, one-on-one advising sessions with students about their individual academic achievements, and the development of explicit documents to outline the expectations of each occasion of complex performance assessment use.

While stakeholders targeted these classroom-based assessment needs for attention over the next year of program development, they deemed cross-curricular assessment practices to be in need of much more immediate efforts. Major cross-curricular assessment programs and their intended uses included: (a) the assessment of student learning outcomes according to a curriculum-external test of German proficiency, both for program feedback/review and student certification purposes; (b) student proficiency assessment for fulfillment of the School of Foreign Service language requirement; (c) curriculum-based writing and speaking performance assessment at the culmination of each GUGD curricular level, for reviewing and improving the appropriateness of curricular expectations, for investigating the degree of comparability between non-intensive and intensive instructional tracks, and for recommending changes in pedagogic materials and activities; and (d) curriculum-based placement assessment for locating students within the newly restructured courses in order to best match their learning needs. Among these intended uses, the latter two were immediately identified within the prioritization session as those areas most in need of work. Little effort was required to negotiate a consensus in this respect, given near universal agreement that existing assessment practices could not meet new assessment demands, and that success of the *Multiple Literacies* curriculum depended in particular on these two assessment programs.

Despite the certain import attributed by departmental stakeholders to a cross-curricular performance assessment program, an even more immediate priority was identified during the meeting in the form of demands for a new curriculum-based placement exam. Widespread discontent had been expressed during stage-setting exercises (e.g., surveys), by both teachers and students, with the lack of alignment between the existing exam (developed several decades prior) and the new curriculum, as well as with the perceived inaccuracies of placement decisions based on it. In addition, it was pointed out that, given the large proportion of students within any given course who entered via a placement exam decision (80-100 students total per exam administration), the potential for a denigrated instructional and learning environment associated with mis-placements might contribute to worse than expected learning outcomes. As such, even before developing a semester-end performance assessment program, it seemed crucial to stakeholders that a new placement assessment program be developed and implemented.

In order to confirm this priority status of a new placement exam over other assessment needs, I queried departmental stakeholders extensively during the prioritization session regarding the potential for revising the existing exam or for incorporating other means of placement decision making. Indeed, the original invitation for my participation by the GUGD had focused on the need for developing and implementing task-based performance assessments (e.g., Norris, Brown, Hudson, & Yoshioka, 1998), but not on other assessment uses. However, stakeholders' responses made clear that the primary perceived assessment practice in need of attention at that time was a systematic means for placing students into the carefully planned and sequenced levels of the new curriculum.

Given wide-spread agreement that the most immediate prioritized assessment need of the GUGD was the development of an entirely new, curriculum-based placement exam, the initial draft specification of intended use for this assessment warrants closer scrutiny (see Appendix B for extended draft). The *general assessment description* emphasized several primary features that were to characterize the GUGD placement exam. The fundamental purpose of the exam was to locate incoming undergraduate students into the most appropriate of four curricular levels based on similarities between their language abilities and those of other students at that level. Language ability was to be *estimated* on the basis of multiple sources of information, and this estimate was to be directly linked with curricular expectations through instruments which tapped the "tasks, texts, and criteria" objectives associated with each level. More specifically, the following assessment-use components (cf. Figure 3 above) fleshed out the details of the new placement program.

1. *Who are the assessment users?* The main users of the placement exam were identified as the GUGD constituents (chair, faculty, instructors, graduate teaching assistants), who sought to ensure an acceptable level of homogeneity in students' language abilities within any given undergraduate course, and who took full responsibility for all aspects of the placement program. Additional users included other departments at the institution, who awarded credit hours or language requirement exemptions based on the placement exam results, and students, who sought exemption from further language study or who sought entry into German courses.

2. *What information is needed to inform interpretations?* Assessment was to provide a basic indication of German language abilities in terms of the expectations of the curricular levels and distinctions among the various levels, and it needed to do so within a relatively short period of time, including a maximum of two hours for gathering information and one day for making and disseminating placement decisions. In addition, content knowledge was explicitly not included in the information to be provided; it was deemed unreasonable to 'reward' or 'penalize' students by basing placement decisions on anything other than language abilities that they had already acquired. Various potential sources of information were proposed as likely candidates for the placement exam, including background information on students' German language learning, scores on other recognized German-language proficiency and achievement exams, and, in particular, curriculum-specific indicators of textual processing, task performance, and related abilities.

3. *What is the purpose of the assessment; how is assessment information used?* Principally, the placement exam was intended be used in adjudicating a recommended curricular-level enrollment for each incoming student, in order to ensure that students were placed into courses appropriate to their German language abilities, to award credit hours for prior learning, and to exempt students from further German language study (where needed). From the point of view of the GUGD, it was hoped that these recommendations would enable the language learning needs of both incoming and advancing students to be most efficiently and effectively addressed within a course, and to enable curricular/instructional focus and planning within courses and at each curricular level. In addition, the mere existence of a curriculum-based, versus a generic or commercial, placement exam was intended to communicate (within the department, to the institution, and beyond) that both students' prior language abilities and the scope and sequence of the curriculum were taken very seriously by the GUGD.

4. *Who or what is impacted by assessment consequences and in what ways?* Finally, numerous possible consequences were identified for various stakeholders. Overall, the curriculum-based placement exam was intended to enable effective teaching and learning in GUGD courses, as well as to encourage awareness of the careful curricular sequence and the need to match students' language abilities to its expectations. For students, intended positive consequences included satisfaction, recognition of prior learning, and academic/language learning success, and negative consequences to be avoided included perceptions of disjuncture between their abilities and instruction, low motivation and boredom, overwhelming learning and performance expectations, and less than expected academic achievement. For the GUGD, consequences focused on both administrative issues, such as impact on enrollment numbers in courses across the curricular levels, the resource demands of using the exam itself, and dealing with inaccurate placements, and on teaching and curriculum issues, including adaptation of instruction to the actual

needs of students placed into courses, the effectiveness of the curricular sequence, and the reputation of the new approach to German instruction.

The specification of intended assessment use also highlighted several questions and constraints for the development of a new curriculum-based placement exam. Chief among these were uncertainties regarding: (a) the specific mechanisms whereby assessment information could be gathered, adjudicated, and disseminated, and via which placement decisions could be enforced; (b) the feasibility of particular assessment techniques that were implied by curricular expectations (e.g., task-based performance assessments), and which among these would prove most directly representative of curricular-level distinctions; (c) the effectiveness, reliability, and perceived appropriateness of assessment instruments and procedures that were feasible within the time and resource constraints of the exam setting; (d) and the extent to which a full-blown placement assessment program could be operationalized within the minimal time available for development (approximately one month). Regarding these last two points, the PIUs verified that language placement exams had to occur within an immutable amount of time, as determined by the university administration, and that a new exam was required for the fall 1999 semester.

Uses. These initial findings were shared among departmental stakeholders who participated in the final specification meeting in May, 1999, and they were also disseminated in written form to all teaching and administrative stakeholders during the following month. Overall, the general assessment policy statements, the specifications of intended uses for assessment within each curricular level, and the specifications for particular cross-curricular assessment uses, served an explicit function as the initial, formalized awareness-raising and consensus-building stages of assessment programs within the GUGD. Furthermore, their development via bottom-up processes, which emphasized participation by all departmental teaching stakeholders, indicated clearly the ownership of, and responsibility for, assessment practices by all educators within the educational context. Finally, through intensive reflection, discussion, and articulation of assessment practices, local educators came to understand not only the importance of attending to the educational functions of assessment in intentional ways, but also the key linkage between uses for assessment and the design of instruments and procedures to meet these uses, and the need to evaluate assessment use according to these specified purposes and qualities. As such, these initial specification and policy efforts served as a touchstone for all assessment considerations, and they were revisited periodically as a heuristic for continual reflection on and improvement of the GUGD's educational assessment efforts.

The specification of intended uses also made clear to departmental stakeholders that considerable changes had to be undertaken in order to bring assessment practices in line with their uses. In concrete terms, this realization was translated into the elimination of a number of practices, including classroom-based activities that had not served any apparent purposes beyond contributing to student grading. In addition, some existing instruments and procedures were modified in order to align them

110

with intended uses, as well as curricular emphases, and this adaptation applied particularly to the writing and speaking performance assessments within and across curricular levels. Finally, as outlined above, other brand new assessment practices were identified for full-scale development, in response to heretofore nonexistent use specifications and, simultaneously, very real existing impetuses to assess.

Of more immediate concern, intended use specifications provided a mandate for assessment development, and they outlined the minimal qualities that would have to be met in order for an assessment program to accomplish what it was intended to accomplish. Similarly, these same specified qualities that were used for developing assessments were also employed as the foundation for subsequent validity evaluation activities. In terms of the prioritized placement exam, the specification of intended uses thus played a key role in directing validity evaluation questions, methods, and uses as it was developed, implemented, revised, and established as a sustained educational assessment program in the GUGD.

6.1.2 Developing a curriculum-based placement assessment program

A pilot version of the placement assessment program was developed through intensive work by a handful of individuals over the course of a few months during the summer of 1999. Primary intended users of evaluation efforts at this stage included me (the evaluation consultant), the department chair, the curriculum developer, and a graduate research assistant assigned to work directly on all test development activities. This core group of intended users acted jointly in utilizing outcomes of the various development efforts to make final decisions on the composition of the placement exam, how it should be pilot-tested, the setting of initial placement standards, and the completion of a final operational version of the exam for use by August, 1999. In addition, several other departmental constituents participated at various points during this development stage, as described below.

Initial efforts during this stage were directed at surveying, identifying, and narrowing down the range of possible assessment instruments and procedures which would most feasibly inform placement exam uses within the time and resource constraints of the administration setting. Two basic strategies were pursued in this regard. First, in order to identify a domain of possible assessment instruments and procedures for meeting the intended uses, PIUs reviewed a range of assessment types with precedented use as placement tests in language programs, including: (a) written and oral performance assessments (e.g., Fulcher, 1997; McNamara, 1996); (b) selected-response tests of vocabulary, collocation, and grammatical knowledge (e.g., Brown, 1989; Schmitt, 1999); (c) integrated-skills tests based on target language use tasks (e.g., Norton, 2000; van den Branden, DePauw, & Gysen, 2002); (d) reduced redundancy measures of L2 proficiency, such as dictation and cloze tests (e.g., Brown, 1981, 1984, 1989, 1993); (e) multiple-choice listening and reading comprehension passages (e.g., Lynch, 1996); and (f) self-assessments of 'can-do' language use statements (e.g., Heilenman, 1991). Available evidence supported the *potential* contribution of each of these alternatives to efficient and accurate placement decision-making.

The second part of this initial narrowing strategy took an explicitly curriculum-based approach. Four representative curricular experts, one each for levels I-IV, were recruited from among GUGD teachers to identify the key features of learner language development that would best distinguish between students at proximate curricular levels. These experts were first asked to provide a brief description of the language knowledge and abilities they thought best characterized a student at the beginning versus the end of the particular level of the curriculum at which they taught. In addition, experts then responded to a questionnaire that consisted of a list of the task, text, and performance types within curriculum documents that formed criterial language use expectations for the end of each of the first three curricular levels; for each item, they provided an estimate of whether or not a student completing their curricular level would be able to meet the language use expectation as described.

Based on information from these two background strategies, the PIUs met and debated which assessment components would best meet placement decision-making needs. At its most basic, the placement decision to be informed was the simple location of a student into one of four available curricular levels, and placement exam information was not intended to inform additional uses (e.g., diagnosis, achievement). Also critical in the choice of appropriate assessment components was the fixed nature of administration and use constraints (mandated by the institution and immutable): (a) the entire exam could last no more than two hours; (b) scores were needed within a very short amount of time, in order to inform decisions and reporting to various interested parties, including students; (c) facilities for administration were not conducive to interactive tasks, audio recording of examinee speech, etc.; and (d) many students would have to be assessed, and their placements decided, within one administration session. After considering the array of possible assessment types, the local experts' recommendations of language abilities that best distinguished among students at the four curricular levels, and these clear constraints, the primary intended users agreed in the end on the development of a listening comprehension test (LCT), a reading comprehension test (RCT), and a C-test as the sub-test components for the new GUGD placement exam (as detailed below), and they also decided to collect background information from examinees about their language learning and use experiences (not addressed in detail here).

In brief, these three sub-test types were all to be based on the selection of texts that represented students' abilities to *process* German language as used in expected ways at the four curricular levels. The LCT and RCT were to be comprised of several such texts each, in conjunction with multiple-choice items that tapped students' abilities to understand details and main ideas in the texts, as well as their abilities to make inferences based on the meaning communicated therein. The C-test presented a constructed-response option for assessing textual processing abilities, and as such it extended examinee performances beyond textual comprehension. C-tests function on the principle of reduced redundancy testing (Klein-Braley, 1985), much like cloze and dictation tests, and as such, they are frequently interpreted as indicators of general language proficiency among literate learner populations (e.g., Grotjahn, 1992a; Klein-Braley, 1997). The basic format of a C-test (for Germanic or Romance languages) requires examinees to complete the second half of words which have been deleted at regular intervals throughout a graduated series of otherwise intact texts that are each around a paragraph in length. The following is an example of what a sentence from one C-test text might look like:

This i___ an exa___ sentence fr___ such a___ exam.

As examinees complete the words, they recreate a meaningful text. However, in order to do so, they obviously have to know both the deleted words and the surrounding words, they have to understand the meaning conveyed by sentences within the text, and they have to understand the grammatical relationships expressed between particular words and between sentences.

Several features of these assessment types, and especially the C-test, spoke in favor of their use within the GUGD. First, it was clear that short-cut *estimates* of language knowledge/ability would be required in order to gather sufficient information across a broad student ability spectrum within a limited amount of testing time. While spoken and written performance assessments might have most thoroughly represented the kinds of learning fostered by the curriculum (Byrnes, 2002), the elicitation and scoring of curriculum-relevant performance tasks would have exceeded considerably the time and resources available for testing and decision making. By contrast, a wide range of curriculum-relevant examinee ability levels could be elicited and scored within a short amount of time on both the comprehension tests and the C-test.

Second, the primary intended users agreed with the local curricular-level experts' recommendation that students' abilities to process a variety of texts provided the most direct indication of differences between curricular levels I-IV, given the explicit literacy focus of the *Multiple Literacies* curriculum. As such, and in accord with the intended use specification for the placement assessment program, the placement sub-tests were to be explicitly *curriculum-based* (Nitko, 1995, 2001), in that test content was to be derived directly from texts representing each curricular level. Thus, specific texts representing students' processing abilities at each of the curricular levels could be sampled into the three tests, with the LCT and RCT providing an indication of students' comprehension of textual meaning in both the aural and written modalities. In addition to such discourse-level comprehension, the C-test would also call upon textual micro-processing abilities, including knowledge of lexical, syntactic, and morphological features of German (Grotjahn, 1996). Finally, the previous success of comprehension tests (e.g., Brown, 1989; Brown & Hudson, 2002; Lynch, 1996) and C-tests (e.g., Bolton, 1992; Jakschik, 1994) for placement purposes in language programs spoke in favor of their potential utility in the GUGD context. The widespread use of C-tests for language placement testing of international students in German universities provided a further degree of authenticity to their implementation in the GUGD, the curricular objectives of which were closely articulated with the development of students' abilities to function in just such language-use environments.

The following concerns of the PIUs motivated the methods pursued in developing these main components of the placement assessment program:

(a) What kinds of texts should be sampled into each of the three sub-tests?
(b) How should examinee responses be elicited on each of the three sub-tests?
(c) How will total scores on each of the three sub-tests be interpreted?
(d) How will final placement decisions be made using the sub-test scores?

Based on empirical evidence gathered in response to these questions, the PIUs sought to construct final operational versions of the placement exam sub-tests, procedures for their administration and scoring, and initial standards for using assessment results to engage in placement decision-making practices.

Methods. Development methods were broken down into three steps: (a) text selection; (b) item writing and test preparation; and (c) pilot-testing (see Appendix C for detailed guidelines for developing the C-test). At each of these steps in development, methods were employed to provide an adequate empirical basis for use by the PIUs in determining the final operational version of the GUGD placement assessment program. Methods followed in the first two steps are reported in some detail here, while pilot-testing procedures are only summarized, as the same methods receive considerable attention in the following section (6.2), which reports on evaluative efforts undertaken during the initial placement implementation stage.

The key problem in developing the LCT, RCT, and C-test sub-tests addressed how *text selection* should proceed, such that individual texts would adequately represent the domain and range of textual processing abilities related to the sequenced GUGD curricular levels. For each sub-test, it was assumed that particular text types could be identified which represented particular curricular levels, and that students who were best matched with a given curricular level would be largely able to engage with the corresponding texts, as well as texts representing lower levels, but not as able to engage with texts representing higher levels. However, at issue was the basis for identifying such texts in the first place, and existing procedures for estimating 'text difficulty' offered little in the way of the close curricular relevance that was being sought.

Thus, for example, in developing C-tests as indicators of 'global L2 competence' (e.g., Connelly, 1997) or 'general language proficiency' (Klein-Braley, 1997), texts have typically been selected to represent authentic, random samples of the general types of language that L2 users encounter, and their difficulty has been estimated intuitively by test developers (Baur & Meder, 1994; Bolton, 1992; Grotjahn, 1992a; Grotjahn, Klein-Braley, & Raatz, 1992; Klein-Braley, 1997). However, in these contexts, researchers have also frequently observed a truncated range of scores and a lack of variance among intermediate and advanced learners (e.g., Grotjahn, 1987, 1992a, 1992b; Huhta, 1996; Köberl & Sigott, 1994), due to a lack of actual 'difficulty' differences between texts. Clearly, in order for the C-test, and the LCT and RCT for that matter, to provide information leading to trustworthy distinctions among learners across multiple levels of ability, *as defined by GUGD curricular differences*, test instruments would have to both elicit a wide range of scores and enable reliable distinctions among learners across this entire score range.

For the GUGD placement exam, it was decided that the texts comprising each of the LCT, RCT, and C-test sub-tests should be purposefully selected to represent the three junctures within the sequenced curriculum where placement decisions needed to be made (i.e., the transition points from level I to II, II to III, and III to IV). Rather than random selection of and intuitive distinctions among texts, the underlying structure of the *Multiple Literacies* curriculum was tapped in order to motivate the identification and selection of texts which would be most likely to differentiate among GUGD students in relevant ways. Therefore, local curricular expertise was sought as the basis for this text selection process from individuals who had participated in the *Multiple Literacies* curriculum and instruction development project. A single expert was recruited to represent each curricular level (from I-IV), based on their understanding of the curricular expectations associated with the given level, as well as substantial experience in teaching courses at that level. In meeting these basic criteria, the selected local experts were considered by the PIUs to fulfill all of the desired qualities of participants in assessment standard-setting efforts, as outlined in Raymond and Reid (2001), including: (a) subject matter expertise, (b) understanding of examinee population, (c) ability to estimate item difficulty, (d) knowledge of instructional environment, (e) appreciation of consequences of standards, and (f) representation of communities of interest.

In order to access systematically these local experts' insights, a basic methodology was drawn from traditions of assessment standard setting which rely on expert judgments in the estimation of students' abilities to perform on different assessment items, tasks, content, etc. (e.g., Angoff, 1971; see also discussion in Loomis & Borque, 2001; Mitzel, Lewis, Patz, & Green, 2001; Zieky, 2001). Therefore, placement exam content, in the form of texts representing the distinct GUGD curricular levels, was determined on the basis of judgments about the likelihood that students completing a given curricular level would be able to process the language within a given set of texts, as follows.

First, level I-III experts individually identified for each sub-test at least three specific texts which they found representative of the kinds of texts that learners at their given level, by and large, should be able to understand and process by the *end* of that level. The Level IV expert made selections that were representative of the kinds of texts that students in the "Text in Context" course should be able to process both upon entering as well as upon completing that course, as a means for 'bracketing' the upper-most processing abilities expected of incoming students. Texts at all levels were selected from a variety of materials related to the content focus of each (newspapers, magazines, novels, stories, radio and television broadcasts, travel guides, fairy tales, public speeches, debates, etc.), and they were left intact (at this point). Overly technical, bizarre, or infrequent texts were avoided (i.e., texts that students would be unlikely to encounter in the day-to-day instruction of the level's courses, even if the language demands seemed appropriate). For the LCT, selections were to include dialogic as well as monologic aural texts of no longer than three minutes duration; for the RCT, coherent multi-paragraph texts were sought; and for the C-test, texts were each to consist of a single paragraph of between 75 and 100 words, the overall meaning of which could be clearly understood without additional supporting material.

Level experts then met to narrow down the overall text pool for constructing subtests. In this meeting, participants reviewed the texts level by level, working from the level I texts upwards. For each proposed text, participants decided whether it seemed appropriate as a representative text for the end of the given level. In other words, participants asked themselves whether they agreed that students completing the second semester of the given level would largely be able to understand and process the text in question while students at lower curricular levels (or beginners, in the case of level I) would be considerably less able to do so. In addition, from among the candidate texts, each participant decided which one or two texts seemed the most appropriate and representative for each level (on each sub-test). Through group discussion about the candidate texts and the favored texts, participants were able to agree upon a final set of texts to be developed into the three pilot placement exam sub-tests: (a) three texts for the LCT, including a dialogue representing level I, a story narration representing level II, and a public service announcement for level III; (b) four texts for the RCT, including two personal narratives for levels I-II, a mass-media report for level III, and a historical essay for level III-IV; and (c) seven texts covering a variety of content areas for the C-test, with one text representing level I, and two texts each for levels II-IV. While more pilot texts would have been preferable (Grotjahn, 1987), available pilot-testing time was limited and the level experts expressed considerable confidence in their selections.

Following text selection, in the *item-writing* and *test preparation* development step, items were drafted, materials and test instructions were assembled, and pilot versions of each test were compiled. For the LCT, in order to gather information about students' abilities as efficiently as possible, it was decided that students would be provided only one listening of each text, no note-taking would be allowed, and ten multiple-choice items would query a balance of main ideas, details, and inferences from each of the texts (for a total of 30 LCT items). Each item included one correct response and three distractor responses, and the four options were randomly assigned a letter from (a) through (d) (to facilitate machine scoring). All item stems and response options were presented in German, and students were allowed sufficient time to read through and respond to the set of items that followed each of the three listening texts—these times were estimated on the basis of an informal pilot test conducted with several volunteers in the GUGD. A script was drafted for the entire LCT, including test instructions to the examinees, the three texts (ordered from lowest to highest represented curricular level), and pauses for completion of items in between, and a master audio-recording was made, using L1-German speakers for voices within each text. Lastly, an examinee LCT booklet was constructed such that examinees would not be able to see the items for a given text until after listening to it, thereby ensuring that examinees would all engage in the same manner of performance on the test (i.e., first listening, then attempting to answer questions).

Test development proceeded along similar lines for the RCT, although with several differences. For the initial level I and II texts, two personal narratives (one paragraph each) had been selected, and multiple-choice items first queried main ideas and details following each text. Subsequently, the same two texts were presented together, and inferences were sought through items which compared the information within each of these two texts. A total of 20 items was created for the texts from these initial two levels. In addition, several glosses were provided for slang terminology where it was deemed beyond the knowledge of level I and II students in the GUGD. For the level III text (three paragraphs), ten multiple-choice items queried main ideas, details, and inferences based on the text, and the same format held for the level III-IV text, for a total of 40 items on the RCT. This last component of the RCT, a particularly difficult and dense text, had been included at the behest of curricular-level experts, as a means of ensuring that they had not underestimated students' curricular-level reading abilities in their choice of the other texts. An RCT test booklet compiled texts and items with instructions to examinees.

Finally, for the C-test, texts and items were prepared following standard recommendations (Grotjahn, 1987), with a few accommodations to the GUGD context (see Appendix C). For each text, the first one or two sentences, as well as the final sentence, were left intact, in order to provide sufficient semantic context for initial processing of the text. Beginning with the second word of the second or third sentence, the second half of each second word was deleted (replacing the letters with a single blank, _____), until 25 deletions had been made. For words with odd numbers of letters, the second half of the word plus one letter was deleted. For compound words, only the second half of the second word in the compound was deleted (e.g., Wirtschaftssys_____, not Wirtscha_____), following Grotjahn (1987); however, this policy was not applied to simple prepositional compounds (e.g., dadurch became dad_____, not dadu_____). Numbers and dates written numerically were not mutilated, nor were acronyms. While these deletion rules were followed as closely as possible, care was also taken during review by the PIUs that deletions reasonably reflected the level of processing difficulty that each text was intended to represent. In several circumstances (e.g., repeated deletion of the same two- or three-letter word in a single text), slight adjustments in the text (adding or removing a word) were deemed by PIUs to result in a more accurate reflection of the curricular expectations.

Given the unfamiliar nature of the C-test for U.S. students, thorough written instructions were provided at the beginning of the C-test. Instructions: (a) explained the kind of responses expected from examinees; (b) provided a clear example in basic German that would be understood by all examinees; (c) clarified the number of letters expected in responses (half or half+one); (d) explained the exception for compound words; (e) emphasized the role played by spelling; (f) enumerated how many texts there were to complete; and (g) indicated how much time examinees had to complete all of the texts (five minutes per text). Texts were arranged in order of difficulty (beginning with the level I text) and labeled "Text 1" through "Text 7". All item response blanks were kept uniform in length. Although examinees were instructed that each response required a specific number of letters, it was hoped that by providing a single underscored blank (instead of individual blanks per letter) students would concentrate on what response made the most sense, rather than on letter counting.

Upon completing the basic development of these three sub-test forms, items, and materials, as well as overall directions for assessment administration, *pilot-testing* activities were undertaken. The pilot placement exam was administered to 30 GUGD study abroad program students in Trier, Germany, during the summer semester prior to initial operational use in August, 1999. These students were selected as the only available group of examinees who reflected, more or less accurately, the likely German abilities of students across the curricular levels at which decisions needed to be made. Although study abroad courses paralleled the *Multiple Literacies* curriculum in terms of content and instructional techniques, they focused in particular on more advanced levels of language study; thus, pilot participants represented students entering only into curricular levels II-IV, with most at III and IV. Furthermore, the pilot exam was administered at the end of a semester of study abroad instruction, to ensure comparability with specific curricular junctures (i.e., administration in the middle of the semester would not have provided much useful information for determining what students can do when they are deemed ready to advance into the next curricular level). In addition to the study abroad learners, four L1-German graduate students completed the pilot placement exam, in order to identify any problematic texts or items in terms of standards of German language use. The pilot placement exam was administered under similar conditions to those expected for the operational assessment, with instructions read aloud to students, time limits placed on the completion of each sub-test, and identification information collected from each participant. Participants were informed that they were assisting the GUGD in an on-going research project, and their consent was secured accordingly, but they did not know that the tests would constitute the new placement exam.

Outcomes from the pilot administration of the placement exam were analyzed for a range of qualities, in order to provide an empirical basis for immediate revisions to tests, items, materials, and directions for use. Besides suggestions for revision from the pilot-test administrator and the L1-German participants on exam formatting and content details, analyses included: (a) descriptive statistics; (b) item quality statistics (item discrimination and facility, item-total correlations, item error and fit estimates); (c) correlations between the three sub-tests; (d) test score reliability estimates; (e) test score standard error estimates; and (f) between-groups comparisons of scores for students at each of the study abroad curricular levels.

Findings. In addition to the assessment products that resulted from empirical development methods, outcomes of pilot-testing activities provided empirical clarification of the extent to which assessment texts and items, as well as administration materials and procedures, would provide trustworthy information in the form of test scores that could be used to meet placement decision-making needs. Pilot-test findings are only summarized very briefly here, for space considerations and due to the reporting of similar analyses on much larger samples of examinees in section 6.2 below.

Pilot-test administrators reported that, overall, administration instructions were clear, examinees understood what was expected of them and engaged readily with the three sub-tests, and that assessment materials functioned as intended with no apparent problems, including the LCT audio-recording. However, they pointed out that no instructions had been included for collecting all test materials, such as test booklets, in addition to examinee response sheets (although they had the presence of mind to do so), an important consideration for security purposes. In addition, they noted that time allowed for the completion of LCT items in response to each of the three aural texts was more than ample, while examinees had requested extra time to complete items for the final texts on both the RCT and C-test. Further feedback from the L1-German students provided key input in several areas. First, throughout all three sub-tests, they observed that recent German spelling reforms had not been attended to, and they suggested exact revisions accordingly. Second, they commented on substantive inaccuracies in several of the texts, given recent historical events (e.g., the timing of the introduction of the Euro as the European Union's common monetary unit). Finally, they pointed out that several of the C-test items could be completed feasibly and correctly with more than one response.

Basic test and item analyses from pilot-testing provided important findings as well. For the LCT, item analyses indicated that all 30 items were functioning within acceptable ranges in terms of facility, discrimination, and fit/error indices, although, due to the imbalance of higher level examinees, items tended towards the easy end of the facility scale. In addition, the average item facility value for the level I text exceeded that found for the level II text, which in turn exceeded that found for the level III text; this finding provided some support for the accuracy of the curriculum-based text-selection procedure. A relatively wide and normal distribution of total scores was found (mean = 20.47, standard deviation = 5.07), but the mean score fell above the mid-point of possible scores, again likely due to the examinee population characteristics. Given the truncated nature and low number of the examinee sample, a Cronbach alpha reliability estimate of 0.85 was interpreted to indicate relatively consistent total test scores based on the full set of 30 LCT items, and the standard error associated with any given score was estimated at plus or minus 2 score points.

For the RCT, item analyses indicated generally acceptable levels of facility, discrimination, and fit/error estimates for items associated with texts at curricular levels I-III; however, very low item facility indices were found for the ten items associated with the final level IV text, indicating that very few of the pilot examinees were able to process this text from the upper curricular levels. In addition, one item from among the first 30 was found to have a negative discrimination index. After removal of this item and the level IV text items, the score distribution for the RCT closely resembled that of the LCT (mean = 19.54, standard deviation = 4.63), and a Cronbach alpha reliability estimate of 0.83 was interpreted to indicated relatively consistent total test scores on the basis of the now 29-item RCT. As with the LCT, average item facility indices were found to decrease, as expected, with increasing curricular level of the associated text. The same amount of standard error was also found at plus or minus 2 score points for any given RCT score.

For the C-test, each text was treated as a single 25-point item for analysis purposes (see discussion in 6.2). Five of the seven texts were found to have high correlations with total test scores, high fit and low error statistics, and average scores reflecting the order intended by text selection—in other words, students' average scores decreased with increasing curricular levels the texts were assumed to represent. However, inconsistencies were found for student performances on the remaining two texts. On the first, a curricular level III text, low item-total correlations and higher error rates suggested that the difficulty of completing the deleted words ranged considerably, yet in unpredictable ways, for the pilot students, and that the text was not providing a consistent indication of their abilities. On the second, a level IV text, all pilot examinees (including the most advanced) scored very low; therefore, the text did not contribute additional score information at the range in which placement decisions needed to be made. Based on the set of five well-functioning texts (including one each from levels I, III, and IV, and two from level II), total test scores produced a high reliability estimate (alpha = 0.91) and a wide distribution of scores (mean = 81.67, standard deviation = 18.53) centered towards the top half of the total point range (125 points for the five texts). Standard error was estimated at plus or minus 5 score points for any given score.

Pearson product-moment correlation coefficients ranged from 0.71 to 0.81 among the total scores on the three sub-tests, indicating that most examinees performed at similar levels of success on each test, but not all. Furthermore, the distribution of total scores on each sub-test for examinees at each curricular level indicated substantial variability within a given level in terms of student performances, based on the small sample of examinees from each level (1 entering level II, 7 at level III, 6 at level IV, and 13 at level V). Accordingly, average test scores for students at each curricular level were interpreted to provide only a very tentative indication of the expected range of scores for students under operational assessment conditions.

Uses. The overarching purpose of activities at this program development stage was to produce assessment instruments and procedures which would fulfill the basic needs for placement decision-making as outlined in the specification of intended assessment use. Obviously, a major objective was accomplished through the products of development activities. More critically, by grounding the entire process in local expertise about the curriculum and the characteristics that local experts thought would best distinguish between its different levels, development outcomes provided for a uniquely curriculum-based response to placement decision-making needs.

At the same time, the assessment instruments and procedures that were pilot-tested with study abroad students represented only a 'bare-bones' response to the placement exam specification, and several additional uses had to be made of empirical development findings in order to bring an operational version of the placement assessment program to fruition in time for the initial official administration of the exam in August, 1999.

First, the PIUs revised and compiled final versions of each of the three sub-tests, their items, associated materials, and test administration instructions. For the LCT, this final version looked very much like the carefully developed pilot test, with aural texts and corresponding items left intact. It was decided that time available for responding to items after each text should be left the same as well, given the likelihood of lower-ability examinees (i.e., who would require more time, ostensibly) in actual placement exam administrations (approximately 20 minutes total audio-tape controlled time). For the RCT, the final level IV text and items were removed, as was the negative-discriminating item, and the remaining 29 test items comprised the full test. Revisions for spelling were made to all reading passages and items, and total test time was left the same (35 minutes), as the removal of the final passage and items was interpreted to resolve timing concerns.

For the C-test, the two poorly functioning texts were removed, and all remaining texts (as well as response blanks) were adjusted according to German spelling reforms and other features identified by L1-German informants. The final test version thus consisted of five texts, ordered from lowest to highest curricular level represented, such that lower ability examinees would not be discouraged too early. Each level was represented by one text, with the exception of two at level II; it was decided that these two should both remain, given their appropriate qualities in pilot-testing, the assumption that decisions associated with level II would be particularly important (due to the unique expectations of the curriculum at that level and beyond), and in order to 'test' the assumption that these and the other texts in fact represented the curricular levels that they were assumed to represent. Total points on the C-test were set at 125, with each text contributing 25 possible points. A total of 25 minutes was provided for completing the C-test.

Explicit and detailed administration instructions were also compiled in order to ensure consistency and security across exam administration settings. These instructions outlined the range of materials necessary for administering the three sub-tests (and the background information form that was to be included in operational testing), and they gave careful instructions on how to copy and compile test booklets. Procedural guidelines were then provided for checking equipment, seating examinees, and distributing and collecting materials. The order of sub-test administration was set as C-test, LCT, RCT, to facilitate the scoring of the C-test, and the timing of each was explained. Finally, oral instructions to be read aloud were spelled out, as well as steps to take in collecting all test response sheets and booklets, and what to do with these following the exam.

Second, beyond final test forms and related details, the PIUs and I put in place the procedures by which examinee responses to each test would be scored and total test scores interpreted. For LCT and RCT multiple-choice responses, machine scoring had been targeted for efficiency purposes. Accordingly, response keys were created for each, and procedures were established for the secure delivery and retrieval of score sheets and examinee score information. For the C-test, with hand-written constructed responses, it was decided that GUGD faculty would be responsible for scoring the exams. A C-test response key was developed based on exact-response scoring, with the exception of a few items where more than one word could feasibly complete the stem. In addition, faculty scorers were to be reminded that 'exactly correct responses' meant that spelling had to be exact as well. Scorers were to mark all incorrect items, tally total correct for each text, and then sum a total correct score for the examinee.

A basic score interpretation strategy was adopted by focusing on the total test score for each sub-test. While this strategy assumed that individual texts and their associated items would contribute very consistent and relatively equivalent types of information regarding examinee abilities—and indeed, that the text-selection approach and item writing had resulted in linearly related ability demands across the texts—initial findings from pilot-test score distributions and reliability estimates suggested that the constellation of texts and items on each sub-test did approximate a consistent set of increasing demands in conjunction with increasing curricular levels represented. As such, the PIUs agreed that total scores for each sub-test would be interpreted to approximate the curricular ability level at which students could process texts.

Finally, the PIUs developed procedures for adjudicating placement recommendations based on the information that would be provided by the three sub-test scores. Clearly, given the unique language learning experiences that students brought with them into the GUGD, there was a high likelihood of differential performances on each sub-test corresponding to the differential processing abilities required (aural receptive, written receptive, written productive). In addition, moderate correlations between test scores had indicated that at least some pilot students performed at differing levels of success on the three sub-tests. Finally, for each sub-test score range, a set of cut-scores would be called upon to link each test performance with an estimate of the appropriate curricular level for student placement. In order to deal with potential discrepancies among sub-test scores, and to translate scores into final placement decisions, the PIUs sought an approach that would meet decision-making needs with both efficiency and accuracy, and which would draw upon existing empirical data from the pilot-test performances of representative students.

First, in order to select cut-score standards for each of the three placement sub-tests, performance data from the pilot administration of the three sub-tests were used to inform a *contrasting groups method* (e.g., Livingston & Zieky, 1982; see also discussion in Brown, 1996; Zieky, 2001), via which expected performance levels (in the form of sub-test scores) were established for the groups of examinees representing each curricular level. Thus, for each sub-test, test-specific cut-score bands were identified by estimating the average performances for students at each level of the curriculum (I – IV), based on the pilot-test performance data. Given the predominance of pilot examinees at levels IV and V of the curriculum (i.e., students at the point of *entering* into these levels), cut-scores were set from the top of the score scale first. Thus, the initial cut-score was set for the decision to place a student into level IV, that is, the highest placement level. This score was identified for each sub-test according to two criteria: (a) no level V pilot examinee had scored below it; and (b) the average score for pilot students at the level IV juncture fell as closely as possible to it. It was decided that the average score for students at the given level, rather than the low score, would provide a more conservative estimate of the bottom range of abilities, due principally to the brief amount of instruction that students received during the study abroad experience (i.e., the PIUs did not trust the average score of these students to reflect more than a minimal level of performance). Subsequently, moving down the score scale for each sub-test, the same basic criteria were used to set the cut-score for placing into level III and into level II of the curriculum. As a result, the three required placement decision cut-score bands were drafted (i.e., for three possible decision junctures: level I/level II, level II/level III, level III/level IV). For decisions about placement into either the first or second semester of instruction at a given curricular level, only the C-test was deemed to provide sufficiently consistent differentiation. For these decisions, the midpoint between two cut-scores was selected as the basis for semester distinctions. Table 2 shows the initial cut-score bands for each sub-test.

Table 2. Cut-score bands for 1999 GUGD placement exam

Placement level	LCT	RCT	C-Test
1.1	0-5	0-5	0-20
1.2			21-39
2.1	6-10	6-10	40-48
2.2			49-55
3.1	11-19	11-19	56-67
3.2			68-79
4	20-30	20-29	80-125

Second, after these cut-score bands had been established, the PIUs agreed upon the following procedures for adjudicating a final placement decision. Three initial placement recommendations were to be made for each examinee by matching that examinees' scores from the three sub-tests with the corresponding cut-score bands representing the GUGD curricular levels. Where the three recommendations were identical, or where two of the three agreed and the third was one semester (for the C-test) or one year (for the LCT/RCT) higher or lower, the student was placed into the agreed-upon level. Where discrepancies were greater than one semester/year, or there were no agreements between sub-tests, the decision was weighted toward the *lowest* recommended curricular level; however, additional information about language experiences collected on a background information form was to be incorporated into these less clear-cut decisions.

These initial decision-making procedures were developed by the PIUs on the basis of the information that was available at that time. Of course, it was acknowledged that, at best, the cut-scores and placement procedures would only serve as a tentative point of embarkation until more data could be collected under operational conditions (indeed, virtually all assessment standard-setting methods have been critiqued due to some persistent degree of arbitrariness; see discussions in Zieky, 2001). Nevertheless, our actions at this point enabled a final operational version of the placement assessment program to be produced in time for official administration in August, 1999. Beyond these basic uses of development information to transform the 'bare-bones' placement exam into a 'barely functional', if curriculum-based, placement program, time did not allow for additional concerns to be addressed at this point. Thus, a variety of potential questions emerging from the specification of intended assessment use were left unanswered until the following stage of program implementation.

6.2 Implementing and revising the placement assessment program

The fully operational form of the GUGD placement exam was first implemented in August, 1999. With this initial operational use, of common and immediate interest was the basic question of whether the placement exam would work as intended—that is, whether it could be administered, scored reliably, and the scores applied for making accurate decisions, all with acceptable levels of procedural consistency and within the constraints imposed by the assessment-use setting. These overarching concerns framed the validity evaluation purposes during this stage of initial assessment program implementation, and they were explicitly prioritized over other concerns, for example, with the consequences of assessment use (see section 6.3).

Beyond the formal evaluation efforts reported below, it is noteworthy that informal findings from the first day of program implementation led to immediate improvements in the use of the placement exam. For example, in one test administration room, located in a 'venerable' campus building, it was discovered that the 19th century architecture proved no match for the noise generated by 20th century garbage removal trucks, whose work coincided with the initial moments of the listening comprehension test. Luckily, the test proctor had the presence of mind to postpone administration until work was finished, and then to recommend the scheduling of future placement exams in a more sound-resistant, if less venerable, location. Similarly, later in the day, after three trips to the campus office for machine-scoring of tests (located, oddly, in the basement of the same venerable building) had failed to produce the individual item response and score data needed for certain test analyses, it became clear that the use of 'automated' exam scoring did not necessarily equate with 'efficient' exam score use. Indeed, GUGD faculty had finished scoring the C-test exams by hand, and finished lunch, by the time the machine-generated scores for the LCT and RCT were available for use, due primarily to the backlog of simultaneous scoring demands from all FL placement exams being administered that day. Although unplanned and informal, these and related observations provided useful insights into the extent to which the GUGD placement exam could be administered, scored, and used with consistency and efficiency, and they were incorporated into improvements in future practice.

In August, 2000, the second fully operational administration of the GUGD placement exam took place, adhering largely to the same procedures as the 1999 exam (with a few exceptions, as discussed below). These two exam administrations, and the academic year that followed each, constituted the "implementation and revision" stage of the placement assessment program. From the outset of assessment development, this initial two-year operational period had been targeted as a sufficient amount of time to ask questions, gather data, and take actions regarding the extent to which the instruments and procedures of the placement exam were functioning effectively and accurately. In order to address this concern as efficiently as possible, formalized validity evaluation efforts at this stage were to be driven by the small group of PIUs, including the department chair, the curriculum developer, the curriculum coordinator, and the consultant evaluator. This group assumed responsibility for the improvement of the assessment program for meeting curricular placement needs. While we sought to represent the interests of other GUGD stakeholders, and to disseminate evaluation information to them, it had been decided in departmental meetings that this small group of individuals would be most able to formulate and direct validity evaluation questions, methods, analyses, etc., and then to report back to the full department with major findings and for input on major decisions.

Accordingly, the PIUs pursued two basic evaluation purposes during the implementation and revision stage, as determined through prioritization meetings. First, they sought to judge whether the instruments and procedures which comprised the placement assessment program were adequate for meeting the decision-making needs defined in the specification of intended assessment use: this evaluation purpose boiled down to judging whether available evidence warranted continuation, adaptation, or suspension of the placement assessment program. Second, the PIUs sought to revise and improve the instruments and procedures of the placement assessment program, where areas in need of immediate change could be identified and where these changes would lead to clear improvements in the accuracy and effectiveness of the placement decision-making process.

In direct pursuit of these two purposes, validity evaluation efforts during this stage focused only on the inferential links between curricular placement decisions and the test-based information that was to inform them, as defined in the specification of intended assessment use, including: (a) qualities of the placement exam instruments, (b) consistency of the procedures via which they were being used for making decisions, and (c) the curricular relevance and accuracy of the decisions being made. Of course, even within this narrowed focus, a wide variety of potential evaluative questions and methods presented themselves, including some traditional measurement validity concerns as well as a range of questions about test usefulness. The PIUs motivated evaluation activities, first and foremost, by asking which questions and methods were *minimally* necessary in order to provide sufficient evidence for meeting the two specific purposes of judging and improving the particular instruments and procedures that defined this placement assessment program. While other aspects of validity might have been investigated—time, resources, and relevance/worth of findings permitting—these minimally necessary efforts had to be prioritized for meeting the immediate demands of ensuring the quality of local assessment use.

Initially, the PIUs determined that basic investigations of several measurement qualities, in the form of test score and item analyses, would provide information necessary both for judging the consistencies of the placement exam sub-tests and for identifying test features in need of improvement. Therefore, these analyses were targeted as one focus of the validity evaluation efforts during this stage. However, given the inferential premises for the placement exam, and in particular the key assumptions that related textual processing abilities to curricular levels, it became apparent to the PIUs that several other questions took precedence over these basic concerns with measurement qualities.

Of foremost concern with initial operational uses of the exam was whether the novel curriculum-based format of the three sub-tests, and their carefully selected texts, could actually be used to distinguish effectively among student abilities across the full range of curricular levels at which placement decisions needed to be made. In addition, the PIUs questioned whether the cut-scores, which had been tentatively established during pilot-testing, would provide accurate standards for these decisions. Lacking evidence for the basic inferential premise for placement decisions, there would be little reason to carry on with additional validity evaluation efforts or additional use of the exam.

However, while they agreed that the most complete sources of evidence would be found in close investigation of student performances on all three placement exam sub-tests, the PIUs also made an explicit choice to focus primarily on the effectiveness of the C-test and the accuracy of its cut-scores in response to this priority. Even though this restriction would limit the comprehensiveness of findings, it was decided that an intensive focus on a single instrument would enable access to the maximum amount of relevant information within the feasible expenditure of departmental time and resources. In addition, the C-test was targeted as the sub-test that best represented the curriculum-based inferential premises, and due to its presumed potential for informing finer-grained distinctions among examinee abilities than the other two sub-tests.

One additional area of concern for evaluation arose during this initial investigation of the effectiveness and accuracy of the C-test, and it prompted the PIUs to postpone additional evaluation efforts until related evidence had been gathered and actions taken. Thus, it became obvious that, regardless of the relative effectiveness of the placement exam sub-tests and the C-test in particular, considerable amounts of unrelated error (i.e., not derived from the test instruments per se) were being introduced during the scoring, decision-making, and student enrollment processes. Anecdotal reports of each of these types of error during the first operational use of the exam led the PIUs to initiate investigations into the sources and the extent of these problems, in order to enact immediate improvements in associated practices.

Obviously, various other possible validity questions were not addressed during this implementation and revision stage of the placement assessment program (although some of these were addressed subsequently; see 6.3 below), and a number of additional questions were generated as a result of these initial efforts. However, it should be equally obvious that all possible questions about the assessment program could not be addressed within time and resource constraints—to attempt to do so would have disabled the process from the outset. Furthermore, all possible validity questions did not need to be addressed, given the explicit and limited intended uses for the particular assessment program within the particular educational context. As such, *for this stage of the assessment program*, the PIUs identified these three foci as the priorities for validity evaluation: the effectiveness and accuracy of the C-test instrument and decision cut-scores (6.2.1), the amount and sources of error in scoring and enrollment practices (6.2.2), and measurement qualities of the test instruments and items (6.2.3).

6.2.1 Evaluating C-test effectiveness and cut-score accuracy

Evaluation findings at this stage were intended to inform the following uses: (a) judgments regarding the continued administration of the C-test; (b) revision of cut-scores for the C-test, if needed; and (c) demonstration to assessment stakeholders, and particularly departmental constituents, of the general accuracy of student placement decisions based on the C-test. In response to these intended uses, investigations were pursued to examine the basic inferential assumptions relating the C-test and decision standards to the GUGD curriculum. According to the specification of intended use, the C-test would provide scores which distinguished consistently among incoming students in terms of similarities/differences with other non-placed (continuing or true beginning) students at each of seven curricular levels (each representing one semester of non-intensive instruction). *If the C-test instrument were effective* in meeting this requirement, it was inferred that:

(a) the C-test would elicit a wide distribution of scores from placement examinees of differing abilities as well as from non-placed students already studying across the range of curricular levels;

(b) C-test scores would distinguish reliably among examinees of differing curricular ability levels within distinct placed and non-placed student populations;

(c) average C-test scores would reflect clear differences between groups of non-placed students from each of the curricular levels at both the beginning and the end of the semester;

(d) average C-test scores would be similar for groups of students at common curricular junctures (e.g., end of previous semester versus beginning of subsequent semester; end of one *year* of non-intensive instruction versus end of one *semester* of intensive instruction);

(e) C-test scores for both placed and non-placed students, and for both intensive- and non-intensive-track students, would increase between the beginning and the end of a semester; and

(f) longitudinal changes in C-test scores would be similar to cross-sectional differences in the C-test scores of students at both the beginning and the end of a semester.

In addition to the effectiveness of the C-test instrument at distinguishing among students, placement cut-score bands for the C-test would also be required to locate students within the curricular levels most appropriate to their abilities. Thus, if the initial placement cut-score bands were accurate, it was inferred that:

(g) non-placed students already studying at a given curricular level would score within the cut-score band for that level on a C-test administered at the *beginning* of a semester of instruction; and

(h) non-placed and placed students would score within the cut-score band for the subsequent curricular level on a C-test administered at the *end* of a semester of instruction.

Methods. In order to investigate inferential assumptions (a) through (h), the following research methods were employed during the Fall 1999 semester, in conjunction with the initial operational use of the placement exam. Instructors of all courses at each of curricular levels 1 through 4 administered the C-test during the first week of classes to all students in their sections who had not enrolled via the placement exam ("non-placed" students), and again to all students ("placed" and "non-placed") during the final week of classes for the 16-week semester. Instructors were to administer the C-test following identical procedures used for the placement exam administration, thereby maintaining equivalent performance conditions. For the semester-beginning administration, students were informed that their test scores would be used for calibrating the placement exam, and that they should therefore perform as well as they could, but they were not informed that they would complete the C-test at the end of the semester. For the semester-end administration, students were informed that a final administration of the C-test was needed in order to investigate their language development over the course of a semester of instruction.

128

Based on pre-post-semester scores, the effectiveness of the C-test score as a predictor variable could be evaluated from the perspective of the single most important (and arguably the only meaningful) criterion variable for its use as a placement decision-making tool, namely the GUGD curricular levels structure. Thus, cross-sectional comparisons between the C-test scores of non-placed students and their corresponding curricular levels would enable interpretations about the extent to which the C-test instrument effectively and consistently distinguished among students representing the full range of curricular abilities. In addition, by adopting a pre-post design around an intervening semester of instruction, longitudinal changes in C-test scores would enable interpretations about the extent to which the instrument was sensitive to learners' curriculum-related language development. Finally, C-test scores for non-placed students at both the beginning and end of a semester of instruction could be compared with placement cut-score bands and the scores of placed students in order to evaluate decision-making accuracy.

Several constraints limited the number and representativeness of students from whom C-test scores were collected. First, instructors of curricular level 1 (first year) students argued that administering the full C-test to true beginning language learners might have a detrimental effect on their motivation and that the results would most likely show very low scores anyway, owing to the fact that these students had very little language learning experience. As such, the C-test was not administered at the beginning of the semester to students in the first-year first-semester course sections (1.1), nor in the first-year intensive course sections (1.Int). However, C-test scores were collected from both groups at the end of the semester, and several students who had completed the C-test during the placement exam did enroll in level 1.1 courses, thereby providing at least some data for investigating abilities and longitudinal change at this level. Second, no sections of the first-year second-semester course (1.2) were offered during fall 1999; therefore, no C-test score data were collected at the beginning or the end of the semester for this curricular level. Furthermore, other 'off-sequence' second-semester course sections for both the second and third years of instruction (2.2 and 3.2) experienced relatively low enrollments in Fall 1999, resulting in considerably fewer C-test scores being collected for these curricular levels in comparison with the 'on-sequence' first-semester, fall course sections for each curricular level (2.1, 3.1, 4). Third, as a result of absenteeism on the days chosen by instructors for administering the C-tests in class, a reduced number of the total enrolled student population completed both the semester-begin and semester-end C-tests.

Despite these unavoidable constraints, C-test scores were collected from a substantial number of students at both the beginning and end of the Fall 1999 semester. Of the 102 students who completed the placement exam, 54 enrolled in fall semester courses, and an additional 95 non-placed students completed the semester-beginning test administration. At the end of the semester, a total of 193 students completed the C-test, 145 of whom were non-placed (note the larger number of students here due to the administration of the C-test to students in level 1 courses at the end of the semester). Finally, 124 students completed both a semester-begin and semester-end test administration. Each C-test performance was scored by GUGD faculty members during a single scoring session at the conclusion of the Fall 1999 semester and following the scoring guidelines from the placement exam. Subsequently, all C-tests were rescored by the consultant evaluator in order to ensure the accuracy of scores for all examinees. Scores for students who had been incorrectly placed and had enrolled in curricular sections higher or lower than warranted were removed from analyses, given the potential that incorrectly enrolled students would perform differentially poorly/well in comparison with other students at the given level.

Several challenges to, and limitations of, the interpretability of evaluation findings were recognized at this stage. The potential for a practice effect on repeated administrations of the C-test was considered by the PIUs. However, it was deemed unlikely that students would attempt or be able to recall particular items from the 125-item constructed-response format test, given that they were allowed only 25 minutes to complete the test and they did not know that they would be taking the test again later in the semester. Further, the 14-week delay between initial and final administrations of the test reassured the PIUs that students would be very unlikely to recall specific items and their correct responses (see also Bolton, 1992, who found that only 4 of 52 students recalled having taken a pre-semester C-test in a 14-week intervention study). More challenging to the interpretability of individual C-test scores was the concern that non-placed students would not complete the test with the same degree of effort as students completing the placement exam, given the different stakes involved. In an effort to ameliorate this potential problem, instructors encouraged students to perform at their best on both administrations of the test. In addition, subsequent analyses of the internal item difficulty structure of the C-test revealed no differences for the various populations of placed and non-placed students who completed the exam, a finding which would not have been expected had students not been attempting to complete all of the items.

Clearly, the greatest limitation on the interpretability of average C-test scores issued from the low numbers of students completing the test at any one level. Highly trustworthy interpretations about scores for a given level were not warranted in most cases, as revealed by the large confidence intervals surrounding many of the average values in the tables and graphs below. Furthermore, additional inferential statistical comparisons between curricular levels (e.g., employing univariate analysis of variance) were not warranted, given the non-normal distributions and low N values within many of the examinee groups. However, the intended uses for evaluation findings during this phase focused on general interpretations about whether or not the C-test instrument was able to distinguish among learners across the curricular levels and whether or not the initial placement cut-score bands approximated actual level ability differences. As such, trends in observations of C-test scores *across* the curricular levels figured much more prominently than did the accuracy of score averages within any given level. Nevertheless, findings were presented to and discussed by the PIUs, and the broader departmental stakeholder group, with the ever-present caveat that the low numbers of test scores did not allow for exact interpretations about the relationship between C-test scores and the typical abilities of students at any given curricular level.

Findings. Inferences (a) and (b) above assumed the effectiveness of the C-test instrument at eliciting a wide range of scores from examinees across the four years of the GUGD curriculum. Descriptive statistics and reliability estimates were calculated for C-test scores from four distinct population samples of students, each of which represented a considerable range of German language ability levels: (a) the placement exam C-test administration to incoming students; (b) the semester-beginning and semester-end administrations of the C-test to non-placed students; and (c) the combined scores from the semester-end administration of the C-test to placed and non-placed students. Table 3 shows descriptive statistics, Cronbach alpha (α) reliability estimates, and standard errors of measurement (SEM) for the four distinct sets of C-test scores.

Descriptive statistics for all four sets of scores confirmed that the C-test instrument effectively elicited a wide range of scores reflecting the broad ability differences within each of the student population samples. Mean scores for each set fell slightly higher than the midpoint of the 125-item test, corresponding to the somewhat larger proportion of advanced students who completed the various administrations. Minimum and maximum scores extended across nearly the entire available scoring range, and consistently large standard deviations (between 21 and 27 score points) indicated considerable variability within both the placed and non-placed student scores and at both the beginning and the end of a semester of instruction.

Table 3. Descriptive statistics and reliability estimates for fall 1999 C-tests

Statistic	Distinct Population Samples			
	Placement Exam Semester-Begin	Non-Pl. Students Semester-Begin	Non-Pl. Students Semester-End	All Students Semester-End
N (examinees)	102	95	145	193
k (items)	125	125	125	125
Mean	77.05	71.86	70.21	74.30
S	26.43	21.15	24.98	24.87
Min	16	16	7	7
Max	125	121	119	119
α	0.96	0.94	0.95	0.95
SEM	±5.29	±5.18	±5.59	±5.56

Note. Table 3 displays descriptive statistics for four distinct groups of students; comparisons should not be drawn among the mean scores for these groups, given the different numbers and participants in each group.

Very high Cronbach alpha reliability estimates for all four sets of scores revealed that this variability was associated with consistent differences among examinees,

131

whose scores could also be trusted on each C-test administration within plus or minus 5.5 score points (one SEM). In sum, based on findings from these initial administrations of the C-test to a variety of both incoming and continuing GUGD students at different points over a semester, the C-test instrument was interpreted to function effectively at eliciting a wide range of scores and at distinguishing reliably among individual students representing all four years of the curriculum.

Inferences (c) and (d) above assumed that average C-test scores would differentiate clearly between groups of students at each of the GUGD curricular levels, that these differences would hold at both the beginning and end of a semester of instruction, and that students at common curricular junctures would exhibit similar scores on the C-test. Average scores and 95% confidence intervals were first calculated for non-placed students at each of the curricular levels for both the semester-beginning and semester-end administrations (see Table 4). Non-placed students' scores were investigated on their own due to the fact that differences could be assumed *a priori* among placed students' scores at each level.

It is clear in Table 4 that average C-test scores differentiated among groups of non-placed students in predicted ways, revealing differences within each group between the beginning and end of the semester as well as substantial and continuous overall increases in C-test scores from the lowest to the highest levels (increasing from an average of 32 to 96 score points from the beginning of level 1 to the end of level 4). However, it is also apparent that students within each level exhibited considerable variability on the C-test, resulting in large standard deviations at all levels (from 8 to 22 score points) and widely ranging minimum and maximum scores (an average range of 39 score points within a single semester level).

The finding that scores for individual students within the non-placed population ranged widely both above and below the average score for a given level did not surprise the PIUs, given the flexibility with which these students had entered into the curricular program over the previous several years and including the Fall 1999 semester. For example, the two non-placed students at level 1.1 for whom semester-beginning C-test scores had been collected had simply enrolled in the introductory German course without registering to take the placement exam, despite the fact that each had already studied German prior to enrollment (their instructor identified them as unique from the other students and administered the C-test to them at the beginning of the Fall 1999 semester). It is possible, then, that several continuing students within each of the levels belonged more appropriately above or below the level at which they were enrolled during Fall 1999, due to such flexible enrollment policies. However, the PIUs also argued that the majority of students at any given curricular level, especially beyond the first year, had entered as continuing students after successfully completing coursework at the previous level of instruction, and that the *central tendency* of students at a given level should adequately estimate the expected learner abilities of that level.

Table 4. C-test descriptive statistics for non-placed students (Fall 1999)

GUGD level		N	Mean	S	Min	Max	95% CI	
							Lower	Upper
1.1	BEG	2	32.00	22.63	16	48	0.00	125.00
	END	27	41.15	19.20	7	83	34.87	47.43
1.2	BEG	--	--	--	--	--	--	--
	END	--	--	--	--	--	--	--
1.Int	BEG	--	--	--	--	--	--	--
	END	19	49.32	12.00	28	78	44.64	54.00
2.1	BEG	19	46.47	15.25	23	76	40.52	52.42
	END	19	61.95	10.27	45	77	57.94	65.96
2.2	BEG	3	57.00	11.14	47	69	38.22	75.78
	END	3	71.67	14.64	56	85	46.99	96.35
2.Int	BEG	4	56.75	8.81	45	64	46.40	67.10
	END	4	73.50	8.96	65	85	62.97	84.03
3.1	BEG	14	71.86	13.27	48	95	65.58	78.14
	END	18	75.39	13.75	49	105	69.88	80.90
3.2	BEG	7	77.86	10.30	63	90	70.31	85.41
	END	7	86.57	7.93	77	98	80.76	92.38
3.Int	BEG	9	73.56	12.47	51	97	65.83	81.29
	END	9	88.67	10.68	78	113	82.05	95.29
4	BEG	36	88.19	12.38	68	121	84.72	91.66
	END	38	96.55	9.61	65	119	93.93	99.17

Note. Very large confidence intervals for mean scores at levels 1.1 and 2.2 are a result of very low numbers of non-placed students who completed the C-test at these levels.

Figure 4 provides a graphic representation of the differences observed between non-placed students' average scores at each level and on the two testing occasions. Note in Figure 4 that average scores are grouped according to common curricular junctures; for example, scores for students from C-test administrations at the *end* of both level 2.2 (second year, second semester) and 2.Int (second year, intensive semester) are grouped with students' scores on administrations at the *beginning* of 3.1 (third year, first semester) and 3.Int (third year, intensive semester), because it was assumed that students at this common point (i.e., the end of the second or the beginning of the third curricular level) would score in similar ways.

Several patterns in Figure 4 underscore the effectiveness of the C-test at differentiating among students, on average, at distinct curricular levels. The overall trend in increasing mean scores across levels is clear, with students at each level scoring higher than students at the previous level, this despite the low numbers and unknown qualities of students at many of the curricular levels. In addition, this increasing trend from curricular level to level is apparent within the sub-sets of semester-beginning scores (white bars) as well as semester-end scores (dark bars). Figure 4 also reveals that non-placed students at similar junctures within the curriculum scored, on average, closer to each other than to students at junctures above or below.

Two discrepancies in these trends are also apparent. First, students at the beginning of the second year intensive semester scored, on average, much closer to students at the mid-year juncture (the end of 2.1 and beginning of 2.2) than to students at the beginning of the year two juncture. This finding was attributed by the PIUs to the fact that relatively advanced students were often advised to enroll in intensive sections slightly below their likely abilities in order to review features of the language and become accustomed to the unique instructional approach. A second discrepancy was identified in the relative lack of difference between students' scores at the beginning and mid-year junctures for level 3. Thus, students at the end of the first semester and at the beginning of the second semester of level 3 did not score, on average, substantially higher than students at the end of level 2 or beginning of level 3. The PIUs attributed this finding to the considerable learning expectations associated with the first semester of the third year of instruction, and they noted that the average scores increased substantially by the end of level three, as predicted. Overall, then, trends in average level scores clearly supported the effectiveness of the C-test at distinguishing between non-placed students at distinct *years* across the curriculum (i.e., beginning of level 2 versus beginning of level 3), while some discrepancies were noted between semesters at the mid-year junctures in levels 2 and 3 (and no data were available for the mid-year juncture in level 1).

In order to further investigate the effectiveness of the C-test at distinguishing between students at proximal curricular levels, additional analyses were carried out on both the scores of the placed students who had enrolled in the Fall 1999 semester and the full set of available cross-sectional score data for the Fall 1999 administrations. Table 5 shows descriptive statistics and 95% confidence intervals around the means for placed students at each curricular level. Similar patterns were observed in the consistent increases in mean scores from level to level and from beginning to end of the semester within each level. While somewhat lower variability was generally apparent among students' scores at the beginning of the semester, due to the fact that they were placed together according to their C-test scores, students' scores at the end of the semester reveal considerable variability and widely ranging minimum/maximum values.

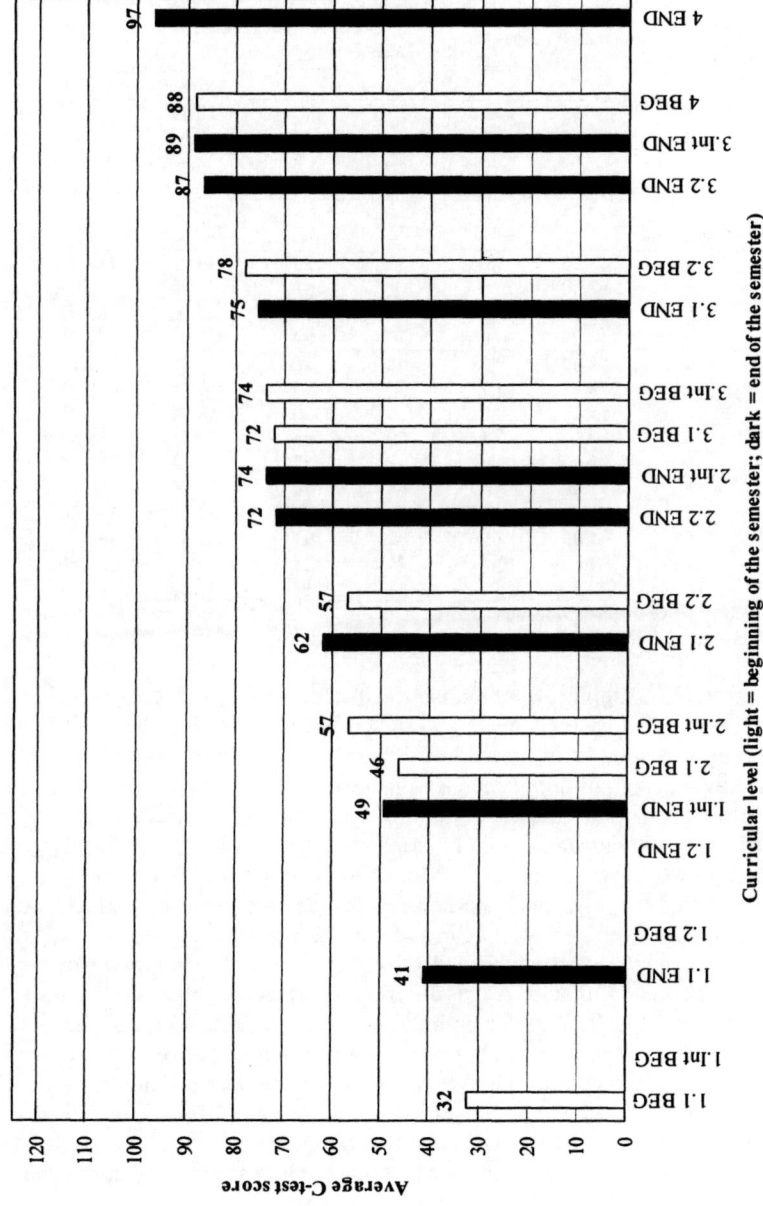

Figure 4. Average C-test scores for non-placed students at the beginning and send of a semester of instruction (Fall 1999)

Table 5. C-test descriptive statistics for placed students (Fall 1999)

GUGD level		N	Mean	S	Min	Max	95% CI	
							Lower	Upper
1.1	BEG	3	34.33	14.36	18	45	10.12	58.55
	END	3	52.00	2.65	49	54	47.54	56.46
1.2	BEG	--	--	--	--	--	--	--
	END	--	--	--	--	--	--	--
1.Int	BEG	--	--	--	--	--	--	--
	END	--	--	--	--	--	--	--
2.1	BEG	4	43.50	8.06	32	50	34.02	52.97
	END	1	57.00	--	--	--	--	--
2.2	BEG	5	60.00	5.24	54	66	55.00	65.00
	END	5	76.00	6.04	70	84	70.25	81.75
2.Int	BEG	4	54.00	9.52	48	68	42.81	65.19
	END	4	78.25	15.73	56	93	59.76	96.74
3.1	BEG	10	65.10	8.84	55	79	59.99	70.21
	END	10	80.10	9.41	59	93	74.65	85.55
3.2	BEG	6	81.00	7.04	72	87	75.25	86.75
	END	6	98.00	9.44	84	108	90.29	105.71
3.Int	BEG	2	66.00	8.49	60	72	28.14	103.86
	END	2	94.00	9.90	87	101	49.83	138.17
4	BEG	19	93.63	12.47	75	121	88.68	98.58
	END	16	102.56	8.56	85	117	98.82	106.31

Note. Very large confidence intervals for mean scores at levels 1.1 and 3.Int are a result of very low numbers of placed students who enrolled at these levels.

Figure 5 provides a graphical comparison of the mean C-test scores for placed students at each of the curricular levels and at the beginning (white bars) and end (dark bars) of the semester. As in figure 4, scores are grouped by common curricular juncture. Once again, the continual increase in mean scores is apparent across the curricular levels in both the semester-beginning and semester-end scores, and substantial differences are apparent within each of the levels, with the largest attributable to the two intensive courses (2.Int = 24 score points difference, 3.Int = 28 score points difference). As with the non-placed students, groups of placed students exhibited similar average C-test scores at common curricular junctures, with a clear exception occurring again at the end of year two and the beginning of year three. It should be noted that average differences observed between semester-beginning and semester-end scores for both the 3.1 level students and the 3.Int level students were of exactly the magnitude expected according to the placement exam cut-score bands (i.e., equivalent to the average scores of the next proximate curricular level, 3.2 for the 3.1 students, and 4 for the 3.Int students). Thus, it would seem that the two groups of level 2 students scored much higher than expected, while the level 3 students performed generally as predicted according to the placement exam uses for the C-test.

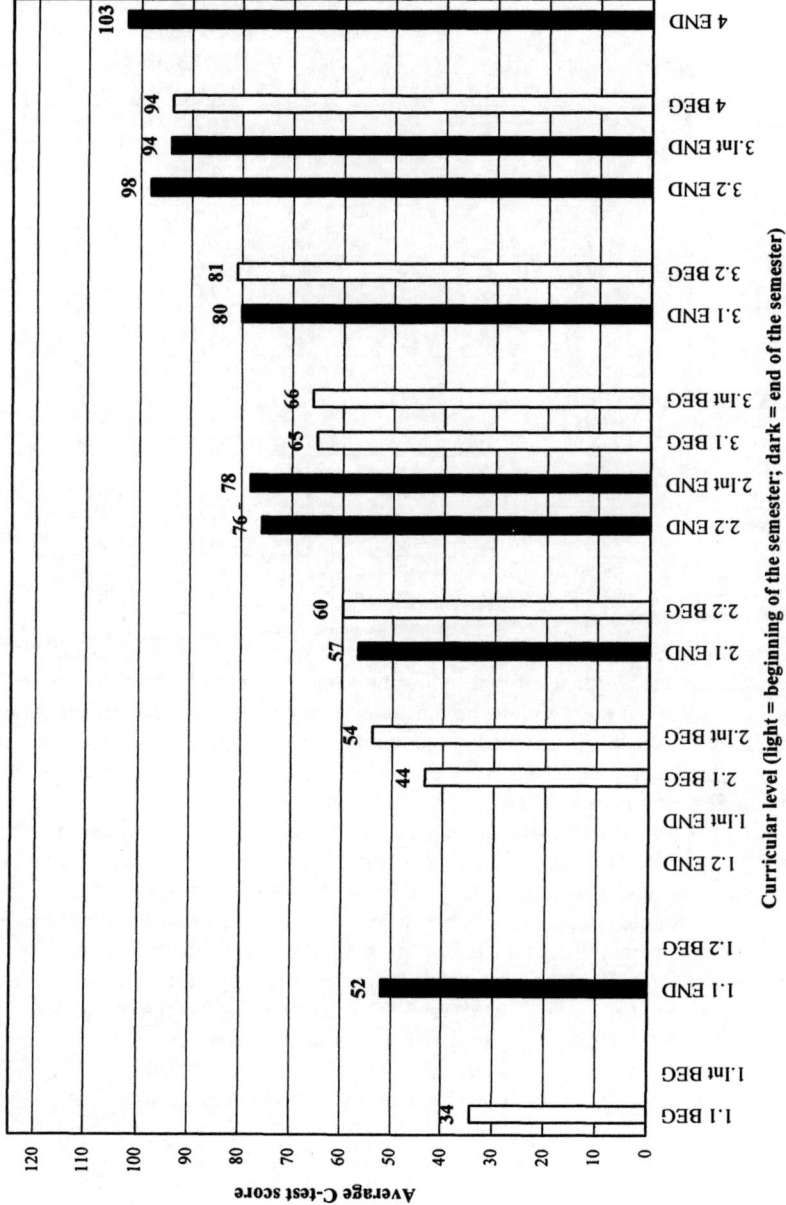

Figure 5. Average C-test scores for placed students at the beginning and the end of a semester of instruction (Fall 1999)

137

Table 6. C-test descriptive statistics for all students combined (Fall 1999)

GUGD level		N	Mean	S	Min	Max	95% CI	
							Lower	Upper
1.1	BEG	5	33.20	15.02	16	47	18.89	47.51
	END	31	41.39	18.78	7	83	35.68	47.09
1.2	BEG	--	--	--	--	--	--	--
	END	--	--	--	--	--	--	--
1.Int	BEG	--	--	--	--	--	--	--
	END	19	49.31	12.00	28	78	44.55	54.08
2.1	BEG	23	45.96	14.16	23	76	40.91	51.01
	END	20	61.70	10.06	45	77	57.81	65.59
2.2	BEG	8	58.88	7.32	47	69	53.50	64.25
	END	8	74.38	9.33	56	85	69.00	79.75
2.Int	BEG	8	55.38	8.62	45	68	49.59	61.16
	END	8	75.88	12.12	56	93	67.73	84.02
3.1	BEG	24	69.04	11.90	48	95	64.89	73.20
	END	28	77.07	12.40	49	105	73.09	81.06
3.2	BEG	13	79.31	8.74	63	90	74.99	83.62
	END	13	91.85	10.19	77	108	86.82	96.88
3.Int	BEG	11	72.18	11.87	51	97	65.70	78.66
	END	11	89.64	10.28	78	113	84.03	95.25
4	BEG	54	89.96	12.66	68	121	87.09	92.84
	END	54	98.33	9.64	65	119	96.14	100.52

In order to provide a more robust representation of student performances for each curricular level, for the purpose of evaluating the extent to which the C-test effectively grouped students at common curricular junctures, the scores of placed students were combined with those of non-placed students at the beginning and end of each curricular level, and descriptive statistics and 95% confidence intervals around the means were calculated for each (displayed in Table 6).

Figure 6 facilitates comparisons among the means and confidence intervals for these combined groups. Note that the mean value for each group is represented by either a minus (semester-beginning scores) or a plus (semester-end scores) symbol in the middle of a vertical bar, and that this bar reflects the magnitude of the confidence interval around each mean. Where these bars overlap, differences between mean values cannot be considered probabilistically unusual (i.e., equivalent to a test of statistical significance at $p < .05$). The overall pattern of similarity in average scores at common curricular junctures, and difference with average scores at the next proximate curricular juncture, is clear, with the confidence intervals around all means at a given juncture overlapping with each other and most progressions to the next level not.

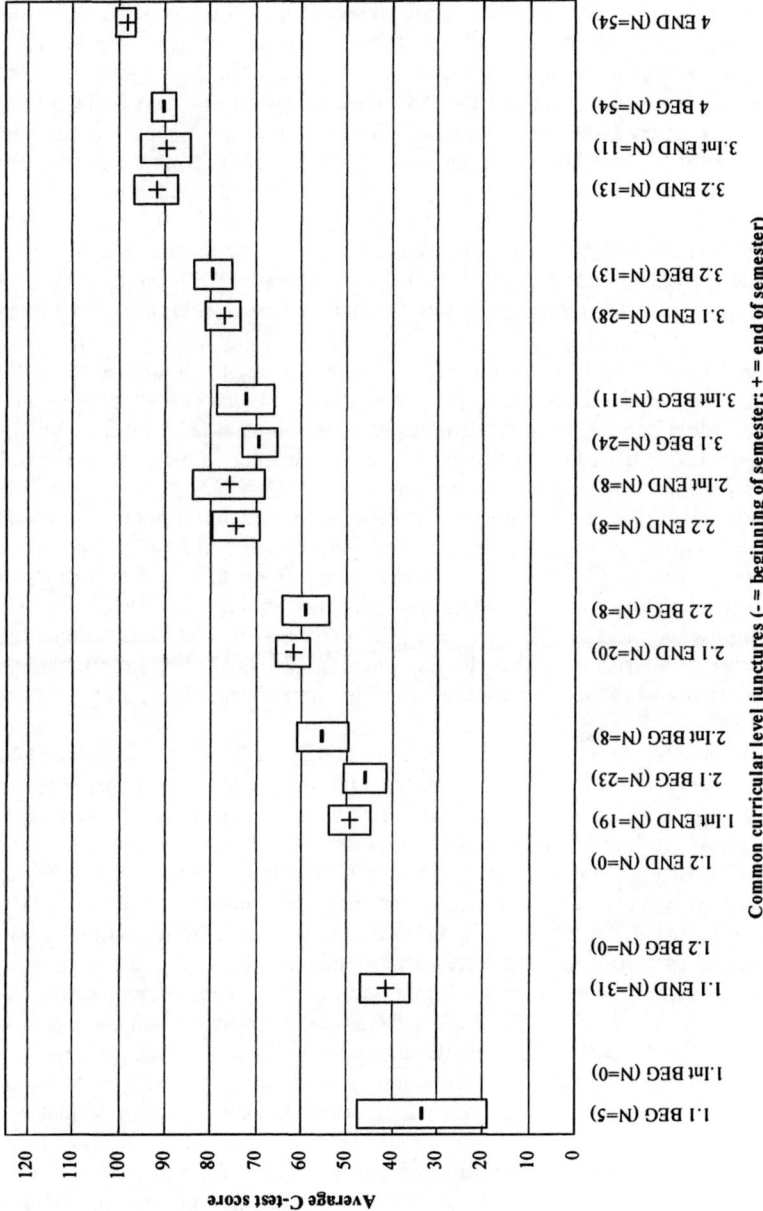

Figure 6. Average C-test scores and 95% confidence intervals at common curricular level junctures (Fall 1999)

Three discrepancies within these overall patterns were noted. First, confidence intervals around average scores for students at the end of the first-year, first-semester (1.1 END) did overlap with those for some of the students at the beginning of the second year of instruction, suggesting that these first-semester students scored somewhat higher on the C-test than expected. Second, the average score for students at the beginning of the second-year intensive (2.Int) course was higher than that for other students at the year 2 beginning juncture, and it overlapped with students' scores at the mid-year juncture. This finding was likely attributable to relatively advanced students who enrolled in the 2.Int course as a review and introduction course. Third, average scores for students at the end of year 2 courses, beginning of year 3 courses, and mid-year 3 courses could not be distinguished probabilistically from each other.

It was clear from these findings that students could be differentiated consistently between each *year* of the curriculum, as scores from both semester-beginning and semester-end C-test administrations demonstrated with substantial and probabilistically rare differences (i.e., non-overlapping confidence intervals) between years 1 and 2, 2 and 3, and 3 and 4. Less certain was the consistency of distinctions made between *semesters* of the curriculum, in particular at the transition between the end of year 2 and beginning of year 3 instruction. Furthermore, the lack of key data points for year 1 students limited the interpretations that could be made about students at that level. However, considering the unknown representativeness of cross-sectional samples of students who completed the various C-test administrations, the overall observed patterns of differentiation encouraged favorable interpretations among the PIUs about the effectiveness of the instrument for use in making placement decisions.

Inferences (e) and (f) above assumed the sensitivity of the C-test instrument to developments in individual students' language abilities, such that consistent increases in C-test scores would be found as a result of one semester of either non-intensive or intensive instruction at each of the curricular levels. In addition, these inferences assumed that longitudinal changes in C-test scores would be similar to cross-sectional differences in scores between proximate curricular levels. Thus, while cross-sectional differences might be detected for any administration of the exam to students sampled from the various curricular levels, due to differences in central tendencies of students' scores at those levels, only a longitudinal investigation of changes in scores for individual students would provide evidence of the extent to which the C-test could estimate curriculum-related *development* in language abilities. It was argued also that a longitudinal investigation would more accurately reflect the magnitude of change attributable to each semester of instruction.

Descriptive statistics and 95% confidence intervals around the means were first calculated for the subset of students at each level (124 total) who completed both the semester-beginning (or placement exam) and semester-end C-test administrations (see Table 7). As with the cross-sectional comparisons, increasing mean values were observed both within each curricular level group and between the levels. In addition, considerable variability was detected among scores within each level on both the semester-beginning and semester-end administrations. Overall increases in group mean scores within the curricular levels also reflected the patterns of change in individual students' scores. For students in non-intensive courses of instruction, scores increased an average of 12.48 points ($S = 9.26$), while the scores of individual students in intensive semesters of instruction increased an average of 18.74 points ($S = 10.91$).

Table 7. C-test descriptive statistics for longitudinal comparisons (Fall 1999)

GUGD level		N	Mean	S	Min	Max	95% CI	
							Lower	Upper
1.1	PRE	4	37.50	13.33	18	47	21.84	53.16
	POST	4	57.50	11.21	49	74	44.33	70.67
1.2	PRE	--	--	--	--	--	--	--
	POST	--	--	--	--	--	--	--
1.Int	PRE	--	--	--	--	--	--	--
	POST	--	--	--	--	--	--	--
2.1	PRE	16	46.19	12.78	24	74	40.60	51.78
	POST	16	62.38	9.84	45	77	58.07	66.68
2.2	PRE	8	58.88	7.32	47	69	53.96	63.79
	POST	8	74.38	9.33	56	85	68.10	80.65
2.Int	PRE	8	55.38	8.62	45	68	49.59	61.16
	POST	8	75.88	12.12	56	93	67.73	84.02
3.1	PRE	21	67.81	12.25	48	95	63.19	72.43
	POST	21	80.52	10.92	59	105	76.40	84.65
3.2	PRE	13	79.31	8.74	63	90	74.99	83.62
	POST	13	91.85	10.19	77	108	86.82	96.88
3.Int	PRE	11	72.18	11.87	51	97	65.70	78.66
	POST	11	89.64	10.28	78	113	84.03	95.25
4	PRE	43	88.81	11.88	68	121	85.77	91.86
	POST	43	98.65	10.24	65	119	96.03	101.27

Means and 95% confidence intervals for pre- and post-semester administrations at each level were compared graphically (see Figure 7). With the exception of curricular level 1.1, where the low number of students ($N = 4$) resulted in large confidence intervals, the patterns of change were consistent across all of the other levels. Average C-test scores increased substantially for students within each level, and these increases resulted in post-semester mean values that differed from pre-semester values to probabilistically rare degrees (i.e., 95% confidence intervals did not overlap within any of the level 2 through level 4 pre- to post-semester comparisons).

Patterns of mean values across the curricular levels revealed considerable consistency for this sample of students. Thus, average C-test scores for students at common curricular junctures did not differ to probabilistically rare degrees, with means falling very close together and 95% confidence intervals overlapping, and this was the case at both the beginning and end of the semester. In addition, average pre-semester scores for students in the intensive semesters of instruction for both levels 2 and 3 fell in between the scores for students beginning the first or second non-intensive semesters of instruction at the given level, but they fell at the same point as scores for students completing the entire year of non-intensive instruction by the end of the semester, a pattern predicted by the curricular structure but not at all a certainty at the outset of this evaluation.

Once again, as with the cross-sectional comparisons, the only exception to this pattern of similar scores at common curricular junctures and different scores between proximate curricular junctures was observed at the transition from year 2 to year 3. While 95% confidence intervals for students completing year 2 (2.2 POST and 2.Int POST) overlapped as predicted with those for students beginning year 3 instruction (3.1 PRE and 3.Int PRE), they also overlapped with scores for students completing the first semester (3.1 POST) and for those beginning the second semester (3.2 PRE) of year 3 instruction. To some extent, this finding may have been attributable to the smaller Ns and larger confidence intervals for the year 2 groups. However, given the repeated finding of non-distinct performances, the PIUs were concerned that the test might not be distinguishing well at this critical transition point within the curriculum or that the placement cut-score bands had incorrectly estimated the approximate point of differentiation between these curricular levels.

Additional evidence regarding the magnitude of change in C-test scores attributable to students at each of the curricular levels was generated via comparisons of average longitudinal changes with average cross-sectional differences in C-test scores and with the magnitude of the GUGD Placement Exam cut-score bands for each curricular level. Table 8 shows the number of score points and standardized effect sizes (d) associated with change or difference at each curricular semester level, as well as the size of the Fall 1999 placement exam cut-score band for each level.

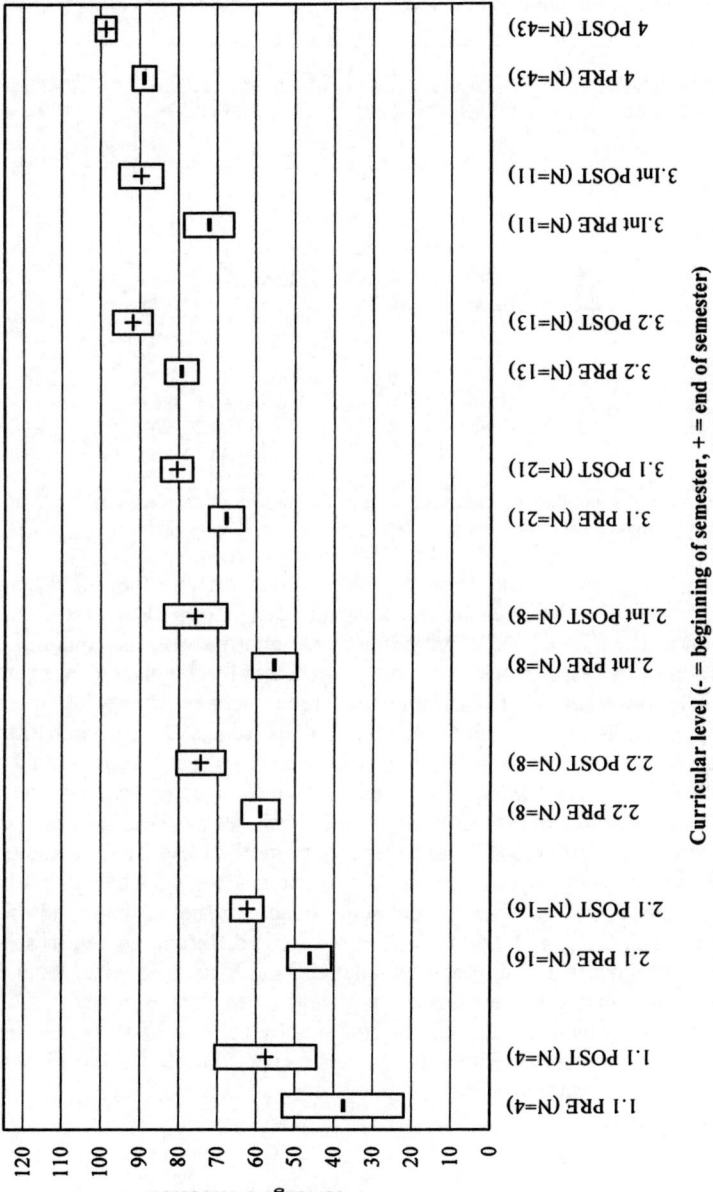

Figure 7. Comparison of average C-test scores and 95% confidence intervals for longitudinal changes over one semester

143

Table 8. Average longitudinal change and cross-sectional difference in C-test scores

GUGD level	Longitudinal change		Cross-sectional difference (Begin)		Cross-sectional difference (End)		Placement band
	points	d	points	d	points	d	points
1.1-1.2	20.00	1.63	--	--	--	--	20
1.2-2.1	--	--	--	--	--	--	20
1.Int-2.Int	--	--	--	--	26.57	2.21	40
2.1-2.2	16.19	1.43	12.92	1.03	12.68	1.29	9
2.2-3.1	15.50	1.86	10.16	0.94	2.69	0.23	7
2.Int-3.Int	20.50	1.98	16.80	1.60	13.76	1.25	16
3.1-3.2	12.71	1.10	10.27	0.95	14.78	1.26	12
3.2-4	12.54	1.32	10.65	0.89	6.48	0.67	12
3.Int-4	17.46	1.58	17.78	1.42	--	--	24
4-4+	9.84	0.89	--	--	--	--	--

Note. The standardized effect size (d) should be interpreted as the number of standard deviation units represented by a given change or difference value.

Several patterns were apparent in Table 8 and helped to explain the differences noted in previous analyses. First, despite the missing data, it was clear that C-test scores for students at curricular level 1 increased substantially over the course of a semester and that these increases were on the order predicted by the placement exam cut-score bands. The observation of a 26-point difference between first-year intensive students and second-year intensive students on the semester-end exam also reflected expected values, given that differences over the second year were predicted to be much less than those over the first year (i.e., had semester-beginning data been available for 1.Int students, a greater difference would have been expected). Second, students at curricular level 2 developed considerably more than had been predicted within the placement cut-score bands. Longitudinal changes for non-intensive students were on the order of nearly twice the cut-score bands for these levels, and this observation helped explain the reduction in cross-sectional difference between second-semester level 2 students and first-semester level 3 students. Likewise, level 3 non-intensive students apparently developed somewhat more than expected, again explaining the reduced difference with level 4 students by the end of the semester. Finally, C-test scores for students in intensive courses increased more for level 2 students and less for level 3 students than might have been expected, based on the placement cut-score bands.

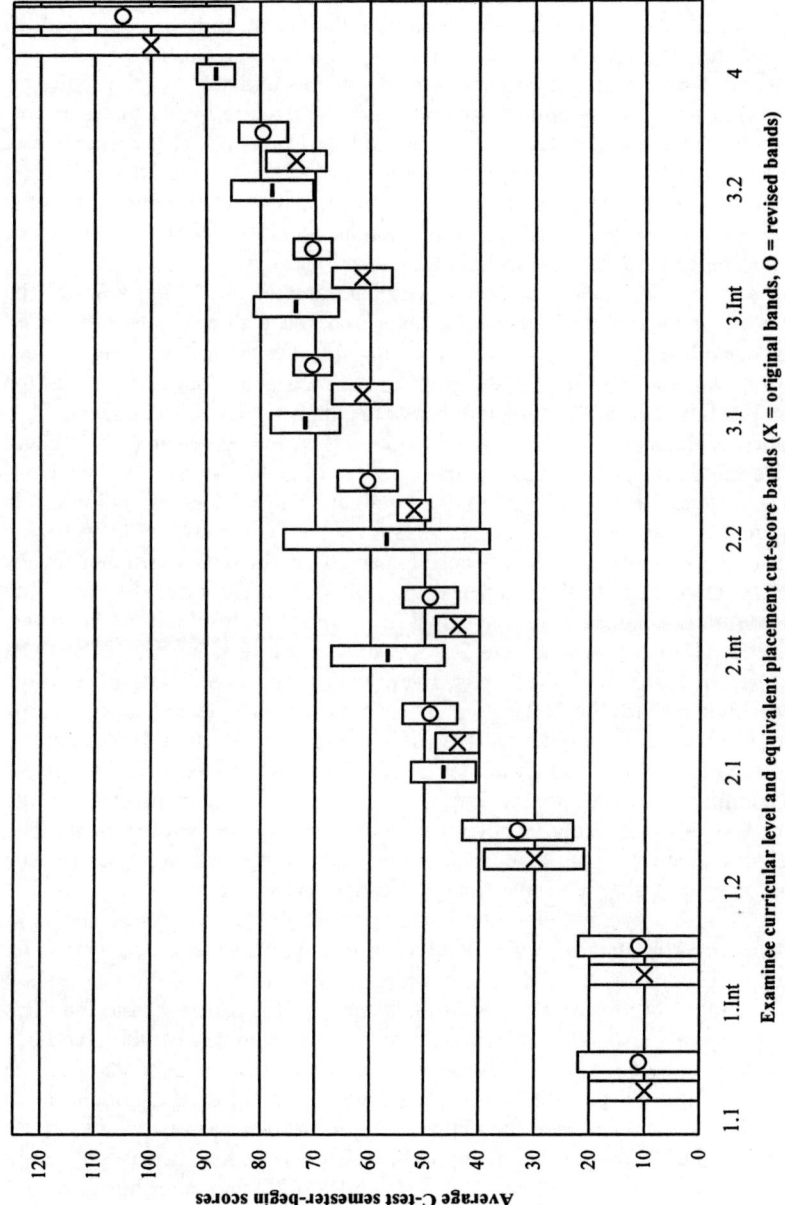

Figure 8. Average non-placed semester-begin C-test scores compared with original and revised placement cut-score bands

145

One final set of analyses provided further evidence for determining the accuracy of placement exam cut-score bands associated with the C-test. Inferences (g) and (h) above assumed that average C-test scores for non-placed students at the beginning of the semester, and for both placed and non-placed students at the end of the semester, would fall within the corresponding placement exam cut-score bands for each curricular level. In order to investigate these assumptions, average C-test scores and 95% confidence intervals for non-placed students at the beginning of the Fall 1999 semester were compared graphically with the original cut-score bands from the placement exam, and the same comparisons were made for the combined scores of placed and non-placed students at the end of the semester.

Figure 8 shows the semester-beginning comparisons. Note in Figure 8 that the Fall 1999 cut-score band at each curricular level (marked with an X) was that used for making determinations about students *entering* into the given level (i.e., the 2.1 cut-score band was used to identify students who should enter into level 2.1 of the curriculum). For this reason, the cut-score bands for intensive courses are identical to the bands for non-intensive courses at the beginning of the semester (i.e., 2.1 and 2.Int have the same semester-beginning cut-score band). Note also that a revised cut-score band is presented for each level (marked with an O; see discussion below). It is clear in Figure 8 that those non-placed students for whom C-test data were available scored on average higher than the cut-score expectations for their curricular levels. At levels 2.2, 2.Int, 3.1, and 3.Int, students' average scores fell above the top of the bands, and confidence intervals only narrowly overlapped with the top of the bands (with the exception of the low-N level 2.2). At all other levels, average scores fell just within the upper limits of the bands. Even level 4 students scored on average considerably higher than the minimum score required for placing into level 4 courses. Based on these observations, the PIUs concluded that Fall 1999 students who were placed into any of the curricular levels above year 1 (for which sufficient semester-beginning data were not available), and particularly those placed into the beginning of year 3, were likely to have been located in courses with students who exhibited slightly higher levels of curriculum-related abilities. In other words, the cut-score bands were probably over-estimating student placements.

Figure 9 compares average semester-end scores for combined placed and non-placed students (marked with a +) with the corresponding placement exam cut-score bands. Combined scores were used in order to provide a more robust representation of students' average abilities by the end of the semester of instruction, and the PIUs reasoned that differences between placed and non-placed students would have been diminished by the end of the semester (for better or worse results, depending on the student). Note in Figure 9 that the Fall 1999 cut-score band at each curricular level (marked with an X) was that used for making determinations about students *exiting* the given level and entering into the next proximate level (i.e., the 2.2 cut-score band was used to identify students who should exit from level 2.1 and enter into level 2.2 of the curriculum). For this reason, the cut-score bands associated with the intensive courses are identical for those associated with the next proximate higher level (i.e., the cut-score band for 2.Int is the same as that for 2.2 at the end of the semester). As with the semester-beginning scores of non-placed students, it was apparent in Figure 9 that the original Fall 1999 cut-score bands fell short of students' average scores on the C-test at the end of each of the curricular levels. In particular, students at 2.1, 2.Int, and 2.2 scored on average substantially higher than the top of the placement cut-score band for the next proximate level by the end of the semester. Students at the end of year 3 courses also scored on average well above the minimum cut-score for entering into level 4 courses.

In sum, two concerns were identified with the accuracy of placement exam cut-score bands. First, average C-test scores for students at both the beginning and the end of the semester exceeded the midpoints of the corresponding cut-score bands at every curricular level, by a low of around ½ of a 5-point SEM (approximately 2 score points higher for students at the beginning of level 2.1) to a high of just over 2 SEMs (approximately 12 score points higher for students at the end of level 2.2). Second, average C-test scores for students within year 2 of the curriculum increased more than predicted by the cut-score bands for year 2 courses; that is, the bands were too narrow to account for students' mean scores at the beginning and the end of the semester. These concerns indicated that original placement exam cut-score bands had likely located incoming students into curricular levels with students of somewhat higher abilities. In response, the PIUs identified an immediate need to revise the existing placement standards prior to additional use of the C-test for placement decision-making purposes.

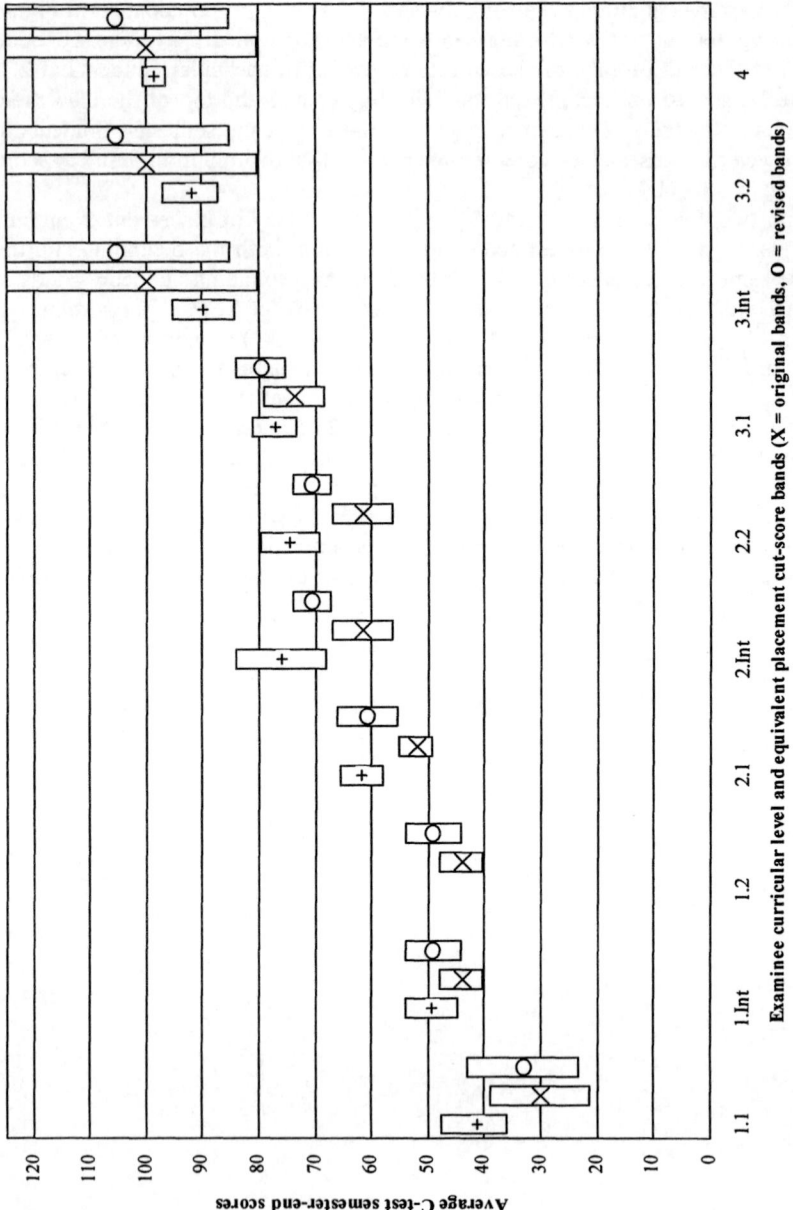

Figure 9. Average semester-end C-test scores compared with original and revised placement cut-score bands (all data)

Uses. The PIUs discussed these findings in light of three intended uses: (a) decisions regarding continued use of the C-test; (b) needed revisions in the C-test and placement cut-score bands; and (c) dissemination of information regarding the effectiveness of the C-test. The PIUs agreed that evidence accumulated from the Fall 1999 studies was sufficient to support interpretations about the effectiveness of the C-test instrument at distinguishing among students across the full range of curricular levels. They interpreted the high reliability estimates and wide-ranging score distributions as evidence that the instrument consistently elicited performances reflective of the range of German language ability levels represented within the GUGD, and they found the cross-sectional and longitudinal comparisons convincing of the extent to which the C-test was able to distinguish between examinees at distinct curricular levels.

Considerable discussion was devoted to likely causes for observed discrepancies at the juncture between levels 2 and 3 of the curriculum, and the PIUs argued that this portion of the curriculum represented the most difficult period of development for students as they acquired advanced language use abilities. The PIUs also expressed concern over the observation that individual students at each curricular level might score substantially higher or lower on the C-test than the central tendency of students at that level, but they speculated that a portion of these students within the non-placed groups in the Fall 1999 studies might not have been truly representative of the curricular levels, given previous inconsistencies in placement and enrollment policies. In a similar vein, they questioned, on the one hand, the extent to which the C-test (or any relatively brief placement test instrument) could be sensitive enough to curriculum-related ability differences to enable interpretations at the mid-year junctures (i.e., between 2.1 and 2.2), and, on the other hand, whether additional placement policies needed to be developed in order to make sure that incoming students took the placement exam and followed placement recommendations. Nevertheless, they agreed that immediate adjustments were required in placement exam cut-score bands for the C-test, in order to bring the average scores for placed students in line with those of non-placed students.

As a result of these discussions, the PIUs decided that the C-test should continue to be administered for placement decision-making purposes. In addition, they raised the possibility of revising the use of the annual fall semester placement exam to adjudicate placement decisions by year only (i.e., into level 1, 2, 3, or 4) but not for recommending 'off-sequence' courses at the mid-year junctures (i.e., into the second semester of each curricular level: 1.2, 2.2, 3.2), given the fact that these courses were only rarely offered during the fall semester. Finally, they suggested that additional placement exam administration and enrollment policies be developed in order to ensure that students were enrolling in the courses most appropriate to their learning needs. Decisions regarding these two placement policy issues were deferred until the evaluation findings could be disseminated and discussed among the full faculty and instructional staff of the department.

The PIUs also initiated immediate revisions to placement exam cut-score bands for the C-test. The resulting revised cut-score bands can be seen in Figures 8 and 9 (indicated with O symbols). First, the overall range of placement decisions was adjusted by raising the highest cut-score (for placing into level 4 courses) one SEM (5 points), from 80 to 85 points. This adjustment placed the highest cut-score point within one SEM of the average scores of students completing the year 3 courses (3.2 and 3.Int semester-end scores) and students beginning year 4 courses (level 4 semester-beginning scores), all of which fell around 90 score points. Second, the cut-score bands were raised for all levels, from between one-half and two SEMs, by adjusting the mid-points of each band to be as equivalent as possible to the average scores for students at both the beginning of that level of instruction and the end of the previous level of instruction. In addition, the width of the cut-score bands for levels 2.1 and 2.2 was increased one-half and one SEM respectively, to account for the observed magnitude of change in C-test scores over the course of a semester at those levels. It was hoped that these adjustments in cut-scores would result in the placement of students into courses where their abilities and needs would be more accurately matched with those of other students.

Evaluation findings and planned revisions to the placement exam cut-score bands for the C-test were further disseminated during a full-department meeting in May 2000. Graphical analyses were used as the primary means for demonstrating the effectiveness of the C-test instrument and the inaccuracies/revisions of the cut-score bands. Response by the departmental stakeholders was generally positive to the continued use of the C-test for placement decision-making purposes, in particular with the recommended adjustments in the cut-score bands which reflected anecdotal reports by several instructors regarding the apparent weaknesses of a few placed students during the beginning of the Fall 1999 semester. Policy changes for the placement exam and enrollment process were also discussed. However, stakeholders decided to postpone any additions or changes until after one more year of placement exam administration in Fall 2000, in order to evaluate better the need for such policies. Finally, a summary of findings from the Fall 1999 evaluation studies, including the analyses reported above, was made available to all departmental stakeholders, and it was decided by them that findings from further investigations would be reported on and disseminated as additions to this initial summary. No further dissemination actions were undertaken at this time (e.g., to students or to department-external stakeholders).

6.2.2 Evaluating scoring consistency and placement/enrollment accuracy

The PIUs identified three principal sources of error which could potentially interfere with the accurate placement and enrollment of students into curricular levels most appropriate to their needs: scoring inconsistency, decision-making inaccuracy, and enrollment infidelity. Each had been observed anecdotally in conjunction with the Fall 1999 exam, although formalized efforts at understanding the nature and extent of error were postponed until two official exams had taken place, in order to provide sufficient data for understanding associated problems. Therefore, following the Fall 2000 exam administration, the PIUs prioritized for evaluation their concerns regarding the extent to which any or all of these error sources might have been contributing to inappropriate placement recommendations and enrollments.

The most obvious source of error was associated with the scoring of examinee performances on the three placement exam sub-tests. For the LCT and RCT sub-tests, machine scoring (Scantron) was used both for marking incorrect responses and for tallying a final test score on each test for each examinee. As such, it was assumed that scoring error would be of little concern for these two sub-tests. However, because students were required to write in the deleted portions of words throughout the C-test, human scoring was called upon to assess the accuracy of their responses and to provide a tally of total correct responses for each examinee. During the placement exam administration, C-test scoring was carried out in a single session by faculty. Although scorers were provided guidelines and a scoring key, the concern remained that, during the rather rapid turnaround required for placement decisions, errors might occur in either the identification of incorrect responses or in the summing of correct responses into a total test score. In order to evaluate these concerns, the PIUs posed the following two questions for investigation:

(a) To what extent did scorers accurately identify correct and incorrect student responses on the C-test?
(b) To what extent did scorers accurately calculate a total score on the C-test?

A second potential source of error within the placement process occurred as decisions were made regarding the most appropriate curricular level for a given examinee, primarily on the basis of information from the three placement exam sub-tests. During the initial Fall 1999 exam, these decisions were made collaboratively by the department chair and the consultant evaluator, following the decision criteria outlined in section 6.1. These decision-making procedures were formalized and passed along to the curriculum coordinator and the department chair for use during the Fall 2000 placement exam administration, with the addition of information regarding the SEM associated with each sub-test (based on the Fall 1999 administrations). The SEMs were to be used for adjudicating ambiguous cases where test scores fell close to the next higher or lower level.

The possibility of error entered into this decision-making process as a result of the inexact system for balancing multiple sources of information (including highly variable language learning experiences) and due to the potential for decision makers to apply the existing procedures inconsistently when deciding among the recommendations from the three sub-tests. Clearly, the result of such errors would take the form of inaccurate placement recommendations made to individual students, as would the result of scoring errors. Unfortunately, because data were not collected on the decision-making processes which had transpired during the two placement exam administrations of interest (due to the fact that related concerns were not raised until after the exams had taken place), existing evidence could not attribute inaccurate placements to either scoring errors or decision-making errors. However, the overall inaccuracy of actual placement recommendations made to students who completed either of the two exam administrations could be estimated by re-assessing the three sub-test scores (revised where necessary) and adjudicating a new recommendation on their basis. Therefore, the concerns of the PIUs could be addressed in part by asking the following question:

(c) What was the impact of scoring and/or decision-making errors on actual placement recommendations made to students?

A third potential source of error was associated with the lack of policies or practices for controlling students' enrollments into GUGD courses. A single relevant policy had been included in the 1999 General Policy Statement on assessment in the GUGD (see Appendix B): "Unless students begin their study of German at Georgetown University or are native speakers of German they will take a placement examination". However, no other departmental policies were in place for requiring students to comply with placement recommendations designated by exam results, nor was there any mechanism for ensuring that students completed the exam or for automatically blocking registration or otherwise restricting students' enrollments. Although most students who intended to enroll in GUGD courses were identified and contacted regarding the need to complete a placement exam prior to initial enrollments, students nevertheless registered for courses in a variety of ways prior to this evaluation study. Faculty and instructors anecdotally reported several cases of students who had enrolled in their courses without taking the placement exam, either on the basis of recommendations by their program major advisors (in other departments) or by simply self-enrolling in whatever courses they thought appropriate. Cases were also reported of students who had taken the placement exam but had ignored the placement recommendation and self-enrolled in a curricular level other than that indicated.

While concrete policies regarding student enrollments, and dependable mechanisms for implementing these policies, would clearly resolve any such errors, departmental stakeholders were hesitant to implement any practices which might be perceived by students as additional bureaucratic impediments. However, stakeholders also perceived problems associated with students enrolling in courses that assumed higher or lower language ability levels, including potential detriments to other students within the course, perceptions of unfairness among students within the department, and institutional and professional reputation regarding the quality of GUGD courses and student learning outcomes. In response to these concerns of stakeholders, the PIUs decided that the degree of error in enrollment first required investigation, and that the source of incorrect enrollments needed to be clarified, prior to any further implementation of enrollment policies. Therefore, the following questions were posed for evaluation:

(d) To what extent did students enroll in non-indicated GUGD curricular levels *due to inaccurate* placement recommendations?

(e) To what extent did students enroll in non-indicated GUGD curricular levels *despite accurate* placement recommendations?

Evaluation findings for questions (a) through (e) above were intended to inform several uses. First and foremost, findings would provide the PIUs with an empirical (versus anecdotal) understanding of both the potential degree of error involved in the placement process, due to inaccuracies in test scoring, and also the actual degree of error observed both in the placement recommendations made to students and in the enrollment actions taken by students. As a result, departmental stakeholders would gain a better understanding of the extent to which students ended up in courses at curricular levels contra-indicated for their likely language abilities and of the probable sources for these enrollment inaccuracies. Second, findings regarding scoring error would be used to raise the awareness of scorers to the potential types of inaccuracies encountered during the process and to revise/improve scoring practices where necessary. Third, findings regarding the extent of error introduced during placement and enrollment decision-making would provide an empirical basis for making decisions about the need for additional placement and enrollment policies and mechanisms, and the forms that these might best take.

Methods. In order to investigate these questions, the following methods were employed. First, to evaluate the potential influence of scoring error, the consultant re-scored all examinee C-test performances from the Fall 1999 and Fall 2000 placement exam administrations, after they had already been scored once by departmental personnel for placement purposes. An exact-response scoring method was employed, based on the C-test scoring guidelines and scoring key. Re-scoring involved the identification of correct/incorrect responses by examinees to the 125 items on each C-test exam, the tallying of total correct responses for each of the five C-test texts (maximum of 25 points each), and the summing of an overall test score (maximum of 125 points). In addition, for any errors identified in the original scoring of a C-test, the type and magnitude of errors were recorded for each exam. Finally, the number of examinees whose placements were potentially impacted by incorrect C-test scores was calculated based on revised placement decisions associated with the new total C-test scores for each examinee. Findings were interpreted as "potentially" incorrect placements because placement decisions were intended to be made on the basis of three unique sources of information (the LCT and RCT, as well as the C-test) and potentially augmented by background information; thus, incorrect scoring of the C-test may or may not have actually influenced the accuracy of the final placement decision.

Second, the impact of scoring and/or decision-making errors on the accuracy of actual placement recommendations was investigated. Revised C-test scores were first translated into curricular level placement recommendations and recorded with the recommendations from each of the LCT and RCT sub-tests for both the Fall 1999 and Fall 2000 exam administrations. Final curricular-level placement recommendations were then re-assessed for all examinees, following the placement procedures

153

outlined above. The total number of inaccurate placement recommendations was then tallied for each level, and the magnitude of mis-placement was recorded (in terms of number of semesters above or below the correct recommendation).

Third, the extent to which scoring and/or decision-making errors led to incorrect enrollments was investigated and compared with the extent to which students enrolled themselves at curricular levels contrary to accurate placement recommendations. Placement-based enrollments (i.e., students who took the placement exam and enrolled in GUGD courses) were first tracked for each curricular level over the academic year of the placement exam, including the Fall and Spring semesters, by identifying the initial course in the GUGD for which the student had registered. Each enrollment was then compared with the final, accurate placement recommendation. Where discrepancies were identified between the actual student enrollment and the accurate placement recommendation, the original placement recommendation was compared with the enrollment. For those incorrect enrollments that matched the original placement recommendations, error was accorded to the placement scoring and decision-making process. For all other incorrect enrollments, error was accorded to the student's own enrollment decision.

Findings. Evaluation points (a) and (b) above questioned the accuracy with which GUGD departmental personnel score the C-tests. Table 9 displays related findings after all placement exam C-tests from the Fall 1999 and Fall 2000 administrations had been re-scored. It is clear that the C-test scoring process incurred considerable error. On each administration, between 65% and 69% of examinees' C-tests had at least one item either falsely marked as incorrect or one incorrect response not marked. In addition, between 9% and 18% of examinees received incorrect total scores as a result of errors in tallying correct responses for each C-test text or errors in summing the total test score.

While numerous exams were affected by scoring error, such errors, if of a small magnitude, would not lead to undue concern, given the fact that the test was comprised of a large number of items (125). Thus, very small amounts of error would be less likely to impact examinees' placements or would impact them to lesser degrees (i.e., fewer semesters incorrect). Table 9 shows that, while numerous errors occurred in marking items as correct/incorrect on both administrations, the average magnitude of marking errors was between 2 and 3 score points (around half the SEM for the C-test). Thus, while the frequency of exams affected was of concern, it was unlikely that resulting misplacements would be greater than a semester higher or lower, even for the worst degree of marking error observed on any single exam (12 points).

Table 9. Type and size of scoring error for two C-test administrations

| | Statistic | Fall, 1999 (N=102) | | Fall, 2000 (N=92) | |
		Addition error	Marking error	Addition error	Marking error
Exams affected	%	18%	65%	9%	69%
by at least 1 error	N	18	66	8	64
Size of error in score points (total k = 125)	Mean	5.28	2.26	14.13	2.32
	S	6.25	1.98	11.99	1.63
	MIN	1	1	1	1
	MAX	20	12	25	7
Potential impact on placement decisions	%misplaced	5%	8%	5%	15%
	Nmisplaced	5	9	5	14
	+3sem	--	--	2	--
	+2sem	--	--	2	--
	+1sem	4	8	--	14
	-1sem	1	1	1	--

Note. Misplacement frequency counts represent placement errors that would have occurred based on C-test scores alone, not including additional information from LCT and RCT scores.

Addition errors, while occurring with much lower frequency, were of a greater magnitude. Addition errors on the Fall 1999 placement exam C-test averaged around one SEM (5 points), but ranged up to 20 score points, and errors on the Fall 2000 C-test averaged more than two SEMs and ranged up to 25 score points. Clearly, depending on the location of an examinee's score within the cut-score bands for the C-test, errors of this magnitude might result in placement inaccuracies of as many as three semesters above or below the correct placement level.

In order to identify the maximum number of students who might have been incorrectly placed as a direct result of scoring inaccuracies on the Fall 1999 and Fall 2000 placement exam C-tests, revised C-test scores which fell within cut-score bands distinct from the original placement exam C-test score were tallied. For both years, the percentage of students with placements potentially affected by either type of C-test scoring error ranged between 5% and 15%, with the maximum percentage of any type of inaccurate placement falling between 13% and 20%. Fall 1999 exams were less affected, both in frequency and magnitude of potential misplacements, with no scores revealing inaccuracies which would shift student placements by more than one semester up or down. A greater frequency and magnitude of potential misplacements occurred in Fall 2000, with four students' potentially misplaced by two to three semesters and numerous others potentially misplaced by one semester. Finally, it is of note that virtually all potential misplacements based on C-test scoring inaccuracies would have resulted in students enrolling in curricular levels higher than appropriate. Clearly, scorers were erring either by not marking incorrect responses where they occurred, or by adding up more than the actual number of correct responses.

In answer to questions (a) and (b), then, the scoring of placement exam C-tests resulted in a high frequency of marking errors and a lower frequency of addition errors, with addition errors resulting in much larger inaccuracies than marking errors. The combined impact of these two types of scoring error had the potential to result in as many as 20% of examinees being misplaced by one semester or more.

Point (c) above questioned the accuracy of actual (versus potential) placement recommendations made to students on the basis of the Fall 1999 and Fall 2000 exams. The sources for such inaccuracies were either scoring errors, of the sort detailed above, or decision-making errors, which occurred in interpreting and comparing scores from the three placement exam sub-tests. Table 10 shows the number, curricular location, and magnitude of inaccurate placement recommendations made to students on the basis of the Fall 1999 placement exam administration. Approximately 15% of students completing the exam received placement recommendations that were, in all likelihood, inaccurate for their level of German language ability as compared with curricular expectations. The majority of misplacements recommended that students enroll one semester level higher than appropriate, and these errors were all located in levels 2.2, 3.1, or 3.2. Several students were also misplaced lower than appropriate. However, no students were actually misplaced by more than one semester level higher or lower.

Table 10. Inaccurate placement recommendations for Fall 1999 Placement Exam

Curricular level	Original placements	Misplacements due to scoring/decision errors (number of semesters)				Revised placements
		-2	-1	+1	+2	
4	47	0	0	0	0	48
3.2	17	0	1	5	0	11
3.1	15	0	0	2	0	18
2.2	10	0	0	4	0	10
2.1	6	0	2	0	0	9
1.2	5	0	1	0	0	4
1.1	2	0	0	0	0	2
Total	**102**	**0**	**4**	**11**	**0**	**102**

Note. Revised placement frequencies show the number of students who should have been placed into each curricular level, based on accurate scoring and decision-making during the GUGD Placement Exam.

Table 11 shows the number, curricular location, and magnitude of inaccurate placement recommendations made to students on the basis of the Fall 2000 placement exam. A more substantial 25% of students completing this exam received placement recommendations that were most likely inappropriate with respect to their German language abilities and the expectations of the curriculum. All but one of these misplacements indicated that students enroll higher than appropriate, and again, the large majority of misplacements were located in levels 2.2, 3.1, or 3.2. In addition, for the Fall 2000 placement exam, four of these students were misplaced by two semester levels higher than appropriate.

Table 11. Inaccurate placement recommendations for Fall 2000 Placement Exam

Curricular level	Original placements	Misplacements due to scoring/decision errors (number of semesters)				Revised placements
		-2	-1	+1	+2	
4	34	0	0	1	0	34
3.2	21	0	1	5	1	15
3.1	20	0	0	8	2	15
2.2	9	0	0	3	1	14
2.1	4	0	0	1	0	8
1.2	2	0	0	0	0	4
1.1	2	0	0	0	0	2
Total	**92**	**0**	**1**	**18**	**4**	**92**

Note. Revised placement frequencies show the number of students who should have been placed into each curricular level, based on accurate scoring and decision-making during the GUGD Placement Exam.

A straightforward interpretation of these findings would attribute the majority of error for actual placement recommendations to the inaccuracies in scoring that were observed for the placement exam C-tests. Thus, the increase in misplacements from 1999 to 2000 could be accounted for, in part, by the increased frequency and magnitude of C-test scoring errors between the two testing occasions. However, C-test scoring errors alone could not account for the entire 10% increase in faulty placement recommendations for Fall 2000. Rather, the additional inaccuracies were in all likelihood attributable to a mistake in the scoring and interpretation of student performances on the LCT and RCT subtests. As it turned out (the consultant was not on hand to oversee the Fall 2000 exam), examinee results from the LCT and RCT had been returned from machine scoring in the form of a single combined score, rather than as two independent scores. Given the quick turnaround time called for in order to disseminate student placement recommendations on the same day as the exam, decision makers had decided to use the combined LCT/RCT scores by also combining the cut-score bands for the two sub-tests. Unfortunately, of course, this strategy resulted in a dramatic reduction of information for placement decision-making purposes. Thus, whether a student performed distinctly better on one of the two sub-tests or equally well on the two was not decipherable from the combined test scores; in fact, the combined scores were virtually uninterpretable as an indication of curricular level abilities, except in the cases of very high or very low scores (i.e., where the student clearly performed very well or very poorly on both sub-tests). As a result, the increased number of misplacements identified for the Fall 2000 administration was at least in part attributable to this error in the scoring and use of the LCT/RCT sub-tests.

The substantial and unexpected proportion of likely misplacements for the two exam administrations provided cause for considerable concern among the PIUs. However, in order to understand the degree to which these inaccurate recommendations translated into actual mis-enrollments, points (d) and (e) above questioned the extent to which students enrolled in contra-indicated curricular levels and the likely source of their decisions for doing so. Tables 12 and 13 show the results of comparisons between students' actual enrollments, their original placement recommendations, and revised placement recommendations after re-scoring of the C-tests. Note in both tables that numbers reflect those students who took the Fall 1999 or Fall 2000 placement exam *and* who enrolled in an initial GUGD course in either the fall or spring semester of the corresponding academic year (i.e., a number of students did not enroll in any GUGD courses during the year following their completion of the placement exam).

Table 12. Inaccurate enrollments from Fall 1999 GUGD Placement Exam

Curricular level	Placement enrollments (F99/S00)	Enrolled *higher* due to misplacement	Enrolled *lower* due to misplacement	Enrolled *higher* than recommended	Enrolled *lower* than recommended
4 (or above)	26	1	0	0	0
3.2	8	0	1	1	1
3.1	12	2	0	2	1
3.intensive	2	0	0	0	0
2.2	5	0	0	0	3
2.1	4	0	0	1	1
2.intensive	6	0	0	0	2
1.2	0	0	0	0	0
1.1	4	0	0	0	3
1.intensive	1	0	0	0	1
Total	**68**	**3**	**1**	**4**	**12**

Note. Students who took the Fall 1999 placement exam could enroll in their first GUGD course in either the Fall 1999 or Spring 2000 semesters.

In conjunction with the Fall 1999 placement exam, only four (6%) of the 68 total students who enrolled did so into incorrect curricular levels as a result of inaccurate placement recommendations, none of which were inaccurate by more than one semester. However, 16 students (24%) self-enrolled in curricular levels higher or lower than recommended. Of these, one enrolled four semesters lower, one enrolled three semesters lower, and five enrolled two semesters higher or lower than recommended. As it turned out, student self-enrollments posed a considerable problem for maintaining homogeneity of students' German language abilities within GUGD courses following the Fall 1999 placement exam.

Table 13. Inaccurate enrollments from Fall 2000 GUGD Placement Exam

Curricular level	Placement enrollments (F00/S01)	Enrolled *higher* due to misplacement	Enrolled *lower* due to misplacement	Enrolled *higher* than recommended	Enrolled *lower* than recommended
4 (or above)	30	1	0	7	0
3.2	9	2	0	0	0
3.1	10	3	0	1	1
3.intensive	3	0	0	0	0
2.2	5	3	0	0	0
2.1	9	1	0	1	3
2.intensive	0	0	0	0	0
1.2	2	0	0	0	0
1.1	0	0	0	0	0
1.intensive	1	0	0	0	0
Total	69	10	0	9	4

Note. Students who took the Fall 2000 placement exam could enroll in their first GUGD course in either the Fall 2000 or Spring 2001 semesters.

In conjunction with the Fall 2000 placement exam, causes for enrollment inaccuracies were somewhat more balanced, no doubt due in part to the increased degree of faulty decision-making based on problems with the scoring of all three placement exam sub-tests. Thus, ten (14%) of 69 students who enrolled did so into one semester level higher as a result of inaccurate placement recommendations. However, once again, a larger number (13) enrolled contrary to placement recommendations; one of these enrolled four semesters higher, and four enrolled two semesters higher than recommended.

In sum, errors in placement exam scoring and decision-making procedures resulted in a substantial number of inaccurate placement recommendations, although these recommendations were almost never on the order of more than one semester higher or lower than the correct curricular level. Furthermore, these inaccurate recommendations did lead a small proportion of students (between 6% and 14%) to enroll in the wrong curricular level, again by no more than one semester higher or lower. More substantial inaccuracies in enrollments were found for students who self-enrolled contrary to placement indications, with between 19% and 24% of students registering for an initial GUGD course at the wrong level, despite ostensibly accurate placement recommendations. Moreover, these mis-enrollments included students who registered for classes up to four semesters higher or lower than the curricular level indicated by the placement exam recommendations.

Uses. Based on the empirical evidence, the PIUs agreed that all three types of error had occurred to a degree that warranted immediate action. However, they also acknowledged that, because the majority of inaccurate student enrollments had located students only one semester higher or lower than appropriate, the overall placement process had not resulted in substantially inappropriate placement recommendations and actions for most students during the 1999-2000 and 2000-2001 academic years (see section 6.3 for further evaluation). Nevertheless, in an effort to reduce the influence of error as much as possible, the PIUs took several actions. Note that their decisions and actions as a result of this evaluation stage, in conjunction with elements from other stages, are summarized in the *GUGD Placement Procedures and Policies* document (Appendix D).

First, scoring error was addressed in the following ways. To remove the possibility of incorrect combinations of LCT and RCT scores, explicit guidelines stressed that "Each of the three placement exam sub-tests is scored *independently*, resulting in three test scores (there is no total or combined score on the placement exam)". Further, the curriculum coordinator was given the specific responsibility of overseeing the placement exam administration to ensure that scoring, decision-making, and enrollment occurred as designed.

In order to improve scorer performance in marking incorrect items and adding up total scores on the C-test, departmental faculty and staff (responsible for scoring the C-test) were first made aware of the severity of inconsistencies observed during the Fall 1999 and Fall 2000 scoring sessions. Findings were disseminated to these stakeholders during a departmental end-of-semester retreat, and they were made available permanently as part of an internal research report. The curriculum coordinator was also placed in charge of the placement exam C-test scoring sessions to ensure that all scorers were aware of the scoring guidelines, and the importance of applying them consistently for all examinees. In addition, the practice of double scoring each C-test was introduced into these scoring sessions in order to provide a check on the accuracy of individual scorer work. Finally, the PIUs decided to initiate the development of a computer-based system for administering and scoring the C-test, in order to eliminate the influence of scoring error altogether.

In order to systematize placement decision-making procedures, the PIUs agreed upon the basic strategies outlined above for interpreting and comparing information from the three placement exam sub-tests as well as any additional information provided by students' language learning backgrounds. These decision-making strategies were outlined in the *GUGD Placement Procedures and Policies* document, and the curriculum coordinator and department chair were placed in charge of making the final placement decisions for each examinee.

Finally, the PIUs perceived the incorrect enrollments of students as the most challenging finding to deal with during this stage. Clearly, the frequency and degree of mis-enrollments called for action, but that action had to be carefully presented as a means for supporting student learning, and it had to avoid perceptions by students and others of restricting students' enrollment options. In addressing this problem, the PIUs first clarified the specific placement and enrollment policies of the GUGD:

- Incoming students with any prior background in German may not enroll in GUGD classes without first taking the placement exam.
- Students' advisors from other departments do not have the authority to make a placement recommendation in lieu of the placement exam.

- Students should enroll in the curricular level into which they were placed, not lower or higher based on their preferences or opinions of their abilities.
- Placement decisions are not immutable and may be revised by the curriculum coordinator or department chair (only) upon recommendation by the student's German Department teacher.

However, in order to implement the basic policy that students should enroll in the curricular level indicated by the placement exam, the PIUs and other stakeholders were careful not to take actions that might reduce enrollments. Thus, they did not implement any restrictions on the actual course registration process (e.g., automatic blocks on students who had not completed the placement exam). Instead, they pursued a strategy of communication, confirmation, and follow-up regarding the placement and enrollment process. For all students who inquired about GUGD courses prior to enrollment, information regarding the placement exam process and enrollment policies was disseminated in the form of a letter which described the exam and how it was used, and which clarified that initial placements should be followed but were not immutable. Following the placement exam and decision-making process, curricular level placement recommendations were disseminated and explained to students in person during a pre-semester enrollment party sponsored by the department, and students were assisted in enrolling in the appropriate GUGD courses.

All placement exam information available for each enrolled student was subsequently distributed to the individual instructors for each GUGD course. Instructors utilized this information to identify students who had placed into their courses (and on what basis), and they collected further information from students on the first day of class which clarified how all students had enrolled in the course. Via this process, the responsibility for accurate enrollments was shifted away from the student and to the instructor of the course. Students who had self-enrolled without taking the placement exam were immediately referred to the curriculum coordinator for exam administration and placement, and the coordinator took pains to explain to students why the placement exam was necessary. Students who had enrolled in contraindicated curricular levels were identified by teachers via the placement exam information, and the teacher explained why the student needed to enroll in the appropriate curricular level. Finally, all students who had enrolled in a given course via the placement exam process were carefully monitored by instructors for the first several weeks of the semester in order to ensure the accuracy of each placement decision.

The PIUs felt that these actions provided the most appropriate means for ameliorating the disconcerting error observed in scoring, decision-making, and enrollment, and they felt that changes would result in improved homogeneity among students' ability levels within courses. In addition, evaluation findings and uses at this stage prompted related concerns. The PIUs began to question the degree to which homogeneity among student abilities could be expected at any of the curricular levels, among either continuing or placed students, given the unique language learning experiences that students brought with them into the program. In addition, they wondered how students who were placed into recommended levels had performed in those courses versus continuing students and students who had been placed or enrolled in contra-indicated curricular levels. However, of immediate concern for evaluation during this implementation and revision stage of the placement exam program was a final set of technical investigations into the measurement qualities of the three placement exam sub-tests and the C-test in particular.

6.2.3 Evaluating measurement qualities of placement exam sub-tests

Beyond their immediate initial concerns with the effectiveness and accuracy of the C-test vis-à-vis the GUGD curricular levels and the sources/amounts of error introduced during the scoring, placement, and enrollment processes, the PIUs and stakeholders more generally questioned the trustworthiness and consistency of the three sub-test instruments. Their questions took the basic forms of "Did the unique text selection, item development, and test construction procedures work for all three sub-tests?", "How reliable are the overall scores on the three sub-tests?", "What is the relationship between scores on the three sub-tests?", and "Do the sub-tests perform consistently on distinct exam administrations?" The PIUs raised these questions for several reasons. First, they desired standard information about the qualities of the test instruments in order to pass final judgments regarding the ongoing use of the placement exam in its new form. Second, they sought any additional information which might be useful in improving individual items and the overall composition of the test instruments. Third, they sought to compare the trustworthiness of the three instruments in order to inform further policies regarding the balance of contributions from each test score for decision making. Fourth, the PIUs assumed that standard measurement quality information would need to be communicated to both internal and external constituents for the purpose of defending the ongoing use of these unique, locally developed test instruments. Finally, they sought baseline information about the measurement qualities of the sub-tests as a means for evaluating the eventual development of parallel forms for each; in other words, they wanted to know whether the in-house test development techniques would produce new test forms of equal quality to these initial placement exam sub-tests.

Investigations proceeded by asking each of the following questions in the following order for each of the three sub-tests:

(a) To what extent did the test elicit an appropriate distribution of examinee scores, and to what extent did this distribution differ between distinct exam administrations?

(b) To what extent did the test produce scores which distinguish reliably among individual examinees, and to what extent did score reliability differ between distinct exam administrations?

(c) To what extent did individual items (or texts, in the case of the C-test) elicit expected response patterns from examinees, and to what extent did these patterns differ between distinct exam administrations?

One final question addressed comparisons between the three placement exam sub-tests:

(d) What was the relationship among overall test scores for the three sub-tests, and to what extent did this relationship differ between distinct exam administrations?

Methods. Data used for investigating questions (a) through (d) consisted of examinee performances on each of the three sub-tests during the two placement exam administrations in Fall 1999 and Fall 2000. Data from each administration were treated independently for all analyses of technical measurement qualities, in keeping with the notion that such qualities do not inhere within test instruments, rather, they reflect the use of test instruments on particular occasions with specific samples of the target population of examinees (see discussion in AERA, APA, NCME, 1999; Feldt & Brennan, 1989; Traub, 1994). Thus, these two groups of examinees were considered unique samples from the population of students who would potentially complete the GUGD placement exam, characterized as adult students enrolled in Georgetown University courses of study and with some amount of German language learning experience. Clearly, within this general population, individuals could vary in a number of ways relevant to their test performances. It was also possible that the parameters of the examinee population itself might change over time (e.g., as incoming students on the whole presented with higher levels of German language preparation). Accordingly, rather than a single set of analyses for the combined examinee performances on the two administrations (i.e., pooling all available test performance data)—which would risk obscuring any differences in measurement qualities associated with specific testing occasions and examinees—distinct analyses were conducted in order to reveal the extent to which measurement qualities would prove consistent across different exam administrations.

There exist, of course, myriad techniques for analyzing test score and item response data (e.g., Bachman, 2004). However, given the conceptual and technical complexity of many of these analytic methods, and the often tiny increments they may offer in additional information for understanding and improving assessment practice *in situ*, their use with the majority of educational assessment constituents would be at best inefficient and at worst debilitating (see related discussion in Davidson & Lynch, 2002; Popham, 2000). As such, only basic analyses from two measurement perspectives were employed in the current study. First, classical test theory (CTT) analyses (Brown, 1996; Henning, 1987; Traub, 1994) provided a straightforward means for quickly estimating the reliability and error associated with overall test scores and with specific test items. By assuming a unitary and normally distributed view of measurement error (as opposed, e.g., to a multifaceted view as in generalizability theory; cf. Shavelson & Webb, 1991), a CTT approach enabled the investigation of simple patterns within existing test performance data using observed raw scores as the unit of analysis.

However, it is clear that CTT analyses based on raw scores may not produce the most accurate or generalizable estimates of measurement qualities underlying test scores, given the actual unequal distribution of error across test items and total test scores (see discussion in Embretson & Hershberger, 1999; McNamara, 1996). Therefore, item response theory (IRT) analyses were also employed to provide a second perspective on measurement qualities. By modeling the relationship between examinees' test performances and the specific patterns and probabilities of response associated with each individual item, and by factoring in the idiosyncratic ability constellations presented by a given population sample, an IRT approach enabled a more exacting analysis of test and item characteristics (Hambleton, Swaminathan, & Rogers, 1991). Specifically, Rasch model IRT analyses (see discussion in Linacre, 1989; McNamara, 1996) provided for measurement and error estimates of examinee abilities and item difficulties. At the same time, even the basic results of these analyses, in the form of logit (logarithmic-odds unit) rather than raw-score estimates, proved much less straightforward for informing the PIUs' interpretations. Therefore, given the benefits and drawbacks of each approach, both CTT and IRT analyses were conducted conjointly in response to each question.

First, in order to investigate the distribution of examinee scores and the reliability of distinctions among examinees on the three sub-tests, descriptive statistics and reliability/error estimates were calculated for the two administrations. Descriptive statistics revealed patterns in the central tendency and dispersion of total test scores, reflecting the effectiveness of the tests at eliciting a range of performances associated with examinees' differing ability levels. CTT estimates of test score reliability (Cronbach alpha, α) and the error associated with raw test scores (standard error of measurement, SEM) provided an indication of the extent to which each test was distinguishing on the whole among student ability levels, and indicated the score range within which a given examinee's test score could be trusted (Brown, 1996). Note that Cronbach α was selected as the most appropriate CTT reliability index for dealing with both the dichotomous items on the LCT/RCT and the polytomous items on the C-test. Thus, each C-test text was treated as a single 25-point 'super-item' for all analyses, given that individual word completions within each text violated the standard assumption of independence among items (i.e., within a single text, performance on one word completion was directly related to performance on other word completions, but this was not the case between texts; see Grotjahn, 1992b). In addition, Rasch model IRT analyses were conducted using FACETS software (Linacre, 1998). These analyses provided overall examinee separation indexes, and standard error estimates, which indicated the extent to which an interval measurement scale modeled for each sub-test was able to distinguish accurately (or 'separate') examinee ability levels (see discussion in McNamara, 1996). Corresponding α equivalents were also calculated for each separation index.

Second, individual items (on the LCT/RCT) and texts (on the C-test) were analyzed in several ways. For dichotomous items on the LCT and RCT, item facility (IF) and item discrimination (ID) estimates provided a CTT perspective on the ease/difficulty of each item and the extent to which an item was able to separate examinees into distinct ability levels (Brown, 1996). Similar patterns were investigated for each of the 25-point C-test texts in the form of descriptive statistics for scores associated with each text. Furthermore, for each of the three sub-tests, Rasch model IRT analyses provided item measure estimates (i.e., an index of item difficulty on the underlying interval scale calculated for each sub-test) and associated estimates of standard error, model fit, and item-total correlations (a Rasch model equivalent to the point-biserial correlation) for each item. Within the FACETS Rasch model program, LCT and RCT sub-test data were modeled dichotomously (i.e., based on the correct/incorrect answers to each item), while a 25-point rating scale model was used for the C-test.

Finally, relationships among examinees' scores on the three sub-tests were investigated by calculating Pearson product-moment correlation coefficients between all pairs of sub-test scores for each exam administration. These correlations enabled interpretations about the extent to which examinees' scores co-varied across the sub-tests and the extent to which any one of the scores might effectively represent the others.

Findings. Evaluation point (a) questioned the extent to which each of the three placement exam sub-tests would elicit a distribution of scores appropriate to the potential range of examinees' German ability levels. Tables 14 and 15 display descriptive statistics calculated for each sub-test on the two exam administrations. For the Fall 1999 administration, minimum and maximum values show that examinees' scores fell across nearly the entire score range for each of the three tests, and large standard deviations confirmed that each test consistently elicited a wide dispersion of scores. However, mean and median values for each test fell well above the mid-point, indicating a potential negative skew for each.

Table 14. Descriptive statistics for Fall 1999 Placement Exam

Statistic	LCT	RCT	C-test
N (examinees)	98	98	102
k (items)	30	29	125 (5 texts)
Mean	20.88	19.56	77.05
Mode	26.00	23.00	48.00
Median	22.00	20.00	78.50
Midpoint	17.50	16.00	70.50
S	6.70	6.72	26.43
Min	5.00	3.00	16.00
Max	30.00	29.00	125.00

Note. Four examinees who missed the scheduled administration of the full placement exam were later administered the C-test only.

Table 15. Descriptive statistics for Fall 2000 Placement Exam

Statistic	LCT	RCT	C-test
N (examinees)	91	91	92
k (items)	30	29	125 (5 texts)
Mean	21.63	19.86	77.99
Mode	21.00	26.00	68.00
Median	22.00	21.00	78.50
Midpoint	20.00	18.00	71.50
S	5.10	5.49	22.34
Min	10.00	8.00	19.00
Max	30.00	28.00	124.00

Note. One examinee who missed the scheduled administration of the full placement exam was later administered the C-test only.

For the Fall 2000 administration, score distributions were more truncated, as examinees scored on the whole at slightly higher mean values than in 1999 and minimum scores increased several points for each test; lower standard deviations for each test also reflected a slightly reduced range and dispersion of scores on this administration. Clearly, a considerable range of scores was elicited from examinees for each test on each exam. However, the fact that mean and median values exceeded midpoint values and were located well above the halfway point on each test, and that differences were observed between the two administrations, prompted additional analyses.

To facilitate a closer analysis of observed raw score patterns, figures 10 through 15 provide the frequency distributions of examinees' scores on each test for each administration. Mean values are indicated by an arrow on the X-axis in each figure. The overall negative skew in the score distribution for the 1999 LCT is apparent in figure 10, and the magnitude of the skew value (skew = -0.67) was found to be larger than two standard errors for skewness (one SES = 0.25), indicating a statistically significant ($p < .05$) negative skew in the score distribution (see formula for SES and discussion in Tabachnick & Fidell, 1996). Thus, while 61% of the scores fell above the mean, they did so within space for only +1.5 standard deviations; however, the 39% of scores below the mean ranged nearly -3 standard deviations to the lowest test score. By comparison, the 2000 LCT score distribution was much more balanced, with 50.5% of scores above the mean and 49.5% below, and the magnitude of the skew (skew = -0.21) was smaller than two standard errors for skewness (one SES = 0.26), indicating no statistical significance ($p < .05$) in the observed skew of the score distribution. However, 2000 LCT score patterns were more truncated, with scores below the mean ranging just over -2 standard deviations, while scores above the mean ranged just under +2 standard deviations. The PIUs interpreted these score distribution patterns to indicate (a) the dominance of more advanced versus more beginning ability examinees completing the placement exams and (b) potential differences between the 1999 and 2000 examinee population samples.

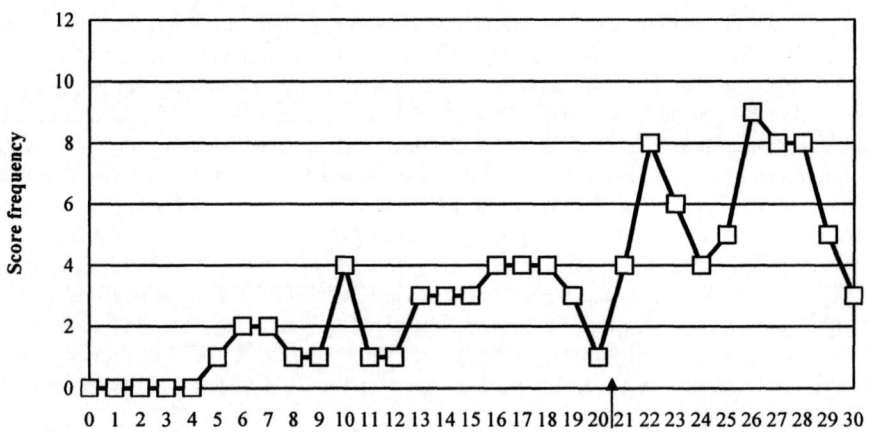

Figure 10. Score frequency distribution on Fall 1999 LCT

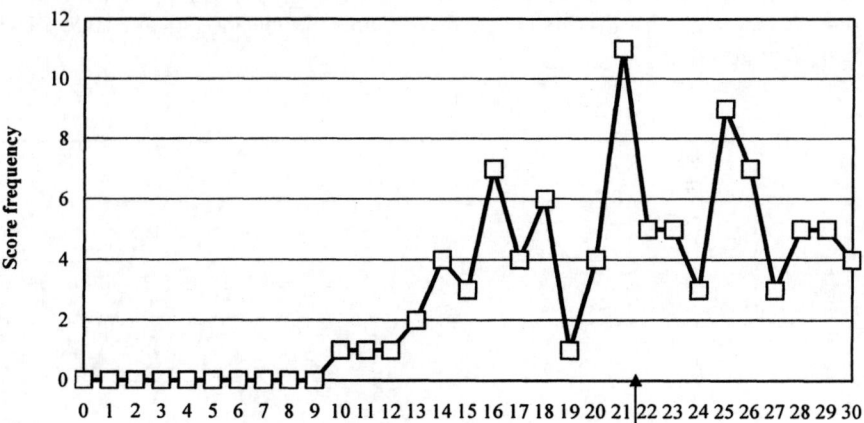

Figure 11. Score frequency distribution on Fall 2000 LCT

Similar score distribution patterns are apparent in figures 12 and 13 for the 1999 and 2000 RCT administrations. Once again, scores were negatively skewed for the 1999 test, and the skew value (skew = -0.52) was found to be statistically significant ($p < .05$) in light of the standard error for skewness (one *SES* = 0.25). A total of 57% of examinees scored above the mean, within +1.5 standard deviations, and 43% of examinees scored below the mean but were spread across approximately -2.5 standard deviations. As with the 2000 LCT, scores on the 2000 RCT were more truncated and less skewed, and the skew value (skew = -0.35) was not greater than two standard errors for skewness (one *SES* = 0.26), with 57% of scores falling above the mean within just under +2 standard deviations and 43% falling below the mean within just over -2 standard deviations. The clear shift to more truncated score distributions and higher minimum and mean values on the 2000 RCT further supported the interpretation that the population sample for the 2000 placement exam included fewer beginning ability examinees.

For both the LCT and RCT, then, score distribution patterns on the two administrations suggested that the tests were capable of eliciting a relatively wide range of examinee ability levels. However the observation that many examinees scored near the maximum possible score on both tests suggested that neither test would be likely to distinguish well among the more advanced students/examinees reflective of the uppermost curricular levels. In addition, differences observed from one administration to the next prompted the question of whether changes in examinee population characteristics over time might eventually supercede the distinctions available within the placement exam sub-tests and, indeed, within the balance of available GUGD curricular offerings.

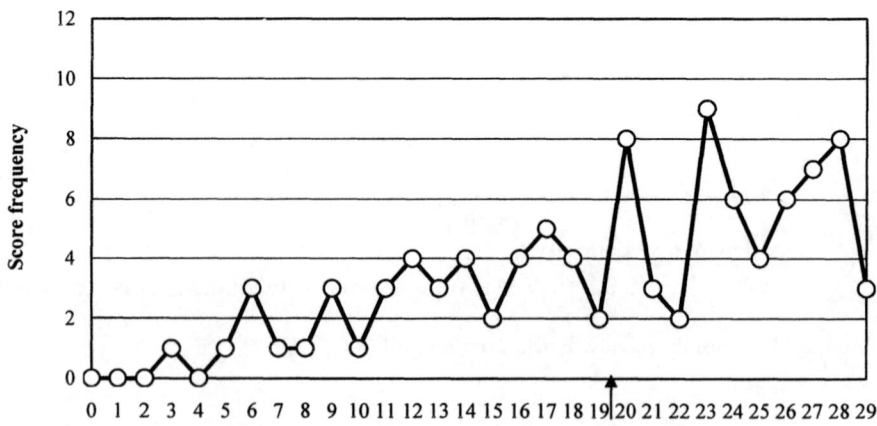

Figure 12. Score frequency distribution on Fall 1999 RCT

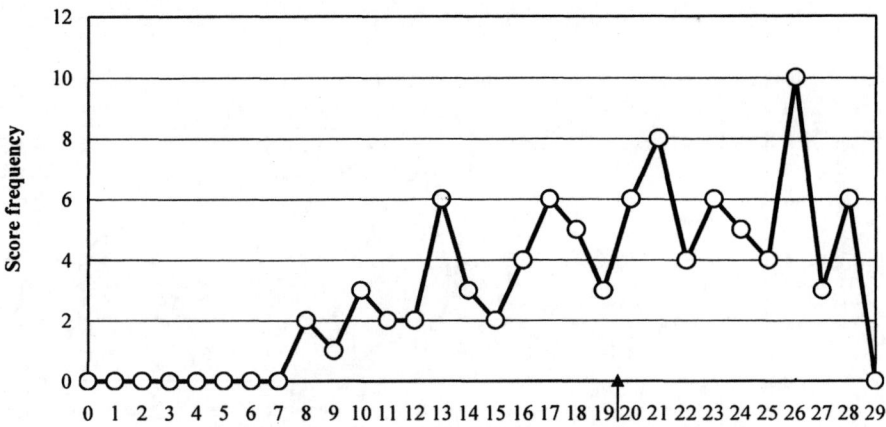

Figure 13. Score frequency distribution on Fall 2000 RCT

Finally, figures 14 and 15 show the score distributions for the 1999 and 2000 C-tests. Scores for both administrations revealed a more balanced distribution than did scores on the LCT and RCT, with much less of a negative skew effect (1999, skew = -0.15; 2000, skew = -0.16). In addition, these small skew values were found to be much smaller in magnitude than two standard errors for skewness (1999, one *SES* = 0.25; 2000, one *SES* = 0.26), indicating no statistical significance ($p < .05$). For the 1999 test, 49% of examinees scored above the mean up to just under +2 standard deviations, while 51% scored below the mean down to just over -2 standard deviations. Similarly for the 2000 test, 48% scored above the mean up to just over +2 standard deviations, and 52% scored under the mean down to approximately -2.5 standard deviations. Thus, while mean scores on the whole, as well as minimum scores, increased slightly from the 1999 to 2000 C-test administrations (reflecting likely population sample differences as observed on the LCT and RCT), scoring patterns remained very similar (with relatively normal distributions) across administrations of this sub-test. The PIUs interpreted the more balanced and consistent score distributions to indicate that the C-test was somewhat more capable of eliciting appropriate distributions of scores from examinees reflecting the entire range of curricular abilities, including the uppermost levels.

169

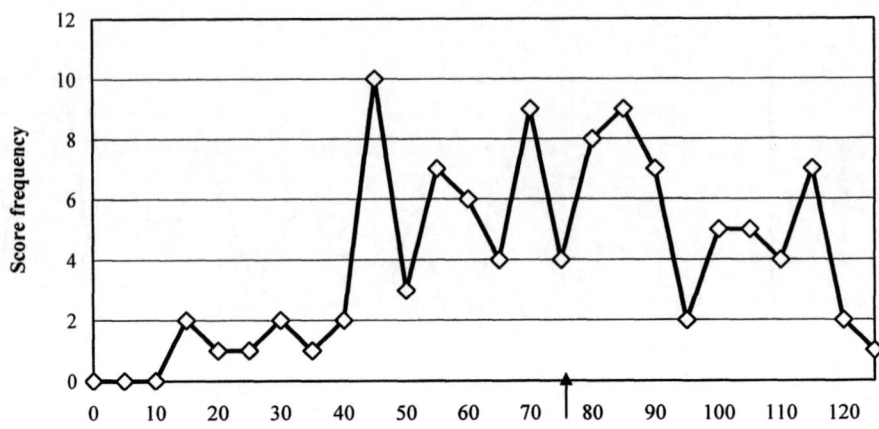

Figure 14. Score frequency distribution on Fall 1999 C-test

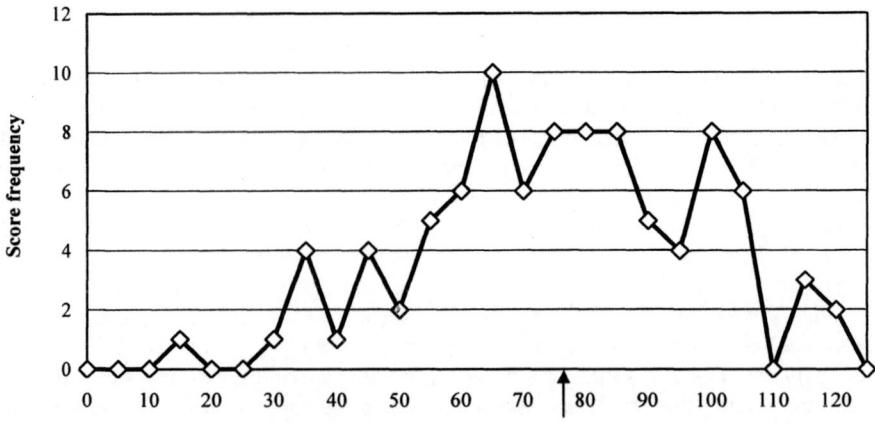

Figure 15. Score frequency distribution on Fall 2000 C-test

While generally appropriate distributions of examinee scores were elicited by the three sub-tests, evaluation point (b) sought to clarify the extent to which individual examinee ability levels could be distinguished reliably within these overall test score patterns. Tables 16 and 17 provide both classical test theory and item response theory estimates of the score reliability associated with each sub-test for each exam administration. Relatively high Cronbach α reliability estimates (with a potential range from 0.00 to 1.00) for the LCT and RCT, and very high α estimates for the C-test, indicated that total raw scores on all three sub-tests were quite effective at distinguishing consistently among individual examinees. Slight decreases from the 1999 to the 2000 exams likely reflected the somewhat reduced variance observed in the 2000 exam score distributions. Note that the higher reliability and lower error estimates observed for the C-test scores may be to some extent attributable to the fact that C-test estimates were based on scale scores (each text worth between 0 and 25 points) versus dichotomous scores on the LCT and RCT (each item worth either 0 or 1 point).

Table 16. CTT and IRT reliability estimates for Fall 1999 placement exam

Statistic	LCT	RCT	C-test
N	98	98	102
k	30	29	125 (5 texts)
α	0.90	0.90	0.96
SEM	±2.12	±2.12	±5.29
IRT examinee separation	2.19	2.22	3.72
IRT separation reliability	0.83	0.83	0.93
IRT standard error	0.58	0.57	0.35

Table 17. CTT and IRT reliability estimates for Fall 2000 placement exam

Statistic	LCT	RCT	C-test
N	91	91	92
k	30	29	125 (5 texts)
α	0.88	0.88	0.95
SEM	±1.77	±1.90	±5.47
IRT examinee separation	1.80	1.91	3.17
IRT separation reliability	0.76	0.79	0.91
IRT standard error	0.59	0.55	0.35

A Rasch model IRT equivalent to test score reliability is provided by the examinee separation index (to be exact, separation is the standard deviation of examinee ability estimates divided by the standard error of measurement, all expressed in logit values; see Wright & Masters, 1982). The separation index is not bounded by the

0.00 to 1.00 range of CTT internal consistency reliability estimates. Thus, the higher the separation, the greater the ability of the test to consistently differentiate individual examinees' abilities. Tables 16 and 17 show that scores on the LCT and RCT produced considerably lower examinee separation indexes than did scores on the C-test. In addition, separation indexes dropped noticeably from the 1999 to the 2000 administrations for all three sub-tests. Based on these separation indexes, examinee separation reliabilities can also be calculated, in order to produce a reliability estimate comparable to Cronbach alpha. Compared with CTT estimates, clearly lower examinee separation reliabilities were found for the three sub-tests in the Rasch model IRT analyses, although the C-test maintained a high degree of consistency in differentiating individual examinees, regardless of the analysis. Of most concern were the lower reliabilities for scores on the 2000 administration of the LCT and RCT sub-tests, where in all likelihood, the reduced range of examinee abilities and a tendency towards high scores resulted in less stable measurement qualities for that administration.

Finally, the standard error of measurement was calculated for scores on each sub-test from both CTT and IRT perspectives. The SEM provides an overall estimate of the amount of error associated with an examinee's score on a given test administration; in other words, it provides a score band (in raw score points) within which an examinee's score can be trusted to 68% certainty (Brown, 1996). Similarly, Rasch model IRT analyses provide an average standard error (in addition to examinee-specific errors) associated with the measurement model calculated for a given set of test scores. Note that the IRT standard error is estimated in logits, and is therefore only interpretable with reference to the other logit-based estimates produced within Rasch model analyses. Tables 16 and 17 show that raw score SEMs for each sub-test indicated approximately plus-or-minus 2 points of error for a given score on the LCT and RCT, and between plus-or-minus 5 and 5.5 points of error for a given score on the C-test. It is important to note that these error estimates indicate that *greater* inconsistency was associated with scores on the LCT and RCT than on the C-test, given the smaller total number of score points on the first two sub-tests (LCT $k = 30$; RCT $k = 29$; C-test $k = 125$). In other words, the error associated with C-test scores was proportionally *lower*, in light of the much larger score scale. This finding was replicated within the more stable IRT estimates, with average standard errors for scores on the LCT and RCT exceeding substantially those for the C-test.

Beyond the measurement qualities associated with total test scores on the three placement sub-tests, the PIUs also questioned the extent to which individual items were functioning as intended at eliciting examinee performances and contributing to these total test scores, as stated in evaluation point (c). Table 18 summarizes CTT estimates of item facility (IF) and item discrimination (ID) calculated for the LCT and RCT items, providing the minimum, average, and maximum values for each index across the items on each sub-test administration. Values for IF can range from 0.00 to 1.00, and they indicate the proportion of examinees who answered the item correctly. Typically, items with IF values between 0.30 and 0.70 are considered to provide the most useful information for norm-referenced tests (i.e., tests which seek to spread examinees out into a broad range of abilities), while items with IF values below or above this range are interpreted as being too difficult or too easy for the given examinee population sample (Brown, 1996). For both the 1999 and 2000 exams, the minimum IF values indicated that none of the items on either test was too difficult for the placement examinees, while maximum IF values indicated that at least some of the items on each test fell within the very easy range above 0.70. Average IF values also suggested that, on the whole, most items on these two tests were answered correctly by the majority of examinees, with the LCT apparently consisting of a greater number of correctly answered items. Note also that the IF values shifted slightly higher from the 1999 to the 2000 administrations for each sub-test, indicating that the test items were slightly less appropriate (i.e., more easy items) for the examinee population sample on the 2000 exam.

Table 18. Classical item analyses for LCT and RCT in 1999 and 2000

sub-test	statistic	1999			2000		
		Min	Mean	Max	Min	Mean	Max
LCT	Item Facility	0.32	0.70	0.92	0.29	0.71	0.99
	Item Discrimination	0.24	0.49	0.85	0.00	0.37	0.61
RCT	Item Facility	0.30	0.67	0.84	0.34	0.68	0.89
	Item Discrimination	0.30	0.52	0.84	-0.05	0.43	0.80

Values for ID can range from −1.00 to +1.00, and they indicate the extent to which the item separates examinees into high and low ability groups; that is, they present the proportion of high-scoring examinees (in this case, the upper third of total test scores) who answered the item correctly to low-scoring examinees (in this case, the lower third of total test scores) who answered the item correctly. For norm-referenced tests, items with higher ID values are considered more useful for spreading examinees out into ability level differences. Following Ebel (1979) and Brown (1996), items with ID values above 0.20 were considered at least marginally acceptable as contributing some useful information for distinguishing among examinees. For the 1999 exam, high average ID values and acceptable minimum values indicated that the majority of items on both sub-tests discriminated well to very well between examinees, with even the easy items (those with high IF values) contributing relatively useful distinctions. However, for the 2000 exam, the average ID and range of ID values dipped considerably lower for items on both tests, with at least some of the items on each contributing virtually no distinctions between higher and lower ability examinees. While more items on the RCT seemed to provide higher discriminatory power than items on the LCT, at least one RCT item revealed a negative ID value. Given the observations of a number of items with very high IF values, and especially the shift to lower ID values from the 1999 to the 2000 exams for both sub-tests, a closer inspection of individual items seemed warranted.

Additional information regarding item characteristics was provided by Rasch model IRT analyses. As with the examinee measures discussed above, Rasch analyses also provide item measure estimates which indicate the probability of a given item being answered correctly by examinees of varying ability levels; the item measure is typically interpreted as the difficulty of an item, and it is estimated in logits according to the same interval scale modeled for examinee measures. Item measure estimates can range from negative values (indicating easier items) to positive values (indicating more difficult items) and do not have maximum or minimum values except as determined by the full range of the interval scale modeled for the given test. For the current analyses, each item measure estimate was accompanied by: (a) standard error values indicating the trustworthiness of probabilities associated with the item; (b) a Rasch model equivalent to the point-biserial correlation indicating the degree of relationship between the individual item and the total test score (ranging from −1.00 to +1.00); and (c) infit/outfit statistics demonstrating the extent to which examinee performances on the item conformed to the predictions of the overall IRT measurement model. Table 19 summarizes these item analyses for each sub-test on the two exam administrations. Note that distinct Rasch model analyses were calculated for each sub-test; that is, the LCT scores on each administration were treated individually, and the RCT scores on each administration were treated individually (for a total of four unique Rasch model analyses). For ease of inspection, outcomes from these analyses are presented in a single table.

Table 19. Rasch model item analyses for LCT and RCT in 1999 and 2000

| sub-test | statistic | 1999 | | | 2000 | | |
		Min	Mean	Max	Min	Mean	Max
	Item Measure	-3.17	-1.21	1.24	-5.07	-1.47	1.39
	Standard Error	0.25	0.31	0.42	0.25	0.36	1.02
LCT	Point-biserial	0.14	0.47	0.78	-0.01	0.35	0.52
	Infit (Zstd)	-4.00	-0.20	2.00	-1.00	0.00	3.00
	Outfit (Zstd)	-3.00	-0.10	3.00	-1.00	-0.20	2.00
	Item Measure	-2.17	-1.02	1.36	-2.58	-1.11	0.83
	Standard Error	0.25	0.29	0.34	0.25	0.29	0.37
RCT	Point-biserial	0.25	0.47	0.66	-0.12	0.36	0.61
	Infit (Zstd)	-2.00	-0.10	3.00	-2.00	-0.10	5.00
	Outfit (Zstd)	-2.00	-0.20	3.00	-2.00	-0.10	4.00

The range and average values for item measures on each sub-test across both administrations confirmed that items were generally answered correctly by the samples of examinees tested, with negative (i.e., easier) item measures predominating. Items on the LCT ranged further into negative values than did items on the RCT, and measures for items on both sub-tests shifted slightly down from the 1999 to 2000 administrations (i.e., items on the whole were apparently 'easier' for the 2000 population sample). Standard error estimates indicated general response consistency and very little difference in error rates among items on both administrations of the RCT and on the 1999 administration of the LCT. However, a very large maximum standard error value was identified for the 2000 LCT administration, indicating that at least one item was associated with considerable inconsistency (see below). Point-biserial correlations were all positive and on average quite high for all items on both tests in the 1999 exam, but minimum values dipped into the negative range on both tests in the 2000 exam, indicating that examinee performances on at least some items were not related with overall test performances. Finally, infit and outfit statistics indicated the extent to which individual items elicited performances which conformed with patterns predicted by the IRT model; *standardized* infit/outfit values are presented in table 19, with an acceptable model fit range from –2 to +2 (Linacre, 1996). It is apparent that on each administration of each test, at least one item exceeded either the minimum or maximum standardized infit/outfit values, suggesting the presence of some items which were not contributing in consistent ways to overall test scores.

Both CTT and IRT item analysis statistics were reviewed next for each individual item, in order to identify potential problem items according to the following criteria: (a) ID < 0.20; (b) Rasch model point-biserial < 0.20; (c) -2.0 > standardized infit/outfit > +2.0. High IF values (greater than 0.70) were not considered necessarily problematic unless they were also associated with one of the other problem criteria. Indeed, the presence of some 'easy' items on each test was deemed essential by the PIUs, given the necessity of testing some (if typically only a few) very low ability examinees and the unpredictable fluctuations in ability levels of examinee population samples from one test administration to the next. Table 20 presents the anomalous items identified according to these criteria on the two administrations of the LCT, and Table 21 presents the anomalous items identified for the RCT.

Table 20. Anomalous items on the LCT in 1999 and 2000

	Item #	CTT Analyses			IRT Analyses			
		Item Facility	Item Discrim.	Item Measure	Stand. Error	Point-biserial	Infit (Zstd)	Outfit (Zstd)
1999	3	0.65	0.85	-0.81	0.33	0.78	-4.00	-3.00
	9	0.77	0.67	-1.58	0.36	0.74	-3.00	-2.00
	23	0.32	0.30	1.24	0.30	0.14	2.00	3.00
2000	2	0.92	0.16	-2.97	0.41	0.23	0.00	0.00
	7	0.93	0.19	-3.15	0.47	0.36	0.00	0.00
	11	0.96	0.13	-3.61	0.53	0.21	0.00	0.00
	12	0.99	0.00	-5.07	1.02	-0.01	0.00	0.00
	13	0.92	0.16	-2.97	0.41	0.24	0.00	0.00
	15	0.98	0.06	-4.35	0.77	0.29	0.00	0.00
	26	0.57	0.32	-0.31	0.29	0.14	3.00	2.00
	30	0.86	0.19	-2.19	0.35	0.14	0.00	0.00

For the LCT, a total of 11 items (3 in 1999 and 8 in 2000) were flagged as potentially problematic, based on the fact that item characteristics met at least one of the criteria above. Interestingly, no item was flagged on both administrations of the LCT, suggesting that problematic item characteristics emerged in interaction with the particular sample of examinees on each administration. Clearly, many more items were identified for the 2000 exam, and this was no doubt due to the apparently higher ability levels of that sample. Closer inspection of the individual flagged items revealed the nature of potential problems in each case. Seven of the eight items on the 2000 exam were flagged due to ID values below 0.20 (and accompanying high standard errors and low point-biserial correlations), indicating a lack of discriminatory power. In each case, this low discrimination was clearly attributable to very high IF values (all above 0.85) and similarly low item measure estimates; in other words, virtually all examinees were answering the items correctly.

The one remaining item on the 2000 exam (#26) and the three items on the 1999 exam were all flagged due to infit/outfit statistics that exceeded the normal range of model fit. For two of these items (#26, #23), positive misfit statistics and very low point-biserial correlations indicated that the items were not being answered in consistent ways, most likely due to misleading wording in the item stem or distractors (Linacre, 1996). Closer distractor efficiency analysis revealed in each case that examinees across all ability levels had selected other distractors to nearly the same degree as other examinees had selected the correct answer, due to somewhat ambiguous wording in the item stems. The final two items flagged on the 1999 LCT exam (#3, #9) both revealed negative misfit, indicating that these items were considered somewhat redundant to the calculation of the underlying measurement model. Note that other item quality characteristics suggested that these were good items, with very high IDs, appropriate IFs, low standard errors, and very high point-biserial correlations. In fact, these were the only two items in the LCT analyses with point-biserial values greater than 0.70. As such, the finding of negative misfit could be explained by the fact that examinee performances on these items were so highly correlated with overall test performance that the items did not provide any additional information for distinguishing among examinees, at least for the purposes of estimating a measurement model from an IRT perspective.

For the RCT, only seven items (2 in 1999, 5 in 2000) were flagged as potentially problematic. The two items on the 1999 exam were both flagged due to slight positive misfit, and each of these items revealed the lowest point-biserial correlations for any items on the 1999 RCT. For item #16, this misfit and low relation to the total score was attributable to somewhat ambiguous wording within the item stem and its distractors; for item #9, misfit seemed simply to be related to anomalous examinee response patterns. Note that item #16 was flagged again on the 2000 exam, this time with more dramatic positive misfit, a negative point-biserial correlation, and a negative ID value.

Table 21. Anomalous items on the RCT in 1999 and 2000

		CTT Analyses			IRT Analyses			
	Item #	Item Facility	Item Discrim.	Item Measure	Stand. Error	Point-biserial	Infit (Zstd)	Outfit (Zstd)
1999	9	0.69	0.30	-1.09	0.30	0.25	2.00	3.00
	16	0.53	0.42	-0.10	0.29	0.25	3.00	3.00
2000	13	0.89	-0.09	-2.58	0.37	0.11	0.00	1.00
	14	0.88	0.13	-2.46	0.35	0.17	0.00	0.00
	15	0.85	0.19	-2.14	0.33	0.17	0.00	0.00
	16	0.51	-0.05	-0.06	0.31	-0.12	5.00	4.00
	24	0.56	0.28	-0.35	0.28	0.13	2.00	2.00

Clearly, examinees were confused by this item, and there was no predictability in their response patterns, with one of the distractors being selected to the same degree as the ostensibly correct answer. Of the remaining items flagged on the 2000 exam, three of them were once again very easy items with low point-biserial correlations due to lack of variance among examinees in their responses to this item (i.e., mostly correct). The final item (#24) revealed a low point-biserial correlation which was associated with inconsistencies in examinee response patterns; distractor efficiency analyses did not reveal ambiguity in item response wording.

In sum, both CTT and IRT analyses indicated that virtually all items on both the LCT and RCT contributed in appropriate ways to total test scores for examinees on the 1999 placement exam. While a few items were found to be quite 'easy' for most examinees or to slightly misfit the IRT measurement model for either test, nearly all items maintained good discriminatory power and appropriate consistency with the total test score. However, for the 2000 exam, analyses indicated more inappropriately 'easy' items, lower average discrimination, and lower item-total consistency, particularly for the LCT. In all likelihood, the apparent reduced quality of items on the two sub-tests from one exam to the next was attributable to a unique examinee population sample in 2000. Only a single item on the RCT was identified as problematic on both exam administrations, indicating that other items on both tests generally performed as intended, at least with the 1999 examinee population sample. As such, immediate concerns with the two sub-tests were not drastic. However, were a recurring pattern to be found of examinee ability levels that could not be captured by the two sub-tests, then additional deliberations would need to be undertaken in order to reconfigure not only the placement exam, but also in all probability the GUGD curricular offerings.

As a final insight into the abilities of each examinee population sample relative to the capacity of items on the two sub-tests, figures 16 through 19 below provide a graphic display of both examinee (column 2) and item (column 3) IRT measure estimates for the two exam administrations. Note that both sets of estimates in each figure are anchored on the same logit interval scale (column 1) and that each star symbol represents either one examinee or one item. In addition, examinee ability level descends from top to bottom as does item difficulty level (more able examinees and harder items are at the top of the figure). Comparing figure 16 to figure 17, it is clear that the range of item difficulties on the LCT accounted well for the lowest to middle ability examinees on the 1999 exam (i.e., the distribution of item measures paralleled the distribution of examinee measures from the bottom of the scale to approximately two-thirds up the scale). However, on the 2000 exam, the overall distribution of examinee measures shifted upwards (i.e., towards higher abilities) relative to item measures. Similar, if less dramatic patterns are apparent in comparing figures 18 and 19 for the two RCT administrations.

```
-----------------------------
|Measr| Examinees | Items|
-----------------------------
+   3 + ***        +        +
|     |            |        |
|     |   *****    |        |
|     |            |        |
|     |            |        |
|     |            |        |
|     |            |        |
+   2 +            +        +
|     |   ******** |        |
|     |            |        |
|     |            |        |
|     |   ******** |        |
|     |            |   *    |
|     |            |        |
+   1 + ********** +   *    +
|     |            |        |
|     |   *****    |        |
|     |            |        |
|     |   ****     |        |
|     |   ******   |        |
|     |            |   **   |
*   0 * ********   *   **   *
|     |   ****     |        |
|     |            |        |
|     |   *        |   **   |
|     |   ***      |   *    |
|     |   ****     |        |
|     |   ****     |   ***  |
+  -1 + ****       +   *    +
|     |            |   **   |
|     |   ***      |   *    |
|     |   ***      |   *    |
|     |   ***      |   ***  |
|     |   *        |        |
|     |   *        |   **   |
+  -2 +            +   *    +
|     |   ****     |   *    |
|     |   *        |        |
|     |   *        |   **   |
|     |            |        |
|     |   **       |   **   |
|     |   **       |   *    |
+  -3 +            +        +
|     |   *        |   *    |
|     |            |        |
|     |            |        |
|     |            |        |
|     |            |        |
+  -4 +            +        +
-----------------------------
```

Figure 16. Examinee and item measures on FACETS ruler for 1999 LCT

179

```
----------------------------
|Measr| Examinees   | Items|
----------------------------
+   3 + ****         +      +
|     | *****        |      |
|     |              |      |
|     |              |      |
|     |              |      |
+   2 + *****        +      +
|     |              |      |
|     |              |      |
|     | ***          | *    |
|     |              |      |
+   1 + *******      + *    +
|     | *********    |      |
|     |              |      |
|     | ***          | ***  |
|     | *****        |      |
*   0 * *****        * *    *
|     | ***********  |      |
|     | ****         | **   |
|     | *            | **   |
|     | ******       | *    |
+  -1 + ****         + *    +
|     | *******      | *    |
|     | ***          | ***  |
|     | ****         | *    |
|     | **           | **   |
+  -2 + *            + *    +
|     | *            | ***  |
|     | *            |      |
|     |              | *    |
|     |              |      |
+  -3 +              + **   +
|     |              | *    |
|     |              |      |
|     |              | *    |
|     |              |      |
+  -4 +              +      +
|     |              |      |
|     |              | *    |
|     |              |      |
|     |              |      |
+  -5 +              + *    +
|     |              |      |
|     |              |      |
|     |              |      |
|     |              |      |
+  -6 +              +      +
----------------------------
```

Figure 17. Examinee and item measures on FACETS ruler for 2000 LCT

180

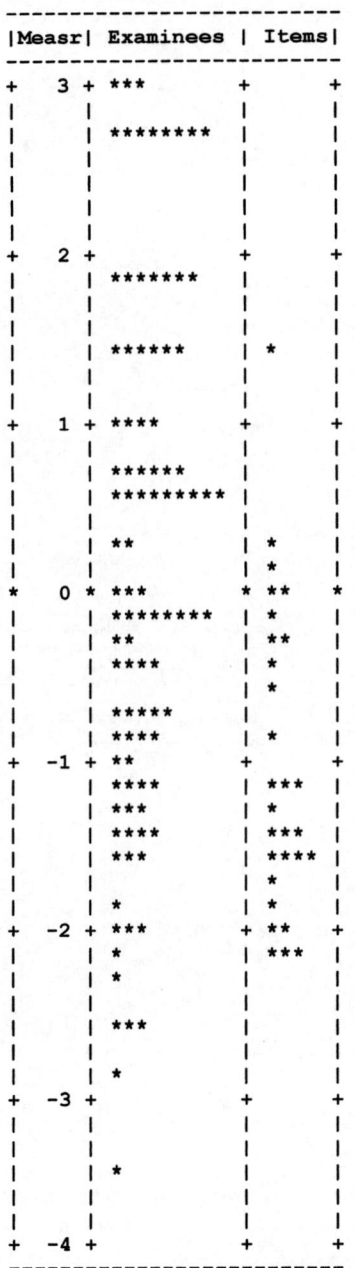

```
-----------------------
|Measr| Examinees | Items|
-----------------------
+   3 + ***        +        +
|     |                     |
|     | *******    |        |
|     |            |        |
|     |            |        |
|     |            |        |
|     |            |        |
+   2 +            +        +
|     | *******    |        |
|     |            |        |
|     |            |        |
|     | ******     | *      |
|     |            |        |
|     |            |        |
+   1 + ****       +        +
|     |            |        |
|     | ******     |        |
|     | *********  |        |
|     |            |        |
|     | **         | *      |
|     |            | *      |
*   0 * ***        * **     *
|     | *******    | *      |
|     | **         | **     |
|     | ****       | *      |
|     |            | *      |
|     | *****      |        |
|     | ****       | *      |
+  -1 + **         +        +
|     | ****       | ***    |
|     | ***        | *      |
|     | ****       | ***    |
|     | ***        | ****   |
|     |            | *      |
|     | *          | *      |
+  -2 + ***        + **     +
|     | *          | ***    |
|     | *          |        |
|     |            |        |
|     | ***        |        |
|     |            |        |
|     | *          |        |
+  -3 +            +        +
|     |            |        |
|     |            |        |
|     | *          |        |
|     |            |        |
|     |            |        |
+  -4 +            +        +
-----------------------
```

Figure 18. Examinee and item measures on FACETS ruler for 1999 RCT

181

```
----------------------------
|Measr| Examinees  | Items|
----------------------------
+  3 +              +       +
|    |              |       |
|    |              |       |
|    | *****        |       |
|    |              |       |
|    |              |       |
|    |              |       |
|    |              |       |
+  2 +              +       +
|    | ***          |       |
|    |              |       |
|    |              |       |
|    |              |       |
|    | **********   |       |
|    |              |       |
|    |              |       |
+  1 + ****         +       +
|    |              | *     |
|    | *****        |       |
|    |              | *     |
|    | ******       |       |
|    |              |       |
|    | ****         |       |
|    |              |       |
*  0 * ********      * **    *
|    |              | **    |
|    | ******       | *     |
|    | ***          | **    |
|    | *****        |       |
|    |              |       |
|    | ******       |       |
|    | ****         | **    |
+ -1 + **           + **    +
|    |              | **    |
|    | ***          |       |
|    | ******       | *     |
|    | **           | ***   |
|    |              | **    |
|    | **           | *     |
|    | ***          | ***   |
+ -2 + *            +       +
|    |              | *     |
|    | **           |       |
|    |              |       |
|    |              | **    |
|    |              | *     |
|    |              |       |
|    |              |       |
+ -3 +              +       +
----------------------------
```

Figure 19. Examinee and item measures on FACETS ruler for 2000 RCT

182

Following item analyses for the LCT and RCT sub-tests, similar CTT and IRT analyses were conducted in order to evaluate the qualities of the five texts comprising the C-test, with each text treated as a single polytomous item. To investigate the difficulty of each text, descriptive statistics were calculated for examinee performances on the five texts for both administrations. Recall that each text had been intentionally sampled under the assumption that it would prove most appropriate to the abilities of examinees at a given GUGD curricular level (and consequently easier or more difficult for examinees at higher or lower curricular levels), with text 1 representing level 1, texts 2 and 3 both representing level 2, text 4 representing level 3, and text 5 representing level 4. Tables 22 and 23 display descriptive statistics for examinee scores on each text across the two administrations.

Table 22. Descriptive statistics for C-test texts on Fall 1999 placement exam

	Text 1	Text 2	Text 3	Text 4	Text 5
k	25.00	25.00	25.00	25.00	25.00
Mean	19.30	16.11	16.05	13.93	11.66
S	4.49	5.55	5.07	6.40	6.71
Min	5.00	2.00	4.00	0.00	0.00
Max	25.00	25.00	25.00	25.00	25.00

Table 23. Descriptive statistics for C-test texts on Fall 2000 placement exam

	Text 1	Text 2	Text 3	Text 4	Text 5
k	25.00	25.00	25.00	25.00	25.00
Mean	19.37	17.09	16.39	13.93	11.21
S	4.14	4.69	4.50	5.51	5.66
Min	4.00	2.00	6.00	2.00	1.00
Max	25.00	25.00	25.00	25.00	24.00

It is clear that examinees performed with decreasing average scores from the first through the fifth texts, as predicted. Furthermore, examinees performed at remarkably similar average score levels for each text on the two distinct administrations, suggesting considerable stability of the C-test structure at eliciting performances related to curricular-level ability differences. In addition, average scores on texts 2 and 3 proved to be very similar to each other on both exam administrations, supporting the assumption that these two texts represented the same student ability level (2) in the GUGD curriculum. Finally, consistently large standard deviations for each text indicated the capacity of the individual texts to distinguish among examinees, albeit at different overall score points. In other words, even though each text was found to be considerably different from the other texts in terms of difficulty, they all apparently did a good job of separating examinees into a broad distribution ostensibly reflective of ability differences.

While average scores on each text provided some support for the predicted underlying structure of the C-test, they did not *confirm* whether each text was consistently discriminating as intended among examinee abilities. Thus, were individual texts functioning as intended, it had been assumed that groups of examinees placed into progressively higher curricular levels would: (a) perform with higher accuracy on *all* five texts than students at the preceding curricular level; and (b) perform with decreasing accuracy from text 1 through text 5, with the exception of texts 2 and 3, where similar average scores were expected within a given curricular level. Accordingly, the average scores of examinees placed into distinct curricular levels were examined independently in order to illuminate the extent to which each text was eliciting predicted differences. Figures 20 and 21 show average score patterns on each C-test text for examinees placed into the seven curricular-semester levels (listed in the legend at right). Assumption (a) was supported on both exam administrations, with increasing average scores on each text at each increasing curricular level (i.e., moving up the graph for any single text), the only exception being equally low average scores on text 5 (the most difficult) for the examinees placed into curricular-semester levels 1.1 and 1.2 during Fall 1999 (note that no students were placed into level 1.1 in Fall 2000).

Assumption (b) was also generally supported on both exam administrations, with overall decreasing scores from text 1 through text 5 by the groups of examinees placed into each curricular level (i.e., moving from left to right along a single line on the figure). However, predicted similarities in scores for texts 2 and 3 were not entirely borne out at each curricular level. For examinees placed into levels 1.1 and 1.2, text 2 proved slightly easier than text 3, while those placed into the middle and upper curricular levels found text 2 slightly more difficult than text 3, albeit with higher overall performance accuracy than examinees at preceding levels. Nevertheless, score patterns by examinees overall and at each of the curricular placement levels clearly supported the basic premise that selected texts represented the GUGD curricular levels by eliciting performances that differed in predicted ways and, therefore, by discriminating effectively among different examinee ability levels.

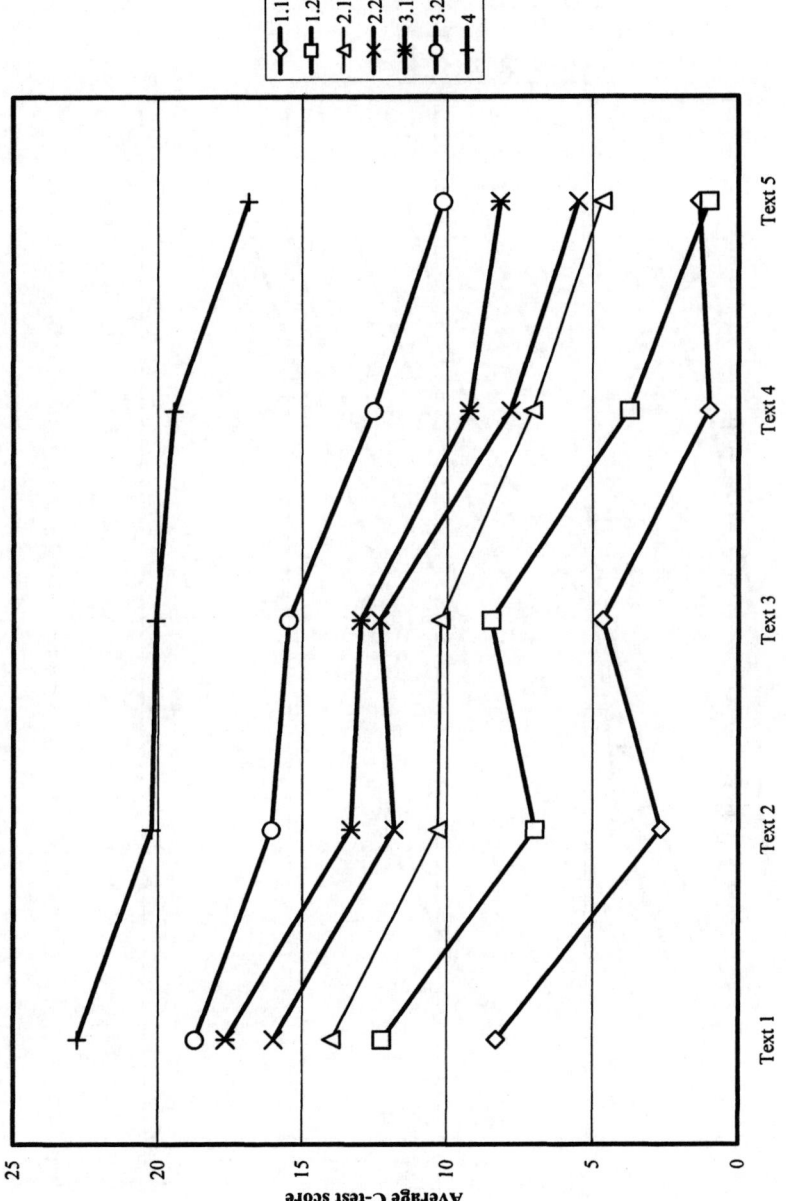

Figure 20. Average performance on five C-test texts by curricular semester-level groups (Fall 1999)

Legend:
- 1.1
- 1.2
- 2.1
- 2.2
- 3.1
- 3.2
- 4

Average C-test score

Text 1 Text 2 Text 3 Text 4 Text 5

186

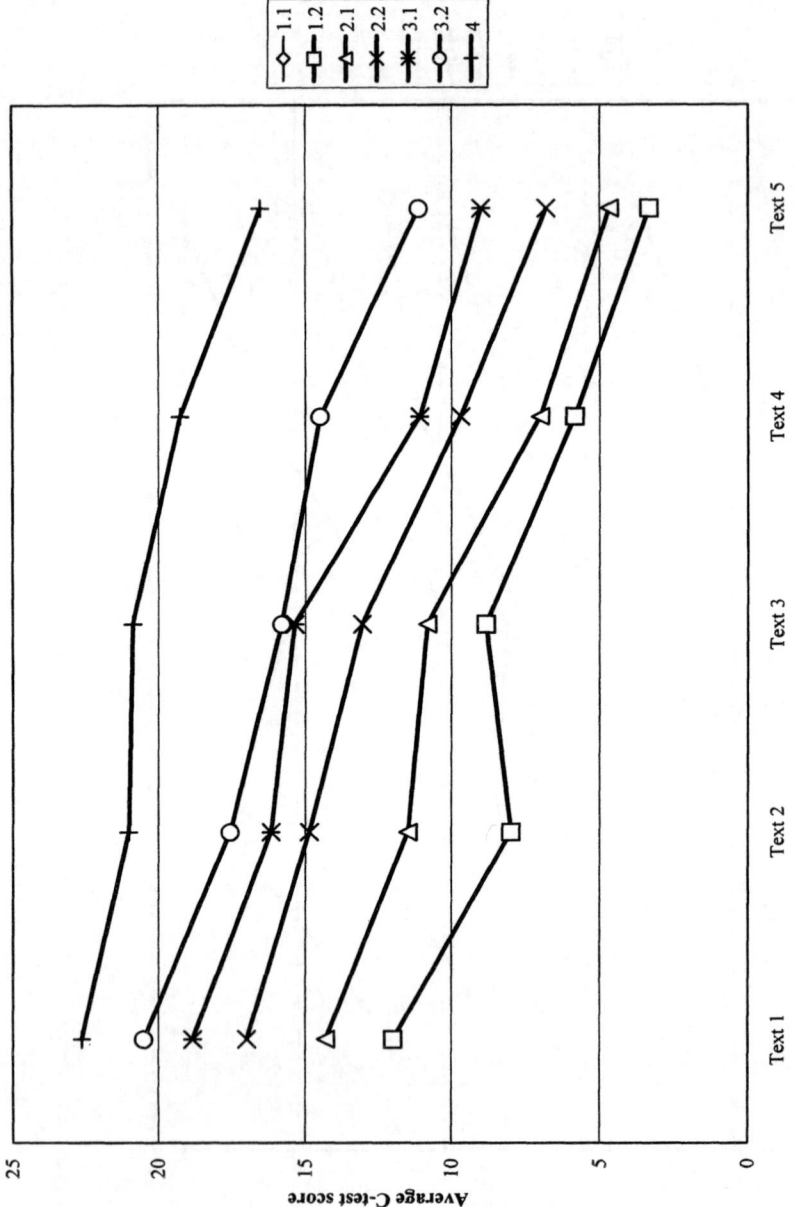

Figure 21. Average performance on five C-test texts by curricular semester-level groups (Fall 2000)

Additional information regarding the qualities of each C-test text was provided by Rasch model IRT analyses for response patterns on the two exam administrations. Tables 24 and 25 display item measure, standard error, infit/outfit, and point-biserial estimates for each text on the two exams. As in the raw score analyses, the apparent difficulties of each of the five texts clearly reflected the predicted pattern on both administrations, with item measure estimates increasing (i.e., texts become more difficult) consistently from text 1 through text 5, and with texts 2 and 3 revealing very similar measure values. In addition, these patterns were replicated to a very similar degree in analyses for both exam administrations.

Table 24. Rasch model item analyses for Fall 1999 C-test texts

C-test Texts	Item Measure	Standard Error	Infit		Outfit		Point-Biserial
			MnSq	Z-Std	MnSq	Z-Std	
Text 1	-1.70	0.06	1.10	0.00	1.20	1.00	0.87
Text 2	-0.75	0.05	1.10	0.00	1.10	0.00	0.89
Text 3	-0.74	0.06	0.70	-1.00	0.80	-1.00	0.92
Text 4	-0.20	0.05	0.90	0.00	0.90	0.00	0.92
Text 5	0.33	0.05	1.00	0.00	1.00	0.00	0.89

Note: Separation: 12.44, Reliability: 0.99

Table 25. Rasch model item analyses for Fall 2000 C-test texts

C-test Texts	Item Measure	Standard Error	Infit		Outfit		Point-Biserial
			MnSq	Z-Std	MnSq	Z-Std	
Text 1	-1.60	0.06	1.10	0.00	1.20	1.00	0.81
Text 2	-0.94	0.06	0.90	0.00	1.00	0.00	0.86
Text 3	-0.75	0.06	0.80	-1.00	0.80	-1.00	0.89
Text 4	-0.16	0.05	1.10	0.00	1.10	0.00	0.86
Text 5	0.47	0.06	0.80	-1.00	0.80	-1.00	0.87

Note: Separation: 12.23, Reliability: 0.99

Standard error estimates were found to be quite low for each text, and standardized infit/outfit statistics fell well within the acceptable range (-2 to +2) for all, indicating that examinees' scores on each text could be fit very well to the underlying measurement model. In addition, strong point-biserial correlation coefficients between each item measure and the total test score indicated that each of the five texts was contributing in equivalent and predicted ways to examinees' overall test scores. A slight across the board decrease in point-biserial values from the 1999 to 2000 exams was the only noticeable difference in item qualities, with the lower values likely attributable to less total variance in examinee performances. However, each text clearly performed very consistently on both administrations in eliciting the predicted examinee performance patterns, despite any differences in the examinee population samples from one year to the next.

Finally, figures 22 and 23 provide graphic displays of both item measures and examinee measures (i.e., estimates of examinees' abilities) according to the common interval scale (represented by logit values in the first column) resulting from Rasch model analyses. Examinees are depicted in the second column of the figure as star symbols (each symbol represents one examinee measure estimate), and the five C-test texts are depicted in the third column of the figure. The predicted differences among the five texts were apparent and very similar for both administrations, with text 1 falling lowest on the scale, texts 2 and 3 falling higher and very close together, and texts 4 and 5 showing substantial increases in difficulty.

Note also that examinee measures were widely distributed across the scale on each administration, with the majority falling between the item measure estimates for texts 1 and 5. Thus, the majority of examinee ability levels were captured within the range of text difficulty estimates. However, it should be pointed out that on each administration a number of examinee measures fell above the item measure estimate for text 5, indicating that these students' actual advanced abilities were not completely captured by the C-test scores. This was not a surprising finding, given that the highest level of interpretation for the placement exam C-test falls at the GUGD curricular juncture between the end of the third year and the beginning of the fourth year of instruction, while many students (including graduate students) who took the placement exam did so with the expectation that they were prepared to enter directly into level-4 or higher classes. Were the C-test intended to capture the entire range of examinee abilities, it would clearly need additional texts that reflected these much higher ability levels. However, because the C-test was designed only to capture abilities (and inform decisions) reflecting the beginning of the first year through the beginning of the fourth year of instruction, the findings supported exactly that use. Furthermore, the observed similarities in text difficulty estimates vis-à-vis examinee abilities from one exam administration to the next suggested considerable stability of the C-test texts for capturing ability differences relevant to the range of placement decisions in the GUGD curriculum.

```
---------------------------------------------
|Measr| Examinees| C-test texts        |
---------------------------------------------
+   4 + *         +                     +
|     | *         |                     |
|     |           |                     |
|     | *         |                     |
|     |           |                     |
|     | **        |                     |
+   3 +           +                     +
|     | **        |                     |
|     |           |                     |
|     | **        |                     |
|     | *         |                     |
|     | *         |                     |
|     | *         |                     |
+   2 + **        +                     +
|     | *         |                     |
|     |           |                     |
|     | ***       |                     |
|     | *****     |                     |
|     |           |                     |
|     | *         |                     |
+   1 +           +                     +
|     | **        |                     |
|     | **        |                     |
|     | *         |                     |
|     | ******    |                     |
|     | ***       | Text 5              |
|     | *******   |                     |
*   0 * ****      *                     *
|     | ***       | Text 4              |
|     | **        |                     |
|     | ******** |                     |
|     | ***       |                     |
|     | **        | Text 2   Text 3 |
|     | *****     |                     |
+  -1 + ****      +                     +
|     | *****     |                     |
|     | **        |                     |
|     | ******** |                     |
|     | ***       |                     |
|     | *         | Text 1              |
|     | *         |                     |
+  -2 + *         +                     +
|     | **        |                     |
|     |           |                     |
|     |           |                     |
|     | *         |                     |
|     | *         |                     |
|     | *         |                     |
+  -3 +           +                     +
---------------------------------------------
```

Figure 22. Examinee and text measures on FACETS ruler for 1999 C-test

```
---------------------------------
|Measr| Examinees | C-test texts|
---------------------------------
+   6 +                +            +
|     |                |            |
|     |                |            |
|     |                |            |
|     | *              |            |
+   5 +                +            +
|     |                |            |
|     |                |            |
|     |                |            |
|     |                |            |
+   4 +                +            +
|     |                |            |
|     | *              |            |
|     |                |            |
|     |                |            |
+   3 +                +            +
|     | **             |            |
|     | *              |            |
|     |                |            |
|     |                |            |
+   2 +                +            +
|     | ***            |            |
|     | ***            |            |
|     |                |            |
|     | *******        |            |
+   1 + **             +            +
|     | *              |            |
|     | *****          |            |
|     | ****           | Text 5     |
|     | ********        |            |
*   0 * *****          *            *
|     | *****          | Text 4     |
|     | ********       |            |
|     | *********      |            |
|     | ******         | Text 3     |
+  -1 + ****           + Text 2     +
|     | *****          |            |
|     | **             |            |
|     | ***            | Text 1     |
|     | **             |            |
+  -2 + **             +            +
|     | *              |            |
|     |                |            |
|     |                |            |
|     |                |            |
+  -3 + *              +            +
---------------------------------
```

Figure 23. Examinee and text measures on FACETS ruler for 2000 C-test

A final investigation during this stage questioned the extent to which scores on the three placement exam sub-tests were related to each other on the two exam administrations (d above). Tables 26 and 27 provide the Pearson product-moment correlation coefficients between all pairs of scores on each exam. While relatively high correlations indicated strong relationships among scores on the three sub-tests, they were not found to be so high as to suggest that information from each test could be interpreted as redundant with the other tests. In other words, for at least some of the examinees, performance on one sub-test was likely substantially better or worse than performance on the other sub-tests, as would be expected from language learners with differing backgrounds in L2 German. Each sub-test, then, seemed to be providing information that was useful in determining the variable profiles with which examinees presented and which would play a role in adjudicating where a given examinee most appropriately belonged within the curriculum.

Table 26. Pearson correlations among placement sub-tests, Fall 1999

	LCT	RCT	C-test
LCT	1.00	0.88	0.82
RCT		1.00	0.86
C-test			1.00

Note. All correlations statistically significant ($p<.05$).

Table 27. Pearson correlations among placement sub-tests, Fall 2000

	LCT	RCT	C-test
LCT	1.00	0.73	0.77
RCT		1.00	0.84
C-test			1.00

Note. All correlations statistically significant ($p<.05$).

It should also be noted that correlation values dropped somewhat from the 1999 to the 2000 placement exams. This change was likely due in part to the overall reduced variance in scores on the three sub-tests for the 2000 examinee population sample. At the same time, it is apparent that the relationship between the LCT and RCT dropped from the highest to the lowest (0.15 points difference), while the relationships between the LCT and C-test (0.05 points) and the RCT and C-test (0.02 points) decreased less dramatically. Of the three sub-tests, then, the C-test seemed to maintain the most stable representation of examinee ability differences captured by the placement exam.

Uses. Findings regarding the measurement qualities of placement exam sub-tests were reported initially to the PIUs in the spring and fall semesters of 2001, during several meetings focused on the status of the placement exam and needed improvements after two years of implementation. Given the technical nature of these investigations, efforts were made to instruct the PIUs in the rationale behind each of the test analyses, the relationship between each analysis and their evaluation questions, and how findings could be interpreted. The figures and tables above constituted the majority of the presentation of findings, and each was accompanied by an explanation, questions, and group discussion. While these evaluation efforts focused to a large degree on simply enhancing the PIUs' understanding of the qualities of the three placement sub-tests, several decisions and further actions were taken on the basis of associated findings.

The PIUs reported general satisfaction with the extent to which each sub-test was capable of eliciting an appropriate range of examinee scores, and they recognized the effects of substantially larger proportions of placement examinees with advanced to very advanced German L2 abilities versus much smaller proportions of lower ability examinees. At the same time, they stressed that the most important placement decisions needed to occur among these lower ranges of examinee abilities, and that, therefore, the placement exam sub-tests would have to maintain a focus on these lower levels, regardless of imbalances or variations in population samples. In addition, given the imbalanced samples of high to low ability examinees, the PIUs interpreted high reliability indices and relatively low error rates as evidence in support of the overall trustworthiness of information provided by the three tests for the decisions to be made. Of particular interest were the higher levels of score reliability and more normal score distributions associated with both of the C-test administrations as compared with the LCT and RCT.

The decision was made to continue operational use of all three sub-tests, as each seemed to be functioning as intended with those examinees about whom decisions needed to be made (i.e., examinees placing into the beginning of the first through the end of the third years of the GUGD curriculum). Based on the observation of somewhat decreasing stability in test score qualities from one exam to the next, especially for the LCT and RCT, the PIUs decided to monitor measurement qualities over subsequent placement exam administrations in order to track any systematic changes in population characteristics and/or patterns of decreasing score reliability.

At the level of individual item analyses, the PIUs were very satisfied with the consistent high qualities found for the five C-test texts on both exams, especially given uncertainties in terms of the text selection and test construction processes. As such, they recommended no revisions in the composition of the C-test. However, they did propose that additional forms of the C-test be developed on the basis of identical text selection procedures, in order to address concerns with test security (i.e., a single operational form could be easily compromised) and to investigate the extent to which replication of the development process would produce an instrument with equivalent measurement qualities.

Greater concerns were expressed in response to the findings of potentially problematic items on the LCT and RCT tests. While continued inclusion of the very easy items was defended in light of the need for some items that could be attempted by low-ability examinees (and the fact that even high facility items discriminated relatively well), revision of the few mis-fitting or low discriminating items was proposed, as was inclusion of more difficult items. However, ensuing discussion revealed that the PIUs were not confident in deciding on revisions to items or changes in the compositions of the two sub-tests based only on the evidence available from the two exam administrations. In light of findings that item qualities could change from one exam to the next, given changes in examinee population sample characteristics, they decided to continue with the use of the same items for several additional placement exam administrations, in order to monitor the stability of individual items over time and potentially unique examinee samples. Thus, they had not been convinced that the sets of items which had functioned in largely appropriate ways for the 1999 exam should be revised on the basis of differences in the 2000 exam alone. Of additional concern in these deliberations was the acknowledgement that substantial item revisions would call for recalibration of the cut-scores associated with curricular placement decisions, since changes would likely result in differing overall test scores. For the time being, then, based on the balance of available information, the PIUs decided to continue with operational use of the unaltered sub-tests and items.

Nevertheless, the PIUs clearly recognized that information being provided by LCT and RCT scores did not offer the same degree of consistency as the information provided by C-test scores. As such, the decision was made to emphasize the C-test score as the primary source of information for placement decisions. First, an initial curricular-*semester* level placement recommendation was to be made on the basis of the examinee's C-test score compared with the cut-score bands. Second, this decision was to be compared with the curricular-*year* level recommendations from the LCT and RCT. Where either or both of these recommendations differed above the recommended level from the C-test, the C-test recommendation was retained as the final placement decision. Where either or both differed below the C-test recommended level by a year or more, the final placement decision was modified downwards according to existing policies.

Finally, during related meetings, several additional questions for potential evaluation were raised or reiterated by the PIUs. First, concerns were voiced regarding students', teachers', and other stakeholders' understandings, on the one hand, and perceptions, on the other hand, of the effectiveness, accuracy, and fairness of the placement exam sub-tests and resulting decisions. Second, the possibility of adding a performative component to the placement exam was again raised, and it was questioned whether the increase in terms of placement decision accuracy and acceptability (e.g., by students) would be worth the additional time/resources required (or even feasible, given existing constraints). Third, interest was expressed again in the relative success of students who had been placed into the various curricular levels versus students who had advanced into them through completion of other GUGD courses, particularly in terms of final course grade differences. Fourth, it was suggested that a longer term research and development agenda be initiated in order to (a) computerize at least a portion of the placement exam, and (b) develop additional test forms in order to address potential security issues and to investigate the effectiveness of the development process itself.

6.3 Sustaining the placement assessment program

After developing, implementing, and revising the GUGD placement exam over a two-year period, the PIUs committed to sustaining the placement program within the *Multiple Literacies* curriculum, and a new stage of validity evaluation began. Given the intense focus during the implementation stage on the relationship between placement instruments and procedures and the accuracy of decisions that were based on them, little attention had been paid thus far to the relationship between these decisions and the actions and consequences they were intended (and not intended) to bring about. Recall that the specification of intended assessment use did not stop with the gathering and interpretation of information about students and the use of that information for making placement decisions, but it incorporated intended consequences for that use as well. Furthermore, after two years of virtually all-consuming attention to the development and implementation of placement and other assessment practices (never mind developments in curriculum and instruction), there was also an explicit interest on the part of GUGD departmental stakeholders, including teachers as well as administrators, to achieve a shift in their daily practices towards a sense of programmatic normalcy.

Accordingly, the focus of validity evaluation efforts was transferred during this stage to the consequential expectations in the initial specification of intended assessment use. One expected outcome of developing and using the placement exam had been the generation of widespread, if basic, awareness and acceptance of a curriculum-based placement procedure (as described in section 6.1), something that had been found clearly lacking in conjunction with the previous exam. Therefore, the PIUs prioritized their concerns that various stakeholder groups, including teachers, students, and others, might not share a clear understanding of the purpose, inferential premise, and effectiveness of the placement exam, or, for that matter, the limitations on decision-making accuracy associated with any short-cut estimate of language ability. Without a general understanding along these lines, it was argued that information available from the placement exam might not be used appropriately by teachers and students, that misconceptions about the relationship between placement decisions and curricular expectations might be perpetuated, and that a variety of unintended consequences might ensue.

Beyond stakeholder perceptions, the PIUs also were interested in the actual academic consequences of placement decisions for students. The most basic purpose of using the placement exam was to locate students in the German courses most conducive to their continued language and academic development, and if actual consequences for placed students indicated otherwise, then there was little point in sustaining the placement assessment program.

These two consequential concerns framed the initial validity evaluation efforts undertaken during this stage of sustained program practice, in order to meet several purposes. First, the PIUs sought to improve the dissemination of information about the placement assessment program among stakeholder audiences by (a) identifying gaps in program understanding and (b) establishing needed lines of communication in order to ameliorate these gaps. In addition, evaluation was intended to locate any residual problems with placement implementation, and associated findings were to inform further improvements in placement practices. Finally, the PIUs sought to triangulate their judgments about the effectiveness of placement decisions with information regarding the consequences of such decisions.

Other areas of concern were raised for potential consideration subsequent to these priorities, including: (a) consequences for any students who did not agree with placement decisions and did not enroll in GUGD courses (and consequences for departmental enrollment figures); (b) the relationship between placement exam decisions and students' German language learning backgrounds; (c) the use of placement decisions for awarding credit in conjunction with *Advanced Placement* test scores; (d) security concerns with the use of a single form of each of the placement exam sub-tests; (e) development and use of parallel forms of the sub-tests; (f) development and use of alternative delivery modes for the placement exam (i.e., computerization); and (g) continued monitoring of the effectiveness and accuracy of the placement exam. In the intervening years, several of these concerns have been addressed in turn. However, only the initial two prioritized concerns for validity evaluation are reported below, in order to exemplify the nature of evaluation during this stage in sustained program practice.

6.3.1 Evaluating stakeholder perspectives on assessment use

Fundamentally at issue during this stage were concerns with whether the placement program was doing what it was intended to do—as defined in the specification of intended assessment use—from the perspective of a given GUGD course, once students had been placed and enrolled in it. The first area of concern addressed basic teacher awareness of the placement assessment program, asking:

(a) To what extent are teachers aware of placement decisions, and other placement exam information, for the students in their classes?
(b) To what extent do teachers understand the purpose and the premise of the placement exam and decisions?

The second area of concern queried the perceived accuracy, effectiveness, and appropriateness of placement decisions:

(c) What are teachers' and students' perceptions regarding the accuracy and effectiveness of placement decisions?

(d) To what extent do teachers perceive continuing versus placed students to present homogeneous learning abilities and needs?

(e) Do teachers agree with the direct placement of incoming students into the more advanced levels of the curriculum, given the unique learning expectations at these levels and assumed learning foundations in the earlier curricular levels?

Finally, a third area of concern addressed problems that might be associated with placement decisions, and solicited suggestions for revising and improving the placement assessment program:

(f) What problems do teachers associate with placement decisions?

(g) In what ways should the placement assessment program be revised, and what additional kinds of information should it provide?

The purpose of validity evaluation at this point was to acquire an initial empirical basis for identifying and understanding major ideas, issues, and problems related to these areas of concern within the GUGD courses into which students were being placed. Resulting information was to be used for triangulating earlier sources of evidence about the effectiveness and accuracy of placement decisions, and to improve communication and understanding about the placement assessment program.

Methods. Semi-structured interviews of current GUGD teachers were selected as the best means to elicit meaningful insights within time and resource constraints. It was argued that interviews, rather than questionnaires, would produce the largest amount of in-depth information within a relatively short period of time, and interviews offered the advantage of probing for details and clarification of uncertainties. It was also argued that teachers would be able to provide useful, if second-hand, insights into student perceptions, given their near daily interaction and the likelihood that students would have raised any placement concerns with their teachers. Thus, in order to minimize disruptions, and in the spirit of returning departmental activities to a sense of normalcy, students were not directly queried during this investigation, but their perspectives were indirectly incorporated via teachers' reported impressions of any student concerns.

Certainly, a single-shot, short-duration interview would not provide sufficient interaction to support the kind of reflexive, grounded interpretation that has come to mark the use of interviews in contemporary ethnographic qualitative research (e.g., Fontana & Frey, 2000; Glesne & Peshkin, 1992). In addition, while rapport was ensured between the PIUs and other teacher informants (given the fact that all were departmental 'insiders' of one sort or another), the interview process could not help but suffer from the biases (both positive and negative) that inhere among colleagues, each with potentially unique stakes in the placement assessment program. Nevertheless, in order to provide initial empirical evidence regarding stakeholders' perceptions of the placement program, and to quickly identify any unanticipated issues or problems with the use of the exam and placement decisions, brief interviews were deemed to offer efficient access to sufficient data. Furthermore, in order to gather the most directly relevant information for these purposes, a semi-structured (as opposed to unstructured) interview format was selected, such that focal areas of concern could be directly queried. Once again, there was a clear bias towards the concerns of the PIUs in this methodological choice. However, the apparent bias was grounded in the premises of the specification of intended assessment use; in other words, the questions being asked and the evidence being sought were driven by a fundamental concern with whether the assessment program was doing what it was intended to do as specified.

Interviews were conducted by the consultant evaluator with 17 individuals, including faculty members ($n = 8$) and graduate teaching assistants ($n = 9$), who comprised the GUGD instructional staff for all undergraduate courses being taught during the fall 2001 semester. Four of the faculty members interviewed also served in departmental administrative roles, and they offered additional insights from that perspective. Given the minimal time available for conducting the interviews and analyzing/interpreting/reporting results, the group of 17 informants was deemed sufficient for the purpose of providing an initial overview of insights into the focal issues. In addition, the targeted group provided good coverage of the multi-level curriculum, with a minimum of three informants representing each of levels I through IV, and they represented distinct amounts of experience within the GUGD, from graduate students teaching their first course, to faculty who had been teaching since the initial use of the placement exam (and much longer, of course, for most faculty respondents).

Interviews were conducted during the eighth week of the Fall 2001 semester, far enough into the course for teachers to have developed a good sense of their students' language abilities and academic progress, but not so far (hopefully) for teachers to have forgotten any concerns that may have arisen during the beginning of the semester. Interviews took place in a private office, in order to minimize interruptions and encourage honesty and responsiveness. The purpose of the interview was briefly explained (as it had been in an initial e-mail statement), with particular emphasis given to the value of teachers' perspectives on the functioning of the placement program. Also explained were the ways in which interviewee responses would be used, that is, for better understanding and, where needed, improving assessment practices in the GUGD. Interviewees were then assured that their responses would be kept anonymous. A hand-held audio tape recorder was then turned on, and interviewees acknowledged verbally their understanding of the purpose of the interview, the guarantee of anonymity of their responses, and their consent for the use of their responses according to the stated purposes.

Several 'warm-up' questions asked about the GUGD curricular levels at which informants were and had been teaching, and to what extent they had participated in any direct way in the placement exam administration or decision-making process.

Subsequently, the first 'perspective' question provided informants with the opportunity to offer any comments that they wanted to raise about the functioning of the placement exam and resulting decisions. This very general question was asked prior to focused questions in order to access any potential issues that teachers found important enough to raise of their own volition. Subsequently, focused questions were posed based on evaluative concerns (a) through (g) above. Details were probed as necessary, in order to maintain clarity of meaning in their comments, but how much informants spoke in response to a given question was left largely to them to decide. Finally, all interviews concluded with a question that provided the informant an opportunity to offer any additional comments about the placement exam and placement decisions.

Tape-recordings of each interview, ranging from 10 to 25 minutes in total (including questions as well as responses), were first transcribed. Subsequently, each informant's response to each of the seven focused questions was identified, extracted, and arranged with responses to the same theme by all other informants. Note that these thematic responses were identified throughout the interviews, wherever they occurred, and not only in association with the specific associated prompt question. In addition, where informants had provided particularly emphatic responses (as identified in my notes and on transcripts, in the form of stress, repetition, etc.), these were noted and interpreted to be of particular importance. Finally, data from the two non-focused questions (i.e., the initial and final questions about major concerns or thoughts, the content of which were self-selected by informants) were analyzed using similar procedures.

Given the one-time and brief nature of these interviews, as well as the purpose of evaluation at this point (i.e., simply to identify teachers' major impressions about several areas of particular concern with assessment use), further in-depth interpretation was neither warranted nor necessary. Rather, findings were synthesized and then reported directly to the PIUs for further action.

Findings. In response to the initial general question, most teachers commented that they really had not spent much time thinking about the placement exam and had little in the way of specific concerns to voice. Several individuals raised particular themes, but no overarching patterns were apparent among them. The four teacher-administrators all brought up their largely positive impressions with the accuracy of the placement decisions that had been made using the new exam, and each also mentioned that procedures and policies still required some attention. Other teachers commented that they found students to be generally well-placed, or they mentioned individual cases of students who had placed into their courses (by and large accurately, in their opinions). Several teachers also noted that they did not really understand how the placement process worked or, for that matter, how students ended up in their particular courses. Two teachers made recommendations for changing specific elements in the exam, either by changing the nature of texts that were used or by adding a performative component.

The first of the focal concerns, (a) and (b) above, questioned teachers' awareness of placement decisions, their understanding of the basic purpose of the assessment, and the inferential premises upon which it was based. In terms of awareness, approximately half of the teachers commented that, at the beginning of the semester, they had not known which students enrolled in their courses on the basis of the placement exam, versus those who had advanced from other courses in the curriculum or who had by-passed the exam and placed themselves. While several of these teachers added that they did become aware of individual cases of placed students, for idiosyncratic reasons, they pointed out that the status of each and every student within a given class was not necessarily known. In addition, even when teachers did know which students in their courses had entered via the placement exam, virtually all reported that they were not aware of their students' specific scores on the placement sub-tests, nor had they received students' self-reported German background information (also collected during the exam).

By contrast, most teachers commented that they wanted to know how students had entered into their courses, either via placement or advancement, and virtually all teachers collected additional sources of student background information during the first week of classes (i.e., beyond that already collected on the background form during the placement exam). Two teachers, both in intermediate-level courses, added emphatically that it was very important to know the nature of student enrollments; both had found that several students had enrolled directly (and incorrectly) into their courses without having taken the placement exam and without having completed any previous courses in the GUGD.

Related information was gathered during the interview of the curriculum coordinator. It was found that the simple curricular-level placement decisions (but not sub-test scores) for all students who completed the placement exam had been reported on the exam day to all GUGD teachers in the form of a master list (i.e., not broken down by class roster). However, as observed by one of the teacher-administrators interviewed, the information was obviously not being used by most teachers, and it therefore needed to be made more explicit and its use "voiced a little more strongly". Thus, although placement decisions were disseminated to teachers at the beginning of the semester, they had not been provided with any specific guidelines for how to use such information. Furthermore, despite their interest in accessing placement exam information about their students, sub-test scores and background information were not provided.

In response to a second set of questions, teachers produced overall consistent notions about what the exam and decisions should accomplish, and they were also consistent in reporting their knowledge about how the exam was actually used to inform placement decisions. Rather uniform responses revealed that teachers agreed on the use of the placement exam for locating students in classes with other students of similar language abilities, such that they would be equally challenged, have a good chance of success, not limit the learning of others, and present similar and largely

anticipated learning needs to the instructors at a given curricular level. One intermediate-level teacher summarized the purpose as follows:

> "Yeah, I think it is to order the students into a group that will allow them to
> learn or will give them the most benefits for learning. Where the group is
> somewhat homogeneous, where they aren't feeling held back by some of the
> students. And aren't feeling intimidated by others. I would say that would be
> where the environment is most conducive to learning."

Furthermore, several teachers commented that the exam should not be expected to
produce 100% correct placements all the time, and that the purpose was to provide a
relatively accurate estimate of where the typical incoming student would be served
best by the instruction available.

A secondary theme, addressed by several respondents, pointed to the programmatic messages that were communicated by the very existence of a placement exam.
From this perspective, in addition to the need for accurate placements, the placement
exam should make clear to students and teachers alike that the intent of the instructional program in the GUGD was to maximize language learning opportunities for
students by articulating their existing language abilities with the unique learning expectations of the curriculum. One teacher-administrator commented:

> "Both with regard to the practice of placing students into the program, but
> equally importantly the entire practice of placement testing sends signals to
> us internally and signals to the students themselves that we take their previ-
> ous language learning seriously and intend to take them seriously as
> learners."

Likewise, a graduate teaching assistant added that the placement exam should provide an introduction to incoming students about the unique, sequential nature of
curriculum and instruction in the GUGD, and that the articulation of placement and
curriculum should be made explicit to them.

Finally, a clear divide was identified in responses to questions about the inferential premises of placement decisions, that is, what was assessed by the three sub-tests
and how that information was used for placing students into specific curricular levels. On the one hand, the four teacher-administrators, all of whom had participated in
decision-making on the basis of the exam, discussed the nature of the three sub-tests,
the kinds of information that they offered in terms of the curriculum, and the ways in
which an appropriate match between student language abilities and the *Multiple Literacies* curriculum could be estimated on the basis of this information. On the other
hand, nearly all other teachers commented that they did not have any insights into
how the exam and decision-making procedures actually functioned (although several
mentioned that they would like to know). Even those who had been involved in the
scoring of the C-test observed that the rest of the placement exam was unclear to

them, as did one long-time teacher: "Personally, I have never even seen the other parts of the placement test, I don't know what they are like." This teacher added that a basic understanding of the exam would be useful, in that "then I maybe would have a better idea about the students and if they are in the right place." Similarly, a multi-year graduate teaching assistant noted: "It's one of those things that, the graduate students don't have much of a role in it, and I think probably the faculty don't either [...] The practice, we just don't know much about it." Thus, just as interview findings indicated that teachers were generally not aware of the placement status or sub-test scores of their students, it also became apparent that they had not been provided with a basic understanding of the inferential premises underlying decisions that were being made about their students.

Moving to questions (c) through (e) above, teachers provided their insights into the accuracy, effectiveness, and appropriateness of decisions based on the placement exam. In terms of the basic accuracy of placement decisions, all interviewed teachers responded that, insofar as they were aware of who had placed into their courses over the previous two and one-half years, placement decisions were nearly always accurate, and this response was repeated across all levels of the curriculum. Furthermore, a follow-up question asked of all informants whether they recalled specific cases of mis-placement or of having to recommend re-placing students into more appropriate curricular levels. This question yielded only three teachers who recalled individual students (over the three administrations of the new exam) who they thought belonged in another curricular level; in addition, one teacher-administrator recalled having to adjudicate "one or two cases" of re-placing students since the initial use of the new placement exam (August, 1999). Additional comments from the perspective of two teacher-administrators highlighted that the use of the placement exam, for locating both Georgetown students and those from other U.S. universities into courses at the GUGD German study abroad program, had been accurate over two years of administration. All in all, then, teachers seemed to perceive very few inaccuracies in placement decisions.

Several additional themes were raised in response to questions about placement accuracy. First of all, several teachers commented that the general accuracy of placement decisions should be communicated to students and teachers alike, but the possibility of inaccuracies and the potential need to re-place students also had to be made explicit. In the words of one informant:

> "I think we should really make some sort of provision to tell people the placement test is very good, actually it's excellent, but somehow every now and then somebody gets into a particular class where he or she shouldn't be. So, consider the placement test as an initial thing. You can be kicked higher or lower."

Several other teachers observed that they found more inconsistencies among students who had *advanced* into their courses versus students who had *placed* in, while over half of the informants commented on differences between students' previous language learning experiences and the unique expectations of curriculum and instruction in the GUGD. However, in each of these cases, teachers reiterated that the original placement decisions had been correct, and that the accuracy of students' placements became clear (to students and teachers) as the semester progressed and students became more attuned to the local language instruction approach. Finally, most informants noted variability among incoming students in terms of 'learning style', 'motivation', 'modality of previous instruction', etc., but they generally added that a brief placement exam could not be expected to address these concerns and that their impact was quickly ameliorated through instruction.

In response to questions about students' general perceptions regarding the accuracy of their placements, approximately half of the teachers reported that they had not discussed placement issues explicitly with their classes, but most also added that they thought students would have approached them with any disagreements about the course or level in which they belonged. Teachers who felt confident in offering insights into students' perceptions uniformly commented that most students found themselves to have been placed appropriately, even those who suffered apparent difficulties with the expectations of a given course. Most of these teachers reiterated the unique challenges that the *Multiple Literacies* curriculum posed to incoming students, and four informants discussed specific cases of students who voiced their concerns that instruction was very dissimilar to their language learning experiences. However, all of these teachers also reported that students in their courses were able to overcome, by mid-semester, initial concerns with this disjuncture. For example, one teacher of upper-level courses observed:

"A couple of the first year students, one in particular, was very concerned. But she has now blossomed [...] For the first time she wrote her reflective journal in German and said right away, 'I feel much more comfortable than I ever did before'. And that comfort level I think could be interpreted along the lines that you interpret it, with regard to am I in the right place."

One teacher-administrator did note that several students had requested permission to enroll in curricular levels lower than their placements, because of a perception that the expectations were too unique and different from their language learning backgrounds. However, this informant also echoed a number of others in adding that these kinds of perceptions on the part of students were probably not concerns with the placement exam and decisions per se, but more of an issue that inhered within the unique approach to language learning; likewise, several teachers recommended that students needed to be provided with an explicit introduction to the curriculum and its instructional means, as a way of responding to such perceptions. Finally, a teacher-administrator commented on the fact that some external users of the C-test (e.g., for students from other universities who sought to participate in the GUGD study abroad program) did not understand the C-test or accept its use as an indicator of their students' German abilities; several study abroad enrollments might have been lost as a result of this perception.

Following up on two related details, teachers also offered their opinions on the extent to which homogeneity among students' abilities and needs could be expected, and they commented on the advisability of placing incoming students directly into the upper levels of the curriculum. Virtually all teachers at all levels reported heterogeneity among students who advanced into their classes as well as those who placed in, and their comments centered around differences in students' language backgrounds, learning 'styles' or 'attitudes', or preparedness to engage with college work. Several informants recommended a more explicit introduction to the nature of teaching and learning in the program, as in the words of one teacher: "And I find that we need almost some kind of buffer zone in the beginning two weeks, to just get these people adjusted." Finally, several teachers at the upper levels commented that increasing diversity among students' abilities, interests, and needs was to be expected in conjunction with increasing levels of the curriculum; one teacher noted:

> "The higher up you are, the more difficult it becomes to answer the question as to whether these people were appropriately placed or not. And the reason for that is quite obvious, because at that level the profile of the learners as aggregate sitting in the class is inherently and always will be extraordinarily diverse."

Nevertheless, respondents agreed that students who exhibit advanced levels of language ability on the placement exam should be placed into the corresponding upper levels of the curriculum. Approximately half of the teachers commented that it would be unfair to place incoming students into courses lower than those suggested by the placement exam, even though the upper levels of the curriculum assumed acquisition of a variety of language, content, and other types of knowledge/ability that had been instructed within the preceding levels. Several teachers also observed that student success at the upper levels of the curriculum depended on variables that couldn't be tested in the placement exam, and therefore, that placements should be subject to modification by the instructor and student, where warranted, as in the words of one teacher:

> "Yeah, if they test in, I'm not sure what the situation is, but I think there should be a certain period where they say, "Can you handle this class?" If you can't or if the instructor doesn't think you can handle this class, then there should be a certain time for them to transfer into a lower class. But I definitely should say that if they test in then they should give it a shot."

The third area of concern, as expressed in questions (f) and (g) above, sought teachers' input on any specific problems as well as suggestions for improving placement. A variety of potential problems was identified by teachers, although there were no patterns raised by the majority. Several teachers observed that students had enrolled in their classes contrary to placement recommendations or without having taken the placement exam, including several transfer and international students, and that these cases had resulted in a disjuncture between the individual's learning needs and the instructional efforts of the teacher and learning efforts of other students. In several instances, it was observed that students' advisors from their major areas of study had explicitly advised them to not take the placement exam and to simply enroll in a given course. One informant commented:

> "Except that two of them didn't take the placement, they just placed themselves [...] And one of them is actually much better, should be at least one level higher, and I've now talked with the coordinator. He gave him the C-test and said he should be at level 4 instead of level 2."

In addition, two of these teachers expressed their lack of knowledge about placement policies and what actions to take in such situations, as in the following case of a student who purposefully enrolled lower than recommended:

> "Because he inquired about what does that mean, what did his placement in the placement test mean, and if he was required to be in that level. And I said no, but you don't want to stay here if this is going to be too easy for you. But he stayed."

Furthermore, teachers pointed out specific problems that arose in their classes in association with students who had enrolled inaccurately. First, teachers raised problems that had been caused for the other students in the class, such as intimidating other students who had lower language abilities, answering questions before other students had the chance to try, and distracting other students by expressing their boredom with the instruction. Problems were also identified for the mis-enrolled students themselves, including poor study habits (and resulting poor academic performances) for students who enrolled too low, and inability to catch up or keep up with learning expectations for students who enrolled too high (resulting in at least one withdrawal).

Turning to questions about needed improvements in placement practices, teachers also offered wide-ranging suggestions, although without particularly unanimous accord and without particular emphasis that any changes needed to be made. The most common suggestion was that more spontaneous and extended performances in German be added to the placement exam, in the form of speaking and writing assessments, although most teachers also acknowledged that time and resource constraints probably ruled out the use of such assessments. Several teachers also recommended the more direct use of information about German language background and learning experiences for placement decision-making, although they had no suggestions regarding how placements might actually differ as a result, in light of the rigid system of courses and curricular levels available for placement. Some teachers emphasized that they would like to receive more information about their students at the beginning of instruction, including test scores and background information, and they suggested that the uses for these kinds of information also should be communicated to all teachers. In addition, several teachers added that clarifications needed to be made and disseminated regarding the concrete policies for placing students, monitoring placed students, and revising placements where necessary. Two graduate teaching assistants also suggested that teachers should be given the opportunity to participate more in the administration, scoring, and decision-making processes of the placement exam, so that they would better understand the basis for students' placements and as a means for professional development.

Clearly, these suggested improvements were associated closely with the primary problem areas that teachers had identified. It is also of note that teachers did not recommend specific changes to the basic test-based information or to the placement decision-making process, beyond the addition of performative elements which they acknowledged to be unfeasible. In summary, one teacher-administrator added the following evaluative comment:

> "I think actually we are fine with what we are getting. One can always gather more information and make all sorts of accurate, and more accurate, and still more accurate placement decisions. But on the practical side of things, especially since we do not offer off-sequence courses any more, it is really either beginning, intermediate, or advanced, and that's really what it is. And then the upper levels. So in some way, the placement exam needs to provide a reasonably good measure of potential success, or potential for a successful learning experience for the student for the particular class that she or he gets placed into. That I think would be what I would want from a placement exam. And I think we are getting that definitely."

Uses. These findings were reported to the PIUs initially in the form of an attached e-mail document sent in early 2002. All were pleased that earlier interpretations about the accuracy and effectiveness of the placement exam and decisions had been supported by teachers' perceptions regarding student placements into their courses. However, beyond this finding in one area of concern, the range of additional issues raised by informants suggested various areas in need of prompt attention, and there ensued a series of e-mail discussions among the PIUs regarding the specific actions to be taken. At the heart of these discussions were the issues of, first, how to improve the implementation of placement decisions such that students ended up in the curricular level where they belonged, and, second, how best to communicate with students, teachers, and other stakeholders about the inferential premises of the exam, its intended uses (as well as those not intended), its effectiveness, and related concerns.

An initial decision was made to draw up a tentative list of recommended policies and practices that, if implemented in conjunction with each use of the placement exam, would address the major potential problems or needs raised within each of the focal concerns. This list was then distributed, along with the interview findings, to the full GUGD faculty and teaching constituency, and the entire matter was scheduled for further discussion during a workshop in May 2002. These initial recommendations are presented below in bulleted format, separated by each area of focal concern. Only two overarching recommendations were made in response to teacher awareness of placement decisions, and the purposes and premises for them:

- Report to teachers for each student placing into their courses: (a) placement exam sub-test scores, (b) placement decisions for each sub-test, (c) overall placement decision, and (d) student language experiences information collected on the background information form.
- In conjunction with the reporting of placement exam outcomes, provide all teachers with a set of guidelines for: (a) interpreting placement exam scores and decisions, (b) using placement exam scores and background information for considering the appropriateness of students' placements, and (c) adjusting students' enrollments where clearly necessary.

Recommendations in the second area of focal concern were broken down by each of the three question topics. First, in response to teachers' and students' perceptions regarding the accuracy and effectiveness of placement decisions, the following recommendations were made:

- It should be made clear to both teachers and students that, while placement decisions have been shown generally to be very accurate, there is always the possibility that a placement recommendation was made in error; students should realize that their placement is not 'set in stone'—teachers may suggest during the first several weeks of classes that they move up or down into courses which better suit their individual learning needs.
- Students and teachers at all levels of the curriculum, and especially at the upper levels (III and IV), should be made aware that, while students may present with language knowledge and abilities appropriate to the given course, they may need a period of planned adjustment into the unique teaching and learning activities, expectations, and requirements of the GUGD program.
- Students need to have a clear introduction to the unique nature of the curriculum, its objectives, the type of instruction that drives it, and, most importantly, the expectations that it assumes of the learner; such an introduction should take place during the initial days of all courses in Levels I-III and Text in Context (Level IV), owing to the fact that students may place directly into courses at each of these levels.

- Students' perceptions of the placement exam and placement decisions should be further investigated via direct query of students, focusing on mid-semester evaluation of placement appropriateness.

Second, in response to teachers perceptions of the homogeneity of students' learning abilities and needs, it was recommended that:

- Teachers at all levels of the curriculum should bear in mind that learners may exhibit very different language abilities, learning styles, motivation, and intellectual capacities regardless of whether they were placed into or advanced into the given course.
- For learners who, because of their advanced language knowledge and abilities, place into the upper levels of the curriculum, there may need to be a formalized period of adjustment built into courses, in order for these students to understand the expectations of the curriculum and teaching/learning that occurs within it.
- Teachers need to be provided with tools for systematically addressing individual differences in both abilities/knowledge and in students' approaches to learning.
- Articulation between the curricular levels, in terms of the types of learning and teaching activities that occur, may need to be revisited, especially between Levels I and II.

Third, in response to teachers' comments on the direct placement of incoming students into the more advanced levels of the curriculum, it was recommended that:

- Teachers should be aware of the potential differences between student backgrounds and experiences with respect to curricular expectations at all levels of the curriculum.
- Teachers should plan explicit strategies for helping individual students to transition into the unique curricular and pedagogic expectations of the *Multiple Literacies* curriculum, especially at the upper levels.
- Students should be made aware that they are being placed into courses on the basis of language abilities, but that they may be faced with a learning setting that is quite unique compared with their experiences.

Finally, recommendations for the third focal concern on problems and improvements were also addressed:

- With the exception of native speakers, all students who have had any German language experience should be required to take the placement exam; policies and procedures for contacting and advising students about this requirement should be reviewed and revised, especially for transfer students, international students, and students from the School of Foreign Service; placement exam policies should be communicated with all relevant external departments and student advisors.

- On those occasions when students enroll in a course without having taken the placement exam, teachers should require that the exam be taken if the students demonstrate obvious ability differences from the others in the class.
- Students should be strongly advised to follow the placement recommendation by enrolling in the corresponding course and level; where courses are not available during the fall semester, students should be advised to postpone enrollment until the spring semester or to consider enrolling in intensive sections.
- External users of the C-test should receive clear communication about the purposes and practices associated with the test, the research which supports decisions on the basis of test scores, and the revisability of all placement decisions by teachers.
- It may be necessary to require students to take (or re-take) the placement exam if they have not studied German at the university level for lengthy periods of time (e.g., more than a year).
- Teachers should be aware that, on rare occasions, students may have been incorrectly placed into their courses due to discrepancies between their German language backgrounds and the language abilities/knowledge measured on the placement exam; for example, naturalistic acquirers of German may perform unusually low on the C-test, due to a lack of literacy development; any suspected cases of mis-placement should be referred to the coordinator of the undergraduate curriculum.
- The purpose and basis for placement decisions needs to be explained to students prior to the administration of the exam; students should also realize that the placement decision represents an initial recommendation that is subject to revision during the first few weeks of the semester.
- Opportunities for involvement in placement exam administration and scoring should be made available to the teaching staff.
- Avenues for more efficient and accurate administration and scoring of the placement exam should be explored, including especially computerized delivery and scoring.

After these tentative recommendations had been disseminated, they were further discussed during a full departmental stakeholder workshop in May 2002. Based on these discussions, specific actions were taken in two overarching areas, and other issues that had been raised were delegated to the curriculum coordinator for subsequent attention. First, placement assessment program policies were revised to incorporate most of the recommendations above and to resolve teacher confusion as well as the problems that had been found with student mis-enrollments. These placement policies were drafted jointly by the consultant and curriculum coordinator and revised by the other PIUs, and then disseminated to all GUGD faculty and teachers (in August 2002) in the form of an official and updated *Placement Procedures and Policies* manual (see Appendix D).

Second, considerable attention was then devoted to the development and dissemination of statements that sought to resolve problems with a perceived lack of understanding about the GUGD placement assessment program. Again, these documents were drafted jointly, and they were subsequently disseminated in a variety of ways, and on a continuing basis, as appropriate to each targeted audience. First, a *General Overview of the Georgetown University German Department Placement Exam* was created (Appendix E), outlining the sub-test components of the exam and their inferential premises, the intended uses for exam scores, and evidence regarding its effectiveness as a curriculum-based placement tool. This document was appended to the *Placement Procedures and Policies* manual, disseminated to all GUGD teachers, and it was posted to the GUGD web site in a prominent location. Second, an *Introductory Statement to Students* was developed in order to present similar information about the placement exam and associated policies to students, and this statement was to be both mailed out to incoming students with departmental information packets and delivered to all students who attended the placement exam administrations each fall. An abbreviated version of this statement was also to be read to students prior to the beginning of each exam administration. Third, an *Overview of the C-test* letter was developed for introducing GUGD-external administrators to the placement exam C-test; in particular, this document was intended to ameliorate the lack of understanding by outside German faculty and students about the nature of the C-test and its use in placing students into the GUGD study abroad program. By disseminating basic information about the placement exam to these key stakeholder audiences, it was hoped that they would come to understand how the placement exam and in particular the C-test functioned, how decisions were made on the basis of the information provide by the exam, and both the effectiveness and limitations of this approach to curriculum-based placement decision-making.

6.3.2 Evaluating the relationship between placements and performance

Beyond stakeholders' awareness, perceptions, and uses of the placement exam, its on-going programmatic implementation gave rise to additional concerns with consequences for student learning and academic performance that might be related to placement decisions. Where students were incorrectly placed, or where they enrolled incorrectly despite placements, it was assumed that their learning needs would not be met as effectively, and that their academic performance would suffer. The PIUs understood, of course, that direct causal outcomes could not be drawn between placement decisions and student academic performance within a class, given the very complex and multivariate nature of questions regarding why students learn and/or perform as they do over the course of a college semester. However, they did express concern with any apparent relationships which might be identified between placements/enrollments and the academic performance of students within corresponding classes. In addition, they questioned the extent to which students who were placed into a given curricular level were performing at similar levels of academic success when compared with students who had advanced into that curricular level. Finally, despite their conviction that incoming students had to be given the opportunity to place as high as appropriate for their language abilities, the PIUs worried that students who placed directly into more advanced levels of the curriculum might suffer a disadvantage at not having advanced through the carefully sequenced (content and language) instructional experiences.

Several specific questions framed an investigation of the relationship between placement/enrollment decisions and student academic performance:

(a) What is the overall academic performance of students who enrolled in the correct German courses, as defined by accurate placement decisions?
(b) What is the overall academic performance of students who enrolled in the *incorrect* German courses, as defined by accurate placement decisions?
(c) How does the academic performance of placement-based students compare with continuing students in German courses overall?
(d) How does the academic performance of placement-based students compare with continuing students at each of the curricular levels?

Methods. Straightforward descriptive and inferential quantitative analyses were employed to investigate questions (a) through (d). However, an initial decision regarding the operationalization of "academic performance" was first required. Potential indicators of students' academic performance included teacher holistic ratings, scores on final exams and semester-end summative writing/speaking tasks, and semester-final course grades. It was decided that semester-final course grades provided the most readily available and comprehensive indicator of a student's overall academic performance. Of course, course grades are themselves susceptible to a variety of potential intervening variables from both the student's (e.g., variable performance over the semester) and the teacher's (e.g., grade inflation) side of the grading equation, leading to instability in the exact meaning of an individual student's grade. Nevertheless, course grades are regularly treated within higher education as a principal indicator for student academic success, and it was reasoned that they should therefore prove appropriate for relative group-level comparisons, if not for interpretation as a direct sign of individual achievement or learning.

At the conclusion of the spring semester of 2001, all course grades from the 1999-2000 and 2000-2001 academic years for all students enrolled in GUGD undergraduate courses from curricular level I through the first course of curricular level IV ("Text in Context") were accessed from university records, and they were arranged in a data-base according to an anonymous numerical identification system. Within this data-base, all students who had completed either the 1999 or 2000 GUGD placement exam were identified, and their corresponding placement recommendations were recorded as well. Furthermore, the *initial* GUGD course in which each of these "placement-based" students had enrolled was identified, and the students were subsequently coded as having "enrolled correctly", "enrolled higher", or "enrolled lower" in this course, based on earlier analyses of student enrollment behaviors as well as the extent of inaccuracies in placement recommendations (see section 6.2). This initial course, then, enabled a 'proving ground' for the efficacy of placement/enrollment decisions, while subsequent courses would not have proved as indicative for investigating consequences of placement/enrollment decisions. Finally, information for all "placement-based" students, including enrollment status and course grade, was grouped within the data-base according to their initial German course/level, along with the course grades for all students who had advanced into the same course from earlier GUGD levels ("continuing" students).

Analyses in response to questions (a) through (d) were conducted on the semester-final course grades of this set of "placement-based" and "continuing" students. Descriptive statistics were first calculated for the course grades of each of four student groups overall for each academic year, including three "placement-based" (enrolled high, enrolled low, enrolled correct) and one "continuing" category. Given the use of a "plus-minus" grading system at Georgetown (with the exception of "A+"), course grades were converted to numeric equivalents using the official institutional four-point scale as in Table 28.

Table 28. Numeric equivalents of semester-final course letter grades

A	A-	B+	B	B-	C+	C	C-	D+	D	D-	F+	F
4.00	3.66	3.33	3.00	2.66	2.33	2.00	1.66	1.33	1.00	0.66	0.33	0.00

Inferential comparisons were then made between average numeric course grades for the overall group of "placement-based" students who had enrolled in the correct level and the overall group of "continuing" students. Due to the very low numbers and unequal distributions of student grades for the other two groups, as well as for students at each curricular level, no other inferential comparisons were warranted or made. For the correct "placement-based" and "continuing" groups, two comparisons were made, one for each of the academic years of interest; these comparisons were kept separate given the slightly different placement standards that had been used in the 1999 versus 2000 placement exams. In other words, it may have been the case that students who were correctly placed/enrolled according to the year 2000 exam results ended up in German courses more conducive to their learning and academic performance, due to adjusted cut-score standards (see section 6.2). Comparisons were drawn between these groups using means and 95% confidence intervals as well as univariate analysis of variance procedures.

Finally, in order to provide an initial, if tentative, indication of potential differences in academic performance success at each of the GUGD curricular levels, average course grades were calculated for the "placement-based" students who had enrolled correctly at each level, and the "continuing" students who had enrolled at the same level. Simple graphic comparisons were used to identify any possible anomalies in expected academic performances across these levels, as inferential comparisons were not warranted due to the low N values.

Findings. Table 29 shows the overall averages and standard deviations of semester-final course grades for each group of "placement-based" and "continuing" students for the two academic years of interest. For both years, students who enrolled in the correct curricular level, as indicated by the placement exam, received on average the highest course grades. Students who enrolled higher than the correct curricular level received lower grades on average than either these students or the group of continuing students, arguably due to the somewhat more challenging nature of the course material vis-à-vis their language abilities.

Table 29. Average course grades for "placement-based" and "continuing" students

Academic Year	Statistic	Placement-based students			Continuing students
		Enroll High	Enroll Low	Enroll Corr.	
	N	7	13	29	117
1999-2000	Mean	3.19	3.46	3.55	3.27
	S	0.31	0.42	0.36	0.71
	N	19	4	30	89
2000-2001	Mean	3.28	3.17	3.43	3.37
	S	0.65	1.00	0.66	0.62

Note. For 1999-2000, 19 additional placement-based students enrolled in courses above level IV, and for 2000-2001, 16 additional placement-based students enrolled in courses above level IV; these students are not included in Table 31.

However, average grades for the group of students who enrolled lower than the correct curricular level, for whom a concomitant academic advantage might have been expected, were found to be the lowest for the 2000-2001 academic year, and lower than that of the correctly enrolled "placement-based students" for the 1999-2000 year. Likewise, continuing students, who were ostensibly the most familiar with the unique instructional practices of the *Multiple Literacies* curriculum, scored on average somewhat below the correctly enrolled "placement-based" students in both years.

Interpretations that might be based on these average course grades are tentative at best, in light of the low numbers of students in each of the incorrect enrollment groups. In addition, substantial variability in course grades was found for all groups in both years, and much more so during the 2000-2001 academic year, indicating that, regardless of their enrollment category, individual students performed at varying levels of academic success. Nevertheless, negative academic consequences certainly were not found to be related to the *accurate* use of the placement exam. In addition, these initial findings did suggest that incorrect enrollments, into courses at both higher and lower curricular levels than indicated, might be associated with somewhat lower levels of academic performance (see associated comments by teachers in the previous section).

While these initial patterns of academic performance could only be interpreted with caution, more robust comparisons were enabled between the continuing students and correctly placed/enrolled students, due to the larger numbers within these groups. Figure 24 compares the average course grades and associated 95% confidence intervals for each of these groups in the two academic years of interest. It is apparent that, for the 1999-2000 academic year, students who enrolled in the correct curricular level for their initial German course received on average somewhat higher semester-final grades than did students who continued from previous curricular levels. Although their confidence intervals just overlap, a univariate analysis of variance procedure identified a statistically significant difference between these group means $(F(1,144) = 4.18, p = .043)$, indicating a relatively trustworthy difference between the average academic performances of each group. For the 2000-2001 academic year, the correctly placed/enrolled students again received higher average grades than did continuing students, but the difference in group means was much smaller, and both the broadly overlapping confidence intervals and a univariate analysis of variance procedure $(F(1,117) = 0.223, p = 0.638)$ indicated no statistically trustworthy difference.

Overall patterns of academic performance supported the interpretation that students who were correctly placed and enrolled in their initial German courses performed at least as well, if not better than, their colleagues who had advanced into courses from previous curricular levels. However, this finding was not overinterpreted, given the uneven representation of students from different curricular levels within the two groups that were compared. Of the students who completed the placement exam in both 1999 and 2000, much larger proportions enrolled in levels III and especially IV of the curriculum than in levels I and II. Accordingly, there was no doubt that a greater percentage of the grades for "placement-based" students came from level III and IV classes than did grades for the "continuing" students, and it is certainly possible that a 'class' or 'level' effect could have accounted for some proportion of the observed differences in favor of the "placement-based" students.

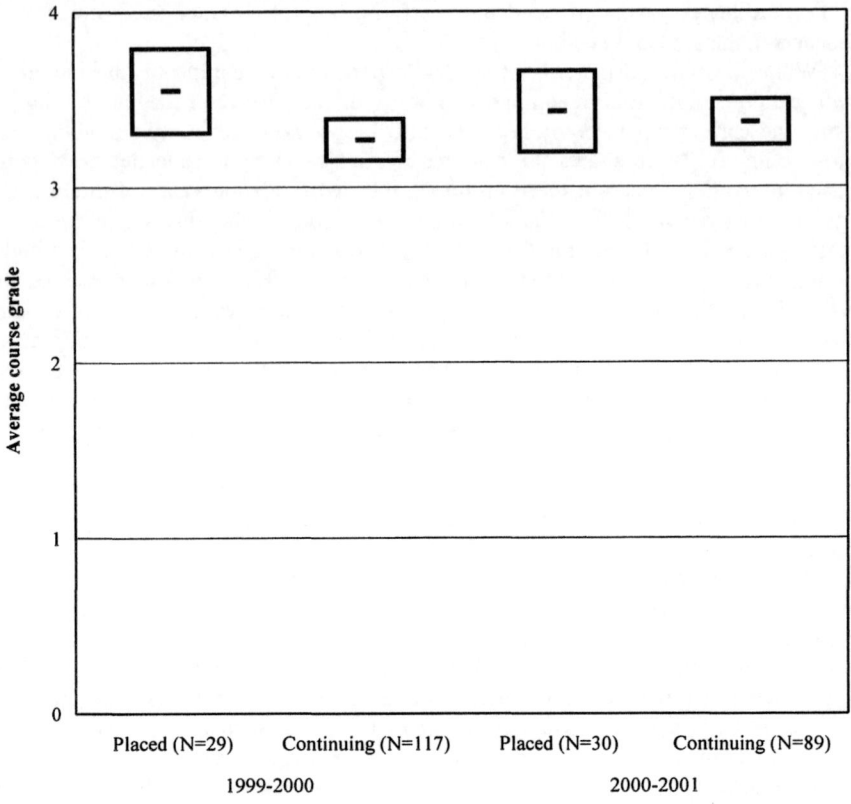

Figure 24. Correctly placed versus continuing students' average course grades

Along similar lines, it remained uncertain to what extent the performance success of correctly placed/enrolled students might be evenly or unevenly distributed across different levels of the curriculum, and the PIUs were particularly concerned about the academic performances of the greater proportion of students who had placed and enrolled in the higher levels of the curriculum.

Figures 25 and 26 show the average semester-final course grades for each group of correctly placed/enrolled students and continuing students at each of the curricular levels for which data were available in the two academic years. Note that these averages should be interpreted with utmost caution, given that data ranged from a low of one student to a high of 15 students in either group for any given curricular level. Despite these interpretive limitations, it is apparent that the students who were correctly placed/enrolled in 1999-2000 performed consistently better than did their continuing student counterparts, at virtually all levels of the curriculum for which data were available. The only exception occurred in both semesters of curricular year III, a strikingly similar finding to the inconsistencies observed at this level in investigations of C-test scores.

In general, the finding of overall higher academic performance at nearly all curricular levels lent additional support to the interpretation that initial placement cut-score standards (for 1999) had been set slightly lower than appropriate. At the same time, it indicated that "placement-based" students who enrolled in the indicated curricular level were performing on average at relatively (and equally, compared with "continuing" students) high levels of academic success across all levels of the curriculum.

For academic year 2000-2001, after placement cut-score standards had been adjusted, patterns of academic performance were found to be more variable, with correctly placed/enrolled students receiving higher average grades at some curricular levels and "continuing" students outperforming them at other levels. However, the key finding in analyses from both of these years, from the point of view of the PIUs, was that students who had correctly placed and enrolled in courses at curricular levels III and IV (the first course at this level) did not perform with noticeably lower levels of academic success than did "continuing" students, and, in fact, they apparently performed consistently better than "continuing" students in the "Text in Context" course at level IV.

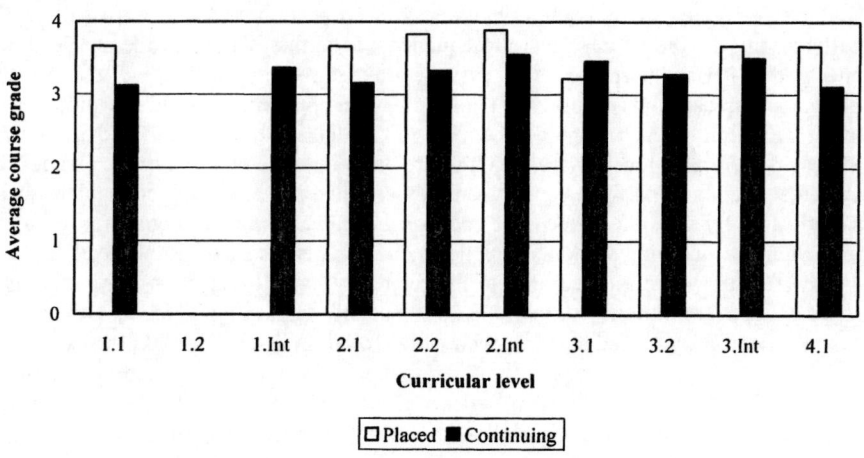

Figure 25. Average course grades by curricular level, academic year 1999-2000

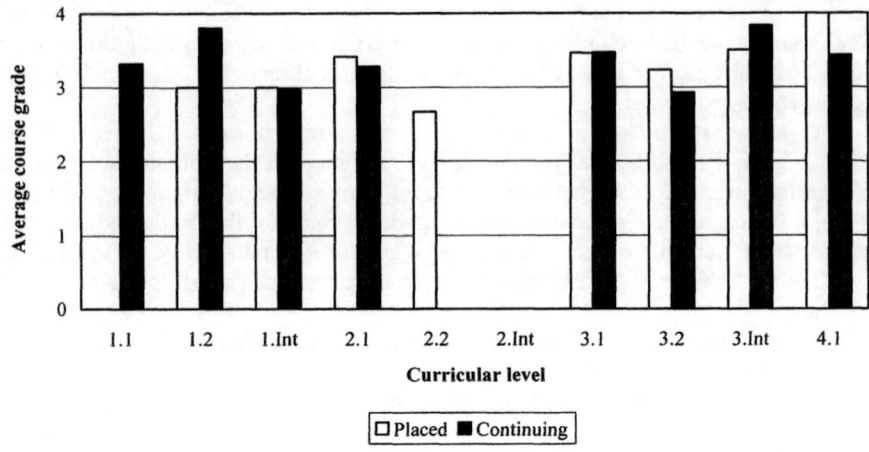

Figure 26. Average course grades by curricular level, academic year 2000-2001

Uses. The original intent of these investigations was to provide a distinct source of evidence regarding the extent to which the placement assessment program was accomplishing what it was intended to accomplish, from the perspective of student academic performance consequences, and to enable further associated judgments about the on-going use of the placement exam. Accordingly, because none of the findings suggested that students who were placed accurately and enrolled correctly suffered any degree of negative consequences, in terms of their academic perform-ances, the PIUs interpreted the evidence as supporting continued use of the placement assessment program. In addition, the apparent if tentative patterns of lower academic success that were found for students who had enrolled in contra-indicated curricular levels were also interpreted to indicate positive consequences for students' academic performances when they enrolled in the correct curricular levels, as indicated by accurate placement decisions. Finally, immediate concerns with the placement of incoming students directly into the upper levels of the *Multiple Litera-cies* curriculum were allayed, due to the relatively high levels of average academic success—at a minimum comparable to those of continuing students—that were found for correctly placed students who had enrolled in level III or IV classes.

Several additional interpretations for patterns in academic performance were proffered by the broader departmental stakeholder audience. First, it was suggested that a lack of motivation and interest might have accounted for the observation of mixed academic performances by students who enrolled in curricular levels lower than recommended by correct placement decisions. As such, and in conjunction with the finding of obviously lower levels of academic performance for those students who enrolled higher than indicated, the importance of ensuring that students enrolled correctly based on accurate placement decisions was reiterated.

Second, some teachers sought to interpret the apparently higher average levels of academic performance on the part of correctly placed/enrolled students (as compared with "continuing" students) to indicate that there might be deficiencies within the curriculum itself. Given the paucity of the data that were analyzed, and especially the fact that a very unequal distribution of curricular levels constituted the two groups being compared, this interpretation was not at all warranted on the basis of the current analyses. As such, the PIUs took pains in the departmental workshop to explain exactly what could and could not be interpreted, and to reiterate that the only intended use of these analyses was for identifying any patterns of negative consequences within the academic performances of correctly placed/enrolled students. All agreed that these had not been identified at this evaluation stage, and that the continued use of the placement exam seemed warranted.

Chapter 7
The implications of validity evaluation

I began this work by questioning how educators might respond to the challenge of ensuring the quality of assessments as they are actually used to meet distinct purposes within teaching and learning contexts. Given the pervasive role of assessment in all walks of education, the fundamental need to evaluate what happens in the name of assessment seems essential—but to what end? In this final chapter, I consider the outcomes of my validity evaluation work in terms of broader implications for the practice of validating educational assessments in foreign language settings and beyond. First, I highlight what happened as validity evaluation processes were pursued by local educators. In addition, I reflect on other process outcomes, in the form of organizational learning and changes in the treatment of assessment within the FL education context. Second, I raise several potential limitations in the validity evaluation approach explored here, from the specific perspectives of program evaluation, educational measurement, and FL education. Finally, I conclude by offering a handful of pragmatic implications for the practice of language assessment validation, based on findings from the current work, and I indicate directions to be taken in future work that seeks to ensure the quality and utility of assessments within language and other education contexts.

7.1 What happened? Intended uses by intended users

Responsibility to evaluate. Perhaps the most basic question that distinguishes an assessment validity evaluation approach from conventional test validation asks who should take responsibility for evaluation of assessments as they are actually used for specific purposes in specific settings. While educational measurement standards (AERA, APA, NCME, 1999) assume that measurement professionals will direct the scientific validation of assessments that they produce, what happens when educational assessments are locally developed in response to the intended uses of local educators, rather than only as measures of construct theories? A *de facto* answer may be that educators who use assessments will be held responsible for that use (by their students, the public, etc.)—regardless of who typically engages in developing assessments or prescribing standards. As such, one intent of the current work was to enable local educators within the targeted FL context to assume responsibility for the validity evaluation of their own assessment practices, and a utilization-focused model was adopted with this intent in mind.

At the same time, important features of the context constrained the extent to which validity evaluation by and for local educators could proceed, and as such, responsibility and participation took different forms for distinct individuals. While it was apparent that the needs, uses, values, priorities, qualities, and constraints in assessment practice could only be identified via direct involvement of the educators themselves, it was also clear that they lacked a framework within which to do so.

Similarly, in order for both assessment development and evaluation to proceed on an empirical and trustworthy basis, rigorous methodological know-how would be required, yet such skills are typically lacking in FL education programs (see chapter 2). Finally, in order for validity evaluation to proceed in a feasible and efficient manner, participation by the full constituency of local educators required careful planning and moderation, such that evaluative action would be enabled through consensus rather than disabled through individual idiosyncrasies or divisiveness.

On the one hand, then, the expertise of local educators was required in order for the validity evaluation process to prove *meaningful* at all in ensuring the relevant qualities of assessments as they were actually used for making decisions and taking actions in support of local FL educational efforts. On the other hand, a degree of methodological expertise in educational assessment and program evaluation was called for in order to support these educators in taking an empirical view of their assessment uses and in driving the evaluation process forward in *feasible* and *useful*, yet rigorous ways. A potential solution was identified through the systematic wedding of local, program-based expertise with external, methodological expertise. Responsibility for validity evaluation, then, fell to both the local educators and to an external consultant, and both sources of expertise conjointly informed all of the steps in validity evaluation of the placement assessment program. A utilization-focused evaluation approach enabled this synthesis, by providing mechanisms for local experts to contribute the substance of program context and evaluation needs, and for the external expert to contribute a methodological framework and associated recommendations. The synthesis of local and external expertise is articulated in Figure 27.

Responsibility for validity evaluation activities took different forms for different individuals. Fundamentally, the empirical focus of all processes and methods was informed by the sustained facilitation of the consultant. At the same time, all of the departmental educators assumed responsibility for their assessment program when they agreed to initiate assessment revisions and to invite a visiting researcher as a consultant on the project. Further, all educators (including faculty, instructors, and teaching assistants) also participated in the fundamental stage-setting, specification, prioritization, negotiation, and consensus-building procedures that occurred intermittently throughout the process. However, in order to facilitate the process in an efficient way, participation in questioning, gathering evidence, and making decisions about the placement assessment program was constrained to a handful of primary intended users who were empowered by the full department to do so. Finally, at each program stage, individual local educators participated in unique capacities: as curricular-level experts and assessment developers, as researchers in gathering relevant data, and in the role of stakeholder informants. In addition, each program stage concluded with full-department meetings in which findings were disseminated, interpretations about the assessment program were discussed, and major decisions about assessment use were adjudicated. Responsibility for assessment validity evaluation *happened*, then, in the form of collaboration between local and external expertise, with each side taking seriously what the other contributed to the process.

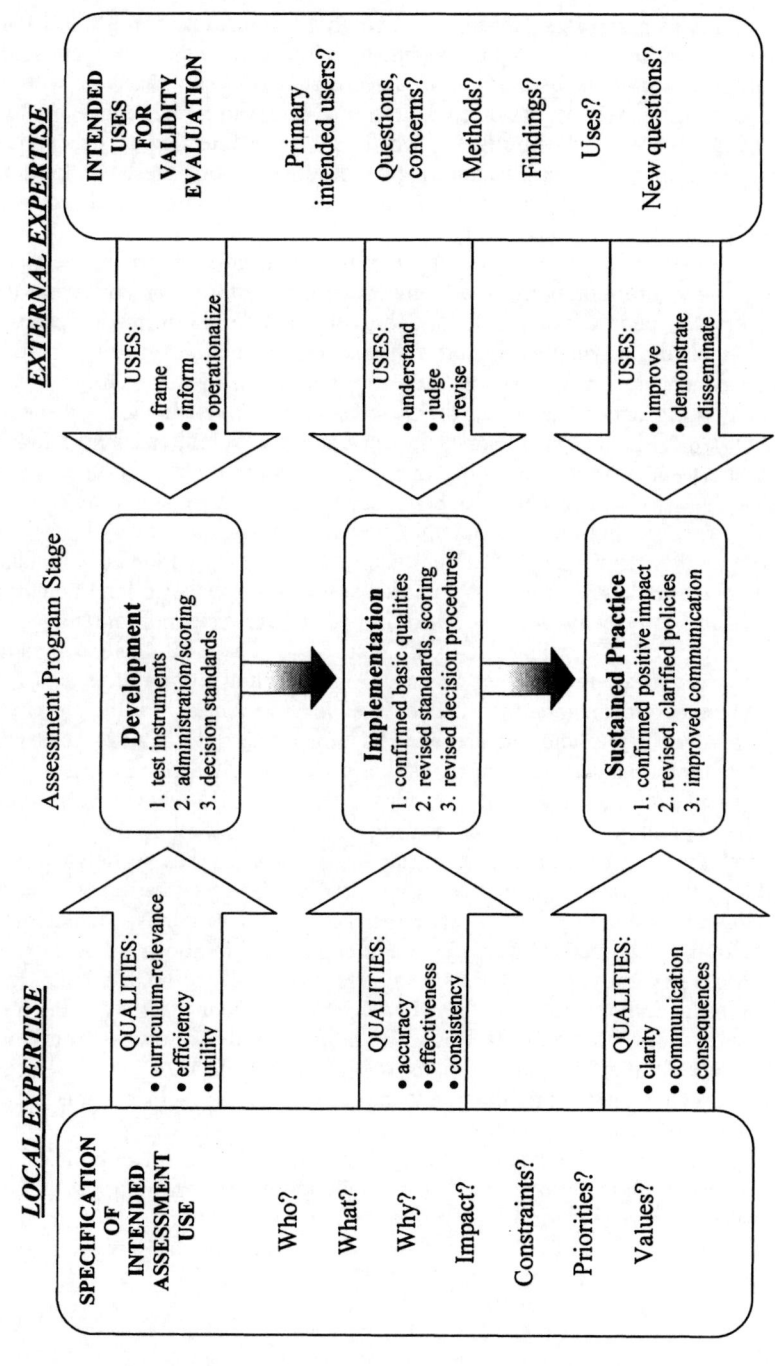

Figure 27. Validity evaluation schematic for the GUGD placement assessment program

Assessments as programs. In adopting a program evaluation approach, a second key question asked how educational assessments might be treated as programs, and in particular, via what means the 'how' of assessment could be articulated with the 'why'. Thus, in order for evaluation to address the extent to which educational assessment programs were accomplishing what they were intended to accomplish, rather than only investigating circumscribed measurement qualities, the local intended uses for assessment had to be made explicit and rationalized from the perspective of the local assessment users.

It was first necessary for the FL educators to reconceptualize their assessment practices as purposeful components of their educational efforts—as endeavors that are undertaken by specific individuals for addressing particular information needs in order to make clearly articulated decisions or take specific actions in bringing about desired consequences. To achieve this transformation, considerable energies were devoted to framing and engaging in the *specification of intended assessment use* (Norris, 2000). That is, before any development, implementation, or investigation of assessment use took place, it was crucial that local FL educators reflect on and make explicit exactly 'why' assessment was being used within their classrooms and curriculum. This specification of the programmatic nature of each and every instance of assessment practice within the GUGD provided the basic foundation for all subsequent assessment activities, including in particular the clear identification of qualities expected of—and to be evaluated and ensured for—each assessment program.

In concrete terms, as summarized in the first row of Table 30, the specification process led to a variety of outcomes as a result of individual, committee, and full-department methods for negotiating intended uses for assessment. For the placement program, educators were able, via the specification process, to achieve consensus regarding the inferential premises, curricular basis, decisions, expected consequences for teaching and learning, and resource constraints that would have to be incorporated into assessment development and investigated via evaluation. In this case, then, *what happened* was agreement among intended users on what was needed and what was feasible in terms of a placement exam. In addition, the specification process enabled GUGD educators to prioritize particular assessment demands, including the placement exam, for immediate development attention, and to allocate resources accordingly. More generally, it also led to awareness-raising and consensus-building in terms of the basic values implied within all GUGD assessment practice, in the form of departmental assessment policies. It is worth noting that these policies themselves pointed to the central importance of outcomes from this stage of assessment use specification, as stated in the introduction to the policies document (see Appendix F):

> Taken together, these documents [use specifications and assessment policies] are intended to guide not only the development and implementation, but also the evaluation and revision of all quizzes, tests, examinations, written and oral performances, and other forms of assessment which play an integral role in the success of the GUGD's educational efforts.

Table 30. Summary of validity evaluation activities for the GUGD placement assessment program

Program stage	Validity concerns/questions	Methods	Findings	Evaluation uses
Specifying intended assessment use	1. Intended uses for assessment: who, what, why, consequences, constraints	1. Individual review & reflection; individual-group transactional negotiation	1a. Specification documents for each assessment 1b. Uncertainties about assessment practice	Organizational learning: awareness, responsibility, consensus on assessment Prioritization: placement exam, changes in other assessments
	2. General practices: values, priorities	2. Committee review & development; committee-department negotiation	2a. Assessment policies 2b. Ranked development priorities	Development mandate: qualities to be met in assessment design Evaluation heuristic: qualities of assessment use to be investigated
Developing instruments and procedures	1. Test selection: possibilities, curriculum-relevance, test-use constraints, feasibility	1. Test type review; curricular expectations review; committee negotiation	1a. Estimates of textual processing abilities meet needs/constraints 1b. Consensus on texts by level	Test selection: curriculum-based LCT, RCT, C-test Text selection: curricular experts identified texts for each level
	2. Test preparation: input materials, response types, scoring, decision making, utility	2. Expert text selection, item writing, test-form development, pilot-testing, committee negotiation of final test forms and procedures	2a. Curricular-level texts 2b. Multiple-choice and fill-in items 2c. Test forms, instructions 2d. Pilot outcomes, problems	Revision: removal of too difficult texts, items; final administration instructions Operationalization: final test forms, scoring procedures, decision cut-scores

(continued)

223

Table 30. (Continued) Summary of validity evaluation activities for the GUGD placement assessment program

Program stage	Validity concerns/questions	Methods	Findings	Evaluation uses
	1. Effectiveness & accuracy: C-test and curricular-level placement decisions	1. Longitudinal, cross-sectional comparisons of placed and continuing students; cut-score comparisons	1a. C-test effective and relatively accurate estimate of cross-curricular differences 1b. Cut-scores too low (students placed too high)	Judgment: confirmed on-going use of C-test, other sub-tests Revision: cut-score standards adjusted higher Development: explicit scoring and decision-making procedures
Implementing the assessment program	2. Amount & sources of error: placement exam scoring, student enrollment	2. Re-scoring, re-placement, and identification of error types and degree	2a. High error in scoring, especially C-test 2b. Higher error in student self-enrollments	Organizational understanding: agreement on curricular-relevance of C-test; need to improve scoring and enrollment error; awareness of potential mis-enrolled students
	3. Measurement qualities: three sub-tests and items	3. Descriptive statistics; CTT & IRT test score and item analyses; correlation	3a. Good reliability, relatively low error on sub-tests 3b. C-test scores more consistent, less error, than LCT & RCT 3c. No consistent item deficiencies 3d. Sub-test scores moderately related, but not homogeneous	Improved practice: prioritization of C-test for semester-level decisions, LCT/RCT for supplemental year-level decisions; carefully structured scoring practices, including dual scoring of C-tests

(continued)

Table 30. (Continued) Summary of validity evaluation activities for the GUGD placement assessment program

Program stage	Validity concerns/questions	Methods	Findings	Evaluation uses
	1. Stakeholder awareness & perceptions: teachers' views	1. Teacher interviews on placement exam awareness, accuracy, effectiveness, purpose, student views, needed revisions	1a. Low awareness about placement exam, decisions, policies 1b. Perceived accuracy, effectiveness 1c. Student heterogeneity, regardless of placement	Development: more explicit documentation of placement policies and procedures; responsibilities outlined for teachers & students, decision-makers Improved communication: public statements to web-site; letters to students & external test users; policies to teachers
Sustaining program practice	2. Stakeholder consequences: students' academic performances	2. Semester grades analyses for placed (correctly & incorrectly), continuing students	2a. No trustworthy difference between placed and continuing overall 2b. Correctly placed students had higher average grades than those placed too high or too low, and than continuing 2c. No trustworthy differences between placed and continuing at individual curricular levels	Program learning: demonstration of no apparent negative consequences for correctly placed students; potentially negative consequences for students who did not enroll as placed Judgment: continued use of placement assessment program

Uses for evaluation. Just as intended uses for assessment were negotiated and specified by local educators, a third key question asked, in turn, how validity evaluation purposes could best be identified, prioritized, and translated into locally relevant, yet rigorous practice. Clearly, in order for validity evaluation to result in utility, feasibility, and meaning for the local FL educators, its purposes would have to be tailored to their particular needs in questioning, investigating, and acting to ensure the qualities of each of their assessment programs. Thus, rather than attempting to embark on an investigation of all possible validity qualities (i.e., "dragnet empiricism", Cronbach, 1989), a utilization-focused approach was employed in order to identify and articulate (a) those particular validity concerns that meant the most to local educators in meeting (b) particular evaluation purposes at (c) particular program stages for (d) particular assessments. As shown on the right-hand side of Figure 27, evaluation expertise played a crucial role in this regard, not by mandating the purposes and methods of validity evaluation, but instead by enabling the elicitation of intended uses for evaluation from intended users (the local GUGD educators).

In practical terms, this process involved interaction and negotiation between a small group of representative primary intended users and an evaluator in determining the minimal necessary evaluation concerns that needed to be addressed in order to meet clearly defined uses—in this sense, validity evaluation was not a never-ending process. Rather, it entailed a series of finite questions that were to be answered with specific empirical methods and to conclude in the use of findings for making intended decisions. Primary intended users offered critical guidance in this process, not only by linking questions to the particular qualities that would be meaningful in evaluating each local assessment use, but also by maintaining the feasibility of evaluation endeavors through their intimate knowledge of the kinds of activities that would and would not work within the educational setting.

For the placement assessment program, this prioritization of intended evaluation uses resulted in a handful of concerns to be addressed at each of three assessment program stages, following the initial specification of intended assessment use. As detailed in Table 30, evaluation was used at the *development* stage for providing an empirical basis in selecting curriculum-relevant test instruments and representative texts, for operationalizing procedures of placement exam administration and scoring within efficiency constraints, and for informing the initial setting of placement decision standards. During the *implementation* stage, evaluation purposes shifted to understanding, judging, and revising the assessment in terms of curriculum-related effectiveness and accuracy of decisions, the extent of error in placement procedures, and several measurement properties of the three sub-tests. Finally, as the placement assessment program entered into *sustained practice*, evaluation concerns shifted again to determining perceptions and awareness of the placement exam, especially on the part of local teachers, and to the consequences for students in terms of their academic performances. Findings were used in demonstrating the impact of, and improving communication and dissemination about, the placement assessment program. *What happened* in prioritizing validity evaluation purposes, then, was the identification of a reasonable number of priority concerns to be investigated in order to meet a finite set of intended uses for helping local educators understand and improve the placement assessment program. What happened was also clearly unique to this one assessment and its specified uses and qualities, while validity evaluation of other assessment programs within the GUGD entailed their own unique prioritized concerns.

Methods of evaluation. The particular empirical methods pursued in validity evaluation of the placement assessment program, then, were likewise tailored to the specific prioritized concerns of primary intended users, but also to the resource constraints of the educational setting, and to the audience of educators who would interpret findings. Thus, as shown in Table 30, methods were selected at each program stage in order to produce findings that would be directly useful for and used by constituents, and they included logical analysis of placement tests and texts in terms of the *Multiple Literacies* curriculum, cross-sectional and longitudinal studies of test performance, scoring and enrollment consistency analysis, classical test theory and item response theory analyses of tests and items, in-depth interviews of teachers, and between-groups comparisons of students' academic performances. *What happened* methodologically, during validity evaluation of the placement assessment program, depended in good part on the expertise contributed by an external evaluator, and this factor was probably essential in ensuring the empirical basis for much of the validity evaluation efforts. Nevertheless, all methods were selected in consultation with primary intended users (indeed, many methods were ruled out by them as being superfluous, along with many potential validity questions), and findings were carefully reported and explained to the local educators, who were fully capable of interpreting them in terms of implications for their assessment program.

Given the intent of informing intended uses for validity evaluation by intended users, the findings at each stage were themselves tailored to the discrete decisions and actions to be taken on their basis. That is not to say that the nature of the findings was somehow manipulated in order to tell the educators what they wanted to hear. In fact, on the contrary, findings presented the local educators with exactly what they did *not* want to hear on multiple occasions, providing a rather strong case against confirmatory bias in the validity evaluation process (i.e., the tendency of internally generated findings to reflect positively on programs). For example, findings that contradicted the qualities expected of the placement assessment program included: (a) inaccurate initial cut-scores; (b) inconsistencies in scoring and enrollment; (c) missing policies for placement-related decisions; (d) negative reactions to the format of the placement sub-tests by external users; and (e) lack of awareness among teachers regarding the placement exam and associated decisions. However, it was exactly these kinds of findings that, when presented in straightforward ways to the local educators, resulted in the most important uses for validity evaluation, in terms of revising and improving the placement assessment program. That is, because the questions, methods, and findings were all tailored *a priori* to meeting the particularly crucial intended uses for evaluation that had been prioritized by the primary intended users, and because of the use of rigorous methods for providing evidence, local educators were able to accept such negative findings as trustworthy empirical sources of evidence and turn them into positive outcomes by continually improving the use of the placement exam.

In the end, of course, the most basic test of the validity evaluation process must be the extent to which findings were used by educators to do something about their assessments. At each stage in validity evaluation of the placement assessment program, findings led to numerous actions on the part of primary intended users and the full departmental constituency. *What was done*, on the basis of validity evaluation, included the judgment to continue using the curriculum-based placement sub-tests; the revision and improvement of scoring, decision-making, and enrollment procedures; and the development of mechanisms for communicating and disseminating placement exam information. What was done also included the identification of additional questions and concerns for later evaluation, the archiving of placement performance data for students, and the generation of new knowledge about both the *Multiple Literacies* curriculum and the placement exam sub-tests. Perhaps most important in what was done, the local educators established their own values and uses for this one assessment program (as well as other assessment programs not detailed in the current work), and they ensured—through intensive evaluation efforts and resulting actions—that the assessment was indeed being used as intended.

As a final observation on what happened in the current work, it is worth noting that, while validity evaluation prioritized the concerns of local educators, it is not necessarily the case that some of the findings cannot generalize beyond the local setting or be of interest to external parties. Arguably the most interesting finding along these lines may have been the extent to which the curriculum-based text-selection and C-test development process resulted in an instrument that could be used to distinguish in robust and reliable ways across student ability differences reflecting fully the four years of a college German-language program. By employing local curricular experts in selecting texts to represent well-defined curricular expectations in terms of students' textual processing abilities, resulting performances by students over several administrations reflected none of the typical attenuation of C-test scores (Grotjahn, 1987, 1992b) among more advanced learners. Given this finding, it may be that a similar approach to C-test development would generalize effectively to other test-use contexts (e.g., in other college FL programs, for other languages), although it is, of course, an *empirical* question whether a C-test could be developed along the same lines for other program curricula and used for meeting the assessment needs of other intended users (the development guidelines in Appendix C might prove helpful in this regard). Clearly, validity evaluation findings within one assessment use context—the GUGD in this case—may contribute useful ideas about assessment development and evaluation to other contexts, but they are not intended to imply 'validity' of assessments beyond the local intended uses by intended users.

7.2 Process uses for validity evaluation

Validity evaluation efforts in the current work focused explicitly on enabling primary intended users—the local educators in the GUGD—to engage in instrumental uses for evaluation, by targeting their immediate concerns about the placement assessment program, gathering evidence that was directly relevant to addressing those concerns, and, especially, encouraging the utilization of findings for informing concrete judgments, decisions, revisions, and improvements in assessment practice (as detailed in Table 30). However, while evaluation procedures were designed with these instrumental uses in mind, it was also apparent that the validity evaluation process itself engendered additional outcomes in the form of considerable organizational learning and change. Thus, as Patton (1998) and others have pointed out, regardless of the uses of actual findings, program evaluations almost inevitably lead to changes of some sort for the program stakeholders and the organizational contexts within which evaluations take place. The direct involvement of stakeholders in utilization-focused evaluations tends to intensify these effects—often referred to as 'process uses'.

In the current work, one lasting impact of the validity evaluation project, and concomitant awareness-raising about the educational roles of assessment, took the form of sustained attention by local educators to articulating the 'how' with the 'why' of assessment practices and programs within the GUGD. Certainly, this shift was engineered deliberately during the period of intensive assessment renovation (from 1999-2002), in the form of *a priori* assessment use specifications which required educators to make explicit the 'why' of all of their assessment practices before revising instruments and procedures accordingly. However, of note is the fact that, in the interim following direct involvement by the consultant, local educators continued to engage in development, implementation, and evaluation of assessment programs in order to meet these intended uses, as initial priorities were met and new priorities emerged. Thus, just as the placement assessment program was articulated and evaluated according to its use specification, so too did local educators devote considerable energies along the same lines to new assessment priorities.

In particular, the curriculum-based performance assessment programs (mentioned in 6.1) in both writing and speaking underwent extensive development, implementation, and evaluation (as described in Byrnes, 2002a, 2002b; Maxim, 2002), in order to meet curricular-level internal uses (i.e., feedback to students and teachers about student development over a semester) as well as cross-curricular summative and formative uses (i.e., understanding student achievement of curricular expectations, revising curriculum and instruction). Furthermore, a curriculum-independent assessment (the *German Speaking Test*, Center for Applied Linguistics, 1995) was used to provide students with widely recognized ratings of their German speaking proficiency, and as one indicator of student learning outcomes in the *Multiple Literacies* program (i.e., for accountability purposes). This assessment met the prioritized need for communicating about student outcomes to external parties, both in a form that is easily understood by other FL programs and audiences, and according to a metric that is thoroughly independent of GUGD-internal teaching and learning (Crane, Maxim, & Pfeiffer, 2003; Norris & Pfeiffer, 2003). Attention to the placement assessment program itself also continued, as a new web-based delivery system was put in place, and revisions made in practices of early placement and the awarding of credit hours based on test performance.

In addition to work on these, and other, on-going assessment programs, process outcomes also took the form of both professional development of local educators in assessment capabilities and a sustained cycle of evaluative thinking vis-à-vis the educational roles of assessment in the GUGD. On the one hand, the curriculum coordinator introduced new assessment components, as well as an overview of the GUGD assessment programs (specifically in the form of the policies and specification documents), into graduate student professional development via a required methods course. Graduate students and faculty alike also participated in a variety of assessment-related workshops and training sessions, focusing on topics such as consistency in scoring and responding to L2 writing, analysis of L2 performance data for interlanguage developmental phenomena, and statistical procedures for interpreting test scores. Several individuals were also certified in the rating of German speaking proficiency according to the ACTFL (1999) guidelines on the *German Speaking Test*.

Furthermore, in order to maintain local educators' awareness of and participation in local assessment activities, considerable attention was paid to making available a historical record and documentation of all related development and evaluation efforts, particularly via the departmental web-site (*Developing Multiple Literacies*, 2003). Critically, the GUGD departmental constituency also took pains to cycle back through key validity evaluation steps and logic (outlined in chapters 5 and 6), in order to maintain an on-going focus on understanding and ensuring the quality of assessments and their uses. For example, during the 2002-2003 academic year, educators undertook the full-scale revision of both the curricular-level intended assessment use specifications and the general departmental policies for assessment (revised version of the latter is shown in Appendix F).

As a result of these efforts, in turn, considerable washback on curriculum and instruction occurred within the GUGD, as the educational functions of assessment were realized. Thus, as educators detailed the intended uses for assessment programs, they identified a variety of curricular and instructional features in need of sharpening and justification. For example, in order for end-of-level writing performance assessments to elicit students' abilities in terms of curricular-level language expectations, those expectations required much greater explication within curricular documents (Byrnes, 2002b). Likewise, in order to treat seriously the general policy that students should be provided ample opportunity to acquire the abilities that are being assessed, instructional activities and materials were revised considerably within each of the curricular levels to better address those abilities targeted in assessment (especially in performance assessment). Finally, outcomes of assessments, specifically findings regarding student language and content-knowledge development within each curricular level, were reviewed by educators in order to recommend changes in instruction, in curricular expectations, and in the assessments themselves (e.g., Byrnes, 2002b; Maxim, 2002; Crane, Maxim, & Pfeiffer, 2003).

Perhaps the most tangible evidence of process outcomes may be found in the array of dissemination efforts that have been associated with the validity evaluation project and subsequent engagement with assessment in the GUGD. As listed on the *Developing Multiple Literacies* (2003) web-site, there have been numerous presentations on assessment-related efforts at professional conferences, as well as invited talks at other college programs, including not only earlier presentations by the consultant, but also dissemination of more recent assessment work by departmental educators (e.g., Byrnes, 2002a; Crane, Maxim, & Pfeiffer, 2003; Maxim, 2002). Publication about assessment efforts has also been evident in professional journals (e.g., Byrnes, 2002b; Norris & Pfeiffer, 2003), and additional publications have incorporated notions initiated within GUGD assessment work into related professional concerns, such as course development (e.g., Eigler, 2001) and the preparation of FL graduate students as educators (e.g., Pfeiffer, 2002).

These dissemination activities demonstrate two key aspects of process uses associated with the initial assessment validity evaluation efforts. First, it is clear that local educators in the GUGD took seriously the important implications of assessment for their own educational efforts and for those of the FL discipline more broadly, and they continued to do so long after the initial three-year collaboration concluded. Second, the fact that this work is being accepted (not to mention solicited) for presentation and publication in key professional forums suggests that it has generated notable interest in the field, not only in terms of the innovative FL curriculum and instruction that emerged out of the *Developing Multiple Literacies* innovation project, but also interest specific to the assessment activities per se (see also Norris 2006a, 2006b). Of course, much closer scrutiny would be required to warrant a causal interpretation regarding the relationship between assessment validity evaluation efforts and subsequent process outcomes at the local educational, as well as FL disciplinary, levels. Nevertheless, the range of observations above can only lend support to the interpretation that validity evaluation processes may indeed be related to positive outcomes for FL educators and education, beyond the basic understanding and improvement of specific assessments.

7.3 Limitations of validity evaluation

It bears emphasis here that, while the local educators posed numerous questions for validity evaluation and findings were used in a variety of ways for understanding and improving the assessment program, other potential validity questions and uses were not pursued. On the one hand, these included additional local concerns with examinees' cognitive response processes on the three sub-tests, students' perceptions of the exam and the accuracy of placement decisions, the relationship between learner backgrounds and placement, the potential contribution to decision effectiveness of additional test information, the extent of agreement between curriculum-based placements and curriculum-independent indicators of learners' German language ability, and others. On the other hand, from a conventional perspective (e.g., Messick, 1989), it could certainly be argued that standard aspects of measurement validity were left un-addressed in the current study. Thus, of the multitude of measurement standards (AERA, APA, NCME, 1999), or even of the 42 characteristics of "test usefulness" proposed by Bachman and Palmer (1996) for evaluation of language tests, it is clear that only a handful were addressed in validity evaluation of the GUGD placement assessment program.

However, these additional aspects of assessment validity (both local and standard) 'did not happen' for purposeful, rationalized reasons. That is, where validation is intended to help specific educators understand and improve specific assessments as they are used for specific purposes, I suggest that the questions, methods, findings, and uses of validation should seek to inform those specific educators about the actual prioritized qualities of their assessments in use, and to do so in feasible ways in light of the constraints that inhere within the given educational context. In the current work, rather than insisting *a priori* on complex psychometric standards in educational assessment—which may or may not add useful iterations to educators' understanding of the extent to which assessments are accomplishing what they were intended to accomplish—a means was sought for identifying and prioritizing those key questions about assessments that would help the local educators to take prioritized actions towards, to actually *do something about*, ensuring assessment quality.

Despite these intentions, and in light of what did and did not happen in the current study, several potential limitations may be discerned for the use of validity evaluation in conjunction with assessments in foreign language, as well as other, educational contexts. Indeed, these limitations should help to contextualize the potential applications of validity evaluation in meeting the challenge of educational assessment across the wide variety of contexts in which it is used and the variety of functions that it assumes.

Program evaluation perspective. In this work, contemporary program evaluation principles were adhered to by accepting multiple possible purposes for evaluation, making explicit the particular uses for evaluating the targeted assessment program, and articulating multiple methods with these explicit uses. However, one particular model, utilization-focused evaluation, was adopted in order to maximize the likelihood that validity evaluation processes would result in actions being taken by local FL educators on the basis of findings. In adopting this model, validity evaluation in the current study incurred several limitations.

The implementation of the utilization-focused model depended very much on the input of a small group of local educational stakeholders, the primary intended users of evaluation, in collaboration with an external evaluation consultant to make critical decisions about the questions, methods, and uses to be pursued in validating assessments. It could certainly be argued that this approach resulted in prioritization of the dominant values of already empowered individuals (i.e., the department chair, the curriculum developer, the curriculum coordinator, and an external evaluator) at the expense of potentially diverging values of other stakeholders (e.g., other teachers, students), as has been suggested of utilization-focused evaluation in general (e.g., Guba & Lincoln, 1988, 1989). As a result, it may have been the case that validity concerns of interest to these other stakeholders were ignored or simply not valued as highly as those of the primary intended users. Clearly, there was a trade-off inherent to this approach between feasibility and utility of the processes, on the one hand, and adequate representation of all stakeholders' views, on the other. Nevertheless, it bears emphasis that efforts were made to reflect on the needs of various stakeholder groups, and the primary intended user group was careful to 'reign in' validity evaluation practices where these were deemed overly intrusive on the teaching and learning mission of the GUGD. In addition, critical findings of validity evaluation were reported to all of the teaching and administrative stakeholders, and major decisions about the placement assessment program were negotiated in full-department meetings, as discussed in chapter 6. At the same time, in order for validity evaluation to proceed at all, not to mention result in practical decisions about and improvements in assessment, a decision was made from the outset to sacrifice a certain degree of representation in order to maximize utility. It is important to note that this decision was made by the departmental stakeholder constituency; as such, the primary intended users and I felt (locally) warranted in driving the validity evaluation process.

Another point of view here (e.g., Scriven, 1997) might suggest that validity evaluation was limited in its scientific rigor and trustworthiness (indeed, the research 'validity' of the process) by entrusting local language educators to determine the purposes of evaluation and to moderate the kinds of questions, methods, and uses of findings that were pursued. It has been argued that a major risk of this kind of self-determination is the prioritization and perpetuation of inappropriate, inaccurate, non-generalizable, inconsistent, and incomplete (even 'messy') scientific practices, due to the lack of knowledge or standards of those participating in the process. While it is certainly true that there was a trade-off between program-internal utilization and program-external generalizability of validity evaluation findings, it is also true that, from the outset, this approach sought nothing more than the generation of locally useful—if empirically sound—knowledge about local uses for educational assessment. Furthermore, while local educators proved essential in determining what would and would not be done via the evaluation process, they did so on the basis of: (a) a clear specification of the intended uses for assessment, which laid out the territory for *relevant* questions, methods, and uses; (b) a clear intent to understand and improve their assessment practices, which kept validity evaluation focused on the fundamental purpose of supporting the GUGD's educational efforts; and (c) the methodological recommendations of an external consultant, which encouraged a rigorous empirical basis for all validity evaluation processes.

Where such conditions apply, and where evaluation participants are committed to the ethical use of research techniques, the charge that locally-driven validity evaluation lacks scientific rigor may be countered with the argument that empirical investigation of *relevant* assessment qualities for *well-defined uses* will result in findings that are more 'valid' for ensuring that assessments are accomplishing their intended uses. Indeed, perhaps the strongest argument against purportedly sloppy, willful, or relativist characteristics of the validity evaluation efforts is the fact that findings throughout were carefully treated (in *all* related reporting, interpretation, and use) as thoroughly contingent upon (a) an understanding of the given assessment program under evaluation and (b) the specific purposes for validity evaluation of that program. Without these critical features of a validity evaluation approach, there is considerable danger that a finding about the 'validity' of a given assessment will be misinterpreted, over-generalized, or otherwise used in unwarranted ways. Validity evaluation incorporates a framework for ensuring that exactly such 'messiness' does not occur in the use of assessment validation.

Finally, it is important to point out that the validity evaluation approach pursued in the current study does not imply that other purposes for evaluating assessments cannot or should not be addressed, and it might be the case that other purposes and contexts for validity evaluation would be better served by models other than the utilization-focused evaluation. This model may have worked particularly well within this college FL education context, due to the well-defined nature of the educational programs there and the fact that the assessment functions within these programs could be thoroughly established via a consensus-building process, not to mention due to the dynamic FL educators within the context. For other settings of assessment use, including in particular large-scale educational assessments that are applied across multiple settings, or assessments designed to measure theoretical constructs for informing research uses, other evaluation models (such as the knowledge-generation approach of more conventional construct theory validation) might prove more appropriate in meeting the needs of associated constituencies. At the same time, by adopting a fundamentally evaluative approach to even these assessments, the specific validity questions to be asked, the methods used for investigating them, and the ways in which findings will be put to use will require careful rationalization and prioritization. In the end, it may be that a validity evaluation approach to ensuring the quality of educational assessments will be most limited by the capacity of educators and measurement professionals to think and act evaluatively and to treat assessments as something more than technical devices.

Educational measurement perspective. It is clear that, by prioritizing the values, concerns, and evaluative purposes of local educators (i.e., those directly responsible for assessment use), only a handful of the many conventional validity qualities of assessments were evaluated, while qualities other than those typically addressed within measurement standards were also included. This selective focus on those aspects of assessment use that were of interest to local educators was intentionally dependent on processes for (a) determining what those local assessment uses were and (b) prioritizing educators' needs in evaluating them, from among the many possible questions or concerns that could have been investigated. From an educational measurement perspective, there is currently very little in the way of mechanisms for or attention to informing such specification and prioritization processes, which require the understanding of educational assessments as programs, and it may be that measurement professionals would therefore find the task of validity evaluation daunting in this respect. Not forthcoming from their standards of practice is how they would prioritize particularly relevant questions and concerns of educators or educational communities, identify key elements of an educational assessment program in need of evaluation, or, most critically, enable something to be done with validation findings by the educators responsible for assessment use.

A more likely reaction from a conventional perspective would be that the selective focus on assessment users' questions and concerns resulted in key validity components not being investigated. Central to this argument of missing validity components, from a unified notion of test validity (Messick, 1989), is the fact that no attempt was made to define a theoretical construct of language ability or knowledge for the assessment in question, to operationalize the construct in the assessment instruments, or to investigate the validity of hypothesized construct interpretations. Certainly, where such knowledge or ability constructs are prioritized as the "*sine qua non*" (Bachman, 2002, p. 6) for validating language and other educational assessments, the current approach to validity evaluation was limited by not assuming or identifying or investigating a construct underlying the placement exam sub-tests. Likewise, without a construct theory, no attention was paid to the extent to which test scores could be assumed to generalize across other contexts of use where such construct interpretations might also be of interest, or to the extrapolations that might be made from test scores to particular aspects of students' language ability. Indeed, without such basic components of a comprehensive measurement validation in the current study, it might be asked how the 'validity' of the placement exam could be interpreted at all by others outside of the immediate GUGD educational context.

The short answer from the validity evaluation approach adopted here is: it shouldn't be. To be clear, while one aspect of language ability, summarized as textual processing ability in German, did inform the placement exam sub-tests, the point of these tests was never to provide a comprehensive indication—or 'measure'—of the construct 'textual processing ability'. Rather, the placement exam was intended to provide enough information, in the form of student performances with texts representing distinct curricular levels, such that a sufficiently trustworthy estimate could be made regarding one central aspect of curricular language-use expectations, in order to identify the most relevant level within the curriculum for placing individual students. Thus, rather than the extent to which the tests provided good or 'valid' measures of a particular language ability construct, much more critical for the current validity evaluation efforts were concerns with the relationship between curricular expectations and actual student performances, the stability of distinctions among curricular levels, and the consistency of procedures for using test-based information. While it might be argued accurately that a "curricular construct" (Nitko, 1995, 1996, 2001) provided the basis for the GUGD placement exam sub-tests, the notion of construct did not enter into the picture from the point of view of the local assessment users, and as such, no constructs were 'validated'. Obviously, there was never any intent that validity evaluation would be used to inform the measurement interpretations of other test users outside of those identified within the GUGD educational context.

Here again, to be absolutely clear, I do not intend to suggest that language ability or other theoretical assessment constructs cannot or should not be addressed in a validity evaluation approach, or that technical approaches to validating measurement constructs should not be pursued where warranted. In language education, there are occasions when assessments are carefully developed and interpreted as measures of theoretical language ability constructs, and careful construct validation is certainly required in such instances (e.g., Norris & Ortega, 2003; Norris, Ortega, & Mislevy, 2003). Furthermore, I am not arguing here that validity evaluation should not attend to the generalizations and extrapolations that are frequently (but certainly *not* always) prioritized for the use of particular language assessments. However, what I am arguing here, and what the current work demonstrated, is that: (a) whatever qualities of assessments are targeted for validation, they should be qualities that are implied in the actual uses of assessments; and (b) for validation to result in information that is relevant to specific audiences of assessment users, and particularly educational audiences, its purposes should be carefully rationalized and carried out in order to enable responsible assessment users to do something as a result.

All too often, unfortunately, educational assessments are 'validated' in prescribed ways according to a construct theory, or they are determined 'valid' for one type of interpretation, and their use is then assumed to be warranted for any circumstances within which that ability or construct is implied (e.g., see the host of articles associated with the ACTFL proficiency guidelines and related assessments in chapter 2). After all, the argument goes, the assessment has been 'validated' (e.g., as a measure of language proficiency), so why shouldn't it apply? What is ignored in this perception and practice of measurement validation is the extent to which any given assessment is appropriate to the particular uses intended by particular users within particular education contexts. While assessments may be 'validated' according to whether or not they are good measures of their constructs, there is much more at stake in seeking to understand and improve assessments that are used programmatically within education.

Foreign language education perspective. As an *a priori* condition for validity evaluation to occur, educators are called upon to be at least somewhat aware of and committed to assessment as a fundamental component of their educational programs, along with curriculum and instruction, a condition that is not particularly pervasive in any educational context today (Popham, 2003a). In addition, for adequate attention to be paid to validity evaluation of assessments, educators will require multiple levels of support and encouragement to do so, not only from their immediate departmental and collegial surroundings, but also from their institutions (schools, universities, etc.) and ultimately their disciplinary milieus.

In the case of assessment in the GUGD, validity evaluation occurred because of a commitment by the entire departmental constituency to program-wide revision of assessment practices in conjunction with curricular innovation. The legitimacy of this undertaking was supported (financially as well as otherwise) by an institution that recognized the clear commitment of this department to improving education in response to student learning needs. Unfortunately, these circumstances may only rarely coincide, especially in college FL programs. College FL educators are generally not aware of assessment as a programmatic educational endeavor, and it is infrequent that curricular thinking of the sort experienced in the GUGD occurs in most FL programs. It is also clear that the discipline has not, to date, treated the role of educational assessment as a central concern, and until it does, it is unlikely that most FL educators or departments or host institutions will be cognizant of the need to engage in validity evaluation of their assessment practices.

Beyond the basic awareness and support required for assessment validity evaluation to occur, it should be clear that considerable time, energy, and other resources may be called upon in implementing validity evaluation throughout the multiple stages of each distinct assessment program at stake. To the extent that FL educators have access to such resources, assessment validity evaluation efforts will be enabled or curtailed. Within the GUGD, all of the local educators contributed substantial time and intellectual energy to validity evaluation efforts, via assessment use specification activities, participation in interviews, meetings, and professional development sessions, and the administration of assessments and collection of data. At the same time, several strategies were adopted in order to maintain the feasibility of evaluation demands in light of practical limitations, as described in chapters 5 and 6. It may be that the cycle of prioritizing a few central evaluation concerns, investigating and acting, then re-prioritizing can enable FL educators to begin to engage to a reasonable degree with assessment validity evaluation despite constraints.

Perhaps the key limitation of validity evaluation, from the perspective of FL educators, is presented by the assessment and evaluation know-how that was called upon within the current work. It is obvious from the methodologies and findings reported in chapter 6 that, in order to address adequately the evaluation concerns of the local GUGD educators, a certain amount and type of technical assessment and research expertise was required, and these kinds of expertise may not currently be available within the majority of FL education contexts. At the same time, the assessment validity evaluation approach also required that local curricular expertise be taken seriously as the source for all substantive decisions and actions. Therefore, it may be that a collaborative approach of the sort explored here, and outlined in Figure 30, can provide the most immediate solution to these limitations on expertise. Until such time as the FL profession takes seriously the development of its educators' capabilities to deal with assessment—well beyond the kinds of assessment knowledge/abilities outlined in current standards for foreign language educators (e.g., ACTFL, 2002)—it may be that external expertise will have to be called upon for assisting in the transformation of FL assessments to educationally purposeful activities. Likewise, while language testers would offer a very useful service in this regard, they will need to take seriously the actual uses for assessment within FL education. In order for validity evaluation to proceed as both a relevant and a rigorous endeavor, both sides of the collaboration will have to respond thoughtfully in determining exactly what assessment qualities need to be evaluated and how exactly the process is intended to contribute to an understanding and improvement of assessment use.

7.4 The future of assessment validity evaluation

In concluding this work, it seems fitting to return to the challenge of educational assessment, as formulated in chapter 1, and to summarize the extent to which the validity evaluation approach explored here can help educators to respond in useful, feasible, and meaningful ways. From the outset of assessment efforts within the focal college FL education context, it was clear that local educators were faced with this same challenge—that is, to *ensure* that appropriate and high-quality assessment practices were being designed, developed, and used in order to meet specific purposes and bring about positive consequences. In addition, they were faced with unique demands in conjunction with curriculum innovation and the need for articulated and supportive assessment practices. As responsible educators, they sought guidance in understanding, developing, using, and improving their assessments, with the concomitant fundamental goal of improving their overall educational efforts.

When provided with a straightforward framework and rationale for doing so, the educators in this FL context were readily able to: (a) identify the actual impetuses for assessment within their classrooms and programs; (b) specify the ways in which assessment instruments and procedures should be used; and (c) develop and engage in assessment practices accordingly. In addition, as new assessments were put into practice in intended ways, educators: (d) prioritized critical questions about the extent to which each assessment was functioning as intended; (e) gathered empirical evidence in response to these questions; and (f) interpreted and acted upon findings in order to understand, judge, revise, improve, develop, and otherwise evaluate their assessments.

The validity evaluation approach helped educators to ensure the prioritized qualities of their assessments by providing them with an empirical basis for decisions and actions at each step along the way. However, obviously, this process did not simply occur of its own accord; rather, it required local educators and an external evaluator alike to rethink their notions of assessment, validation, and the educational relevance of both. Along these lines, and based on the outcomes of the current study, the following pragmatic recommendations can be made to FL educators and others seeking to engage in validity evaluation of their assessments:

1. Dispense with the notion that 'good measurement' is all that is needed for 'good educational assessment'; treat assessments programmatically, just like curriculum and instruction.
2. Link the 'how' with the 'why' of assessment by specifying the intended uses (who, what, why, consequences, constraints) for each assessment instance within the educational context.
3. Consider assessment development, use, and evaluation to be integrated facets of a single process which should be informed by the clear *a priori* specification of intended use.
4. Realize that different assessment uses will require distinct assessment practices—there is no 'one-size-fits-all' measure of language ability (or proficiency), and assessments developed, used, and 'validated' for one context may not be appropriate for use in another.
5. Rationalize the purposes for evaluating assessments and prioritize the questions and concerns that make the most sense to assessment users, prior to adopting any validation methods; take seriously the expertise offered by local educators as well as the potential need for external expertise.
6. Take a cyclical approach to assessment validity evaluation within a given educational setting; prioritize which assessments and which questions are most in need of attention.
7. Enable validation to play an educationally meaningful role, rather than posing a debilitating burden, by considering the audiences for evaluation, their information demands, and the contextual constraints in articulating evaluative methods.
8. Follow through with the intended uses for evaluation, by reporting and interpreting findings, and by incorporating procedures for building consensus among assessment users on needed actions in revising, improving, or perpetuating assessments.

Just as validity evaluation along these lines requires FL educators to think about assessment in unique ways compared with their traditions of practice, so too will it require language testers and other educational assessment professionals to rethink why we are validating assessments and what it is about assessment that needs validation in the first place. To date, responsibility for and ownership over assessment validation has been posited as the concern of measurement professionals, and their practices are based on particular areas of technical expertise and a focus on psychometric qualities of assessments. From this perspective, validity has been portrayed persistently as an "evaluative judgment" (Messick, 1989, p. 13) of the extent to which tests are measuring what they are intended to measure, even if what it means to 'measure' has expanded considerably in recent years.

However, "judgment" is only one of many evaluative functions, as program evaluators have made clear over the course of the 20th century (e.g., Cronbach, 1982, 1989; Patton, 1997). We evaluate to judge, certainly, but we also evaluate to generate knowledge, to understand, to improve, to illuminate, to clarify and specify, to develop, to initiate changes, to advocate, and for many other reasons in pursuit of the betterment of programs and society. For those professionals working at the interface of education and assessment, it may be that the pragmatic recommendations above can also help facilitate their reconceptualization of assessment validation as a process that may beneficially pursue any and all of these evaluative uses—but always in very intentional ways. That is, in order for validation to attain educational relevance, we will need to offer principled reasons for asking important questions about particular qualities of assessments as they are used, rather than simply appealing to the *judgmental* predilections of professional standards. In addition, we will need to provide principled mechanisms for finding relevant answers to these questions, and, most crucially, we will need to enable the use of those answers in justifying and informing actions by individuals seeking to ensure the quality of educational assessments.

Finally, in further pursuing this challenging agenda, several directions in research may be motivated by the arguments and outcomes of the current work. Within college FL education, and other education contexts, it would be very useful to survey and identify the actual impetuses for assessment, and to clarify their programmatic implications in the form of specifications of intended use. Based on such specifications, language testers and other educational measurement professionals alike would be provided with critical information regarding the areas in need of research and development, and the extent to which their current efforts are relevant to the actual demands placed on assessment users. Without such specifications, it is likely that educational assessments will continue to be used in unintended ways, from the classroom-based to the institutional to the statewide and national assessment programs that will no doubt persist.

Research would also beneficially address the ways in which communities of assessment users, whether in college FL programs or across public schools or within particular research domains, might best be engaged in the process of evaluating their assessments. How might the interests and values of various stakeholders for an assessment best be elicited and determined? How should particular questions, concerns, or qualities be prioritized for evaluation? What purposes tend to mark the evaluation needs of assessment users? What information demands and constraints should dictate how investigations are conducted and findings reported? Via what processes can the *use* of validity information be encouraged and enabled in order to actually do something about assessment quality? Through consistent attention to such questions, accumulated research findings would illuminate the particular approaches to evaluation that seem to prove the most useful in enabling educators, and other assessment users, to understand and improve their assessments. Cronbach (1989) made similar recommendations for the meta-evaluation of assessment validation itself, focusing on the quantity, quality, expense, and utility of validity investigations in determining whether they should be incorporated into standard practice. Work of this sort should help particular communities of assessment users and evaluators to better understand the processes that will lead to intended outcomes, and help them sift through professional standards for those recommendations that make the most sense for meeting their actual needs.

A final direction in related research might explore the nature of process outcomes (Patton, 1998) that are associated with the validity evaluation of educational assessments. Apparent positive, if unintended, effects of validity evaluation in the GUGD were identified in organizational learning about assessment, improved understanding of curriculum and instruction, dissemination and generation of interest in assessment within the FL education community, and professional development of graduate students and faculty alike. Investigations of related outcomes from other validity evaluation studies would provide insights into how such processes might be planned in order to effect positive changes within FL education and other contexts.

In the end, it is my hope that the extensive rationale, arguments, and evidence presented here make a convincing case for the potential of assessment validity evaluation to meet the criterion of educational relevance. Fundamentally, in foreign language as well as other educational contexts, assessments are only good insofar as their use does good, in terms of supporting educational efforts and outcomes, and it is my intent that validity evaluation helps to ensure that they do.

APPENDIX A
INITIAL DRAFT OF GUGD ASSESSMENT POLICIES

GERMAN DEPARTMENT, GEORGETOWN UNIVERSITY (July 17, 1999)
GENERAL POLICY STATEMENT

The policies stated below describe the intended use of assessment in the German Department in order to clarify its role and nature for those who perform the assessment (e.g., teachers and the German Department as a whole) and for those who use the outcomes of assessment (e.g, teachers, students, various administrative units within the university, outside constituents), and to delineate its use for evaluating the curriculum as a whole, particularly in its sequenced courses in Levels I-III and in the small group of Level IV courses.

The following principles guide assessment use and the role of assessment:

1. All assessment, whether formative or summative, embedded in the curriculum or independent of it, focuses on students' abilities to use the language in various communicative settings.

2. Unless students begin their study of German at Georgetown University or are native speakers of German they will take a placement examination. This assessment instrument and placement procedure is based on the content- and task-focus of the curriculum and reflects its goals and emphases in the various content areas that have been agreed upon for reading, listening, writing, and speaking

3. Students can place out of courses up to and including Level III, Stories and Histories.

4. Reflecting the long-term developmental and cumulative nature of acquiring the curriculum's German studies content and an academic level of literacy, both instruction and assessment practices have a strong process and developmental character. That means that students have repeated opportunities for building up content and linguistic knowledge and for improving their performance in a range of communicative tasks, particularly through carefully planning and executing more extensive tasks for which they have received careful guidance, criteria for assessment, and feedback.

5. Because of this developmental nature of any learning, but particularly language learning, assessment is also used to evaluate students' sustained engagement with the content of a course, inside and outside the classroom.

6. To assure fairness to the students but also assessment validity and program quality, the Department places particular emphasis on the clarity of assessment criteria, their suitability for the level of language acquisition and the tasks that occur during instruction at a given level, their appropriateness for the overall goals of the curriculum, and the uniformity of grading practices at a given level. While all instructors have the responsibility of attending to these issues, special responsibilities fall to the Level Coordinators and to the Supervisor. Recommended activities are: the collaborative construction of syllabi, cooperative exchange of documents which detail assessment practices in the various modalities for major task types and genres, recommendations regarding efficient and effective feedback, scheduling of grading sessions during the semester, joint grading of the semester final, and feedback at the end of the year.

7. The complexity of language use requires multiple assessment sources (e.g., quizzes, midterms, final examinations, individual and group projects) and also various conditions under which language is assessed (planned vs. unplanned, individual vs. group, interactive vs. non-interactive). Because of the curricular focus on linking content and language in language use, both holistic assessments that gauge students' ability to attain broad communicative goals and local, highly targeted assessments that focus on specific aspects of content and language form need to be incorporated. The differences between these two foci in assessment and their use in particular assessment situations need to be communicated to students.

8. Although different courses place different emphases on listening, reading, speaking, and writing and focus on different aspects of performance (e.g., accuracy, fluency, and complexity) in particular tasks, assessment practices in all courses must signal to students the importance of developing language abilities in a balanced fashion in order to facilitate continued interlanguage development toward professional-level performance.

9. In line with the content-focus of the curriculum both content and language will be assessed throughout the entire undergraduate sequence. As a consequence content is an assessment criterion beginning with Level I courses and quality of language use is explicitly evaluated all the way through Level V courses. It is understood that the weight of content knowledge increases with each instructional level. It follows that the assessment criteria at each of the sequenced levels and in all Level IV and V courses must specify the role and weighting of content and language performance within specific assessment events.

10. One of the goals of the curriculum is that students should become active and independent learners. To encourage and enable students to take responsibility for their learning, criteria for evaluation of different types of performance in various

assessment contexts should be make explicit and, as appropriate, should be jointly constructed between instructors and students. Similarly, students should be aware of the uses of assessment. Joint formulation of what constitutes a quality performance for a whole range of tasks in all four modalities and knowledge of the use of assessments not only reduces the seeming arbitrariness of assessment, a significant source of anxiety, misdirected attention, and even resentment, but also enables students to establish realistic learning goals on their own, something that becomes increasingly important in the upper levels of the curriculum. Such an approach should enhance students' motivation, enjoyment of learning, and likelihood of success. The ultimate aim is to motivate students to continue to use German after they have left the University, perhaps even to improve it under the right circumstances.

11. The outcomes of assessment should be conveyed to the test takers in rich feedback that goes beyond grades or scores. Rich feedback is indispensable since it provides diagnostic information about language performance to the student and suggests future actions for improving language abilities.

12. As much as possible, assessment is related to instructional practices and instructional emphases. In particular, assessment and pedagogical approaches and content emphases should be seamlessly connected, an approach that reflects the performance- and task-orientation of the pedagogies employed within a German studies, content focus for the curriculum.

13. Ongoing course-based assessment, but also final assessment and grades for a course, always combines three aspects:
    - a criterion-reference that assures attainment of course and curriculum goals and maintains overall program quality;
    - the assessment of student progress toward individual goals within the goals of a course, over the period of a semester; this aspect of self-directed or jointly negotiated individual student performance gains, receives greater importance at the higher levels of the curriculum.
    - recognition of students' level of engagement in his or her German studies as a way that most classes comprise students with a range of student profiles who may have to show particular commitment and effort in order to attain the goals of the course or their personal goals.
The interrelationship between these foci and their incorporation into assessment must be clarified to the students.

14. Assessment also takes place in order to assign grades or to provide other verbal descriptors for language performance. This need to respond to both institutional and extra-institutional expectations and requirements grows out of and supple-

ments the Department's emphasis on process and multiple ways of reporting back to test users.

15. The notion of task as it has been explicated in the second language acquisition and language testing literature is particularly suitable at levels I - IV as a means for organizing pedagogical interventions and for conceiving of assessment practices and criteria. Therefore, departmental activities will assure a high degree of knowledge by all teaching staff of this concept and its uses for fostering efficient, effective, and balanced acquisition of accuracy, fluency, and complexity of language use. Such uses should also be tempered relative to an overall understanding of interlanguage development.

16. The multi-section courses at Levels I - III, in their intensive and non-intensive tracks, will conduct a semester final examination that is jointly constructed by all teachers at the level. The purpose of this common final is to ascertain
    - the extent to which the Level objectives were attained
    - the degree of similarity in outcomes of non-intensive and intensive courses, something that is critical for students' ability to shift between tracks,
    - the need for adjustments in materials and pedagogies for the level/course.

17. Given the nature of our curricular objectives, particularly our emphasis on performance in all modalities and our process approach to learning and assessment, course-final assessment is not inherently to be equated with or limited to a scheduled final examination period. Nor do all modalities need to be assessed once more beyond the cumulative record students have already compiled over the course of the semester. In other words, the writing and speaking components of this end-of course assessment might be handled through the cumulative evidence or through an end-of semester oral test, while reading, listening, and short-answer writing might be assessed in a separate examination.

18. While all assessment is linked to instructional decisions, the results of end-of semester assessment in the sequenced courses in Levels I-III should be formally analyzed and evaluated for possible washback effects on curricular goals and content and pedagogical approaches. The Supervisor, in conjunction with the Level coordinators, assembles the results of end-of semester and end-of year-assessment, analyzes the data, and presents a report to the entire teaching staff of the Department. This report addresses the following issues through data and/or narrative:
    - the extent to which students at each level have attained the level goals as these have been stated in the overall curriculum and in the course-specific syllabi;
    - the degree of comparability between student achievement in the non-intensive and the intensive sections at a specific level;

    - recommendations regarding possible changes or adjustments in emphasis in the modalities, in materials, in pedagogical tasks, or in instructional interventions that have a specific focus (e.g., on accuracy, fluency, complexity).
    - implications for the placement examination and actual placement practices.
    - recommendations for revision of assessment practices in general.

19. Given the complexity of assessment, all members of the Department's teaching staff pledge themselves to cooperating in various aspects of creating guidelines, administering tests, assessing language performance, and sharing information about test results.

20. Finally, the Department makes every effort to assure that all members of the teaching staff are knowledgeable about the peculiarities of assessment within a content-based and task-oriented curriculum that also has a distinct process focus. This ongoing need for considering assessment practices and their uses is addressed through the Department's mentored TA development program as well as through a variety of faculty development activities that include presentations by departmental faculty and invited speakers.

APPENDIX B
DRAFT SPECIFICATION OF INTENDED
ASSESSMENT USE FOR THE GUGD
PLACEMENT EXAM

FIRST DRAFT: USE SPECIFICATION FOR GEORGETOWN UNIVERSITY GERMAN DEPARTMENT PLACEMENT EXAM PROGRAM
May, 1999

General assessment description

A combination of information sources is utilized to determine placement of incoming students into appropriate courses at Levels I-IV of the German language program at Georgetown University. Absolute beginning German language students (placed into the 1st semester of Level I) as well as students who speak German as their first language (exempted from courses at Levels I-III), are not expected to take the placement exam. Assessment instruments and procedures estimate students' German language abilities in order to locate them in courses with other students at similar stages within the language acquisition process. Assessment is based on German language tasks, texts, and criteria defined within the integrated and sequenced curricular objectives from each program level; assessment therefore directly references the specific curriculum driving the German language program.

Specification of intended use components

Who are the assessment users?

German department: The German Department (comprised of a department chair, full-time faculty and staff, and graduate teaching assistants) utilizes the assessment to place students into appropriate courses of study, relative to the sequential and integrated curriculum. The German Department seeks an appropriate level of homogeneity among students within individual courses in order to facilitate the language teaching and learning process. The German Department may also utilize information from the placement exam for on-going curricular evaluation and revision. Assessment development, administration, scoring, and reporting of results are the responsibility of the German Department.

University programs: Various university programs utilize the assessment in conjunction with AP exam results in order to award credit hours and exempt students from portions of program-specific language requirements. Specific policies vary from program to program.

Students: Students who have taken AP exams can use placement exam results in order to exempt from further language requirements for particular courses of study and to receive up to six university credit hours. Students may also be interested in receiving feedback on their general level of German ability relative to the Georgetown University German language program., and students will, of course, seek entry into the curriculum at fitting levels.

Uncertainties to be addressed:
--are results communicated appropriately for interpretation by various users?
--are assumptions (by various users) about the relationship between AP exam results and placement exam results reliable and warranted?
--is curriculum-related diagnostic information from the placement exam to be used within the German Department (by teachers or students), or are only placement exam results (i.e., scores) utilized?

What information is needed to inform interpretations?

General interpretations: Assessment should provide basic trustworthy information for estimating students' German language abilities relative to level-specific curricular objectives. Students' language abilities are interpreted simply in terms of relative distinctions between the abilities that characterize a given curricular level and those above or below that level. Information must be gathered within two hours, then synthesized, and reported within a total available time frame of one day. Content knowledge cannot be expected to play a role in placement interpretations.

Potential information needed for specific interpretations:

Background in German:

German language learning experience: To what extent (number of semesters) has the student engaged in formal study of German at the high school and/or college level?

Residency in a German language environment: To what extent (years, months) has the student resided in environments where a substantial proportion of day-to-day communicative events transpired in German?

Academic study in German language environment: To what extent has the student undertaken academic work in German (e.g., German-language high school)?

Results of recognized German assessment instruments:

Advanced Placement exam, German
Scholastic Aptitude Test II, German

ACTFL/FSI Oral Proficiency Interview
CAL Simulated Oral Proficiency Interview
Goethe Institut Sprachdiplom?

GU German Department Level I-IV curriculum-specific information:

Level-specific textual processing ability: Can the student demonstrate ability to comprehend and otherwise process German language texts (written, aural) representative of particular curricular levels?

Level-specific task performance ability: Can the student demonstrate evidence of ability to use German in successfully performing skills-integrative (reading, listening, writing) tasks representative of particular curricular levels?

Cross-curricular task ability: For tasks that are common to multiple curricular levels, can the student demonstrate evidence of ability to use German in performing them as well as would be expected from students leaving a given curricular level course (i.e., a Level I second semester performance)?

Self-reflective view of task-related, text-related, and general purpose German language ability: How does the student evaluate her/his own abilities to accomplish curriculum-related tasks (and especially oral communication tasks) and to comprehend curriculum-related texts? How does the student evaluate her/his own 'general purpose' language ability?

Uncertainties to be addressed:

--what domains of tasks are representative of what curricular levels (these will be used to sample exam items)?
--what text and task types cut across the curricular levels, and what are the performance expectations for these tasks which distinguish among levels (and semesters)?
--what text types and processing abilities are representative of what curricular levels?
--what is the relationship between background information, other recognized German L2 assessment types, and curriculum-specific assessment (e.g., grad. v. undergrad. differences; general academic ability as a moderating variable on some tasks and texts; naturalistic acquirers or heritage learners versus classroom learners, etc.)?
--are level- and program-specific interpretations warranted, based on the information provided within this system?
--given the time constraints, how can information necessary for the required interpretations be most efficiently and effectively gathered (what about short-cut estimations)?
--how is the placement exam related to the semester final exam system?
--how are scores from other recognized exams submitted/gathered?

--is there any registration process for students enrolling in German courses, or does everything occur during the placement exam time period? (is there no other time to collect information from them? If so, how does this occur?)

What is the purpose of the assessment; how is assessment information used?

General purpose: The assessment is used to ensure that students are placed into courses appropriate to their German language abilities, to award credit hours, and to exempt students from further German language study.

German Department purpose: To maintain consistency of students' German-language abilities within courses at particular curricular levels so that their language learning needs may be most efficiently and effectively addressed. To enable curricular/pedagogic focus within courses and across curricular levels. To gather information about the language learning experiences and abilities of students entering into the program for the purpose of on-going curriculum development. To communicate that students prior abilities are taken seriously and that the scope and sequence of the curriculum is likewise taken seriously by the department.

Programs of study purpose: To ensure that students who have taken AP exams should receive university credit hours towards fulfilling language components within their program degree requirements.

Student purposes: To exempt from some or all of their degree program language requirements. To gain access to higher level courses. To receive acknowledgment of their language learning experiences. Possibly to receive feedback about their German language abilities.

Uncertainties to be addressed:
--how do programs of study perceive outcomes of process (satisfied with student abilities, don't care, etc.)?
--are placements into courses/levels appropriate in terms of curricular focus of these courses/levels?
--are information sources sufficiently reliable for assessment purposes?

Who or what is impacted by assessment consequences in what ways?

General: An explicitly curriculum-based placement exam should engender understanding and acceptance of the curricular sequence and the need to match students' language abilities with its expectations. Accordingly, it should result in both effective teaching and learning within each undergraduate course.

Students: Incoming students have the greatest stakes in the process. Positive consequences should be: ensuring that students are placed into courses appropriate to their German language abilities; ensuring that students receive acknowledgment and credit for language learning experiences; providing students with a good idea of their German language abilities in light of university/departmental expectations; enabling academic and language learning success. Negative consequences may be: perception of inaccurate placement; disjuncture between perceived abilities (based on language learning experiences) and tested abilities relative to the German Department curriculum; placement into courses inappropriate for meeting their needs; boredom, low motivation, overwhelming expectations, etc.; decreased academic achievement.

German Department: Enrollment may be positively or negatively impacted by results of the placement exam. Time and resources must be devoted to development, administration, scoring, reporting, record-keeping, and evaluation of the exam. Teachers must develop/adapt courses in response to the needs of students placed into them by the assessment; hence the link between the placement decision and the course objectives/content should be apparent (especially to students). Teachers may be adversely affected by misplacements. The reputation of the department in the eyes of the students, other university programs, and the institution in general, may depend in part on appropriate admissions/placement decisions and the face validity of the assessment process. Teachers and administration must deal with any disagreements with the assessment process (e.g., on the part of students, other programs, etc.).

German Department curriculum: Curricular changes may be induced by information gathered on the exam, or the effectiveness of courses in meeting curricular objectives may be confirmed in part by information gathered on the exam.

Programs of study: Students awarded credit hours based on the combination of AP and placement exam results may or may not meet the language ability expectations of the program of study.

Uncertainties to be addressed:

--how do different stakeholders perceive the effectiveness of the placement exam system?
--do actual positive consequences outweigh actual negative consequences for all impacted by the assessment process?
--are there unintended/unforeseen consequences of assessment use?
--is there a system for evaluating the actual consequences of assessment use for various stakeholders?

APPENDIX C
CURRICULUM-BASED C-TEST DEVELOPMENT
GUIDELINES

GEORGETOWN UNIVERSITY GERMAN DEPARTMENT
C-TEST DEVELOPMENT GUIDELINES

These guidelines outline the general procedures followed in developing the original C-test for the current GUGD placement exam (Summer, 1999). Procedures are broken down into four sections: (a) text selection, (b) text preparation, (c) pilot-testing, and (d) analysis and calibration. For the purposes of developing future parallel C-tests for placement purposes, it is recommended that these guidelines be followed as closely as possible. However, given the potential for new demands, constraints, and needs associated with the placement exam, each section in this document also provides alternatives and suggestions for further C-test development work within the GUGD.

Text selection

1. *Participants*: Recruit curriculum level experts who will identify potential C-test texts. Level experts should have a good understanding of the curricular expectations associated with a given level as well as substantial experience in teaching courses at both semesters of that level. Minimally, one expert participant will be necessary for each of the first four curricular levels (Introductory, Intermediate, Advanced, and Level IV). In addition, a test developer will participate by coordinating all of the activities, including the recruitment of other participants.

2. *Text identification*: Level experts each identify at least three authentic written texts representative of the kinds of texts that learners at the given level should be able to largely understand and process by the end of that level (i.e., experts should be envisioning students who are successfully completing the second semester of study within the given level, such as Intro-2, Intermediate-2, etc.). The Level IV expert should identify texts that are representative of the kinds of texts that students in the "Text in Context" course should be able to process. Texts may be selected from a variety of sources (newspapers, magazines, novels, travel guides, fairy tales, etc.) and should remain unaltered (at this point). Text content may reflect the specific content areas that are treated within a given level; however, overly technical, bizarre, or infrequent texts should be avoided (i.e., do not include texts that students would be unlikely to encounter in the level, even if the language demands seem appropriate). In addition, texts should be avoided if they feature extensive use of proper nouns with which students may not be familiar (e.g., place names). Finally, texts should represent relatively free-standing narrative, descriptive, exposi-

tory, or related units, in the form of a single paragraph of between 75 and 100 words. The meaning of the unaltered text should be clear without additional supporting material. For example, a 75-word section of dialog from *Der Zerbrochene Krug* would not be appropriate, as it requires surrounding text in order to be understood. However, a descriptive paragraph from *Die Chronik der Sperlingsgasse* would probably provide an appropriate text (if matched to a particular curricular level).

3. *Text selection*: Level experts and the test developer meet and select between seven and ten texts for initial inclusion in the pilot C-test. Prior to meeting, copies should be made of the various candidate texts identified by the level experts. In the meeting, participants review the proposed texts level by level, working from the Introductory texts upwards. For each text, participants need to decide whether it seems appropriate as a representative text for the end of the corresponding level; in other words, participants ask themselves whether they agree that students completing the second semester of the given level would be largely able to understand and process the text in question (or, at Level IV, whether students in TinC would be able to process the text). In addition, from among the candidate texts, each participant should decide which one or two texts seem the most appropriate/representative for each level. Through open discussion about the candidate texts and the favored texts, participants as a group decide on one or two texts from each level which should be selected for inclusion in the pilot C-test. At least two texts (and possibly 3) should be included from the Intermediate curricular level.

Alternatives and suggestions:

- The identification of texts might be delegated to all of the teachers working at a given curricular level, as a sort of professional development activity. However, including all teachers will certainly reduce the efficiency of the process, and it may not be the case that all teachers working within a given will share sufficient experience with and understanding of the curricular expectations at that level. Another possibility for increasing participation would be for the individual representative of the particular level to simply solicit suggestions and feedback from level-teachers about the representativeness of particular texts.
- During the text selection meeting, it might be interesting/worthwhile for individual participants to actually record their votes or ranks for the texts they find the most appropriate at each level, prior to openly discussing the texts. This would provide an idea of the extent to which practitioners across the curriculum share internalized notions of the expectations at particular levels of the curriculum. Average ratings for the texts would also prove helpful in selecting a final text for inclusion in the pilot C-test (e.g., the text ranked the highest on a "level representativeness" scale).
- Seven texts were operationalized in the pilot version of the original C-test. Two of these texts were discarded after pilot-testing. The objective is for the final op-

erational C-test to include 5 texts. Depending on the conditions wherein a new set of C-test texts will be piloted, minimally seven but possibly more texts will need to be included. However, it may be the case that including more than seven texts will lead to examinee fatigue and unstable results.

Text preparation

1. *Deletion*: For each text, leave the first sentence intact. Beginning with the second word of the second sentence, delete the second half of the word (replacing the letters with a single blank, _____). Continue deleting the second half of every second word until 25 deletions have been made. Each text should have exactly 25 deletions. For words with odd numbers of letters, delete the second half of the word plus one letter. For compound words, delete only the second half of the second word in the compound (e.g., Wirtschaftssys_____, not Wirtscha_____); however, do not follow this policy for simple da- and wo- compounds. Numbers and dates written numerically should not be deleted, nor should acronyms. The text should generally conclude with a final intact sentence or a substantial part of the final sentence intact.

2. *C-test assembly*: Provide written instructions at the beginning of the C-test. Instructions should: (a) explain the kind of item responses expected from examinees; (b) provide a clear example in basic German that will be understood by all examinees; (c) clarify the number of letters expected in responses (half or half+one); (d) explain the exceptions for compound words; (e) emphasize the importance of spelling; (f) enumerate how many texts there are to complete; and (g) give an indication of how much time examinees have to complete all of the texts. After the instructions, arrange the pilot texts in order of difficulty (beginning with the Introductory text). Label the texts "Text 1" through "Text N". Utilize a relatively large font size (e.g., Times New Roman, 14-point), and be sure to provide sufficient space for examinees to write out full responses to all words (around 9 underscored spaces seems sufficient). Make sure that all item response blanks are uniform in length.

Alternatives and suggestions:
- While the deletion rules should be followed as closely as possible, deletions should also reasonably reflect the level of processing difficulty that the text is intended to represent. For example, it may be the case that the same word (e.g., "zu") is repeatedly deleted within a single text. Under such circumstances, slight adjustments in the text (adding or removing a word) may result in a more accurate reflection of the kinds of understandings required by the text; reasonableness vis-à-vis the curricular expectation of the given level should be the final criterion for making deletion decisions.

- Test instructions may be borrowed virtually intact from the existing C-test, although the time allowed for completing the pilot-test will need to be extended. Texts should each require on average five minutes to complete.
- It may be worth exploring some changes in the instructions; namely, whether telling examinees explicitly how many letters to provide results in substantial differences in performance results. In the current C-test, examinees are directed explicitly to provide either exactly the same number of letters as the first half of the word, or the first half plus one (with the compound exception explained as well). It has been argued that this may cause examinees to pay undue attention to counting letters for each word, as opposed to processing the overall meaning of the text. An alternative set of instructions might be beneficially explored. Such instructions would simply direct examinees to complete the blank with the letters for the word that makes the most sense in the passage, without explaining how many letters to expect. In order to investigate such changes in instructions, the current version and the new version would each be distributed randomly across half of the pilot participants, and resulting performances compared (see pilot-testing alternatives for further thoughts on this issue).

Pilot-testing

1. *Participants*: Participant students should be recruited from across the first four years of the GUGD curriculum to whatever extent possible; that is, students should be enrolled in classes that are directly tied to a particular level of the GUGD curriculum. Minimally, participants are needed to represent the junctures between Introductory/Intermediate, Intermediate/Advanced, and Advanced/Level IV. As a rule, more is better in terms of the number of participants; practically speaking, at least ten per juncture should be taken as a minimum amount (although many more would be better). For piloting the original C-test, students in the Georgetown-Trier study abroad program were recruited.
2. *Timing*: It is absolutely essential that the pilot C-test be administered either at the very beginning or the very end of a semester of instruction and that all participants be administered the test at the same time. If the test is administered during a semester, interpretations cannot be linked to the junctures between the curricular levels, where placement decisions need to be made. Careful records must be kept about when the pilot test was administered and what GUGD courses students were enrolled in at the time of testing (this is best accomplished by including identification information on the pilot C-test form itself).
3. *Administration*: For the test administration session, examinees will only need a pencil (better than a pen for changing responses, which may happen a lot for some examinees). Explain to students that they will be taking an exam which is intended solely for research purposes. They should understand that

their scores will be kept anonymous and will have no bearing on their course grades or otherwise. Request that students do their best on the exam, so that the results will be trustworthy (e.g., "we are interested in seeing how well GU students can do on an exam like this"). After distributing the exams, read through all instructions and work through the examples with students. Query students regarding their understanding of the instructions and address any uncertainties. Advise students that they should not take too long on any one text (around 5 minutes each should be about right); however, be flexible in allowing students to complete the entire exam (if many students are still working after the allotted time, allow more time). It will be essential for all students to try to complete all of the texts. Make sure that students know how many texts there are (front and back of pages), and let students know approximately how much time they have left (e.g., in increments of 5 minutes from the beginning of the exam session); this will encourage them to progress through each of the texts.

4. *Security*: Make only as many copies of the exam(s) as will be needed for the test administration. Count the number of copies that you distribute, and count the number that you pick up at the end of the session to make sure that all students handed back an exam. Do not tell students that the C-test is a pilot version of a new test that will be used for placement purposes; students should understand that this is a test that is being researched, but nothing more.

Alternatives and suggestions:
- Where additional variables are being investigated (such as two different sets of instructions), more participants will need to be recruited in order for comparisons among groups to be trustworthy. A good rule of thumb is to double the number of participants for each additional variable.
- For investigating alternate sets of instructions as well as for drawing comparisons between the original and the new C-tests, administration will need to be carefully controlled. First, if two sets of instructions are being investigated, the instruction types will need to be equally divided across both the new and the old C-tests (i.e., there should be equal numbers of old C-tests that have the original instructions and the new instructions; same for the new C-test). Second, all student participants should be administered both the old and the new C-test, in order for the most accurate comparisons to be made between the two tests. Third, it will probably be best for a single participant to receive only one type of instructions (either spelling out the number of letters or not). Once examinees have seen one set of instructions, it would only introduce confusion to have them respond to a different type on the subsequent test. Therefore, exactly half of the students from each level of the curriculum should be administered one set of instructions and half should be administered the alternate set of instructions. Students from within each level should be randomly assigned to receive one or the other set of instruc-

tions (obviously, this implies the need for substantial numbers of students within each level). Fourth, the two tests should probably be administered on subsequent days, because fatigue would surely affect their performances if students were asked to complete the two tests during the same session. It would probably be a good idea to counter-balance the order of administration of the two tests (i.e., half of the students work the old test first, and the other half work the new test first).

- Time permitting, it may be worthwhile to ask students to rank order the C-test texts according to how difficult they found them to be. At the end of the session, after all students have completed the exam, simply direct them to write a number (from 1-n, depending on number of texts) beside each text label. In addition, students might be asked to indicate which of the C-test texts they found to be the closest to their level of ability (something like "which of the texts did you find to be neither too easy for you to complete nor too difficult"). Students could simply circle their particular choice.

Analysis and calibration

[NOTE: Relatively advanced technical expertise will be required for conducting adequate analyses of the pilot-test results and for using these analyses for the purpose of producing a final operational C-test, associated cut-scores, and related decision rules/policies. The following guidelines summarize the kinds of analyses needed. However, for pilot-test research, it would be advisable to contact the author of this document or to involve an assessment development specialist.]

1. *Descriptive statistics*: Calculate mean, standard deviation, min, max, etc. for full test performances by all examinees, independently for each set of examinees from a given level, and independently for each C-test text. Stats will show the extent to with the various texts and the full-length test are differentiating among a wide range of examinees. Stats will also provide an initial impression of the functioning of each text in relation to the other texts, as well as each group of students in relation to the other groups. Graphing distributions for each text and each group will provide the most easily interpreted indication of how the texts seem to be functioning.

2. *Text difficulty analyses*: In addition to descriptive statistics, item response theory (IRT) statistics should be calculated in order to provide an estimate of the difficulty of the various pilot texts. Text difficulty estimates should be compared with predictions regarding which curricular level the text is intended to represent. Texts which seem overly difficult or overly easy for the majority of the examinees or for the level they are intended to represent will be good candidates for removal.

3. *Reliability analyses*: Traditional and IRT reliability statistics should be calculated for the full test (treating each text as a single 25-point item) and for each

text. Point-biserial correlations will show the relationship between each text and the full test performance. Texts with low point-biserials and low item reliabilities (or high standard error estimates and low model fits in IRT analyses) will be good candidates for rejection.

4. *Between-groups comparisons*: Average performance by each level of examinees on each text should be compared with average performances by all of the other levels of examinees on each text. These comparisons should seek to identify which texts do the best job of distinguishing between the various curricular levels.

5. *Text retention*: Five texts should be selected for retention as the operational C-test, based on the statistical properties of each text. The preceding analyses should be repeated for the final set of five retained texts in order to estimate full-test reliability and to establish average performances expected from each curricular level for the full-length test.

6. *Cut-score decisions and analyses*: Based on average performances for each curricular level on the full-length test, initial cut-scores should be set (e.g., taking the mid-point between two curricular levels as a starting point). Three initial cut-scores will be needed: for distinguishing Introductory from Intermediate, Intermediate from Advanced, and Advanced from Level IV. Where sufficient data are available, additional cut-scores may be investigated for first and second semester within a given level. Reliability, decision dependability, and standard error estimates should be calculated for each cut-score, and adjustments in the cut-scores (up or down) should then be investigated in order to identify the optimal cut-score location for each placement decision.

Alternatives and suggestions:

- If parallel versions of the C-test are being investigated, then a full test equating study will need to be conducted on the basis of the pilot investigations, in order to determine whether scores on the two tests can be used interchangeably and whether particular decision points on each test (cut-scores) are comparable and dependable.
- Likewise, if different versions of test instructions are being investigated, careful within- and between-groups comparisons will need to be conducted in order to determine what, if any, effect the different instructions may have on test performance.

APPENDIX D
PLACEMENT PROCEDURES AND POLICIES

GEORGETOWN UNIVERSITY GERMAN DEPARTMENT
PLACEMENT PROCEDURES AND POLICIES (updated Summer, 2002)

This document outlines the procedures by which incoming students are placed into courses in the Georgetown University German Department (GUGD). It also clarifies departmental policies regarding placement decisions and the potential adjustment of students' enrollments. All departmental teachers, and especially teachers new to the department, should familiarize (or reacquaint) themselves with these procedures and policies prior to each fall semester placement exam administration and the first day of classes.

1. Overview of the GUGD Placement Exam

Except for students who are native speakers of German or absolute beginning learners of German, all incoming students are required to take a departmental placement exam in order to determine where they would most appropriately enroll within the available courses offered by the department. In the summer of 1999, a new placement exam was developed in order to provide an efficient and accurate estimate of the curricular level most suited to a learner's German language abilities. Appendix A to this document provides an overview of the three placement exam sub-tests, as well as why and how they are used. Those teachers not familiar with the placement exam should read Appendix A before continuing with this document. For those interested in accessing additional information about research and development efforts associated with the placement exam, several reports and summaries are available in the Assessment folder on the departmental J-Drive.

2. Placement exam administration and scoring

    a. The <u>Curriculum Coordinator</u> is responsible for administering the placement exam.

        ➤ The exam is administered in two back-to-back morning sessions, once a year, several days prior to the beginning of the fall semester, typically on the Monday before the Wednesday when classes begin; each administration requires two hours.
        ➤ Step-by-step administration guidelines are available and should be reviewed by the curriculum coordinator and anyone assisting in the administration.

➢ All GUGD faculty assist in the administration. Graduate student teachers are welcome to observe and assist, and new teachers are encouraged to do so (contact the curriculum coordinator).

➢ There is no spring semester administration of the placement exam; however, individual administrations of the exam can be scheduled with the curriculum coordinator where necessary (e.g., for mid-year transfer students).

➢ At the beginning of the placement exam administration, students are made aware of the nature of the three exam sub-tests, the scoring and decision-making process, when they will receive their scores, and the fact that they will be monitored by teachers during the first few weeks of the semester in order to ensure the accuracy of their placements.

b. The <u>Curriculum Coordinator</u> and <u>department faculty</u> are responsible for scoring the exams.

➢ Each of the three placement exam sub-tests is scored **independently**, resulting in three test scores (there is no total or combined score on the placement exam).

➢ Students' responses to the Listening and Reading Comprehension tests are machine scored using scan-tron answer sheets; scoring is completed in the Registrar's office in the basement of White Gravenor, immediately following exam administration.

➢ Students' responses to the C-tests are scored by hand by faculty and additional teachers as necessary, immediately following administration; prior to scoring, all participants should review the C-test scoring guidelines and clarify any ambiguities with the curriculum coordinator.

➢ The three total scores for each sub-test are entered into a computer spreadsheet for each student, by student name and identification number.

c. NOTE: Research and development efforts are currently underway to revise the administration and scoring of the three placement exam sub-tests; future administrations will be computer-administered and –scored; the curriculum coordinator will update the department regarding these developments.

3. Placement decisions and enrollment policies

a. The <u>Curriculum Coordinator</u> and <u>Department Chair</u> are responsible for making final placement decisions and recommendations for each student.

➢ Each of the three individual sub-test scores is compared with the score bands for GUGD curricular levels I-IV (see Appendix B to this document); three preliminary placements are made for each student, based on each sub-test.

> The Standard Error of Measurement for each sub-test is considered for students whose scores are close to the cut-score between two curricular levels.
> For students where at least two of the sub-test placements are in agreement, and the third is no more than one semester higher or lower, the student is placed into the corresponding curricular level.
> For students whose sub-test scores do not agree, placement is weighted towards the lowest score; however, student background information (e.g., language learning experience) is also taken into account in the decision.
> Final placement recommendations for each student are compiled by the curriculum coordinator prior to the departmental placement/enrollment party.
> Final placement recommendations are matched against the latest class rosters to identify any students who have pre-registered for the wrong class. Discrepancies are noted on the posting of placement recommendations at the departmental/enrollment party and in the placement information given to each instructor in order to alert students and teachers alike of the need to be registered for the class into which one was placed.

b. Students are responsible for complying with the following departmental enrollment policies.

> Incoming students with prior background in German may not enroll in GUGD classes without first taking the placement exam.
> Students' advisors from other departments do not have the authority to make a placement recommendation in lieu of the placement exam.
> Students should enroll in the curricular level into which they were placed, not lower or higher based on their preferences or opinions of their abilities.
> Placement decisions are not immutable and may be revised by the curriculum coordinator or department chair (only) upon recommendation by the student's German Department teacher.
> Students who apply for credit by exam or Advanced Placement credit are required to take the placement exam; they will receive credit only up to the level indicated by their placement exam scores.
> Students who take the placement exam in August and place into off-sequence courses not offered that fall (e.g., Intro II, Intermediate II) are advised either to enroll in the intensive section of that curricular level or to wait until the spring semester when the off-sequence courses are offered. Depending on students' scores on each sub-test and their background in German, the curriculum coordinator or department chair can revise the initial placement recommendation to be in line with each semester's course offerings.

4. Placement information conveyed to teachers

a. <u>Teachers</u> will receive the following information for each student in their course/section by the first day of classes.

  ➢ Scores for each of the three placement exam sub-tests
  ➢ Placement recommendations based on each sub-test
  ➢ Final overall placement recommendation from the curriculum coordinator, including identification of students who, based on their placement exam results, are pre-registered for the wrong course.
  ➢ Copy of the background information form filled out by each student

5. German department placement/enrollment party

a. <u>Teachers</u> and <u>students</u> are encouraged to attend the departmental placement/enrollment party held on the afternoon of the same day as the placement exam administration.

  ➢ Final placement recommendations for each student are posted at the party, including identification of students who, based on their placement exam results, are pre-registered for the wrong course.
  ➢ The party gives students the opportunity to interact with teachers, seek advice, and decide about enrolling in GUGD courses.
  ➢ Teachers should have access to the information listed in #4 above for all students; actual final class enrollments will not be available until the first day of classes.
  ➢ Teachers should make a point of advising students whose placement recommendation indicates they are pre-registered for the wrong course.
  ➢ Students who have questions about their placements at this time should be referred to the curriculum coordinator or department chair.

6. Confirming student enrollment status—first day of classes

a. <u>Teachers</u> are responsible for confirming that students who enroll in their classes are where they should be.

  ➢ All students indicate on the Class Enrollment Information Form how they entered into the class (for <u>level I</u>: absolute beginner, placed in, other; for <u>levels II-IV</u>: advanced in, placed in, other). Teachers may also elect to have students complete a more extensive survey to supplement the questionnaire completed as part of the placement exam.
  ➢ Teachers identify any cases of 'self-enrollment', including: (a) students who identify themselves as 'others' (i.e., they simply enroll themselves into a

course without taking the exam); (b) students who enroll higher than the curricular level suggested; (c) students who enroll lower than the level suggested. All students identified as 'others' should be referred by the teacher to the curriculum supervisor so that they can take the placement exam. Those students enrolled in the wrong course need to be advised to enroll in the course into which they were placed.

➤ Teachers submit a completed Class Enrollment Information Form to the curriculum coordinator after each of the first three class periods.
➤ Curriculum coordinator interviews students to find out why they did not take the exam, then administers the exam and places students.
➤ In case teachers are missing information about particular students, all language background questionnaires from the placement exam will be kept in a binder in the departmental secretary's office.

7. Monitoring placed students and adjusting enrollments

a. <u>Teachers</u> are responsible for identifying students who were clearly mis-placed.

➤ While rare, it is possible that a student will be placed into a curricular level that is inappropriate (too high or too low) for that student's language abilities.
➤ Teachers should monitor for the first several weeks of the semester those students who placed into their classes in order to identify any clear misplacements (based on obvious differences from other students in class).
➤ Teachers, and especially new teachers, should bear in mind that there will be a large degree of naturally occurring heterogeneity among students within their courses.
➤ Where a teacher suspects possible misplacement, placement exam scores and background information should be reviewed prior to further action.

b. The <u>Curriculum Coordinator</u> and/or the <u>Department Chair</u> are responsible for adjusting students' enrollments.

➤ Only the curriculum coordinator or department chair may adjust students' enrollments in German courses.
➤ The teacher should meet with the student in order to discuss the possibility of adjusting enrollment prior to submitting a recommendation to the curriculum coordinator.
➤ Where teachers identify students who they think are clearly misplaced, they may submit a written recommendation to the curriculum coordinator stating exactly why they think the student would be better served in a different curricular level/course.

- ➢ The curriculum coordinator meets with the student and discusses an appropriate adjusted enrollment.
- ➢ Where students express dissatisfaction with their placement into a given course, teachers should refer the student to the curriculum coordinator for further action.

APPENDIX E
OVERVIEW OF THE GUGD PLACEMENT EXAM

General Overview of the Georgetown University German Department Placement Exam (2002)

The Georgetown University German Department (GUGD) Placement Exam consists of three sub-tests: the Listening Comprehension Test (LCT), the Reading Comprehension Test (RCT), and the C-test. Each of these sub-tests was designed to provide information about how well entering students are able to understand and process German language texts (both aural and written) like those found at various levels within the German Department's "Multiple Literacies" curriculum. The three sub-tests were also designed to provide this information as quickly and efficiently as possible. Students' scores on these sub-tests are used for the sole purpose of deciding where students most appropriately fit within the set of courses offered in the "Multiple Literacies" curriculum—that is, at what curricular level students would benefit the most from instruction. Based on their placement exam scores, students may be placed into one of the first three years of sequenced instruction (Beginning, Intermediate, and Advanced courses), or, with high enough scores, they may be placed out of the first three years of instruction. Given the very broad range of language abilities reflected in these decisions, the three sub-tests were designed to contain both texts and items that range considerably in the amount of difficulty they may pose for students. Accordingly, most entering students should generally not expect to be able to answer all of the test items correctly.

The straightforward multiple choice format for items on the LCT and RCT will be familiar to most students. These items test students' abilities to understand details and main ideas in the texts, as well as their abilities to make inferences based on their understanding of the meaning communicated in the texts.

The C-test format will probably be less familiar to most students, although it appears at first glance to be similar to a fill-in-the-blank test. However, the C-test is not a simple fill-in-the-blank test. The C-test asks examinees to complete the second half of words which have been deleted at regular intervals throughout a series of otherwise intact texts that are each around a paragraph in length. This i___ an exa___ sentence fr___ such a___ exam. As examinees complete the words, they recreate a meaningful text. However, in order to do so, they obviously have to know both the deleted words and the surrounding words, they have to understand the meaning conveyed by sentences within the text, and they have to understand the grammatical relationships expressed between particular words and between sentences. All of these abilities figure into the accurate completion of a C-test text; as such, the C-test presents students with a very challenging language task. Again, only very advanced language learners will be able to correctly answer all of the items in each C-test text, although certain texts will be easier or more difficult than others, depending on which level of the "Multiple Literacies" curriculum they represent.

The C-test format (and the multiple choice formats for the LCT and RCT, for that matter) may appear somewhat 'artificial' in terms of the kinds of communicative language abilities that students are expected to develop in college foreign language contexts. Indeed, the activities that students engage in on these placement tests should not be taken to reflect the kinds of communication they will be doing in Georgetown German classes. However, it should be understood that these tests are not intended as achievement or proficiency tests—rather, their sole purpose is to inform a quick and accurate placement decision. Several sources of evidence support the use of the C-test for placement purposes in college German language programs and in the GUGD:

1. C-tests have enjoyed a long history of successful use as placement exams in a number of foreign language programs in German universities, where this testing format was originally developed. Extensive research there has shown that: (a) scores on C-tests consistently provide good estimates of examinees' abilities, (b) placement decisions based on C-tests equal and often surpass the accuracy of other placement tests combined (such as oral interviews, written essays, grammar and vocabulary tests), and (c) C-tests provide accurate estimates and inform decisions in much less time than most other placement exam formats.
2. The GUGD placement exam was carefully developed such that the accuracy of placement decisions into the "Multiple Literacies" curriculum would be maximized. Research on this placement exam has shown that: (a) individual students' scores on the C-test improve consistently and as predicted as they advance through the levels of the curriculum; (b) average student scores on the C-test differ from curricular level to level as predicted; (c) graduate students and other very advanced German learners consistently place out of the sequenced courses in the curriculum; (d) scores on the C-test, LCT, and RCT are closely related as predicted; and, perhaps most importantly, (e) students and teachers almost always agree with a student's placement based on the exam.

These and other sources of evidence support the use of the C-test and the full GUGD placement exam as a tool for making quick and accurate decisions about where, within the available German Department courses, incoming students most appropriately belong. Of course, as with any placement decision, there is always a small chance of students being placed into a course which does not provide the best fit for their language learning needs. Accordingly, placement policy in the GUGD treats the first several weeks of a typical semester (for study abroad, the first several days) as a probationary period for all placed students. During this period, teachers provide numerous opportunities for students to display their language knowledge and abilities, and they carefully compare their observations of placed students with the language learning demands that characterize the particular curricular level and course. On those occasions when a student and a teacher agree that the student would probably be better served in a lower or higher level course, placement decisions may be adjusted accordingly by the undergraduate curriculum coordinator or the department chair. While such changes happen rarely, this policy is in place in order to make sure that students benefit maximally from their time in the Georgetown University German Department.

Finally, it should be emphasized that it is not the expectation of the GUGD that incoming students will present homogenous German language knowledge and abilities which match exactly the abilities of other students and the coursework in particular classes. In fact, while the "Multiple Literacies" curriculum was designed to foster certain kinds of continuing advanced language development throughout all levels of the program, it also recognizes the variable abilities that students will develop as they pursue their individual interests in using the German language for various communicative purposes. As such, the GUGD placement exam was designed to provide an efficient 'best-fit' estimate for incoming students. It was not designed to profile all of a student's strengths and weaknesses in using German for meeting various communicative ends. It should go without saying that, once the placement decision has been made, it is up to the learner and the teacher to make sure that related language learning needs and objectives are met.

APPENDIX F
REVISED GUGD ASSESSMENT POLICIES STATEMENT

GERMAN DEPARTMENT, GEORGETOWN UNIVERSITY
(September 12, 2002)

GENERAL POLICY STATEMENT

This document summarizes assessment policies in the Georgetown University German Department (GUGD). Originally drafted in the spring of 1999, and revised in summer 2002, these policies reflect extensive deliberations by the Department's entire teaching/administrative staff about the purposes for assessment within the *"Developing Multiple Literacies"* undergraduate curriculum, at both the classroom and program levels. In addition to these overall policies, assessment practices particular to each of the four sequenced curricular years (levels I-IV) are spelled out in a *Specifications of Intended Test Use* document for each level and in separate guidelines for the assessment of speaking and of writing. Also, guidelines that pertain to the development of writing and its assessment were separately developed. Taken together, these documents are intended to guide not only the development and implementation, but also the evaluation and revision of all quizzes, tests, examinations, written and oral performances, and other forms of assessment which play an integral role in the success of the GUGD's educational efforts.

1. All assessment, whether formative or summative, embedded in the curriculum or independent of it, focuses on students' abilities to use the language meaningfully in various settings.

2. All students entering the program take a placement examination; exempted are students beginning their study of German at Georgetown University or native speakers of German. Placement test instruments and decision-making procedures are explicitly based on the unique content-, task-, and textual-focus of the *Multiple Literacies* Curriculum. Separate instructions and guidelines govern administration and scoring of the placement test and actual student placement.

3. Assessment is explicitly linked to curricular goals and instructional practices and emphases. In particular, in line with the content-focus of the curriculum, both content and language will be assessed throughout the entire undergraduate sequence. As a consequence, content is an assessment criterion beginning with Level I courses, and quality of language use is explicitly evaluated all the way through Level V courses. Furthermore, assessment, content emphases, and peda-

gogical approaches should mirror the performance and task orientation of the entire curriculum.

4. The Department emphasizes the clarity of assessment criteria, their suitability for the level of language acquisition and the instructional tasks of a particular level, and their appropriateness for the overall goals of the curriculum. Clarity, suitability, and appropriateness of assessment criteria are the basis for uniformity of grading practices. While all instructors share a responsibility of attending to these issues, special responsibilities fall to the Level Coordinators and to the Curriculum Coordinator. Recommended activities are: the collaborative construction of assessment instruments and procedures, cooperative exchange of documents which detail assessment practices in the various modalities for major task types and genres, recommendations regarding efficient and effective provision of feedback, scheduling of grading sessions during the semester, joint grading of the semester final, and feedback about assessment at the end of the year.

5. In line with the long-term developmental and cumulative nature of acquiring the curriculum's German studies content and an academic level of literacy in German, both instruction and assessment practices have a strong process and developmental character. Therefore, students have repeated opportunities for building up content and language knowledge and for improving their performance in a range of genres and tasks, particularly through planning and executing more extensive tasks for which they have received guidance, criteria for assessment, and feedback. Because of the developmental and creative nature of language learning students' sustained engagement with a course (e.g., via homework and class participation) is also assessed.

6. The complexity of language use requires multiple assessment sources (e.g., quizzes, midterms, final examinations, individual and group projects) and various conditions under which language is assessed (planned vs. unplanned, individual vs. group, interactive vs. non-interactive, scaffolded vs. unscaffolded, formally assessed vs. informally assessed). Because of the curricular focus on linking content and language in language use, both holistic assessments that gauge students' ability to attain broad communicative goals and local, highly targeted assessments that focus on specific aspects of content and language form need to be incorporated. The differences between these two foci in assessment and their use in particular assessment situations need to be communicated to students.

7. Ongoing course-based assessment as well as final assessment and grades for a course always combine three aspects:
    - a criterion reference that emphasizes attainment of course and curriculum goals and maintains overall program quality;

- an individual reference that emphasizes progress toward a student's personal goals within the goals of course, over the period of a semester; this aspect of self-directed or jointly negotiated individual student performance gains and receives greater importance at the higher levels of the curriculum;
- an individual reference that recognizes students' level of engagement in their German studies; this aspect recognizes that most classes are comprised of students with a range of learner profiles resulting in differing levels and types of commitment and effort in order to attain the goals of the course as well as their personal goals.

The interrelationship between these foci and their incorporation into assessment must be clarified to students at the beginning of a course.

8. One of the goals of the curriculum is that students should become active and independent learners. Assessment can play an important role in attaining that goal inasmuch as an awareness of criteria for evaluation of different types of performance in various assessment contexts and the uses of assessment outcomes can encourage and enable students to take responsibility for their learning. Clear articulation and demonstration of what constitutes a quality performance for a whole range of tasks in all four modalities and knowledge of the use of assessments not only reduces the apparent arbitrariness of assessment (a significant source of anxiety, misdirected attention, and even resentment), but also enables students to establish realistic learning goals on their own, something that becomes increasingly important in the upper levels of the curriculum (and beyond). Such an approach enhances students' motivation, enjoyment of learning, and likelihood of success. The ultimate aim is to motivate students to continue to use German after they have left the University, perhaps even to continue to improve it under the right circumstances.

9. The outcomes of assessment are conveyed to learners in substantive feedback that goes beyond grades or scores. Such feedback is indispensable since it provides diagnostic information about students' language performance, guides future action by both instructors and students, and contributes to enhancing students' motivation to improve their language abilities.

10. Assessment is a vital foundation for the assignment of grades and for evidence about language development and levels of language abilities. This need to respond to both institutional and extra-institutional expectations and requirements grows out of and supplements the Department's emphasis on learning as a process..

11. The multi-section courses at Levels I - III, in their intensive and non-intensive tracks, conduct semester-final assessments that are jointly constructed by all teachers at the level. The purpose of these assessments is to ascertain:

- the extent to which the Level objectives and expectations were attained by students
- the degree of similarity in outcomes of non-intensive and intensive courses, an assumption that is critical for enabling students' to shift between tracks,
- the need for adjustments in materials and pedagogies, as well as learning and performance expectations, for the level/course.

12. Given the nature of the Department's curricular objectives, particularly the emphasis on performance in all modalities and the process approach to learning and assessment, student performance is assessed extensively over the course of the semester. In particular, the department has developed separate guidelines and assessment task sheets for task-based assessment of writing and of speaking in the sequenced curricular levels I - IV. As a consequence speaking is no longer separately assessed at the end of a course or curricular level. However, to assure continued adherence to the curricular goals all instructors must familiarize themselves with the principles, procedures, and practices for assessing writing and speaking and their impact on instruction as well as their relationship to semesterfinal assessments during the scheduled final examination periods and also for the assignment of grades.

13. All members of the Department's teaching staff cooperate fully in creating guidelines, administering tests, assessing language performance, and sharing information about test results.

14. All assessment practices related to the *Multiple Literacies Curriculum* will be subjected to periodic validity evaluation, in order to determine the extent to which assessment is accomplishing what it is intended to accomplish and to identify assessment practices in need of revision. The Curriculum Coordinator directs these evaluation efforts.

15. Finally, the Department makes every effort to assure that all members of the teaching staff are knowledgeable about assessment within a content-based and task-oriented curriculum. In particular, the notions of genre and task as explicated in the literature on instructed second language acquisition and language testing offer insights and practice-oriented recommendations for structuring courses, for organizing pedagogical interventions, and for conceiving of assessment practices and criteria. Therefore, departmental activities will assure a high degree of knowledge by all teaching staff of these concepts and their potential role in fostering efficient, effective, and balanced acquisition of accuracy, fluency, and complexity of language performance and development toward meaning-oriented language use. Naturally, such uses will be tempered relative to an overall understanding of interlanguage development within instructed settings. Accordingly, the Department provides a mentored development program for

teaching assistants as well as a variety of faculty development events. In addition, documents, policies, reports, and other information pertaining to assessment practices in the Department are organized and maintained in a format accessible to instructors internally via the departmental network. Where appropriate, information about departmental assessment practices is made available to external interested parties via the departmental web site. All such information is updated periodically, in order to reflect current practice.

REFERENCES

"100 days--100 languages": ACTFL receives new testing contract from DLIFLC. (2003). *Foreign Language Annals, 36*(1), 147.

Alderson, J. C., Clapham, C. C., & Wall, D. (1995). *Language test construction and evaluation.* New York: Cambridge University Press.

Alkin, M. C. (1990). *Debates on evaluation.* Thousand Oaks, CA: Sage.

American Council on the Teaching of Foreign Languages. (1982). *ACTFL Provisional Proficiency Guidelines.* Yonkers, NY: American Council on the Teaching of Foreign Languages.

American Council on the Teaching of Foreign Languages. (1986). *ACTFL Proficiency Guidelines.* Yonkers, NY: American Council on the Teaching of Foreign Languages.

American Council on the Teaching of Foreign Languages. (1987a). ACTFL Chinese Proficiency Guidelines. *Foreign Language Annals, 20,* 471-487.

American Council on the Teaching of Foreign Languages. (1987b). ACTFL Japanese Proficiency Guidelines. *Foreign Language Annals, 20,* 589-603.

American Council on the Teaching of Foreign Languages. (1988). ACTFL Russian Proficiency Guidelines. *Foreign Language Annals, 21,* 177-197.

American Council on the Teaching of Foreign Languages. (1989). ACTFL Arabic Proficiency Guidelines. *Foreign Language Annals, 22,* 373-392.

American Council on the Teaching of Foreign Languages. (1999). *ACTFL Proficiency Guidelines--speaking, revised.* Yonkers, NY: American Council on the Teaching of Foreign Languages.

American Council on the Teaching of Foreign Languages. (2002). *Program standards for the preparation of foreign language teachers.* Yonkers, NY: American Council on the Teaching of Foreign Languages.

American Educational Research Association, American Psychological Association, & National Council on Measurement in Education. (1985). *Standards for educational and psychological testing.* Washington, DC: American Educational Research Association.

American Educational Research Association, American Psychological Association, & National Council on Measurement in Education. (1999). *Standards for educational and psychological testing.* Washington, DC: American Educational Research Association.

American Psychological Association. (1954). Technical recommendations for psychological tests and diagnostic techniques. *Psychological Bulletin, 51,* 201-238.

American Psychological Association, American Educational Research Association, & National Council on Measurement in Education. (1966). *Standards for educational and psychological tests and manuals.* Washington, DC: American Psychological Association.

American Psychological Association, American Educational Research Association, & National Council on Measurement in Education. (1974). *Standards for educational and psychological tests.* Washington, DC: American Psychological Association.

Anastasi, A. (1986). Evolving concepts of test validation. *Annual Reviews of Psychology, 37,* 1-15.

Anastasi, A. (1990). Ability testing in the 1980s and beyond: Some major trends. *Public Personnel Management, 18*(4), 471-485.

Angelo, T. A., & Cross, P. K. (1993). *Classroom assessment techniques: A handbook for college teachers* (2nd ed.). San Francisco: Jossey-Bass.

Angoff, W. H. (1971). Scales, norms, and equivalent scores. In E. L. Thorndike (Ed.), *Educational measurement* (2nd ed., pp. 508-600). Washington, DC: American Council on Education.

Angoff, W. H. (1988). Validity: An evolving concept. In H. Wainer & H. Braun (Eds.), *Test Validity* (pp. 19-32). Hillsdale, NJ: Lawrence Erlbaum Associates.

Aschbacker, P. (1991). Performance assessment: State activity, interest, and concerns. *Applied Measurement in Education, 4,* 275-288.

Azevedo, M. M. (1990). Professional development of teaching assistants: Training versus education. *ADFL Bulletin, 22*(1), 24-28.

Bachman, L. (1990). *Fundamental considerations in language testing.* Oxford: Oxford University Press.

Bachman, L. (2002). Alternative interpretations of alternative assessments: Some validity issues in educational performance assessments. *Educational Measurement: Issues and Practice, 21*(3), 3-18.

Bachman, L., & Savignon, S. J. (1986). The evaluation of communicative language proficiency: A critique of the ACTFL Oral Interview. *Modern Language Journal, 70,* 380-390.

Bachman, L. F. (2000). What, if any, are the limits of our responsibility for fairness in language testing? In A. J. Kunnan (Ed.), *Fairness and validation in language assessment: Selected papers from the 19th Language Testing Research Colloquium, Orlando, Florida* (pp. 39-41). New York: Cambridge University Press.

Bachman, L. F. (2004). *Statistics for language testing.* New York: Cambridge University Press.

Bachman, L. F., & Palmer, A. S. (1996). *Language testing in practice.* Oxford: Oxford University Press.

Bardovi-Harlig, K., & Hartford, B. (Eds.). (1997). *Beyond methods: Components of second language teacher education.* New York: McGraw-Hill.

Barnes, B., Klee, C., & Wakefield, R. (1990). A funny thing happened on the way to the language requirement. *ADFL Bulletin, 22*(1), 35-39.

Barnett, M. A., & Cook, R. F. (2000). The seamless web: Developing teaching assistants as professionals. In J. C. Walz (Ed.), *Development and supervision of teaching assistants in foreign languages* (pp. 85-111). Boston, MA: Heinle & Heinle.

Barnhardt, S., Kevorkian, J. A., & Delett, J. S. (1998). *Portfolio assessment in the foreign language classroom.* Washington, DC: National Capital Language Resource Center.

Barnwell, D. P. (1996). *A history of foreign language testing in the United States.* Tempe, AZ: Bilingual Press.

Baur, R. S., & Meder, G. (1994). C-Tests zur Ermittlung der globalen Sprachfähigkeit im Deutschen und in der Muttersprache bei ausländischen SSchülern in der Bundesrepublik Deutschland. In R. Grotjahn (Ed.), *Der C-test: Theoretische Grundlagen und praktische Anwendungen* (Vol. 2, pp. 151-178). Bochum, Germany: Brockmeyer.

Berk, R. A. (Ed.). (1984). *A guide to criterion-referenced test construction.* Baltimore, MD: The Johns Hopkins University Press.

Bernhardt, E. (2002). A language center director responds. *Modern Language Journal, 86*(2), 246-248.

Bernhardt, E., & Deville, C. (1991). Testing in foreign language programs and testing programs in foreign language departments: Reflections and recommendations. In R. V. Teschner (Ed.), *Assessing foreign language proficiency of undergraduates* (pp. 43-59). Boston: Heinle & Heinle.

Bernhardt, E., & Hammadou, J. (1987). A decade of research in foreign language teacher education. *Modern Language Journal, 71*, 289-299.

Birckbichler, D. W. (Ed.). (1990). *New perspectives and new direction in foreign language education.* Lincolnwood, IL: National Textbook Company.

Bitter, G. G., & Pierson, M. E. (2002). *Using technology in the classroom.* Boston: Allyn & Bacon.

Bolton, J. (1992). Wie schwierig is ein C-Test? Erfahrungen mit dem C-Test als Einstufungstest in Hochschulkursen Deutsch als Fremdsprache. In R. Grotjahn (Ed.), *Der C-test: Theoretische Grundlagen und praktische Anwendungen* (Vol. 1, pp. 193-204). Bochum, Germany: Brockmeyer.

Bond, L. (1995). Unintended consequence of performance assessment: Issues of bias and fairness. *Educational Measurement: Issues and Practice, 14*(4), 21-24.

Borsboom, D., Mellenbergh, G., & van Heerden, J. (2004). The concept of validity. *Psychological Review, 111*(4), 1061-1071.

Breiner-Sanders, K. E., Swender, E., & Terry, R. M. (2002). Preliminary proficiency guidelines--writing: Revised 2001. *Foreign Language Annals, 35*(1), 9-15.

Brennan, R. L. (1998). Misconceptions at the intersection of measurement theory and practice. *Educational Measurement: Issues and Practice, 17*(1), 5-9, 30.

Brennan, R. L. (2001). Some problems, pitfalls, and paradoxes in educational measurement. *Educational Measurement: Issues and Practice, 20*(4), 6-18.

Brennan, R. L., & Johnson, E. G. (1995). Generalizability of performance assessments. *Educational Measurement: Issues and Practice, 14*(4), 9-12.

Brière, E. (1971). Are we really measuring proficiency with our foreign language tests? *Foreign Language Annals, 4*(3), 385-391.

Brisolara, S. (1998). The history of participatory evaluation and current debates in the field. In E. Whitmore (Ed.), *Understanding and practicing participatory evaluation* (pp. 25-41). San Francisco: Jossey-Bass.

Brookhart, S. M. (2003). Developing measurement theory for classroom assessment purposes and uses. *Educational Measurement: Issues and Practice, 22*(4), 5-12.

Brown, J. D. (1981). Newly placed versus continuing students: Comparing proficiency. In J. C. Fisher, M. A. Clarke, & J. Schachter (Eds.), *On TESOL '80 building bridges: Research and practice in teaching English as a second language* (pp. 111-119). Washington, DC: TESOL.

Brown, J. D. (1984). A cloze is a cloze is a cloze? In J. Handscombe, R. A. Orem, & B. P. Taylor (Eds.), *On TESOL '83: The question of control* (pp. 109-119). Washington, DC: TESOL.

Brown, J. D. (1989). Improving ESL placement tests using two perspectives. *TESOL Quarterly, 23*, 65-83.

Brown, J. D. (1993). A comprehensive criterion-referenced language testing project. In D. Douglas & C. Chapelle (Eds.), *A new decade of language testing research: Selected papers from the 1990 Language Testing Research Colloquium* (pp. 163-184). Alexandria, VA: TESOL.

Brown, J. D. (1996). *Testing in language programs.* Upper Saddle River, NJ: Prentice Hall Regents.

Brown, J. D., & Hudson, T. (2002). *Criterion-referenced language testing.* New York: Cambridge University Press.

Brown, J. D., Hudson, T., & Kim, Y. (2001). *Developing Korean language performance assessments.* Honolulu, HI: Second Language Teaching & Curriculum Center.

Bryan, C., & Clegg, K. (eds.) (2006). *Innovative assessment in higher education.* London: Routledge.

Bryk, A. S. (1998). Misuse of standardized achievement tests. *Education Week*(March 25).

Buck, K., Byrnes, H., & Thompson, I. (Eds.). (1989). *The ACTFL oral proficiency interview: Tester training manual.* Yonkers, NY: American Council on the Teaching of Foreign Languages.

Buck, P. H. (1964). Examinations: A retrospective view at Harvard. In L. Bramson (Ed.), *Examining in Harvard College* (pp. 4-37). Cambridge, MA: Committee on Educational Policy, Harvard University.

Byrnes, H. (1998b). Introduction: Steps to an ecology of foreign language departments. In H. Byrnes (Ed.), *Learning foreign and second languages: Perspectives in research and scholarship* (pp. 1-22). New York: Modern Language Association.

Byrnes, H. (2000). Shaping the discourse of a practice: The role of linguistics and psychology in language teaching and learning. *Modern Language Journal, 84*, 472-494.

Byrnes, H. (2001). Reconsidering graduate students' education as teachers: "It takes a department!". *Modern Language Journal, 85*(4), 512-530.

Byrnes, H. (2002a, November 23). *Task-based writing in a curricular context: Specifying goals, pedagogies, and assessment criteria.* Paper presented at the AATG/ACFTL conference, Salt Lake City.

Byrnes, H. (2002b). The role of task and task-based assessment in a content-oriented collegiate foreign language curriculum. *Language Testing, 19*(4), 419-437.

Byrnes, H., & Canale, M. (Eds.). (1986). *Defining and developing proficiency: Guidelines, implementations, and concepts.* Lincolnwood, IL: National Textbook Company.

Byrnes, H., & Kord, S. (2001). Developing literacy and literary competence: Challenges for FL departments. In V. Scott & H. Tucker (Eds.), *SLA and the literature classroom: Fostering dialogues* (pp. 31-69). Boston: Heinle & Heinle.

Campbell, D. T. (1957). Factors relevant to the validity of experiments in social settings. *Psychological Bulletin, 54*, 297-312.

Campbell, D. T. (1960). Recommendations for APA test standards regarding construct, trait, or discriminant validity. *American Psychologist, 15*, 546-553.

Campbell, D. T. (1969). Reforms as experiments. *American Psychologist, 24*, 409-429.

Campbell, D. T. (1991). Methods for the experimenting society. *Evaluation Practice, 12*, 223-260.

Campbell, D. T. (1996). Can we overcome worldview incommensurability/relativity in trying to understand the other? In R. Jessor, A. Colby, & R. Shweder (Eds.), *Ethnography and human development: Context and meaning in social inquiry* (pp. 153-172). Chicago: University of Chicago Press.

Campbell, D. T., & Fiske, D. W. (1959). Convergent and discriminant validity in the multitrait-multimethod matrix. *Psychological Bulletin, 56*, 81-105.

Campbell, D. T., & Stanley, J. C. (1966). *Experimental and quasi-experimental designs for research.* Chicago: Rand McNally.

Canale, M. (1984). Testing in a communicative approach. In G. A. Jarvis (Ed.), *The challenge for excellence in foreign language education* (pp. 79-92). Middlebury, VT: Northeast Conference on the Teaching of Foreign Languages.

Canale, M., & Swain, M. (1980). Theoretical bases of communicative approaches to second language teaching and testing. *Applied Linguistics, 1*, 1-47.

Carduner, J. (2002). Using classroom assessment techniques to improve foreign language composition courses. *Foreign Language Annals, 35*(543-549).

CARLA Assessment Team. (1998a). *Minnesota Language Proficiency Assessments: Contextualized Reading Assessment (CoRA): Intermediate-high level, German.* Minneapolis, MN: University of Minnesota, The Center for Advanced Research on Language Acquisition.

CARLA Assessment Team. (1998b). *Minnesota Language Proficiency Assessments: Contextualized Speaking Assessment (CoSA): Intermediate-low level, German.*

Minneapolis, MN: University of Minnesota, The Center for Advanced Research on Language Acquisition.

CARLA Assessment Team. (2000a). *Minnesota Language Proficiency Assessments: Contextualized Listening Assessment (CoLA): Intermediate-high level, German.* Minneapolis, MN: University of Minnesota, The Center for Advanced Research on Language Acquisition.

CARLA Assessment Team. (2000b). *Minnesota Language Proficiency Assessments: Contextualized Writing Assessment (CoWA): Intermediate-mid level, German.* Minneapolis, MN: University of Minnesota, The Center for Advanced Research on Language Acquisition.

Carroll, J. B. (1961). Fundamental considerations in testing English proficiency of foreign students. In C. f. A. Linguistics (Ed.), *Testing the English proficiency of foreign students* (pp. 30-40). Washington, DC: Center for Applied Linguistics.

Center for Applied Linguistics. (1995). *The German Speaking Test.* Washington, DC: author.

Chalhoub-Deville, M. (1996). Performance assessment and the components of the oral construct across different tests and rater groups. In M. Milanovic & N. Saville (Eds.), *Performance testing, cognition and assessment: Selected papers from the 15th Language Testing Research Colloquium, Cambridge and Arnhem* (pp. 55-73). Cambridge: Cambridge University Press.

Chalhoub-Deville, M., Sweet, G., Schmidt, K., & McCollum Lozier, V. (1996). *Qualitative and quantitative review of the University of Minnesota CLA Language Spanish Entrance and Graduation Proficiency Tests.* Minneapolis, MN: University of Minnesota, The Center for Advanced Research on Language Acquisition.

Chapelle, C. (1999). Validity in language assessment. *Annual Review of Applied Linguistics, 19*, 254-272.

Chapelle, C., & Douglas, D. (1993). Foundations and directions for a new decade of language testing. In D. Douglas & C. Chapelle (Eds.), *A new decade of language testing research: Selected papers from the 1990 Language Testing Research Colloquium* (pp. 1-22). Alexandria, VA: TESOL.

Chapelle, C. A. (1998). Construct definition and validity inquiry in SLA research. In L. F. Bachman & A. D. Cohen (Eds.), *Interfaces between second language acquisition and language testing research* (pp. 32-70). Cambridge: Cambridge University Press.

Chelimsky, E. (1997). The coming transformations in evaluation. In E. Chelimsky & W. Shadish (Eds.), *Evaluation for the 21st century: A handbook* (pp. 1-26). Thousand Oaks, CA: Sage.

Christie, C. A., & Alkin, M. C. (1999). Further reflections on evaluation misutilization. *Studies in Educational Evaluation, 25*, 1-10.

Chun, M. (2002). Looking where the light is better: A review of the literature on assessing higher education quality. *Peer Review*(Winter/Spring), 16-25.

Cizek, G. (1991). Effusion confusion: A rejoinder to Wiggins. *Phi Delta Kappan, 73*, 150-153.

Cizek, G. (2001). More unintended consequences of high-stakes testing. *Educational Measurement: Issues and Practice, 20*(4), 19-27.

Cizek, G. (2003). Rejoinder. *Educational Measurement: Issues and Practice, 22*(1), 40-44.

Clark, J. L. D. (1988). Validation of a tape-mediated ACTFL/ILR-scale based test of Chinese speaking proficiency. *Language Testing*(5), 197-205.

Clark, J. L. D., & Clifford, R. (1988). The FSI/ACTFL proficiency scales and testing techniques: Development, current status, and needed research. *Studies in Second Language Acquisition, 10*, 129-147.

Cohen, A. (1994). *Assessing language ability in the classroom* (2nd ed.). Boston: Heinle & Heinle.

Coleman, A. (1929). *The teaching of modern foreign languages in the United States*. New York: Macmillan.

College Entrance Examination Board. (1937). *Thiry-seventh annual report of the secretary*. New York: College Entrance Examination Board.

Connelly, M. (1997). Using C-Tests in English with post-graduate students. *English for Specific Purposes, 16*(2), 139-150.

Cook, T. D. (1985). Postpositivist critical multiplism. In R. Shotland & M. Mark (Eds.), *Social science and social policy* (pp. 21-62). Beverly Hills: Sage.

Cook, T. D. (1997). Lessons learned in evaluation over the past 25 years. In E. Chelimsky & W. Shadish (Eds.), *Evaluation for the 21st century: A handbook* (pp. 30-52). Thousand Oaks, CA: Sage.

Cook, T. D., & Campbell, D. T. (1979). *Quasi-experimentation: Design and analysis issues for field settings*. Chicago: Rand McNally.

Cousins, J. B. (1996). Consequences of researcher involvement in participatory evaluation. *Studies in Educational Evaluation, 22*(1), 3-27.

Cousins, J. B., & Earl, L. M. (1995). *Participatory evaluation in education: Studies in evaluation use and organizational learning*. London: Falmer.

Cousins, J. B., & Whitmore, E. (1998). Framing participatory evaluation. In E. Whitmore (Ed.), *Understanding and practicing participatory evaluation* (pp. 5-23). San Francisco: Jossey-Bass.

Crane, C., Maxim, H., & Pfeiffer, P. (2003, November 22). *Linking curriculum-based and curriculum-independent assessment: Articulation and accountability*. Paper presented at the ACTFL/AATG conference, Philadelphia.

Cronbach, L. J. (1963). Course improvement through evaluation. *Teachers College Record, 64*, 672-683.

Cronbach, L. J. (1969). Validation of educational measures, *Proceedings of the 1969 Invitational Conference on Testing Problems: Toward a theory of achievement measurement* (pp. 35-52). Princeton, NJ: Educational Testing Service.

Cronbach, L. J. (1971). Test validation. In R. L. Thorndike (Ed.), *Educational measurement (2nd ed.)* (pp. 443-507). Washington, DC: American Council on Education.

Cronbach, L. J. (1980). Validity on parole: How can we go straight?, *New directions for testing and measurement: Measurement achievement over a decade. Proceedings of the 1979 ETS Invitational Conference.* (pp. 99-108). San Francisco: Jossey-Bass.

Cronbach, L. J. (1982). *Designing evaluations of educational and social programs.* San Francisco: Jossey-Bass.

Cronbach, L. J. (1986). Social inquiry by and for earthlings. In D. W. Fiske & R. Shweder (Eds.), *Metatheory in social science: Pluralisms and subjectivities* (pp. 83-107). Chicago: University of Chicago Press.

Cronbach, L. J. (1988). Five perspectives on validity argument. In H. Wainer & H. Braun (Eds.), *Test validity* (pp. 3-17). Hillsdale, NJ: Lawrence Erlbaum Associates.

Cronbach, L. J. (1989). Construct validation after thirty years. In R. L. Linn (Ed.), *Intelligence: Measurement theory and public policy* (pp. 147-171). Urbana: University of Illinois Press.

Cronbach, L. J. (1990). *Essentials of psychological testing* (5th ed.). New York: Harper & Row.

Cronbach, L. J., & Associates. (1980). *Toward reform of program evaluation.* San Francisco: Jossey-Bass.

Cronbach, L. J., & Meehl, P. E. (1955). Construct validity in psycholgical tests. *Psychological Bulletin, 52,* 281-302.

Crookes, G. (1997). What influences what and how second and foreign language teachers teach? *Modern Language Journal, 81*(1), 67-79.

Cross, K. P. (1999). Assessment to improve college instruction. In S. Messick (Ed.), *Assessment in higher education: Issues of access, quality, student development, and public policy* (pp. 35-45). Mahwah, NJ: Lawrence Erlbaum Associates.

Cumming, A., & Berwick, R. (Eds.). (1995). *Validation in language testing.* Philadelphia: Multilingual Matters.

Cureton, E. E. (1951). Validity. In E. F. Lingquist (Ed.), *Educational measurement* (pp. 621-694). Washington, DC: American Council on Education.

Dandonoli, P., & Henning, G. (1990). An investigation of the construct validity of the ACTFL proficiency guidelines and oral interview procedure. *Foreign Language Annals, 23,* 11-22.

Davidson, F., & Lynch, B. K. (2002). *Testcraft: A teacher's guide to writing and using language test specifications.* New Haven: Yale University Press.

Davies, A. (1990). *Principles of language testing.* Cambridge, MA: Basil Blackwell.

Davis, H. R., & Salasin, S. E. (1975). The utilization of evaluation. In E. L. Streuning & M. A. Guttentag (Eds.), *Handbook of evaluation research* (Vol. 1, pp. 621-666). Beverly Hills, CA: Sage.

Delandshere, G., & Petrosky, A. (1998). Assessment of complex performances: Limitations of key measurement assumptions. *Educational Researcher, 27,* 14-24.

Delett, J. S., Barnhardt, S., & Kevorkian, J. A. (2001). A framework for portfolio assessment in the foreign language classroom. *Foreign Language Annals, 34*(6), 559-568.

Denzin, N. K. (1978). *Sociological methods.* New York: McGraw-Hill.

Developing multiple literacies (2003). Georgetown University German Department. Available: http://www.georgetown.edu/departments/german [2004, January 15].

Dewey, J. (1938). *Logic: The theory of inquiry.* New York: Henry Holt.

Di Pietro, R. J., Lantolf, J. P., & Labarca, A. (1983). The graduate foreign language curriculum. *Modern Language Journal, 67,* 365-373.

Ebel, R. L. (1979). *Essentials of educational measurement* (3rd ed.). Englewood Cliffs, NJ: Prentice-Hall.

Education Sciences Reform, Pub. L. No. 107-279 (2002).

Egbert, M., & Maxim, H. (1998). Incorporating critical thinking and authenticity into business German testing. *Modern Language Journal, 82*(1), 19-32.

Eigler, F. (2001). Designing a third-year German course for a content-oriented, task-based curriculum. *Die Unterrichtspraxis, 34*(2), 107-118.

Eisenhart, M., & Towne, L. (2003). Contestation and change in national policy on "scientifically based" education research. *Educational Researcher, 32*(7), 31-38.

Eisner, E. W. (1999). The uses and limits of performance assessment. *Phi Delta Kappan, 80*(9), 658-660.

Elliot, E. J. (2003). *Assessing education candidate performance: A look at changing practices.* Washington, DC: NCATE.

Embretson, S. E., & Hershberger, S. L. (Eds.). (1999). *The new rules of measurement.* Mahwah, NJ: Lawrence Erlbaum.

Feldt, L. S., & Brennan, R. L. (1989). Reliability. In R. L. Linn (Ed.), *Educational measurement* (Vol. 3, pp. 105-146). New York: Macmillan.

Fetterman, D. M. (Ed.). (1988). *Qualitative approaches to evaluation in education: The silent scientific revolution.* New York: Praeger.

Fetterman, D. M. (1994a). Empowerment evaluation. *Evaluation Practice, 15*(1), 1-15.

Fetterman, D. M. (1994b). Steps of empowerment evaluation: From California to Cape town. *Evaluation and Program Planning, 17*(3), 305-313.

Fetterman, D. M. (2001). *Foundations of empowerment evaluation.* Thousand Oaks, CA: Sage.

Fetterman, D. M., Kaftarian, S., & Wandersman, A. (Eds.). (1996). *Empowerment evaluation: Knowledge and tools for self-assessment and accountability.* Thousand Oaks, CA: Sage.

Finocchiaro, M., & Sako, S. (1983). *Foreign language testing: A practical approach.* New York: Regents Publishing Company.

Foucault, M. (1979). *Discipline and punish: The birth of the prison.* New York: Vintage.

Fox, C. A. (2000). Toward a revised model of TA training. In J. C. Walz (Ed.), *Development and supervision of teaching assistants in foreign languages* (pp. 191-207). Boston, MA: Heinle & Heinle.

Frederick, P. (2002). The need for alternative authentic assessments in online learning environments. *Journal of Instructional Delivery Systems, 16*(1), 17-20.

Frederiksen, J. R., & Collins, A. (1989). A systems approach to educational testing. *Educational Researcher, 18*(9), 27-32.

Freed, B. F. (1984). Proficiency in context: The Pennsylvania experience. In S. J. Savignon & M. S. Berns (Eds.), *Initiatives in communicative language teaching: A book of readings* (pp. 211-240). Reading, MA: Addison-Wesley.

Freed, B. F. (1987). Preliminary impressions of the effects of a proficiency-based language requirement. *Foreign Language Annals, 20*, 139-146.

Freed, B. F. (1992). The foreign-language requirement. In W. Rivers (Ed.), *Teaching languages in college: Curriculum and content* (pp. 41-55). Chicago: National Textbook Company.

Freeman, H. E. (1977). The present status of evaluation research. In M. A. Guttentag & S. Saar (Eds.), *Evaluation studies review annual* (Vol. 2, pp. 17-51). Beverly Hills: Sage.

Freire, P. (1970). *Pedagogy of the oppressed.* New York: Seabury Press.

Fries, C. C. (1945). *Teaching and learning English as a foreign language.* Ann Arbor, Michigan: University of Michigan Press.

Fulcher, G. (1996). Invalidating validity claims for the ACTFL oral rating scale. *System, 24*, 163-172.

Fulcher, G. (1997). An English language placement test: Issues in reliability and validity. *Language Testing, 14*(2), 113-138.

Geertz, C. (Ed.). (1973). *The interpretation of culture.* New York: Basic Books.

Genesee, F., & Upshur, J. A. (1996). *Classroom-based evaluation in second language education.* New York: Cambridge University Press.

Ginther, A., & Stevens, J. (1998). Language background, ethnicity, and the internal construct validity of the Advanced Placement Spanish Language Examination. In A. J. Kunnan (Ed.), *Validation in language assessment: Selected papers from the 17th Language Testing Research Colloquium, Long Beach* (pp. 169-194). Mahwah, NJ: Lawrence Erlbaum Associates.

Glaser, R. (1994). Criterion referenced tests: Part I. Origins. *Educational Measurement: Issues and Practice, 13*(4), 9-11.

Glaser, R., & Silver, E. (1994). Assessment, testing, and instruction: Retrospect and prospect. *Review of Research in Education, 20*, 393-419.

Glisan, E. W. (2002b). NCATE approves new teacher preparation program standards. *Foreign Language Annals, 35*(6), 689, 696.

Glisan, E. W. (2002c). NCATE standards expected to have significant effect on foreign language teacher preparation. *Foreign Language Annals, 35*(2), 249, 253.

Gould, S. J. (1981). *The mismeasure of man*. New York: W. W. Norton.

Gradman, H. L., & Reed, D. J. (1997). Assessment and second language teaching. In K. Bardovi-Harlig & B. Hartford (Eds.), *Beyond methods: Components of second language teacher education* (pp. 198-213). New York: McGraw-Hill.

Graman, T. (1988). Education for humanization: Applying Paulo Freire's pedagogy to learning a second language. *Harvard Educational Review, 58*, 433-448.

Green, B. F. (1995). Comparability of scores from performance assessments. *Educational Measurement: Issues and Practice, 14*(4), 13-15.

Green, D. R. (1998). Consequential aspects of the validity of achievement tests: A publisher's point of view. *Educational Measurement: Issues and Practice, 17*(2), 16-19, 34.

Greene, J. C. (1988). Stakeholder participation and utilization in program evaluation. *Evaluation Review, 12*(2), 91-116.

Greene, J. C., & Abma, T. A. (Eds.). (2001). *Responsive evaluation*. San Francisco: Jossey-Bass.

Gronlund, N. E., & Linn, R. L. (1990). *Measurement and evaluation in teaching* (6th ed.). New York: Macmillan.

Grosse, C. U. (1993). The foreign language methods course. *Modern Language Journal, 77*, 303-312.

Grotjahn, R. (1987). How to construct and evaluate a C-test: A discussion of some problems and some statistical analyses. In R. Grotjahn, C. Klein-Braley, & D. K. Stevenson (Eds.), *Taking their measure: The validity and validation of language tests* (pp. 219-254). Bochum, Germany: Brockmeyer.

Grotjahn, R. (1992a). Der C-test. Einleitende Bemerkungen. In R. Grotjahn (Ed.), *Der C-test: Theoretische Grundlagen und praktische Anwendungen* (Vol. 1, pp. 1-18). Bochum, Germany: Brockmeyer.

Grotjahn, R. (1992b). Der C-Test im Französischen. Quantitative Analysen. In R. Grotjahn (Ed.), *Der C-Test: Theoretische Grundlagen und praktische Anwendungen* (Vol. 1, pp. 205-255). Bochum, Germany: Brockmeyer.

Grotjahn, R. (1996). 'Scrambled' C-Tests: Untersuchungen zum Zusammenhang zwischen Lösungsgüte und sequentialler Textstruktur. In R. Grotjahn (Ed.), *Der C-test: Theoretische Grundlagen und praktische Anwendungen* (Vol. 3, pp. 95-125). Bochum, Germany: Brockmeyer.

Grotjahn, R., Klein-Braley, C., & Raatz, U. (1992). C-Tests in der praktischen Anwendungen. Erfahrungen beim Bundeswettbewerb Fremdsprachen. In R. Grotjahn (Ed.), *Der C-Test: Theoretische Grundlagen und praktische Anwendungen* (Vol. 1, pp. 263-296). Bochum, Germany: Brockmeyer.

Guba, E. G., & Lincoln, Y. S. (1988). Do inquiry paradigms imply inquiry methodologies? In D. M. Fetterman (Ed.), *Qualitative approaches to evaluation in education: The silent scientific revolution* (pp. 89-115). New York: Praeger.

Guba, E. G., & Lincoln, Y. S. (1989). *Fourth generation evaluation*. Thousand Oaks, CA: Sage.

Guilford, J. P. (1946). New standards for test evaluation. *Educational and Psychological Measurement, 6*, 427-439.

Guion, R. M. (1977). Content validity: The source of my discontent. *Applied Psychological Measurement, 1*, 1-10.

Guion, R. M. (1980). On trinitarian doctrines of validity. *Professional Psychology, 11*, 385-398.

Gulliksen, H. (1950). Intrinsic validity. *American Psychologist, 5*, 511-517.

Guntermann, G. (Ed.). (1993). *Developing language teachers for a changing world.* Lincolnwood, IL: National Textbook Company.

Haertel, E. H. (1999). Performance assessment and education reform. *Phi Delta Kappan, 80*(9), 662-672.

Halleck, G. (1995). Assessing oral proficiency: A comparison of holistic and objective measures. *Modern Language Journal, 79*, 223-234.

Hambleton, R. K. (1984). Validating the test scores. In R. A. Berk (Ed.), *A guide to criterion-referenced test construction* (pp. 199-230). Baltimore: Johns Hopkins University Press.

Hambleton, R. K., Swaminathan, H., & Rogers, H. J. (1991). *Fundamentals of item response theory.* Newbury Park , CA: Sage.

Hammadou, J. (1993). Inquiry in language teacher education. In G. Guntermann (Ed.), *Developing language teachers for a changing world* (pp. 76-104). Lincolnwood, IL: National Textbook Company.

Hammerly, H. (1991). Two philosophies of language program and language testing design. In R. V. Teschner (Ed.), *Assessing foreign language proficiency of undergraduates* (pp. 61-78). Boston: Heinle & Heinle.

Haworth, J. G. (Ed.). (1996). *Assessing Graduate and Professional Education: Current Realities, Future Prospects* (Vol. 92). San Francisco: Jossey-Bass Publishers.

Heilenman, L. K. (1991). Self-assessment and placement: A review of the issues. In R. V. Teschner (Ed.), *Assessing foreign language proficiency of undergraduates* (pp. 93-114). Boston: Heinle & Heinle.

Henmon, V. A. C. (Ed.). (1929). *Achievement tests in the modern foreign languages, prepared for the Modern Foreign Language Study and the Canadian Committee on Modern Languages.* New York: Macmillan.

Henmon, V. A. C. (1934). Recent developments in the construction, evaluation, and use of tests in the modern foreign languages. In A. Coleman (Ed.), *Experiments and studies in modern language teaching* (pp. 191-218). Chicago: University of Chicago Press.

Henning, G. (1987). *A guide to language testing: Development, evaluation, research.* New York: Newbury House.

Henning, G. (1990). Priority issues in the assessment of communicative language abilities. *Foreign Language Annals, 23*, 379-384.

Henning, G. (1992). The ACTFL oral proficiency interview: Validity evidence. *System, 20*, 365-372.

Henry, G. T. (2000). Why not use? In V. J. Caracelli & H. Preskill (Eds.), *The Expanding Scope of Evaluation Use* (Vol. 88, pp. 85-98). San Francisco, CA: Jossey-Bass.

Hernon, P., Dugan, R. E., & Schwartz, C. (eds.) (2006). *Revisiting outcomes assessment in higher education*. Westport, CT: Libraries Unlimited.

Higgs, T. (Ed.). (1981). *Curriculum, competence, and the foreign language teacher*. Lincolnwood, IL: National Textbook Company.

Higgs, T. (1984a). Introduction: Language teaching and the quest for the Holy Grail. In T. Higgs (Ed.), *Teaching for proficiency: The organizing principle* (pp. 1-9). Lincolnwood, IL: National Textbook Company.

Higgs, T. (Ed.). (1984b). *Teaching for proficiency: The organizing principle*. Lincolnwood, IL: National Textbook Company.

House, E. R. (1995). Principled evaluation: A critique of the AEA Guiding Principles. In W. R. Shadish, D. L. Newman, M. A. Sheirer, & C. Wye (Eds.), *Guiding principles for evaluators* (pp. 27-34). San Francisco: Jossey-Bass.

House, E. R., & Howe, K. R. (1999). *Values in evaluation and social research*. Thousand Oaks, CA: Sage.

Huba, M. E., & Freed, J. E. (2000). *Learner-centered assessment on college campuses: Shifting the focus from teaching to learning*. Needham Heights: Allyn and Bacon.

Huberman, M., & Cox, P. (1990). Evaluation utilization: Building links between action and reflection. *Studies in Educational Evaluation, 16*, 157-179.

Hudson, T. (1993). Nothing does not equal zero: Problems with applying developmental sequences findings to assessment and pedagogy. *Studies in Second Language Acquisition, 15*, 461-593.

Hudson, T. (2000). *2000 Summer Institute evaluation: Computer-based tests for less commonly taught languages*. Honolulu, HI: Second Language Teaching and Curriculum Center.

Hughes, A. (1989). *Testing for language teachers*. New York: Cambridge University Press.

Huhta, A. (1996). Validating an EFL C-test for students of English philology. In R. Grotjahn (Ed.), *Der C-test: Theoretische Grundlagen und praktische Anwendungen* (Vol. 3, pp. 197-234). Bochum, Germany: Brockmeyer.

Hymes, D. (1967). Models of the interaction of language and social setting. *Journal of social issues, 23*(2), 8-38.

Jaeger, R. M. (1995). Setting standards for complex performances: An iterative, judgmental policy-capturing strategy. *Educational Measurement: Issues and Practice, 14*(4), 16-20.

Jakschik, G. (1994). Der C-Test für Erwachsene Zweitsprachler als Einstufungsinstrument bei der Schulausbildung. In R. Grotjahn (Ed.), *Der C-test: Theoretische Grundlagen und praktische Anwendungen* (Vol. 2, pp. 259-278). Bochum, Germany: Brockmeyer.

James, C. J. (Ed.). (1984). *Foreign language proficiency in the classroom and beyond*. Lincolnwood, IL: National Textbook Company.

Jarvis, G. A., & Taylor, S. V. (1990). Reforming foreign and second language teacher education. In D. W. Birckbichler (Ed.), *New perspectives and new direction in foreign language education* (pp. 159-182). Lincolnwood, IL: National Textbook Company.

Johnson, M. (2001). *The art of non-conversation: A reexamination of the validity of the Oral Proficiency Interview*. New Haven, CT: Yale University Press.

Johnson, R. B. (1998). Toward a theoretical model of evaluation utilization. *Evaluation and Program Planning, 21*(1), 93-110.

Joint Committee on Standards for Educational Evaluation. (1994). *The program evaluation standards: How to assess evaluations of educational programs* (Vol. 2). Thousand Oaks, CA: Sage.

Jonson, J. L., & Plake, B. S. (1998). A historical comparison of validity standards and validity practices. *Educational and Psychological Measurement, 58*, 736-753.

Kane, M. T. (1992). An argument-based approach to validity. *Psychological Bulletin, 112*(3), 527-535.

Kane, M. T. (2001). Current concerns in validity theory. *Journal of Educational Measurement, 38*(4), 319-342.

Kane, M. T., Crooks, T., & Cohen, A. (1999). Validating measures of performance. *Educational Measurement: Issues and Practice, 18*(2), 5-17.

Keeton, M. (1999). Assessing and credentialing learning from prior experience. In S. Messick (Ed.), *Assessment in higher education: Issues of access, quality, student development, and public policy* (pp. 47-56). Mahwah, NJ: Lawrence Erlbaum Associates.

Kenyon, D. (1997). Further research on the efficacy of rater self-training. In A. Huhta, V. Kohonen, L. Kurki-Suonio, & S. Luoma (Eds.), *Current developments and alternatives in language assessment: Proceedings of LTRC 96* (pp. 257-273). Jyvässkylä, Finland: University of Jyvässkylä.

Kenyon, D., & Malabonga, V. (2001). Comparing examinee attitudes toward computer-assisted and other oral proficiency assessments. *Language Learning & Technology, 5*(2), 60-83.

Kenyon, D. M., Malabonga, V., & Carpenter, H. (2001). Response to the Norris commentary. *Language Learning & Technology, 5*(2), 106-108.

Kenyon, D. M., & Tschirner, E. (2000). The rating of direct and semi-direct oral proficiency interviews: Comparing performance at lower proficiency levels. *Modern Language Journal, 84*(1), 85-101.

Khattri, N., Reeve, A., & Kane, M. (1998). *Principles and practices of performance assessment*. Manwah, NJ: Lawrence Earlbaum Associates.

Klein-Braley, C. (1985). A cloze-up on the C-test: A study in the construct validation of authentic tests. *Language Testing, 2*, 76-104.

Klein-Braley, C. (1997). C-Tests in the context of reduced redundancy testing: An appraisal. *Language Testing, 14*(1), 47-84.

Köberl, J., & Sigott, G. (1994). Adjusting C-test difficulty in German. In R. Grotjahn (Ed.), *Der C-test: Theoretische Grundlagen und praktische Anwendungen* (Vol. 2, pp. 179-192). Bochum, Germany: Brockmeyer.

Kondo-Brown, K. (2002). A FACETS analysis of rater bias in measuring Japanese second language writing performance. *Language Testing, 19*(1), 3-32.

Kondo-Brown, K., & Brown, J. D. (2000). *The Japanese placement tests at the University of Hawaii: Applying item response theory.* Honolulu, HI: Second Language Teaching & Curriculum Center.

Kramsch, C., & Kramsch, O. (2000). The avatars of literature in language study. *Modern Language Journal, 84,* 553-573.

Kunnan, A. J. (Ed.). (1998). *Validation in language assessment: Selected papers from the 17th Language Testing Research Colloquium, Long Beach.* Mahwah, NJ: Lawrence Erlbaum.

Kunnan, A. J. (2000). Fairness and justice for all. In A. J. Kunnan (Ed.), *Fairness and validation in language assessment: Selected papers from the 19th Language Testing Research Colloquium, Orlando, Florida* (pp. 1-14). New York: Cambridge University Press.

Kuo, J., & Jiang, X. (1997). Assessing the assessments: The OPI and the SOPI. *Foreign Language Annals, 30*(4), 503-512.

Kymlicka, W. (1991). *Liberalism, community and culture.* New York: Oxford University Press.

Lado, R. (1961). *Language testing: The construction and use of foreign language tests.* London: Longmans.

Lafayette, R. C. (1993). Subject-matter content: What every foreign language teacher needs to know. In G. Guntermann (Ed.), *Developing language teachers for a changing world* (pp. 124-158). Lincolnwood, IL: National Textbook Company.

Lalande, J. (1991). Advancing the case for an advanced methods course. In S. S. Magnan (Ed.), *Challenges in the 1990s for college foreign language programs* (pp. 151-166). Boston, MA: Heinle & Heinle.

Landy, F. J. (1986). Stamp collecting versus science: Validation as hypothesis testing. *American Psychologist, 41,* 1183-1192.

Lane, S., Parke, C. S., & Stone, C. A. (1998). A framework for evaluating the consequences of assessment programs. *Educational Measurement: Issues and Practice, 17*(2), 24-28.

Lantolf, J. P., & Frawley, W. (1985). Oral proficiency testing: A critical analysis. *Modern Language Journal, 69,* 337-345.

Lantolf, J. P., & Sunderman, G. (2001). The struggle for a place in the sun: Rationalizing foreign language study in the twentieth century. *Modern Language Journal, 85,* 5-25.

Lariviere, R. W. (2002). Language curricula in universities: What and how. *Modern Language Journal, 86*(2), 244-246.

Larson, J. W., & Jones, R. L. (1984). Proficiency testing for the other language modalities. In T. Higgs (Ed.), *Teaching for proficiency: The organizing principle* (pp. 113-138). Lincolnwood, IL: National Textbook Company.

Lazaraton, A. (1992). The structural organization of a language interview: A conversation analytic perspective. *System, 20,* 373-386.

Lee, J., F., & VanPatten, B. (1995). *Making communicative language teaching happen.* New York: McGraw-Hill.

Leviton, L. C., & Hughes, E. F. X. (1981). Research on the utilization of evaluations: A review and synthesis. *Evaluation Review, 5*(4), 525-548.

Light, R. (2001). *Making the most of college: Students speak their minds.* Cambridge, MA: Harvard University Press.

Linacre, J. M. (1989). *Many-facet Rasch measurement.* Chicago: MESA Press.

Linacre, J. M. (1996). *A user's guide to Facets Rasch Measurement Computer Program.* Chicago: MESA Press.

Linacre, J. M. (1998). *FACETS Computer program for many-facet Rasch Measurement.* Chicago: Mesa Press.

Lincoln, Y. S. (2001). Varieties of validity: Quality in qualitative research. In J. C. Smart (Ed.), *Higher education: Handbook of theory and research* (Vol. XVI, pp. 25-72). New York: Agathon Press.

Linn, R. L. (Ed.). (1989). *Educational Measurement* (3rd ed.). New York: American Council on Education and Macmillan.

Linn, R. L. (1997). Evaluating the validity of assessments: The consequences of use. *Educational Measurement: Issues and Practice, 16*(2), 14-16.

Linn, R. L. (1998). Partitioning responsibility for the evaluation of the consequences of assessment programs. *Educational Measurement: Issues and Practice, 17*(2), 28-30.

Linn, R. L., Baker, E. L., & Dunbar, S. D. (1991). Complex, performance-based assessment: Expectations and validation criteria. *Educational Researcher, 20*(8), 15-21.

Liskin-Gasparro, J. E. (1984a). The ACTFL proficiency guidelines: A historical perspective. In T. Higgs (Ed.), *Teaching for proficiency: The organizing principle* (pp. 11-42). Lincolnwood, IL: National Textbook Company.

Liskin-Gasparro, J. E. (1984b). The ACTFL proficiency guidelines: Gateway to testing and curriculum. *Foreign Language Annals, 17*(5), 475-489.

Liskin-Gasparro, J. E. (1995). Practical approaches to outcomes assessment: The undergraduate major in foreign languages and literatures. *ADFL Bulletin, 26*(2), 21-27.

Livingston, S. A., & Zieky, M. J. (1982). *Passing scores: A manual for setting standards of performance on educational and occupational tests.* Princeton, NJ: Educational Testing Service.

Lodeman, A. (1887). The modern languages in university, college and secondary schools. *Modern Language Notes, 1,* 97-109.

Loevinger, J. (1957). Objective tests as instruments of psychological theory. *Psychological Reports, 3*, 635-694.

Long, M., Doughty, C., Kim, Y., Lee, J., & Lee, Y. (2003). *Task-based language teaching: A demonstration module*. Honolulu, HI: Second Language Teaching & Curriculum Center.

Loomis, S. C., & Bourque, M. L. (2001). From tradition to innovation: Standard setting and the National Assessment of Educational Progress. In G. Cizek (Ed.), *Setting performance standards: Concepts, methods, and perspectives* (pp. 175-217). Mahwah, NJ: Lawrence Erlbaum Associates.

Lopez, C. (1998). Assessment of student learning. *Liberal Education, 84*(3), 36-43.

Lowe, P. J. (1988). The unassimilated history. In P. J. Lowe & C. Stansfield (Eds.), *Second language proficiency assessment* (pp. 11-51). Englewood Cliffs, NJ: Prentice Hall Regents.

Lozano, A. S., Sung, H., Padilla, A. M., & Silva, D. M. (2002). Evaluation of professional development for language teachers in California. *Foreign Language Annals, 35*(2), 161-170.

Lundeberg, O. K. (1929). Recent developments in audition-speech tests. *Modern Language Journal, 144*(3), 193-202.

Lynch, B. K. (1996). *Language program evaluation: Theory and practice*. New York: Cambridge University Press.

Mabry, L. (Ed.). (1997). *Evaluation and the postmodern dilemma*. Greenwich, CT: JAI.

Madaus, G. F. (1990). *Testing as a social technology*. Boston: Boston College.

Madaus, G. F., & O'Dwyer, L. M. (1999). A short history of performance assessment. *Phi Delta Kappan, 80*(9), 688-695.

Magnan, S. (1987). Rater reliability of the ACTFL oral proficiency interview. *Canadian Modern Language Review, 43*, 525-537.

Magnan, S. S. (1991). Just do it: Directing TAs toward task-based and process-oriented testing. In R. V. Teschner (Ed.), *Assessing foreign language proficiency of undergraduates* (pp. 135-161). Boston: Heinle & Heinle.

Maki, P. (2002). Using multiple assessment methods to explore student learning and development inside and outside of the classroom. *NetResults*(January), Retrieved January 8, 2003, from http://www.naspa.org/NetResults/article.cfm?ID=2558.

Maki, P., & Borkowski, N. (eds.) (2006). *The assessment of doctoral education: Emerging criteria and new models for improving outcomes*. Sterling, VA: Stylus Publishing.

Mason, K. (2000). Beyond the methods course: Designing a graduate seminar in foreign language program direction. In J. C. Walz (Ed.), *Development and supervision of teaching assistants in foreign languages* (pp. 113-134). Boston, MA: Heinle & Heinle.

Maxim, H. (2002, November 8). *Developing a curriculum-based approach to oral assessment*. Paper presented at the Annual Meeting of the German Section of the

American Association of University Supervisors and Coordinators, Ann Arbor, MI.

McCarthy, A., Scott, K., Shiba, K., & Thornton, P. (1998). *Tools for the articulation of Japanese language instruction: Standards, a curriculum framework, benchmarks, and sample assessments*. Minneapolis, MN: University of Minnesota, The Center for Advanced Research on Language Acquisition.

McCollum Lozier, V., & Chalhoub-Deville, M. (1997). *Preliminary item response theory analysis of the University of Minnesota CLA Language Proficiency Tests in French, German, and Spanish*. Minneapolis, MN: University of Minnesota, The Center for Advanced Research on Language Acquisition.

McMillan, J. H. (2003). Understanding and improving teachers' classroom assessment decision making: Implications for theory and practice. *Educational Measurement: Issues and Practice, 22*(4), 34-43.

McNamara, T. (1996). *Measuring second language performance*. New York: Longman.

McNamara, T. (2000). *Language Testing*. Oxford: Oxford University Press.

Mehrens, W. A. (1992). Using performance assessment for accountability purposes. *Educational Measurement: Issues and Practice, 11*(1), 3-9, 20.

Mehrens, W. A. (1997). The consequences of consequential validity. *Educational Measurement: Issues and Practice, 16*(2), 15-18.

Mehrens, W. A. (1998). Consequences of assessment: What is the evidence. *Educational Policy Analysis Archives, 6*(13), Available at: http://olam.ed.asu.edu/epaa/v6n13.html.

Mellow, J. D. (1996). On the primacy of theory in applied studies: A critique of Pienemann and Johnston (1987). *Second Language Research, 12*, 304-318.

Messick, S. (1975). The standard problem: Meaning and values in measurement and evaluation. *American Psychologist, 30*, 955-966.

Messick, S. (1980). Test validity and the ethics of assessment. *American Psychologist, 35*, 1012-1027.

Messick, S. (1981). Constructs and their vicissitudes in educational and psychological measurement. *Psychological Bulletin, 89*, 575-588.

Messick, S. (1989). Validity. In R. L. Linn (Ed.), *Educational Measurement* (3rd ed., pp. 13-103). New York: American Council on Education and Macmillan.

Messick, S. (1994). The interplay of evidence and consequences in the validation of performance assessments. *Educational Researcher, 23*(2), 13-23.

Messick, S. (1995). Standards of validity and validity of standards in performance assessment. *Educational Measurement: Issues and Practice, 14*(4), 5-8.

Miller, M., & Legg, S. (1993). Alternative assessment in a high-stakes environment. *Educational Measurement: Issues and Practice, 12*, 9-15.

Milleret, M., Stansfield, C., & Kenyon, D. (1991). The validity of the Portuguese Speaking Test for use in a summer study abroad program. *Hispania, 74*, 197-207.

Mishler, E. G. (1990). Validation in inquiry-guided research. *Harvard Educational Review, 60*, 415-442.

Mitzel, H. C., Lewis, D. M., Patz, R. J., & Green, D. R. (2001). The bookmark procedure: Psychological perspectives. In G. Cizek (Ed.), *Setting performance standards: Concepts, methods, and perspectives* (pp. 249-281). Mahwah, NJ: Lawrence Erlbaum Associates.

Mohan, R., Bernstein, D. J., & Whitsett, M. D. (Eds.). (2002). *Responding to sponsors and stakeholders in complex evaluation environments*. San Francisco: Jossey-Bass.

Morrow, K. (1984). Testing performance in oral interaction. In S. J. Savignon & M. S. Berns (Eds.), *Initiatives in communicative language teaching: A book of readings* (pp. 203-209). Reading, MA: Addison-Wesley.

Moss, P. A. (1992). Shifting conceptions of validity in educational measurement: Implications for performance assessment. *Review of Educational Research, 62*(3), 229-258.

Moss, P. A. (1994). Can there be validity without reliability? *Educational Researcher, 23*(2), 5-12.

Moss, P. A. (1996). Enlarging the dialogue in educational measurement: Voices from interpretive research traditions. *Educational Researcher, 25*(1), 20-28.

Moss, P. A. (1998). The role of consequences in validity theory. *Educational Measurement: Issues and Practice, 17*(2), 6-12.

Moss, P. A. (2003). Reconceptualizing validity for classroom assessment. *Educational Measurement: Issues and Practice, 22*(4), 13-25.

Moss, P. A., Beck, J. S., Ebbs, C., Matson, B., Muchmore, J., Steele, D., Taylor, C., & Herter, R. (1992). Portfolios, accountability, and an interpretive approach to validity. *Educational Measurement: Issues and Practice, 11*(3), 12-21.

Moss, P. A., & Schutz, A. (1999). Risking frankness in educational assessment. *Phi Delta Kappan, 80*, 680-687.

Muirhead, B. (2002). Relevant assessment strategies for online colleges and universities. *USDLA Journal, 16*(2), Available at:
http://www.usdla.org/html/journal/FEB02_Issue/article04.html.

Munby, J. L. (1978). *Communicative syllabus design*. Cambridge: Cambridge University Press.

Murphy, J. A. (1991). The graduate teaching assistant in an age of standards. In S. S. Magnan (Ed.), *Challenges in the 1990s for college foreign language programs* (pp. 129-150). Boston, MA: Heinle & Heinle.

Musumeci, D. (1997). *Breaking tradition: An exploration of the historical relationship between theory and practice in second language teaching*. New York: McGraw-Hill.

Muyskens, J. A. (1984). Preservice and inservice teacher training: Focus on proficiency. In T. Higgs (Ed.), *Teaching for proficiency: The organizing principle* (pp. 179-200). Lincolnwood, IL: National Textbook Company.

National Research Council. (2001). *Knowing what students know*. Washington, DC: National Academy Press.

National Standards in Foreign Language Education Project. (1996). *Standards for foreign language learning: Preparing for the 21st century.* New York: National Standards in Foreign Language Education Project.

NCATE. (2002). *Professional standards for the accreditation of schools, colleges, and departments of education.* Washington, DC: NCATE.

Nitko, A. J. (1995). Is the curriculum a reasonable basis for assessment reform? *Educational Measurement: Issues and Practice, 14*(3), 5-10.

Nitko, A. J. (1996). *Educational assessment of students.* Englewood Cliffs, NJ: Prentice-Hall.

Nitko, A. J. (2001). Conceptual frameworks to accommodate the validation of rapidly changing requirements for assessments. In D. Scott (Ed.), *Curriculum and assessment* (pp. 143-163). Westport, CT: Ablex.

No Child Left Behind, Pub. L. No. 107-279 (2001).

Norris, J. M. (1996). *A validation study of the ACTFL Guidelines and the German Speaking Test.* Unpublished master's thesis. Honolulu: University of Hawaii.

Norris, J. M. (1997a). The German Speaking Test: Utility and caveats. *Die Unterrichtspraxis, 30*(2), 148-158.

Norris, J. M. (1997b). Native speaker judgments as indicators of L2 oral proficiency: Redefining the role of the native speaker in proficiency guidelines. *University of Hawai'i Working Papers in ESL, 16*(1), 47-95.

Norris, J. M. (2000). Purposeful language assessment. *English Teaching Forum, 38*(1), 18-23.

Norris, J. M. (2001a). Concerns with computer-adaptive oral proficiency assessment. *Language Learning & Technology, 5*(2), 99-105.

Norris, J. M. (2001b). Use of address terms on the German Speaking Test. In K. Rose & G. Kasper (Eds.), *Pragmatics in language teaching* (pp. 248-282). New York: Cambridge University Press.

Norris, J. M. (2006a). Assessing foreign language learning and learners: From measurement constructs to educational uses. In H. Byrnes, H. Weger-Guntharp, & K. Sprang (Eds.), *GURT 2005: Educating for Advanced Foreign Language Capacities: Constructs, Curriculum, Instruction, Assessment* (pp. 167-187). Washington, DC: Georgetown University Press.

Norris, J. M. (2006b). The why (and how) of student learning outcomes assessment in college FL education. *Modern Language Journal, 90*(4), 590-597.

Norris, J. M., Brown, J. D., Hudson, T. D., & Yoshioka, J. K. (1998). *Designing second language performance assessment.* Honolulu: University of Hawai'i Press.

Norris, J. M., & Ortega, L. (2003). Defining and measuring SLA. In C. J. Doughty & M. H. Long (Eds.), *Handbook of second language acquisition* (pp. 717-761). Malden, MA: Blackwell.

Norris, J. M., Ortega, L., & Mislevy, R. (2003, March 24). *Seeking design solutions for measurement problems in instructed SLA research.* Paper presented at the American Association for Applied Linguistics conference, Arlington, Virginia.

Norris, J. M., & Pfeiffer, P. (2003). Exploring the use and usefulness of ACTFL Guidelines oral proficiency ratings in college foreign language departments. *Foreign Language Annals, 36*, 572-581.

Norton, B. (2000). Writing assessment: Language, meaning, and marking memoranda. In A. J. Kunnan (Ed.), *Fairness and validation in language assessment: Selected papers from the 19th Language Testing Research Colloquium, Orlando, Florida* (pp. 20-29). New York: Cambridge University Press.

Nuessel, F. (1991). Foreign language testing today: Issues in language program direction. In R. V. Teschner (Ed.), *Assessing foreign language proficiency of undergraduates* (pp. 1-20). Boston: Heinle & Heinle.

Oller, J. W., Jr. (1971). Dictation as a device for testing foreign language proficiency. *English Language Teaching, 25*, 254-159.

Omaggio, A. C. (1984). The proficiency-oriented classroom. In T. Higgs (Ed.), *Teaching for proficiency: The organizing principle* (pp. 43-84). Lincolnwood, IL: National Textbook Company.

Omaggio, A. C. (Ed.). (1985). *Proficiency, curriculum, articulation: The ties that bind.* Middlebury, VT: Northeast Conference on the Teaching of Foreign Languages.

Omaggio, A. C. (1986). *Teaching language in context: Proficiency-oriented instruction.* Boston: Heinle & Heinle.

Omaggio-Hadley, A. C. (2001). *Teaching language in context* (3rd ed.). Boston: Heinle & Heinle.

Ortega, L. (1999). Language and equality: Ideological and structural constraints in foreign language education in the U.S. In T. Huebner & K. A. Davis (Eds.), *Sociopolitical perspectives in language policy and planning in the USA* (pp. 243-266). Amsterdam: John Benjamins.

Patton, M. Q. (1978). *Utilization-focused evaluation.* Beverly Hills, CA: Sage.

Patton, M. Q. (1986). *Utilization-focused evaluation* (Second ed.). Beverly Hills, CA: Sage.

Patton, M. Q. (1997). *Utilization-focused evaluation: The new century text* (Third ed.). Thousand Oaks, CA: SAGE Publications, Inc.

Patton, M. Q. (1998). Discovering process use. *Evaluation, 4*(2), 225-233.

Peterson, M. W., & Einarson, M. K. (2001). What are colleges doing about student assessment? *Journal of Higher Education, 72*(6), 629-669.

Pfeiffer, P. (2002). Preparing graduate students to teach language and literature in a foreign language department. *ADFL Bulletin, 34*, 11-14.

Phelps, R. P. (1998). The demand for standardized student testing. *Educational Measurement: Issues and Practice, 17*(3), 5-23.

Phillips, J. K. (2003). Implications of language education policies for language study in schools and universities. *Modern Language Journal, 87*(4), 579-586.

Pienemann, M. (1998). *Language processing and second language development: Processability theory.* Philadelphia: John Benjamins.

Pienemann, M., Johnston, M., & Brindley, G. (1988). Constructing an acquisition-based procedure for second language assessment. *Studies in Second Language Acquisition, 10,* 217-243.

Popham, W. J. (1981). *Modern educational measurement.* Englewood Cliffs, NJ: Prentice-Hall.

Popham, W. J. (1990). *Modern educational measurement* (2nd ed.). Englewood Cliffs, NJ: Prentice-Hall.

Popham, W. J. (1994). The instructional consequences of criterion-referenced clarity. *Educational Measurement: Issues and Practice, 13*(4), 15-18.

Popham, W. J. (1997). Consequential validity: Right concern--wrong concept. *Educational Measurement: Issues and Practice, 16*(2), 9-13.

Popham, W. J. (1999). Where large scale assessment is heading and why it shouldn't. *Educational Measurement: Issues and Practice, 18*(3), 13-17.

Popham, W. J. (2000). *Modern educational measurement: Practical guidelines for educational leaders* (Third ed.). Boston: Allyn & Bacon.

Popham, W. J. (2003a, April). *Curriculum, instruction, and assessment: Amiable allies or phony friends.* Paper presented at the National Council on Measurement in Education, Chicago, Illinois.

Popham, W. J. (2003b). Seeking redemption for our psychometric sins. *Educational Measurement: Issues and Practice, 22*(1), 45-48.

Popper, K. R. (1962). *Conjectures and refutations: The growth of scientific knowledge.* New York: Harper & Row.

Posse, M., Shifman, R., & Sweet., G. (1999). *Tools for the articulation of Russian language instruction: Standards, a curriculum framework, sample assessments, and teacher resources.* Minneapolis, MN: University of Minnesota, The Center for Advanced Research on Language Acquisition.

Preskill, H., & Torres, R. T. (2000). The learning dimension of evaluation use. In V. J. Caracelli & H. Preskill (Eds.), *The Expanding Scope of Evaluation Use* (pp. 25-37). San Francisco, CA: Jossey-Bass.

Quellmalz, E. (1991). Developing criteria for performance assessments: The missing link. *Applied Measurement in Education, 4,* 319-331.

Rawls, J. (1971). *A theory of justice.* Cambridge, MA: Belknap.

Raymond, M. R., & Reid, J. B. (2001). Who made thee a judge? Selecting and training participants for standard setting. In G. Cizek (Ed.), *Setting performance standards: Concepts, methods, and perspectives* (pp. 119-157). Mahwah, NJ: Lawrence Erlbaum Associates.

Reason, P. (Ed.). (1988). *Human inquiry in action: Developments in new paradigm research.* London: Sage.

Reckase, M. (1998). Consequential validity from the test developer's perspective. *Educational Measurement: Issues and Practice, 17*(2), 13-16.

Reichardt, C. S., & Cook, T. D. (1979). Beyond qualitative *versus* quantitative methods. In T. D. Cook & C. S. Reichardt (Eds.), *Qualitative and quantitative methods in evaluation research.* Beverly Hills, CA: Sage.

Reid, W. (1994). Reframing the epistemological debate. In E. Sherman & W. Reid (Eds.), *Qualitative research in social work.* New York: Columbia University Press.

Reid, W., & Hanrahan, P. (1982). Recent evaluations of social work: Grounds for optimism. *Social Work, 27,* 328-340.

Report of the Task Force on the Commonly Taught Languages. (1978). *ADFL Bulletin, 10*(1), 1-7.

Report to the president from the president's Commission on Foreign Language and International Studies. (1980). *Modern Language Journal, 64,* 9-57.

Rivers, W. (1992a). The program director or coordinator, the LTCS, and the training of college language instructors. In W. Rivers (Ed.), *Teaching languages in college: Curriculum and content* (pp. 295-319). Chicago: National Textbook Company.

Rivers, W. (Ed.). (1992b). *Teaching languages in college: Curriculum and content.* Chicago: National Textbook Company.

Rivers, W., Dell'Orto, K. M., & Dell'Orto, V. (1988). *Teaching German: A practical guide.* Lincolnwood, IL: National Textbook Company.

Rog, D. J., & Fournier, D. (Eds.). (1997). *Progress and guture directions in evaluation: Perspectives on theory, practice, and methods.* San Francisco: Jossey-Bass.

Rogers, P., Hacsi, T. A., Petrosino, A., & Huebner, T. A. (Eds.). (2000). *Program theory in evaluation: Challenges and opportunities.* San Francisco: Jossey-Bass.

Rorty, R. (1979). *Philosophy and the morror of nature.* Princeton, NJ: Princeton University Press.

Rorty, R. (Ed.). (1982). *Consequences of pragmatism.* Minneapolis: University of Minnesota Press.

Rossi, P. H., Freeman, H. W., & Lipsey, M. W. (1999). *Evaluation: A systematic approach* (6th ed.). Thousand Oaks, CA: Sage.

Ryan, K. E., & DeStefano, L. (Eds.). (2000). *Evaluation as democratic process: Promoting inclusion, dialogue, and deliberation.* San Francisco: Jossey-Bass.

Ryan, K. E., & Johnson, T. D. (2000). Democratizing evaluation: Meanings and methods from practice. In K. E. Ryan & L. DeStefano (Eds.), *Evaluation as democratic process: Promoting inclusion, dialogue, and deliberation* (pp. 39-50). San Francisco: Jossey-Bass.

Salaberry, R. (2000). Revising the revised format of the ACTFL Oral Proficiency Interview. *Language Testing, 17,* 289-310.

Sasaki, M. (1996). *Second language proficiency, foreign language aptitude, and intelligence: Quantitative and qualitative analyses.* New York: Peter Lang.

Savignon, S. J., & Berns, M. S. (Eds.). (1984). *Initiatives in communicative language teaching: A book of readings.* Reading, MA: Addison-Wesley.

Schafer, W. D., & Lissitz, R. W. (1987). Measurement training for school personnel: Recommendations and reality. *Journal of Teacher Education*(May/June), 57-63.

Schmitt, N. (1999). The relationship between TOEFL vocabulary items and meaning, association, collocation and word-class knowledge. *Language Testing, 16*(2), 189-216.

Schrier, L. L. (1993). Prospects for the professionalization of foreign language teaching. In G. Guntermann (Ed.), *Developing language teachers for a changing world* (pp. 105-123). Lincolnwood, IL: National Textbook Company.

Schulz, R. A. (1988). Proficiency-based foreign language requirements: A plan for action. *ADFL Bulletin, 19*(2), 24-28.

Schulz, R. A. (2002). Changing perspectives in foreign language education: Where do we come from? Where are we going? *Foreign Language Annals, 35*(3), 285-292.

Schwandt, T. A. (1997). The landscape of values in evaluation: Charted terrain and unexplored territory. In D. J. Rog & D. Fournier (Eds.), *Progress and future directions in evaluation: Perspectives on theory, practice, and methods* (pp. 25-39). San Francisco: Jossey-Bass.

Scriven, M. (1967). The methodology of evaluation. In R. W. Tyler, R. M. Gagne, & M. Scriven (Eds.), *Perspectives of curriculum evaluation* (pp. 39-83). Chicago: Rand McNally.

Scriven, M. (1969). An introduction to meta-evaluation. *Educational Product Report, 2*(5).

Scriven, M. (1972). Objectivity and subjectivity in educational research. In L. G. Thomas (Ed.), *Philosophical redirection of educational research*. Chicago: National Society for the Study of Education.

Scriven, M. (1991). *Evaluation thesaurus*. Newbury Park, CA: Sage.

Scriven, M. (1997). Truth and objectivity in evaluation. In E. Chelimsky & W. Shadish (Eds.), *Evaluation for the 21st century: A handbook* (pp. 477-500). Thousand Oaks, CA: Sage.

Shadish, W., Cook, T. D., & Leviton, L. C. (1991). *Foundations of program evaluation: Theories of practice*. Newbury Park, CA: Sage.

Shanahan, D. (1997). Articulating the relationship between language, literature, and culture: Toward a new agenda for foreign language teaching and research. *Modern Language Journal, 81*(2), 164-174.

Shavelson, R., & Huang, L. (2003). Responding responsibly to the frenzy to assess learning in higher education. *Change, 35*(1), 10-19.

Shavelson, R. J., & Webb, N. M. (1991). *Generalizability theory: A primer*. Newbury Park, CA: Sage.

Shaw, I. F. (1999). *Qualitative evaluation*. Thousand Oaks, CA: Sage.

Shepard, L. A. (1993). Evaluating test validity. *Review of Research in Education, 19*, 405-450.

Shepard, L. A. (1997). The centrality of test use and consequences for test validity. *Educational Measurement: Issues and Practice, 16*(2), 5-8, 13, 24.

Shepard, L. A. (2000). The role of assessment in a learning culture. *Educational Researcher, 29*(7), 4-14.

Shohamy, E. (1990). Language testing priorities: A different perspective. *Foreign Language Annals, 23*, 385-394.

Shohamy, E. (1992). New modes of assessment: The connection between testing and learning. In E. Shohamy & A. R. Walton (Eds.), *Language assessment for feedback: Testing and other strategies* (pp. 7-28). Dubuque, Iowa: Kendall/Hunt.

Shohamy, E. (1994). The validity of direct versus semi-direct oral tests. *Language Testing, 11*, 99-123.

Shohamy, E. (1998). Evaluation of learning outcomes in second language acquisition: A multiplism perspective. In H. Byrnes (Ed.), *Learning foreign and second languages: Perspectives in research and scholarship* (pp. 238-261). New York: Modern Language Association.

Shulha, L. M., & Cousins, J. B. (1997). Evaluation use: Theory, research, and practice since 1986. *Evaluation Practice, 18*(3), 195-208.

Spolsky, B. (1973). What does it mean to know a language? Or how do you get someone to perform his competence? In J. W. Oller, Jr. & J. Richards (Eds.), *Focus on the learner* (pp. 164-176). Rowley, MA: Newbury House.

Spolsky, B. (1985). The limits of authenticity in language testing. *Language Testing, 2*, 31-40.

Spolsky, B. (1995). *Measured words*. Oxford: Oxford University Press.

Spolsky, B. (2000). Language testing in *the Modern Language Journal*. *Modern Language Journal, 84*(4), 536-552.

Stake, R. E. (1980). Program evaluation: Particularly responsive evaluation. In W. B. Dockrell & D. Hamilton (Eds.), *Rethinking educational research* (pp. 72-87). London: Hodder & Stoughton.

Stake, R. E. (1991). Retrospective on "The countenance of educational evaluation". In M. McLaughlin & D. Phillips (Eds.), *Evaluation and education at quarter century*. Chicago: University of Chicago Press.

Stake, R. E. (1997). Advocacy in evaluation: A necessary evil? In E. Chelimsky & W. Shadish (Eds.), *Evaluation for the 21st century: A handbook* (pp. 470-476). Thousand Oaks, CA: Sage.

Stake, R. E. (2000). A modest commitment to the promotion of democracy. In K. E. Ryan & L. DeStefano (Eds.), *Evaluation as democratic process: Promoting inclusion, dialogue, and deliberation* (pp. 97-106). San Francisco: Jossey-Bass.

Stansfield, C. (1996). *SOPI test development handbook*. Washington, DC: Center for Applied Linguistic.

Stansfield, C., & Kenyon, D. (1992). Research on the comparability of the oral proficiency interview and the simulated oral proficiency interview. *System, 20*, 347-364.

Stansfield, C., Kenyon, D., Paiva, R., Doyle, F., Ulsh, I., & Cowles, M. (1990). The development and validation of the Portuguese Speaking Test. *Hispania, 72*, 641-651.

Stenhouse, L. (1993). The teacher as researcher. In M. Hammersley (Ed.), *Controversies in classroom research*. Buckingham: Open University Press.

Stevenson, D. K. (1985). Authenticity, validity, and a tea party. *Language Testing, 2*, 40-47.

Stiggins, R. (1987). Design and development of performance assessments. *Educational Measurement: Issues and Practice, 6*(3), 33-42.

Stiggins, R. J. (1988). Revitalizing classroom assessment: The highest instructional priority. *Phi Delta Kappan, 69*, 363-368.

Stiggins, R. J. (1999). Evaluating classroom assessment training in teacher education programs. *Educational Measurement: Issues and Practice, 18*(1), 23-27.

Stiggins, R. J. (2001). The unfulfilled promise of classroom assessment. *Educational Measurement: Issues and Practice, 20*(3), 5-15.

Stiggins, R. J., & Bridgeford, N. J. (1985). The ecology of classroom assessment. *Journal of educational measurement, 22*, 271-286.

Stiggins, R. J., & Conklin, N. F. (1992). *In teachers' hands: Investigating the practice of classroom assessment.* Albany, NY: State University of New York Press.

Stronach, I., & MacLure, M. (1997). *Educational research undone: The postmodern embrace.* Philadelphia: Open University Press.

Stufflebeam, D. (1966). A depth study of the evaluation requirement. *Theory Into Practice, 5*, 121-134.

Stufflebeam, D. L. (2001). *Evaluation models.* San Francisco: Jossey-Bass.

Suskie, L. (Ed.). (2000). *Assessment to promote deep learning.* Washington, DC: American Association for Higher Education.

Swain, M. (1984). Large-scale communicative language testing: A case study. In S. J. Savignon & M. S. Berns (Eds.), *Initiatives in communicative language teaching: A book of readings* (pp. 185-201). Reading, MA: Addison-Wesley.

Tabachnick, B. G., & Fidell, L. S. (1996). *Using multivariate statistics* (3rd ed.). New York: HarperCollins.

Taleporos, E. (1998). Consequential validity: A practitioner's perspective. *Educational Measurement: Issues and Practice, 17*(2), 20-23, 34.

Tedick, D. J. (Ed.). (1997). *Proficiency-oriented language instruction and assessment: A curriculum handbook for teachers.* Minneapolis, MN: University of Minnesota, The Center for Advanced Research on Language Acquisition.

Tedick, D. J. (Ed.). (2002). *Proficiency-oriented language instruction and assessment: A curriculum handbook for teachers (Rev Ed.).* Minneapolis, MN: University of Minnesota, The Center for Advanced Research on Language Acquisition.

Tedick, D. J., & Walker, C. L. (1994). Second language teacher education: The problems that plague us. *Modern Language Journal, 78*, 300-312.

Tedick, D. J., & Walker, C. L. (1995). From theory to practice: How we prepare teachers for second language classrooms. *Foreign Language Annals, 28*, 499-517.

Tenopyr, M. L. (1977). Content-construct confusion. *Personnel Psychology, 30*, 47-54.

Tenopyr, M. L. (1996). *Construct-consequences confusion.* Paper presented at the Annual meeting of the Society for Industrial and Organizational Psychology, San Diego.

Terry, R. M. (2000). Improving inter-rater reliability in scoring tests in multisection courses. In J. C. Walz (Ed.), *Development and supervision of teaching assistants in foreign languages* (pp. 229-262). Boston, MA: Heinle & Heinle.

Teschner, R. V. (1987). A profile of the specialization and expertise of lower division foreign language program directors in American universities. *Modern Language Journal, 71*, 28-35.

Teschner, R. V. (Ed.). (1991). *Assessing foreign language proficiency of undergraduates.* Boston: Heinle & Heinle.

The College Board. (1996). *Articulation and achievement: Connecting standards, performance, and assessment in foreign language.* New York: College Entrance Examination Board.

The quiet revolution in language teaching: Still growing, still exciting, after all these years. (2002). *Foreign Language Annals, 35*(5), 581, 589-593.

Thompson, I. (1996). Assessing foreign language skills: Data from Russian. *Modern Language Journal, 80*(1), 47-65.

Thorndike, E. L. (1904). *Introduction to the theory of mental and social measurements.* New York: Teachers College.

Torres, R. T., & Preskill, H. (1999). Ethical dimensions of stakeholder participation and evaluation use. In J. L. Fitzpatrick & M. Morris (Eds.), *Current and emerging ethical challenges in evaluation* (pp. 57-66). San Francisco: Jossey-Bass.

Toulmin, S. (1990). *Cosmopolis: The hidden agenda of modernity.* New York: Free Press.

Traub, R. E. (1994). *Reliability for the social sciences: Theory and applications.* Thousand Oaks, CA: Sage.

Tschirner, E., & Heilenman, L. K. (1998). Reasonable expectations: Oral proficiency goals for Intermediate-level students of German. *Modern Language Journal, 82*(2), 147-158.

Tulou, G., & Pettigrew, F. (1999). Performance assessment for language students. In M. Kassen (Ed.), *Language learners of tomorrow* (pp. 189-231). Lincolnwood, IL: National Textbook Co.

Valette, R. M. (1992). Testing as a guide to student and teacher: Placement, achievement, proficiency. In W. Rivers (Ed.), *Teaching languages in college: Curriculum and content* (pp. 199-223). Chicago: National Textbook Company.

van den Branden, K., DePauw, V., & Gysen, S. (2002). A computerized task-based test of second language Dutch for vocational training purposes. *Language Testing, 19*(4), 438-452.

van Ek, J. A. (1976). *Significance of the threshold level in the early teaching of modern languages.* Strasbourg: Council of Europe.

Vanderplaat, M. (1995). Beyond technique: Issues in evaluating for empowerment. *Evaluation, 1*(1), 81-96.

Vanderplaat, M. (1997). Emancipatory politics, critical evaluation, and government policy. *Canadian Journal of Program Evaluation, 12*(2), 143-162.

VanValkenburg, J., & Arnett, C. (2000). The professionalization of teaching assistants: Can it be accomplished? *Die Unterrichtspraxis, 33*(1), 1-6.

Weir, C. (1990). *Communicative language testing.* New York: Prentice Hall.

Weiss, C. H. (1980). Knowledge creep and decision accretion. *Knowledge, Creation, Diffusion, Utilisation, 1*(3), 381-404.

Weiss, C. H. (1998a). *Evaluation* (2nd ed.). Upper Saddle River, NJ: Prentice Hall.

Weiss, C. H. (1998b). Have we learned anything new about the use of evaluation? *American Journal of Evaluation, 19*(1), 21-33.

Whitmore, E. (Ed.). (1998). *Understanding and practicing participatory evaluation.* San Francisco: Jossey-Bass.

Wiggins, G. (1989). A true test: Toward more authentic and equitable assessment. *Phi Delta Kappan, 70,* 703-713.

Wiggins, G. (1993a). *Assessing student performance: Exploring the purpose and limits of testing.* San Francisco: Jossey-Bass.

Wiggins, G. (1993b). Assessment: Authenticity, context, and validity. *Phi Delta Kappan, 75,* 200-214.

Wiggins, G. (1998). *Educative assessment: Designing assessments to inform and improve student performance.* San Francisco: Jossey-Bass.

Wiggins, G., & McTighe, J. (1998). *Understanding by design.* Alexandria, VA: Association for Supervision and Curriculum Development.

Wiley, D. E. (1991). Test validity and invalidity reconsidered. In R. E. Snow & D. E. Wiley (Eds.), *Improving inquiry in the social sciences: A volume in honor of Lee J. Cronbach* (pp. 75-107). Hillsdale, NJ: Elrbaum.

Wise, S. L. (Ed.). (1993). *Teacher training in measurement and assessment skills.* Lincoln, NE: Buros Institute of Mental Measurements, University of Nebraska.

Wolf, D. P. (1993). Assessment as an episode of learning. In R. E. Bennett & W. C. Ward (Eds.), *Construction versus choice in cognitive measurement* (pp. 213-240). Hillsdale, NJ: Lawrence Erlbaum.

Wolf, D. P., Bixby, J., Glenn, J., & Gardner, H. (1991). To use their minds well: Investigating new forms of student assessment. *Review of Research in Education, 17,* 31-74.

Wright, B. D., & Masters, G. N. (1982). *Rating scale analysis: Rasch measurement.* Chicago: Mesa Press.

Yalow, E. S., & Popham, W. J. (1983). Content validity at the crossroads. *Educational Researcher, 12*(8), 10-15.

Yao, T., & Ning, C. (1998). *CATRC (Computer-Adaptive Test for Reading Chinese).* Honolulu, HI: Second Language Teaching & Curriculum Center.

Young, R. (1995). Conversational styles in language proficiency interviews. *Language Learning, 54,* 3-42.

Young, R., & He, A. W. (Eds.). (1998). *Talking and testing: Discourse approaches to the assessment of oral proficiency.* Philadelphia: John Benjamins.

Zieky, M. J. (2001). So much has changed: How the setting of cutscores has evolved since the 1980s. In G. Cizek (Ed.), *Setting performance standards: Concepts, methods, and perspectives* (pp. 19-51). Mahwah, NJ: Lawrence Erlbaum Associates.

Zimmerman, M. A., & Rappaport, J. (1988). Citizen participation, perceived control, and psychological empowerment. *American Journal of Community Psychology, 16*(5), 725-750.

Language Testing and Evaluation

Series editors: Rüdiger Grotjahn and Günther Sigott

www.peterlang.de

Peter Lang · Internationaler Verlag der Wissenschaften

David Marsh / Dieter Wolff (eds.)

Diverse Contexts – Converging Goals

CLIL in Europe

Frankfurt am Main, Berlin, Bern, Bruxelles, New York, Oxford, Wien, 2007.
362 pp., num. fig., tab. and graph.
Mehrsprachigkeit in Schule und Unterricht.
Edited by Gerhard Bach, Stephan Breidbach and Dieter Wolff. Vol. 6
ISBN 978-3-631-56905-4 · pb. € 39.80*

CLIL, 'a dual-focussed educational approach in which an additional language is used for the learning and teaching of both content and language' can be viewed as an example of curricular integration. This publication is one example of how this is being achieved. It serves to articulate why, and how, good practice can lead to the positive outcomes increasingly reported across Europe. It results from selected presentations given at the Helsinki CLIL 2006 conference "CLIL Competence Building for Globalization: Quality in Teaching Through a Foreign Language". The 28 contributions to this book, which originate from countries across the European Union, are divided into six sections covering classroom practice, evaluation, research, and programme management.

Contents: Basic CLIL issues in Europe · Implementing CLIL in the education systems · Investigating CLIL · Integrating and evaluating language and content · Practising CLIL · Documenting joint European CLIL activities · Conclusions

Frankfurt am Main · Berlin · Bern · Bruxelles · New York · Oxford · Wien
Distribution: Verlag Peter Lang AG
Moosstr. 1, CH-2542 Pieterlen
Telefax 0041(0)32/3761727

*The €-price includes German tax rate
Prices are subject to change without notice

Homepage http://www.peterlang.de